A MISSOURI

RAILROAD
PIONEER

Missouri Biography Series
William E. Foley, Editor

The Missouri Biography Series focuses on citizens who were born in the state and those whose careers had significant impact on the region. From baseball great Stan Musial to renowned musician Scott Joplin to former president Harry S. Truman, this series highlights the lives of some of the notable individuals who have called Missouri home.

A MISSOURI
RAILROAD
PIONEER

THE LIFE OF LOUIS HOUCK

Joel P. Rhodes

University of Missouri Press   Columbia

Library of Congress Cataloging-in-Publication Data

Rhodes, Joel P., 1967–
   A Missouri railroad pioneer : the life of Louis Houck / Joel P. Rhodes.
      p.   cm.
   Summary: "Examines the life of a self-taught Cape Girardeau railroader whose
network of more than five hundred miles of track transformed southeastern
Missouri in the late nineteenth century. Louis Houck also helped establish the
college now known as Southeast Missouri State University and wrote a noted
history of Missouri"—Provided by publisher.
   Includes bibliographical references and index.
   ISBN 978-0-8262-2141-4 (paperback : alk. paper)
   1. Houck, Louis, 1840–1925.   2. Pioneers—Missouri—Biography.
3. German Americans—Missouri—Biography. 4. Businessmen—Missouri—
Biography.   5. Railroads—Missouri—History.   6. Southeast Missouri State
University—History.   7. Historians—Missouri—Biography.   8. Cape Girardeau
(Mo.)—Biography.   I. Title.
   F466.H86R48 2008
   977.8'03092—dc22
   [B]

2007052626

Designer: Jennifer Cropp
Typefaces: Palatino, Mesquite, and Willow

Publication of this book has been generously assisted by generous donations,
in memory of James C. Olson, made by Adolf E. and Rebecca B. Schroeder
and by Mel and Meta George.

To Jeanie,
MUSE

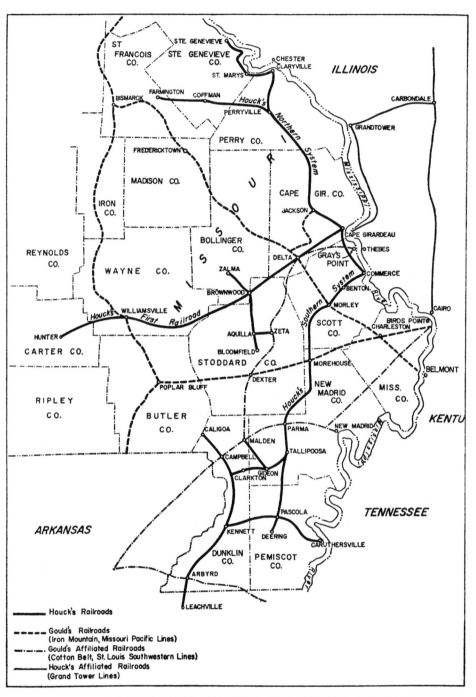

MAP SHOWING EARLY RAILROADS IN SOUTHEAST MISSOURI

CONTENTS

ACKNOWLEDGMENTS

Since first committing to a biography of Louis Houck—a notion born out of a collaborative effort to write the history of Cape Girardeau but actually determined by a February conversation with my wife, Jeanie, in the hot tub—I have crossed paths with a great many folks whose invaluable contributions must be recognized. Jeanie is chief among these, as both inspiration and reviewer for my first adventure in biography. Over the past three years she listened patiently each night as I read every word of that day's modest writing, "talking history" much the way Louis did a century before. Her earnest questions and critiques served as the first line of revisions. Likewise, our children Alex, Olivia, and Ella curiously tolerated Dad's obsession with the old railroader. In fact, our youngest daughter Ella has never known a time in her life when Daddy was not working on "Uncle Louis" as he affectionately became known around the Rhodes' house.

I certainly could never have begun or completed my research without Louis's own family, Jeanette and Andy Juden, Ronald Reed, and Patrick and Cheryl Evans. In particular, I want to thank Jeanette, who graciously gave me access to the Houck world and allowed me to sit at her dining room table every Friday morning for many months distilling Louis's writings into my laptop. Similarly, Ronald's insight into his great grandfather's legal and political talents contributed a great deal to the study as well as some lively conversations over Italian food. I am also very appreciative for the Evans' invitation to tour the beautiful Elmwood mansion, certainly one of the oldest, if not the oldest, continuing residences by one family in Missouri.

My colleagues in the history department at Southeast Missouri State University also contributed their time and considerable talents during a number of faculty seminars, through review of various chapters, and perhaps more importantly by just allowing me to pop my head in their offices with a quick question or clarification. In this regard I particularly thank

Frank Nickell, Bonnie Stepenoff, Eric Clements, and Joe Werne. Kay Kimmich-Choate, our able administrative assistant, also deserves recognition, whether for making copies, getting images scanned, or sincerely listening to my latest Houck-isms. I should probably also thank my Missouri history and historic preservation students—especially my graduate assistant Ben Simmons—who over the past six or seven semesters have heard almost every historical discussion somehow wind its way back to Louis Houck.

Across campus in Special Collections, Lisa Speer and her archivists facilitated the bulk of my research with their archival expertise and cheerful willingness to lug dozens of heavy boxes out to me. I owe them all a great deal of gratitude. In particular, I want to thank Lisa Graham, but also, and in no particular order, Cindy Boehlke, who processed the 172 linear feet of the Houck collection, Ellen Ryan, Sam Sampson, Brooke Culler, Anna Powell, Sarah Stephens, Kylie Maxcy, Margaret Harmon, Julie Elgin, Robyn Mainor, Bill Baehr, Garret Kremer-Wright, and Carla Jordan. Speaking of archivists, thanks also to Laura Jolley, Greg Olson, and Ken Winn at the Missouri State Archives and the State Historical Society of Missouri's Richard S. Brownlee Fund Award that got me there. The same goes for Bruce Ketchum at the Deutscheim State Historical Site, Karen F. Stanley, and of course Bill Foley, whose interest and encouragement from the outset emboldened me.

Well, Louis, here it is, exactly one hundred years since your histories. I hope I got it right.

A MISSOURI
RAILROAD
PIONEER

CHAPTER 1

Wanderjahre

I gradually became familiar with all parts of the printing business and my father allowed me to run the printing office after I was about sixteen years old almost as I pleased.

Louis Napoleon Hauck shivered as his father Bartholomeaus told him about the Cossacks again. Since first publishing the *Belleviller Zeitung* in 1849, Bartholomeaus had worked alongside his nine-year-old son in the family's printing office, teaching him every aspect of publishing a German-language newspaper while regaling the boy with marvelous stories of his adventures and travels in the old country. Of all Bartholomeaus's recollections of Bavaria—about famous generals and royalty in the Hauck family tree—the story of the Cossacks seemed to impress young Louis most of all. As they labored, Bartholomeaus earnestly recounted how, as a child almost Louis's age, he had watched the fierce warriors, loyal only to the czar, ride through his village on their way home to Russia after tormenting Napoleon Bonaparte's retreating army across Europe. There, at the fifteenth-century stone bridge spanning the Main River in Würzburg in the winter of 1813, the soldiers had dismounted and chopped through the ice to bath in the freezing water. For Bartholomeaus, a feeble boy who could not walk until after his fifth birthday, and then only after doctors painfully embedded his slender legs in hot sand, the memory of the will and discipline of these powerful men resonated deeply, already spanning continents. Now, in passing it on to his oldest son, the crippled printer hoped it would span generations.[1]

1. Louis Houck, "Some Reminiscences of Louis Houck," 1.

Bartholomeaus Hauck was born on August 24, 1805, St. Bartholomew's Day, in Heidingsfeld, near the historic fortified city of Würzburg, in what is today a region known for its vineyards in southwestern Germany.[2] The son of a Bohemian weaver, Bartholomeaus's frail physical condition, probably the result of polio, made his childhood burdensome with frequent visits to the doctors at Würzburg's celebrated sixteenth-century Julius hospital. While his brother Franz pursued a university education and a career in law among the Romanesque cathedrals and baroque palaces of Würzburg, the Haucks apprenticed young Bartholomeaus to the Archiepiscopal printing office in the city in 1819. Arranging a standard apprenticeship, the family paid an up front fee of 700 florins with the stipulation that the fourteen-year-old serve for seven years without pay.

At the conclusion of his servitude, Bartholomeaus embarked on his "wanderjahre," or years of travel, a lengthy journey of discovery customary for young workmen to complete their education and become a master. For the next three years, he painstakingly made his way on foot throughout central Europe, strengthening his legs and honing his craft by working with a succession of master printers.

Bartholomeaus's wanderjahre took on a transatlantic dimension when he began reading the emigration literature becoming popular in Germany during the late 1820s. In these promotional accounts of America, the roaming printer discovered a vibrant New World, unlike the old one where he could see firsthand how population pressure and the oncoming Industrial Revolution were already threatening the traditional economy. In particular, Gottfried Duden's influential *Report of a Journey to the Western States of North America*, published the year Bartholomeaus emigrated, painted an alluring picture of the now midwestern portion of the United States, especially the state of Missouri with its steep river bluffs and rolling wooded hills.[3] Here was a land at once somehow familiar and yet new, a country where equality of opportunity offered an unstratified society that rewarded daring and hard work. In 1829, Bartholomeaus Hauck made his way to the port of Hamburg and walked up a gangplank onto a ship bound for Baltimore.

Like most German immigrants of the era, Bartholomeaus did not linger in the port of entry. Short of money and sleeping in doorways, the newcomer searched in vain for a German printing office, eventually settling for

2. The general story of Bartholomeaus's and Anna's early life is taken from Houck, "Reminiscences," 1–3.

3. The general outline of Missouri's German population is based on Perry McCandless, *A History of Missouri, Volume II 1820–1860.*

railroad work and drifting around the region before finally ending up in Wilkes-Barre, Pennsylvania. Determined to find gainful employment as a German-language printer, Bartholomeaus headed for the Midwest and the "German Triangle," an area with a heavy concentration of his countrymen staked out by the vertices of Cincinnati, St. Louis, and Milwaukee.[4] He arrived in Cincinnati around 1833, but despite the growing German population in that city, he again struggled to catch on at a print shop. By mid-decade Bartholomeaus boarded another steamboat, bound this time for St. Louis, and the state he had read travel writers describe as Deutscheim, or German Home.

Clearly Missouri's premier city in terms of population, trade, and culture, St. Louis's location below the confluence of the Missouri and Mississippi rivers positioned it historically as the commercial clearinghouse of river trade in the interior of the continent, and after the Louisiana Purchase in 1803 as the gateway for western expansion. At the time Bartholomeaus climbed up its crowded and slippery stone levee—where moored steamboats stretched out as far as his eyes could see—St. Louis was also the regional epicenter of a substantial German migration to the interior of the continent just then under way. Coming up the Mississippi River from the port of New Orleans, tens of thousands of German immigrants would eventually flow through the city. While thousands stayed, significant numbers settled farther west along the Missouri River and south along the Mississippi. Still others crossed the Mississippi into Illinois, moving first up to Chicago and then later concentrating in the southern portion of the state.[5]

Amid what became the largest immigrant population in antebellum Missouri, Bartholomeaus finally found newspaper work printing the *Anzieger des Westens* (Western Gazette). He also became acquainted with Anna Senn Deppler, a recently widowed German immigrant. Born June 10, 1804, in the village of Villigen, on the Limat River in the Canton Argau region of Switzerland, Anna came to America with her husband Jakob Deppler around 1829 as well, stopping briefly in Philadelphia and Pittsburgh before finding their way to St. Louis. The young couple mingled with other Germans moving through St. Louis on their way into the Missouri hinterland to settle and probably made the determination to follow. In 1835 Jakob sailed back to

---

4. Roger Daniels, "The Immigrant Experience in the Gilded Age," in Charles W. Calhoun, ed., *The Gilded Age: Essays on the Origins of Modern America*, 72, 76.

5. Theodore Calvin Pease, *The Story of Illinois*, 134; Arthur Charles Cole, *The Centennial History of Illinois, Volume III: The Era of the Civil War, 1848–1870*, 23.

Switzerland to resolve their affairs and sell off all their assets in order to raise the necessary capital. Anna anxiously waited in St. Louis for months, only to receive news that her husband had died of cholera on a Mississippi riverboat within miles of completing his journey. Adding to her considerable distress, Anna discovered that of the $7,000 she knew Deppler was carrying in his belt, only $1,500 was returned to her.

During this difficult period, Bartholomeaus befriended Anna, first helping the illiterate woman arrange her finances and later comforting her as best he could. The couple married two years later in 1837.

The first of Bartholomeaus and Anna Hauck's five children, Louis, was born on April 1, 1840, in tiny Mascoutah, in St. Clair County, Illinois, some twenty-five miles east of St. Louis. Throughout Louis's early childhood, fierce competition among German-language newspapers compelled Bartholomeaus to ply his craft at a number of ephemeral presses around St. Louis and in central and southern Illinois. By the mid-nineteenth century, every German enclave of any size in the region supported a daily paper, usually aligned with the Democratic Party in the years before slavery divided political loyalties. But few communities could support more than one, which meant that once a German press firmly established itself, rivals found it nearly impossible to start another.[6]

Accordingly, Bartholomeaus, who was primarily a printer and publisher rather than an editor, led an almost itinerant existence during the 1840s, frequently moving from one Democratic paper to the next as the family grew with almost every stop. While Louis was still an infant, Bartholomeaus left the *Anzieger des Westens* for another job in Red Bud, Illinois, where Louis's brother Julius was born in 1841. By 1845, circumstances once again relocated the family—which now included a daughter, Louisa Appolona, born in 1843—to Quincy, Illinois. Here, 140 miles north of St. Louis along the Mississippi River, Bartholomeaus published the *Stern des Westens* (Western Star). Following the birth of their third son, George, in 1846, the restless Haucks made a brief return to the St. Louis area, with Bartholomeaus, by this time an artisan of some local repute, printing first the *St. Louiser Zeitung* (St. Louis Newspaper) and later *Cosmopolite*. In 1848, with some difficulty they were back in Quincy where a fourth son, John, was born.

Curiously, in the interim, Bartholomeaus briefly tried his hand at farming in 1843, purchasing land in the heavily German region along the Gas-

6. Pease, *Story of Illinois,* 134; Cole, *Centennial History of Illinois,* 17, 23, 26, 453; McCandless, *History of Missouri,* 40.

conade River near the community of Hermann, Missouri. And although Louis worked in his father's various printing offices nearly all the time while growing up, it was the Haucks' rocky hillside farm, located fifteen to twenty miles south of the Missouri River in Gasconade County, that provided the setting for the boy's earliest memories. Only three years old, Louis, known to most as Louie, remembered delighting his parents in the amusing way only a toddler can: helping out by hoeing up freshly planted corn and obstinately refusing to collect eggs from the scary barn loft despite fervent and careful prodding from Anna.

Yet aside from quaint reminiscences, Louis also vividly recalled traveling by steamboat up the Missouri River to Hermann where a rented skiff took the family up the Gasconade to their farm. During the trip he marveled at the unspoiled timber-covered bluffs that rose above the river and the isolated farms clinging to the water's edge. Writing more than seventy years later, he warmly recalled how "the people along the bank, hunting and spearing for fish, were a great revelation to me."[7] This personal connection, however brief, to what was still a relatively rough and unpolished part of the world, began a lifelong fascination with the landscape, heritage, and folkways along the rivers of frontier Missouri. Later as a historian of the state's territorial period, Louis obviously wrote with a twentieth-century nostalgia and longing for the authenticity of the vanishing wilderness and the bygone pioneers he observed as a boy in central Missouri.

In December 1848, Bartholomeaus finally put down some roots for his wife and five small children, trading the erstwhile farm in Missouri for a house in Belleville, Illinois, where he started publishing the *Belleviller Zeitung* (Belleville Newspaper). The *Zeitung,* which first appeared in January 1849, marked a reunion between Bartholomeaus and Theodore Engelmann, an intellectual refugee of the recently failed democratic unrest in Germany. The two had briefly worked together five years earlier on the *Belleville Beobachter* (Belleville Observer) before Engelmann sold that operation to Bartholomeaus when the former's duties as circuit clerk diverted his time and energies away from editing. For this second go-around at the *Zeitung,* the two duplicated their previous working arrangement, with Engelmann again taking up the editor's pen and Bartholomeaus serving as his foreman.[8]

From their office, probably located somewhere near the bustling public square, Engelmann and Hauck would have chronicled a dynamic period

7. Houck, "Reminiscences," 3, 6.
8. Robert C. Fietsam, Jr., Judy Belleville, and Jack Le Chien, *Belleville: 1814–1914,* 17.

in Belleville's early history. Founded in 1814 in a cornfield on the high ground inland from the Mississippi River roughly where East St. Louis is today, Belleville had grown sparingly in the early years of Illinois statehood. Yet by the middle of the nineteenth century, Belleville was establishing itself as a minor political, judicial, and commercial center in the agricultural region of southern Illinois. And most of these transformations could be traced directly to the arrival of what local politicians were already referring to as the "German element." At a time when railroad construction and shifting populations were quickly erasing the frontier atmosphere of Illinois—with enterprising settlers leaving for California and Colorado and even larger numbers of immigrants replacing them—the town's population nearly quadrupled from two thousand in 1840 to seventy-five hundred in 1860. Two-thirds of these newcomers were German-speaking, placing Belleville alongside Chicago, Galena, Quincy, Alton, Peoria, and Peru as the towns having the highest concentrations of Germans in the state. The town was in fact the St. Clair County seat, a county well on its way to becoming one of only a handful in Illinois with almost half its population foreign born.[9] It is little wonder that Belleville's thriving milling and mining operations were increasingly overshadowed by its reputation throughout the Midwest for breweries, beer gardens, and superb lager.

When the Haucks returned to Belleville, the impressionable Louis soon came to especially appreciate the "old Virginia style" courthouse adjacent to the public square. At the *Zeitung*, Bartholomeaus and Louis supplemented their newspaper work by printing custom jobs, including many of the "blanks," or legal forms used by the county and circuit court clerks. While delivering blanks to the circuit clerk's office upstairs in the courthouse, Louis often peered into the windows of the courtroom on the main floor, studying the lawyers as they paced the brick floor in front of the bar and the audience arranged in amphitheater style to the sides. The judge, seated behind a slightly elevated bench affixed with a brightly painted Illinois coat of arms, probably called to mind his father's stories of Uncle Franz, by now a judge himself back in Würzburg.

Thoroughly impressed by the spectacle and drama of the law, Louis also came to recognize the desirability of a more formal education while making one of his deliveries at the courthouse. On this particular occasion, Louis submitted the proof of a legal blank to circuit court clerk William Thomas for his approval. Too small to see over Thomas's desk as the clerk carefully proofread the document out loud in German, Louis pulled up a

9. Pease, *Story of Illinois,* 134; Cole, *Centennial History of Illinois,* 17, 23.

stool and listened. When Thomas reached the end, he recited "A.D. 18—." Looking over his spectacles, he earnestly asked, "Louie, what does A.D. mean?" Owing in part to his nomadic upbringing and printing chores, Louis's schooling had been piecemeal and sporadic, attending various German parochial schools whenever possible and, now in Belleville, occasionally attending classes held at the local Odd Fellows Hall. The boy sheepishly replied he did not know. "Louis," the clerk instructed, "that means Anno Domini, year of our Lord." Impressed that two letters could mean so much, Louis left the courthouse to ask his father about the possibility of getting some type of "special instruction."[10]

Sometime in 1852, Bartholomeaus consented to a compromise, arranging with friends back in Gasconade County for twelve-year-old Louis to study under the private tutelage of Eduard Muehl, an iconoclastic printer and scholar in Hermann. For the next two years, Louis lived and worked with Muehl's family in Hermann, a collection of some ninety predominantly brick buildings and vineyards nestled at the foot of the hills along the Missouri River near its confluence with the Gasconade. Founded just fifteen years earlier as a settlement colony by immigrants from Pennsylvania hoping to preserve their language and heritage in Duden's Missouri, Hermann was, in Louis's words, "altogether a German town." He later remembered only one American among its several hundred inhabitants.[11]

The surroundings were certainly familiar enough, and for the most part so was the curriculum. Eduard Muehl, a graduate of the University of Leipzig and trained Lutheran minister, published the *Wochenblatt* (Weekly Paper) in the basement of a home built by his brother-in-law Carl Procopius Strehly. The Strehly and Muehl families shared the white neoclassical-style house, now part of the Deutscheim State Historical Site, and during his tenure as Louis's teacher, Muehl spent mornings training his young apprentice on the technical art of publishing and afternoons working through comprehensive lessons in German.

But perhaps the most significant education Louis received in Hermann lay outside the Washington hand-press he learned to print on or the romantic literature he read. Eduard Muehl embraced the philosophy of "rationalism" and had left the pulpit to follow this movement committed to finding truth through reason and factual analysis rather than faith, dogma, supernatural revelation, or the other fundamentals of organized

10. Houck, "Reminiscences," 4, 5, 6.
11. Dorothy H. Shrader, *The City of Hermann, Missouri Presents Hermann: 1836 A Dream in Philadelphia, 1986 A Town in Missouri;* Houck, "Reminiscences," 7.

Christianity. The philosophical *Wochenblatt,* like his *Lichtfreund* (Friend of Light) before it, addressed the major issues of the day, but the paper Louis helped Muehl print interpreted them from a rationalist perspective, using deductive reasoning to discover the essential self-evident truths thought to be inherent to all reality.

After the day's printing was completed, Muehl—whose shoulder-length hair and ever-present Jacobin beret bespoke his revolutionary politics— often played host to informal gatherings of like-minded intellectuals. Many of these "liberals"—certainly by the conservative and doctrinaire standards of German Lutherans and Catholics in nineteenth-century Missouri—were members of a rationalist group known as the "Union of Free Men." Some, like Theodore Engelmann in Belleville and Frederick Muench, a close friend of Muehl's who later became a Missouri state senator, were political idealists who had left Germany in the wake of failed revolutions against an undemocratic government in the early 1830s.[12] In Muehl's basement office or in the open area between the house and Strehly's adjacent vineyard they engaged one another in a sustained dialectic encompassing a heady range of subjects including religion, philosophy, politics, physical science, and history.

During Louis's time in their midst, these conversations were increasingly dominated by the peculiar institution of slavery, and in particular the recently published *Uncle Tom's Cabin,* which the devoutly anti-slavery *Wochenblatt* translated in serial form. No doubt at their urging, Louis devoured *Uncle Tom's Cabin,* and while not fully recognizing at the time how strangely out of place this was in the strongly pro-slavery region of central Missouri, he listened intently as the rationalists analyzed its message.

He personally disagreed with their abolitionism and equality of the races doctrines, which in time would help these rationalists find their way into the new Republican Party. But the whole exercise inspired Louis, and he eagerly began reading other serial stories routinely published by German newspapers on their front page. In time he could follow three or four of these stories at once, published in as many different newspapers. "These stories were mostly historical," he recalled, "and I think by reading the different serial stories and keeping the plots in mind, I unconsciously trained my memory and also thus acquired a taste for historical reading."[13]

12. Informal conversations with Bruce Ketchum, Historic Site Specialist 3, Deutscheim State Historical Site: Hermann, Mo., April 14, 2005, July 15, 2006; McCandless, *History of Missouri,* 38–39.
13. Houck, "Reminiscences," 7.

When not reading, contemplating, or listening to his teacher play the guitar, Louis climbed the hill above the Strehly home with Muehl's oldest son, Thuisko, to gaze out at the endless parade of steamboats navigating the Missouri River. There, near the Lutheran church overlooking the river and surrounding countryside, the boys passed the days in Hermann, deciphering the English names painted on the big boats. Sometimes the two climbed down to surreptitiously pick peaches and grapes they then sold to passengers landing on the wharf.

In the late spring of 1854, Bartholomeaus abruptly retrieved his son from Hermann as a cholera epidemic ravaged the town. Among the nearly seventy eventual casualties were Eduard Muehl and his daughter Rosa, who died on the same day, July 7, 1854. It is difficult to precisely determine what impact his time in Hermann had on Louis, but it seems certain this was an influential period in his formative years. He acknowledged that it sparked his interest in serial stories, which in turn he believed placed his feet on the path toward becoming, many believed, the principal Missouri historian of his day. Likewise, surveying the panoramic riverscape from his perch above town certainly underscored his idyllic affinity for frontier life in Missouri. These two persistent threads in his life, later affectionately woven into five volumes of colonial Missouri history, probably began intertwining on that hill above Hermann.

What influence his exposure to colloquial rationalism had is less clear as he naturally never demonstrated anything like a fixed adherence to any one formal philosophy. In fact over the course of his life, Louis at times based critical decisions on what could more appropriately be considered an empiricist's preference for personal experience and introspection, a strategy fundamentally at odds with the rationalist's reliance on deductive reasoning. On the other hand, consistent with the rationalist aversion to organized religion, he always stopped just short of joining a church, despite living most of his life in Cape Girardeau, a highly religious community with a rich array of faiths and denominations.

All things considered, it would be fair to say that this small coterie of German intellectuals in Hermann steeped Louis in their appreciation for the liberating nature of learning and knowledge in a free society. And while their liberal politics and abolitionism apparently never swayed him, their polemics trained him to think clearly, regardless of the subject. Later in law and business, the rationalist influence is most discernible in the skillful way Louis quickly raised salient questions and then precisely formulated well-reasoned solutions based on evidence and available alternatives. Still, in the grand scheme of things, perhaps Hermann's most enduring legacy was fostering in Louis a sustained pursuit of knowledge for its own sake and an abiding appreciation for the intrinsic worth of ideas.

Louis probably resumed his place at the *Belleviller Zeitung* in May 1854, the same month Congress passed the highly charged Kansas-Nebraska Act. Easily the preeminent national issue of its time, the act, and the political context in which it unfolded in Illinois, forged his core political beliefs just as Muehl shaped his intellectual development.[14] Bartholomeaus raised Louis a Jacksonian Democrat, and the boy "always took a very deep interest in politics," working most of his young life in an atmosphere of political idealism that characterized the German press. The various editors who wrote for the *Zeitung* in the 1850s championed the simple rural democracy that prevailed in antebellum Illinois and Missouri. But at the time he was coming of age politically—printing propaganda for some of the state's most prominent Democrats and occasionally writing editorials under a pseudonym—the Democratic Party in Illinois and the nation were figuratively, and soon literally, being torn apart by impending civil war.

The Democratic Party in mid-1830s Illinois crystallized around supporters of Andrew Jackson's renewal of Jefferson's democratic principles. As Jacksonianism swept across Illinois and neighboring Missouri, those with a healthy ethnic and agrarian suspicion of government and special interests put aside the local issues and feuds which clouded state politics to build a formal party machinery. Organizing more or less around their collective commitment to small government, strict construction of the constitution, states' rights, and the primacy of ordinary citizens, Illinois Democrats dominated the less organized, less unified Whigs and effectively controlled state politics throughout the 1830s and 1840s.

But in the 1850s, slavery dramatically shifted the state's political landscape, with sharp divisions erupting between anti-slavery Democrats in the north and their pro-slavery counterparts in the southern, or Little Egypt, portion of the state. To keep the weakened party together, most Illinois Democrats rallied behind their senator, Stephen A. Douglas, who took the lead nationally in attempting to mitigate the issue of slavery, and thereby avoid sectional hostilities, through his principle of "popular sovereignty" in determining the status of the peculiar institution in the opening of the West. By young Hauck's fourteenth birthday in 1854, Douglas crafted his Kansas-Nebraska Act, which unequivocally repealed the Mis-

---

14. Ibid., 8. The general outline of Illinois political history is based on Cole, *Centennial History of Illinois* and Pease, *Story of Illinois*.

souri Compromise's prohibition of slavery in those two new territories. The linchpin was popular sovereignty, leaving any decision on the status of slavery up to the residents of these soon-to-be states.

Ultimately, the Kansas-Nebraska Act satisfied no one, touching off fierce sectional debates over the precise interpretation and course of popular sovereignty. Along the Kansas and Missouri border, harsh words escalated into guerrilla warfare, considered the opening salvos of the Civil War. Fall-out over Kansas-Nebraska also destabilized the two-party political system between the Whigs and Democrats at the national and state level, decimating the Whigs, fracturing the Democrats, and giving rise to the new Republican Party.

In Illinois, the ripple effect from the Kansas-Nebraska Act created a volatile and confusing political landscape where politicians formed new allegiances only to quickly realign as leaders jumped ship and changed their political stripes. Divisions within the Democrats finally burst open. The party split almost sectionally between "Anti-Nebraska" factions in northern Illinois who opposed its repeal of the Missouri Compromise, and "Pro-Nebraska groups" in the south who supported the act's concept of popular sovereignty. German Democrats, as a whole vehemently anti-slavery, loudly voiced their opposition to the Kansas-Nebraska Act. Their presses, which had previously supported Douglas, now lambasted the senator and his concept of popular sovereignty.

So too did the *Zeitung* come to take a stand against the Kansas-Nebraska Act. Louis remembered that during the agitation over the law, both Lyman Trumbull, a prominent resident of Belleville, and Lieutenant Governor Gustavus Koerner, a lifelong friend of Engelmann who increasingly contributed most of the paper's editorials on American politics, frequently wrote anti-Nebraska articles critical of Douglas for the *Zeitung*. Trumbull in particular, who was running as an anti-Nebraska candidate for Congress in a largely pro-Nebraska part of the state, eagerly sought the Haucks' help in gaining the support of like-minded Germans in the surrounding Alton congressional district.

While there are no *Zeitung* editorials extant from this era, it seems that Louis's evolving politics were being distilled through some form of free-soilism—the prevention of slavery's geographic expansion in order to keep the West open for white settlement only—and the racial sensibilities of his day. He considered himself foremost a patriot, steadfastly loyal to the party and committed to the democratic ideals of state's rights, national union, and peace. As such, Hauck shared the prevailing sentiment within the Democratic ranks that disloyal "abolition hordes" threatened the

Republic like Vandals from antiquity while likewise preferring negotiations with the South based on the stipulation that slavery could remain there, but not be allowed to spread.[15]

By 1856, Bartholomeaus's health apparently began declining and Louis recalled running the printing office "almost as I pleased," despite being just sixteen years old and by his own admission understanding English "only indifferently."[16] That same year, the presidential election forced the divided Democrats to finally choose between their principles and their party. Many anti-slavery and anti-Nebraska Democrats hesitated at first to leave the party of Jackson, and Germans in particular found it difficult to let go of the word "democrat" and its powerful connotations. But after the defection of what Illinois historian Theodore Calvin Pease called "the brains and conscience of the Democratic Party"—men like Koerner and Trumbull—disaffected Democrats began migrating en masse into the Republican ranks.[17]

The state of Illinois now became sharply divided between the two parties, Republicans generally dominating northern Illinois while Democrats held sway in the south. The only exceptions to this strict demarcation were the Democratic bloc of northern counties between the Mississippi and the Wabash rivers and the southern Republican outposts of Edwards, Madison, Bond, and St. Clair.[18] Thus with the political ground having shifted underneath him, Louis found himself in a curious, at times awkward, and ultimately dangerous, position: he was a German Democrat in a largely Republican county.

Most immigrant groups tended to vote as a bloc, which meant that given their numbers—more than 130,000 by 1860—and concentrations in counties like St. Clair, German voters held the balance of power in Illinois politics.[19] Accordingly, both parties, first the Whigs and Democrats, and after 1856 the Democrats and Republicans, aggressively campaigned to win their hearts and minds. Sometimes patronage was used to curry their

15. Luke H. Hite to Louis Houck, October 17, 1863, in possession of Patrick and Cheryl Evans, Cape Girardeau, Mo.; Cole, *Centennial History of Illinois*, 25.

16. Houck, "Reminiscences," 4.

17. Pease, *Story of Illinois*, 158.

18. Cole, *Centennial History of Illinois*, 146, 151; Pease, *Story of Illinois*, 158–59.

19. Cole, *Centennial History of Illinois*, 17, 23. In 1860, the German population of Illinois stood at 130,804, principally concentrated in the cities of Chicago, Belleville, Galena, Quincy, Alton, Peoria, and Peru. That same year, St. Clair and Monroe counties counted between 40 to 50 percent of its population as foreign born, while surrounding Madison and Clinton counties were between 30 to 40 percent and Washington and Randolph counties 20 to 30 percent.

favor, and in other instances traditional leaders like Koerner, a onetime Democrat now turned Republican, and clergy were cultivated so that they in turn could use their authority—political, religious, or otherwise—to influence the German community.[20]

The German press offered English-speaking politicians perhaps the most invaluable conduit into the potentially decisive German immigrant constituency. Naturally political in nature, German-language newspapers, and their editors, were routinely enlisted to translate platforms and influence readers with their vigorously preachy editorials, just as political heavyweights such as John Reynolds, William H. Bissell, Trumbull, and Koerner regularly did at the *Zeitung*. Of the scores of local newspapers established each year during the Civil War era, many were German political organs begun specifically to take up a party banner. Most of these nascent presses served the Republicans, reflecting and reinforcing the fact that the majority of German Protestants in Illinois had transferred their allegiance to the GOP by the late 1850s. This left Democrats desperate to recruit editors of their own in order to reclaim the German vote, especially in heavily contested Republican counties with sizable German populations like St. Clair.

In this way, local Democratic leaders most likely encouraged Louis and John Reis, who worked for the Haucks at the *Zeitung*, to commence printing a newspaper in Alton, in neighboring Madison County, another German stronghold now tenuously held by the Republicans. In January 1857, with money advanced by Bartholomeaus, the *Illinois Beobachter* (Illinois Observer) went to press under Louis's editorial direction. By his own confession just a "half-grown boy," Louis managed the paper with his partner Reis throughout 1857. But while political currents ran hot leading up to the next year's critical statewide General Assembly elections and the first showdown between Douglas and Abraham Lincoln, Louis increasingly found his attention drawn back to more scholarly pursuits.

Since leaving Hermann, he had continued to read voraciously, complementing serial stories with biographies written by seventeenth-century German historian Johann Christoph Wagenseil. Bartholomeaus had purchased a two-volume set of Wagenseil's works to enhance his son's obvious interest in the celebrated characters from history. And he was not disappointed. Louis found the handsomely illustrated books invaluable, the scholarship, in the style of Plutarch, rewarding, and the heroic stories

20. Ibid., 69, 123, 150–51, 292.

inspiring. The subjects of those biographies also seemed to have had the unintentional effect of stirring in him a desire to see a future beyond the printing press.

Although an accomplished printer, Louis was conceivably feeling anxious over being trapped in his father's unpredictable profession. While he may not have explicitly articulated this worry to Reis, the two obviously conferred at great length about Louis's budding interest in becoming a lawyer, and it was Reis who acted as a catalyst to crystallize in Hauck's mind the notion of attending college as a means toward that end. "Reis talked to me much about the University of Wisconsin at Madison, where he had lived and interested me greatly in that Institution," recalled Louis, "and I made up my mind principally on account of what he said, to take the money I had earned and go to Wisconsin University." In November 1857 he sold his interest in the *Beobachter* for the not inconsequential sum of $800.[21] As Louis transacted the sale, his thoughts may well have returned to one of the illustrations in Wagenseil's histories, given that when assessing this period of his life years later, he made specific reference to Sesostris, an Egyptian monarch from the second century B.C. In Louis's recollection, Sesostris stood in his chariot "to which some subjugated kings were hitched to pull it and that when he observed one of the kings watching the turning wheel of the car he asked what he was thinking about, and he answered that the fortunes of men turned like those wheels." "This observation," Hauck intentionally noted, "I never forgot."[22]

Louis enrolled at the University of Wisconsin in early 1858 expressly to, in his words, "perfect myself in English and whenever I got far enough in my education [would] study law."[23] For the next fifteen months, he boarded at the University Club House on campus with another prospective law student, John E. Hand. Studying English, German, Latin, and Greek, Louis joyfully devoted a great deal of his time outside the classroom to the literary Hesperian Society, clearly thrilled by the intellectual give and take of this new community of scholars. In their spare time, Louis, Hand, and Fielding Mansfield played chess and tended to the houseplants that filled their room. Louis practiced his English on Hand and Mansfield. They all practiced their Latin on one another.[24]

21. Indenture between Louis N. Houck and George Weigler, November 11, 1857, in possession of Patrick and Cheryl Evans, Cape Girardeau, Mo.

22. Houck, "Reminiscences," 7.

23. Ibid., 8.

24. John E. Hand to Louis Houck, September 8, 1858, in possession of Patrick and Cheryl Evans, Cape Girardeau, Mo.

Nonetheless, sometime in the spring of 1859 the $800 ran out, and Louis once again looked to take up his place at the printing press. On a regular visit to Belleville later in the year, he was summoned to a meeting with Illinois Speaker of the House William Ralls Morrison. Already one of the most powerful politicians in the state, the old Jeffersonian was similar in character and demeanor to his friend Abraham Lincoln, and had the distinction of being one of only a handful of state Democrats to have survived the last three elections.[25] Morrison must have been familiar with Louis's work from his days at the *Illinois Beobachter* in Alton, because at this meeting he, and probably State Senator William H. Underwood, proposed that Louis return to Belleville to publish a German newspaper "in the interest of the Democratic party." In reminding Louis of the Republican ascendancy in St. Clair County, they probably also expressed growing optimism that some of those Democratic "bolters" were now having second thoughts because of the violent perversion of popular sovereignty in Kansas.[26] With the pivotal 1860 election on the horizon, the English-speaking *Belleville Democrat* was already working assiduously to shepherd those wayward Democrats home, and, frankly, the party needed Louis to come home quickly and fill the void in the German-speaking community left after Bartholomeaus had inexplicably moved on to Kansas.

Perhaps reluctant to detour so broadly from his long-term goals, Louis evidently needed some convincing, deliberately using the word "induced" when describing Morrison's and Underwood's proposition. Given his later appointment in the Illinois General Assembly, it seems clear that part of this inducement included the prospect of patronage.[27] Within two years Louis was also studying law in the office of Underwood, an established Belleville attorney who had served as circuit court judge before his election to the General Assembly in 1856. Perhaps the men were already aware of his legal and political ambitions and tailored their overture accordingly. Whatever understandings they reached, the meeting seems to have concluded satisfactorily for all parties, establishing a political association between the three men and commencing Louis Hauck's tumultuous tenure as editor and publisher of the *Belleville Volksblatt*.

25. Franklin D. Scott, *The Political Career of William R. Morrison*, 5, 6, 8.
26. *Belleville Democrat*, March 27, 1858.
27. Houck, "Reminiscences," 8.

CHAPTER 2

Volksblatt

The Belleville *Advocate* of June 28th, says that the *Volksblatt*, edited and published for five years by me in this city, was "a violent disunion sheet." Unwilling to waste many words, I simply pronounce the assertion an unmitigated falsehood, and the writer a contemptible scoundrel.

—Louis Hauck, *Belleville Democrat,* July 29, 1865

After a two-year hiatus from editorializing on Illinois politics, Louis Hauck opened the Belleville office of the *Volksblatt* (People's Sheet) in the summer of 1860 during what Illinois historian Arthur Cole described as "a period of storm and stress for the journalistic profession" in that state.[1] On the eve of one of the most critical presidential elections in American history, political activity was intensifying, with candidates and partisan speakers already canvassing the region. The debut of Hauck's *Volksblatt* meant that no fewer than six newspapers competed to indoctrinate the voters of St. Clair County. Irascible Democratic and Republican editors in English and German fired across the others' bows with hortative columns as the sectional crisis over slavery was hardening positions on both sides and steadily moving the nation closer to war.

Two years before in Illinois, the statewide General Assembly elections had essentially been a referendum over what course the state would follow regarding slavery. With Douglas's Senate seat at stake, the campaign ultimately came down to a choice between the Democrat Douglas's moderate popular sovereignty or the Republican nominee Abraham Lincoln's aggressive free-soilism. Stumping along the political circuit in 1858, Lin-

1. Cole, *Centennial History of Illinois,* 456.

coln and Douglas engaged in a classic series of frontier-style debates, including an October meeting in Alton. Many from Belleville were in attendance that day, some to hear Douglas speak of traditional Jacksonianism and his party's dedication to maintaining the Union through compromise, while others came for Lincoln's impassioned moral critique of slavery and proclamation that the time had arrived to stop accommodating the institution.[2] In the end, neither politician could truthfully claim a clear victory in their debates, but the Democrats ultimately recaptured the General Assembly behind Douglas's spirited campaign and returned him to the Senate.

From a national perspective, the 1858 Illinois state election effectively positioned Douglas and Lincoln as the front-runners of their respective parties for president in 1860. And while copies of the *Belleville Volksblatt* could not be found in the historical record, judging from its English-speaking counterpart, the *Belleville Democrat*, Hauck wasted no time weighing in on behalf of Douglas Democracy. In reaching out to German Republicans who had been led astray, he denounced Lincoln as a dangerous abolitionist and probably shared a personal observation with his readership to paint the Republican candidate as disrespectful to Germans. Louis had missed the Lincoln-Douglas debate in Alton, but had seen both men speak in Belleville on separate occasions. In 1856 Hauck remembered being "very much disgusted" by Lincoln's remark that "I like the Dutch because the Dutch like me" during a speech in which the politician concluded with the earnest sentiment, "God Bless the Dutch." Thinking it an unsightly "reflection on a German to be called a Dutchman," Louis almost certainly would have used this perceived slight to his editorial advantage.[3]

At William Ralls Morrison's urging, Louis also delivered his first political speeches in support of Douglas to German audiences in Monroe County and across Illinois, even venturing into Indiana. In St. Clair County his speeches included an endorsement of William H. Underwood's reelection to the state senate.[4] His commitment and outspokenness on behalf of the Democrats raised Louis's profile in Belleville for better or worse and expanded his circle of friends within the party's local hierarchy. Nonetheless, he and the *Volksblatt* could not reverse the political winds sweeping the entire northern portion of the country. Abraham

2. *Belleville Democrat*, October 16, 1858.

3. Houck, "Reminiscences," 4; Fietsam et al., *Belleville*, 25.

4. *Belleville Democrat*, June 2, 9, 1860; John E. Hand to Louis Hauck, November 29, 1860, in possession of Patrick and Cheryl Evans, Cape Girardeau, Mo.

Lincoln ultimately united voters across the Northeast, Midwest, and Far West under the Republican banner on his way to the presidency. He carried his home state by some twelve thousand votes and while virtually all of southern Illinois went for Douglas, St. Clair, Madison, and Bond counties stayed Republican.

Lincoln's election in 1860 immediately set in motion a secessionist movement that had been brewing in the South for nearly a decade. Threatened by Republican abolitionism and Lincoln's assurance that the nation must "become all one thing, or all the other," southern states concluded that to preserve slavery they would have to leave the Union, preferably in peace, but through force if necessary. In the months before Lincoln's inauguration, politicians in Washington grasped at possible compromise solutions to preserve the Union at the very time leaders in the South created a separate Confederate nation. In Illinois, Louis joined fellow Democrats in declaring his loyalty to the Union and the *Volksblatt* made appeals to cool the abolitionist passions he thought were propelling the nation toward civil war. Even after the Confederate attack on the federal arsenal at Fort Sumter, South Carolina, in April 1861, touched off that Civil War, Louis continued to write principled editorials encouraging North and South to once again walk a middle ground.

By his own admission "not very enthusiastic in favor of the war," Louis became in the context of Civil War Illinois a "peace Democrat" who never gave up hope for some type of negotiated settlement.[5] As opposed to either the rabid Southern-leaning "anti-war Democrats" who sought to hamper the Northern war effort or the loyal "war Democrats" who put country before party and supported Lincoln, Hauck considered himself simply an "unconditional unionist" who ached at how enthusiastically and patriotically men tore it asunder.[6] Even another Republican friend, himself a Union officer whom Louis did not exactly see eye-to-eye with politically, conceded that at the heart of Louis's opposition to the war was an "unarterable [sic] attachment to the government of [his] fathers."[7] This steadfast faith in Jeffersonian democracy and his basic conservatism convinced him that the gravest threat to the future of his country was not the South's "War of the Rebellion," but rather Northern extremism: first in the

5. Houck, "Reminiscences," 8.
6. Cole, *Centennial History of Illinois,* 258, 260; Pease, *Story of Illinois,* 168, 169.
7. Robert A. Halbert to Louis Hauck, September 28, 1862, John E. Hand to Louis Hauck, September 20, 1861, in possession of Patrick and Cheryl Evans, Cape Girardeau, Mo.

form of the "Abolition Devil" and eventually in Lincoln's provocative handling of the rebellion and capricious use of war powers.

Regardless of exactly where he fell on the ideological spectrum of
wartime Democrats, his caustic editorials put him at considerable odds
with the prevailing pro-war and pro-Lincoln sentiment in Belleville. I
"became very unpopular on account of my opposition to Lincoln," Louis
recalled of publishing a partisan newspaper in a region increasingly sensitive to any hint of treason and disloyalty among Democrats.[8] Republican
friends and even Democratic allies increasingly pressured him to, in the
words of his college roommate John Hand, "change your mind about
Democracy and Politics long before the next Presidential Election." During the 1860 campaign, Hand, a staunch Republican with abolitionist ten-
dencies, had expressed how isolated Louis was becoming among fellow
German Republicans. "Mr. Baer [apparently a prominent local German
Republican] has come out rather strong against you since you commenced
editing a Democratic newspaper," Hand reported to Louis. "He says and
told me to tell you so that 'you are a poor miserable fellow.' He and ____
think it an unpardonable offense to introduce so much 'schimpfereisn'
[vulgarity, cursing] into a public journal, and think that if you keep on
your 'Volksblatt' will 'caput gehen' [fall apart]."[9]

Robert Halbert grew up with Louis in Belleville, and while the two men
were roughly the same age and shared the same legal ambitions, their paths
diverged significantly on the politics surrounding the war. Both were
Unionists, but Halbert could not understand Louis's willingness to hold
out an "olive branch" to the treacherous South. Halbert chose to preserve
the Union through force of arms, volunteering and eventually reaching the
rank of captain in Company H of the 117th Illinois Infantry. Expressing his
regret at Louis's position, Halbert offered his hope "that the charge of disloyalty whih [sic] has been urged against your party may prove to be
untrue." "It is no time now to make war with the administration," he
pleaded upon reporting the news that Vicksburg had been taken.[10]

Their often heated exchanges left Halbert to marvel at how "political
opponents could be personal friends, and them who have been my most
[dear] have been politically opposed to me." In capturing a sentiment so

8. Houck, "Reminiscences," 8.
9. John E. Hand to Louis Hauck, November 29, June 7, 1860, in possession of Patrick
and Cheryl Evans, Cape Girardeau, Mo.
10. Robert A. Halbert to Louis Hauck, November 6, December 2, 1862, in possession
of Patrick and Cheryl Evans, Cape Girardeau, Mo.

closely associated with the Civil War, he acknowledged Louis's resolve and appealed for the two to call a truce. "Eschewing all political [disagreements]," Halbert beseeched his friend to "let us keep alive the friendship that has hertofore [sic] existed between us."[11] Louis placed a high premium on loyalty when it came to friends and family, and he obviously saw the wisdom in Halbert's exhortation. For the remainder of the war, the two carried on their correspondence, replacing political matters with critiques of Milton's *Paradise Lost* and Halbert's observations on the lonely Southern belles he encountered while fighting in Alabama.

Curiously, Halbert often described warfare itself for Louis in grandiose terms, as if his civilian friend were regrettably missing out on this momentous spectacle. Aside from a few anxious moments over the draft and his service in the St. Clair County Home Guard, Halbert's letters were as close as Louis ever got to the fighting. Yet, Hauck seems to have been genuinely conflicted about military service. Publicly, he probably expressed, as many Democrats did, that this was a Republican war to be fought by Republicans. Privately, however, it appears Louis initially questioned whether his volunteering could actually contribute to the preservation of his beloved Union. It was only after the awful carnage of the Civil War steadily drove him to see volunteering as madness that in all likelihood he reached the conclusion that he could better serve the Union by means other than his own "useless death."[12]

Halbert never begrudged Louis his conscientious decision to not enlist, and in fact, evidently believed that had political circumstances allowed, Louis's temperament would have obliged him to join the bloody fray. In one particularly telling passage about one of the last battles of the Civil War, Halbert—a hardened veteran of several campaigns—clearly acknowledged Hauck's penchant for tales of gallant warriors on history's battlefields. "I would like to see you, Louis in a grand charge like that on [Fort] Blakely [Alabama]," he wrote, perhaps communicating a need in his friend to ride with these warriors at least vicariously. "You would be in the Seventh Heaven."[13]

Although Louis's courage of conviction strained one of his oldest friendships almost to the breaking point, his pragmatism and developing polit-

11. Robert A. Halbert to Louis Hauck, July 7, 1863, in possession of Patrick and Cheryl Evans, Cape Girardeau, Mo.
12. William H. Barnum to Louis Hauck, March 15, 1863, in possession of Patrick and Cheryl Evans, Cape Girardeau, Mo.
13. Robert A. Halbert to Louis Hauck, May 11, 24, June 15, 1865, in possession of Patrick and Cheryl Evans, Cape Girardeau, Mo.

ical instincts allowed him enough moral latitude to continue his support of William Ralls Morrison despite his political ally's conflicting position as a "war Democrat." When hostilities began, Morrison, the former Speaker of the Illinois House and the man most responsible for Hauck publishing the *Belleville Volksblatt*, followed his friend Stephen A. Douglas in throwing his support behind the new president and the war. At the request of Republican Governor Richard Yates, Morrison lent "moral force" to the Northern military cause among Democrats by organizing the 49th Illinois infantry regiment. After Morrison was seriously wounded during some of the bloodiest fighting of the war at Fort Donelson, Tennessee, in February 1862, Seventeenth District Democrats responded by nominating him as their candidate for the U.S. Congress.

In reaching out to his political friends in the district, Morrison naturally contacted Louis to ensure the *Volksblatt*'s favorable translations and editorials even though the two men now differed on the pivotal political question of the war's continuance. Faced with an interesting political dilemma, Morrison was savvy enough to know that in this predominantly Republican district, even with his distinguished war record, any stance short of advocating the complete destruction of the rebellion might taint him with the stain of disloyalty and doom his chances for election. Yet, conversely, he understood that the majority of Democrats in the district took a far more moderate approach and most were, like Louis, in fact peace Democrats favoring a negotiated settlement. Accordingly, Morrison rather disingenuously wanted Hauck to "spin" his position (to borrow a term from modern politics) so that peace Democrats could in good conscience send him to Congress. In asking this favor of Louis, the slippery Morrison assured the editor that in all his statements and correspondence regarding the war, "there is nothing which should frighten a patriot."[14] Reading between the lines, Louis would have taken this to mean that while the two could privately differ, there was nothing in Morrison's record to publicly betray Hauck's integrity or embarrass the *Volksblatt*.

On election day, Hauck probably believed that whatever misgivings he had about Morrison's actual stance, he was after all the best candidate for the job. District voters tended to agree, making Morrison one of only a very few Democrats seated in the U.S. Congress during the war. In "squinting" somewhat on his beliefs and endorsing Morrison, however,

14. Scott, *Political Career of William R. Morrison*, 6, 7, 9; William Ralls Morrison to Louis Hauck, October 25, 1862, in possession of Patrick and Cheryl Evans, Cape Girardeau, Mo.

Hauck demonstrated a keen grasp of how things really got done in politics, apparently engaging in a bit of horse-trading with the congressman. It seems very reasonable that the *Volksblatt'*s unwavering support for Morrison in the fall of 1862 positively influenced Hauck's "appointment" as the enrolling and engrossing clerk of the Illinois General Assembly the next year. Perhaps this election simply completed a deal already struck during their 1859 meeting when Morrison "induced" Louis to start the *Volksblatt;* a bargain that had been postponed after Morrison failed to run for reelection to the Illinois House of Representatives in 1860. What is certain, after Morrison's election in 1862, is that Louis specifically requested that the congressman nominate both his younger brothers George and John to the U.S. Naval Academy.[15] Just twenty-two years old, already Louis appreciated the strategic value of being in the confidence of powerful officeholders who asked for, and in turn granted, favors, especially leaders like Morrison who were on a first-name basis with the president of the United States.

Louis maintained a similarly advantageous relationship with Circuit Court Judge William H. Underwood, a close political confidant of Morrison's who was reelected state senator with the *Volksblatt'*s backing in 1860. Underwood had likely helped Morrison persuade Louis to edit the *Volksblatt* by offering the prospective law student a chance to study in his thriving Belleville legal firm. At a time before the increasing complexity of corporate law professionalized the legal field, apprenticing with an established jurist such as Underwood was still the traditional means of becoming a lawyer and would have therefore negated Hauck's need for law school. At any rate, in September 1861, while very much at the helm of the *Volksblatt,* Louis officially hung out his shingle as an "Attorney at Law," working in the basement offices of the firm Underwood & Noetling in the newly completed Greek Revival–style courthouse that dominated Belleville's public square.[16]

Under Morrison's and Underwood's wings, in January 1863 Louis also finally got his first taste of legislative politics, albeit as the enrolling and engrossing clerk for the Illinois General Assembly in Springfield. Ostensi-

15. Regrettably, despite Louis's sizable expenditures of time, money, and political capital to get his brothers into the Academy, neither gained admittance. George failed his examination due to deficiencies in speaking and writing English, while John's nomination by Morrison was rescinded on a politically motivated technicality. William Ralls Morrison to Louis Hauck, November 17, 1862, in possession of Patrick and Cheryl Evans, Cape Girardeau, Mo.

16. *Belleville Democrat,* September 14, 1861; Fietsam et al., *Belleville,* 50.

bly an elected post, this clerical position was traditionally filled through the process of patronage whereby the majority party rewarded loyal friends and supporters with government jobs. The duties of enrolling and engrossing clerk certainly suited a man with Louis's background. Basically taking the rough copies of bills written by the legislators themselves, he printed a formal "engrossed" version for the General Assembly to consider. After a bill passed both chambers of the General Assembly, he then copied another "enrolled" version for the governor to sign. In addition to his services in this capacity, Louis also took on the added responsibility of mailing legislative documents back to the *Belleville Democrat* and *Volksblatt* and for extra pay procuring other German newspapers for the legislators.[17]

Louis often found his "irksome duties" monotonous, but embraced his work as a learning experience and critical step in realizing his inchoate political aspirations. Intimidated at first by "the distinguished personages" making policy in the chambers of the Illinois capital, Hauck quickly figured out that for all their reputation and bombast, these politicians looked "just like other men."[18] For an energetic and affable—largely bilingual—clerk who took the initiative to make their acquaintance, printing bills and fetching newspapers could yield a great many new friends.

Louis also confided to his friend James Slade that although Underwood served in the state senate, he, Louis, was "not satisfied with the doings" of that body and that a wise man could learn far more of "how affairs are managed" by availing himself of that "august assemblage," the state house.[19] This decision to follow the representatives gave him an invaluable insider's look at one of Illinois's most dynamic legislative sessions because even as the tide of battle was turning toward the Union in 1863, Lincoln's Emancipation Proclamation and heavy-handed curtailment of wartime civil liberties helped people the Illinois General Assembly with rabid antiwar and peace Democrats. And in their caucus rooms and from the gallery, Hauck watched the Democrats use their majority to enact a legislative agenda based on their shared conviction that the war was a mistake.[20]

In this climate of heightened emotions, historian Arthur Cole observed that "it was easy enough to construe specific items in the democratic

17. Informal conversations with Kim Efird, Illinois State Archives, January 13, April 13, 2005; Houck, "Reminiscences," 8; *Belleville Democrat,* January 31, 1863.

18. William H. Barnum to Louis Hauck, June 9, 1863, in possession of Patrick and Cheryl Evans, Cape Girardeau, Mo.

19. James Park Slade to Louis Hauck, January 22, 1863, in possession of Patrick and Cheryl Evans, Cape Girardeau, Mo.

20. Pease, *Story of Illinois,* 170; Cole, *Centennial History of Illinois,* 298, 299, 300.

indictment of the administration policies as incontrovertible evidences of disloyalty." "Every democrat," Cole points out, "who did not openly and actively support the administration and the war was labeled a venomous 'copperhead,' at once a southern sympathizer and a traitor to the union."[21] Throughout Illinois, alarm over rampant "copperheadism" undermining the war effort increasingly led to pro-Union regulators silencing the most outspoken critics of government through vigilante violence and intimidation. As Louis sent legislative materials home to the *Volksblatt* for publication, he was well aware that freedom of the press in particular was taking a fierce beating, literally and figuratively. Democratic editors, some of whom he knew, faced lawful suspension of mail privileges and arrest, in addition to extralegal boycotts and in extreme cases assault by Union mobs and soldiers.

Louis was somewhat insulated from this harassment while in Springfield, but when he returned to Belleville periodically to check on the affairs of the *Volksblatt* that spring, he heard rather ominous whispers of "copperhead" around the public square and from those passing his office, which may have been located nearby on Northern Illinois Street. Some readers were canceling their subscriptions, judging the newspaper "too strong secesh."[22] Still others made thinly veiled threats about dealing with snakes accordingly. Not one to tread lightly, Louis ultimately ran afoul of these pro-Union Bellevillites by continuing to use the inflammatory rhetoric they found so dangerous in his editorials.

On March 3, 1863, the U.S. Congress passed the Enrollment Act, also known as the Conscription Act because it enlisted—technically drafted— into military service all able-bodied Union men between the ages of twenty and forty-five. The controversial law touched off fierce protest in the North, mainly among immigrant groups who declared that a war to free blacks was not their fight. While it is not clear whether Louis based his condemnation of the act on this particular line of reasoning, three days later pro-Union vigilantes wrenched open a window at the *Volksblatt* in the predawn hours and rudely relocated most of the office's contents into the muddy streets.

The next day unknown parties defaced the notice Louis tacked to the *Volksblatt* which read

21. Cole, *Centennial History of Illinois,* 300, 302.
22. William H. Barnum to Louis Hauck, March 15, 1863, in possession of Patrick and Cheryl Evans, Cape Girardeau, Mo.; Houck, "Reminiscences," 8.

Well done.
TO THE PUBLIC,
The type and several forms of the "Volksblatt"
were destroyed by *PATRIOTS* last
night. The paper will not appear to-day.
                    L. Hauck.
Served him right.

The English words "Well done" had been added to Louis's original sign in German, just as the phrase "Served him right" was inserted in Hauck's own native language. On the initial version, Louis had written "scoundrels," over which someone had also pasted a piece of white paper with the word "Patriots."[23]

Outwardly unfazed by this increasingly widespread assault on the First Amendment, Louis caught a train to St. Louis the morning after the attack to purchase new fonts of type, and had the *Volksblatt* presses up and running within a week before resuming his clerical duties at the capital. But by June his appointment as enrolling and engrossing clerk likewise fell victim to political malice as Governor Richard Yates prorogued, or discontinued, the legislative session rather than contend further with obstinate Democrats controlling the General Assembly.

Nevertheless, when asked by John Hand "whether you have learned enough to make your sojourn at the capital pay for the time spent," Louis could truthfully answer in the affirmative.[24] For one thing, he purchased a revolver and began sleeping in the *Volksblatt* office. Yet, more important, in the face of continued harassment, his anxiety for his safety and that of his press actually mixed awkwardly with a renewed hopefulness over his own political prospects. Inspired by his experiences in Springfield, he vigorously resumed his editing and speechmaking on behalf of the Democratic Party, now with a tentative eye toward running for the Illinois house himself in 1864. His law practice, affiliated as it was with Underwood, complemented his legislative work in the eyes of constituents and further positioned him advantageously among the legal and business community of the county. If his friend and fellow "good Democrat" William Barnum's generous accolades are any indication at all, Hauck's optimism concerning his "Electoral aspirations" was not wholly unfounded. In commenting

23. *Belleville Democrat,* March 7, 1863.
24. John Hand to Louis Hauck, February 18, 1863, in possession of Patrick and Cheryl Evans, Cape Girardeau, Mo.

on a political speech Louis gave at Prairie du Rocher in the summer of 1863, Barnum noted that it was "electrical in its effect upon the audience." "You produced a very brilliant impression," he wrote to Louis, "and if you will only follow it up you will certainly become the most popular politician in Illinois."[25]

Politics notwithstanding, Louis came of age during the Civil War, and as a man in his early twenties his interests ranged far beyond the county courthouse or state capital. Exceedingly well read, Louis and an informal coterie of friends—Barnum, Hand, James Park Slade, and Luke Hite—fancied themselves as members of Belleville's resident intelligentsia. By day, most were neophyte lawyers, but outside their law offices the informal group put aside the legalese of their profession to engage one another in a nearly endless colloquium of Greek mythology, American and European history, philosophy, and classical literature, ardently exchanging erudite observations on the latest essays read and lectures attended.

While not the only one with some college education, Hauck nonetheless assumed a central role in these exchanges, often dominating their gatherings and correspondence. English-speaking members of the circle, like Barnum, attributed his passion for learning and decided intellectual advantage, at least in part, to Louis's ability to draw on the best that had been written or thought in "the two noblest of living languages." "How I wish I could cross with you," Barnum once enviously wrote, "the bridge spanning the channel between English literature and the high poetic, historic and philosophic realms of Germany."[26] In jest, Louis suggested he learn German by subscribing to the *Volksblatt.*

Even in rural Illinois, these intellectual pursuits were not as uncommon as one might imagine. In fact, many of the failed German revolutionaries who immigrated to St. Clair County came from highly educated and professional backgrounds and maintained a strong commitment to advancing knowledge. Some, like the "Latin Farmers" of the nearby Shiloh Valley— so-called because of their collective use of the ancient Roman language while working the land—diligently labored to keep Old World culture alive through education and a public library.[27] In this spirit, Hauck's young friends formed their own "intellectual improvement society" to bring their

25. William H. Barnum to Louis Hauck, April 13, August 17, 1863, in possession of Patrick and Cheryl Evans, Cape Girardeau, Mo.

26. William H. Barnum to Louis Hauck, December 19, 1864, in possession of Patrick and Cheryl Evans, Cape Girardeau, Mo.

27. Fietsam et al., *Belleville,* 16.

literary appreciation and collegial debate to Belleville.[28] During one public lyceum indicative of the society's work, Hauck and Barnum rose from their seats in the audience during the oration to lead an impromptu discussion on whether the conquests of Alexander had been beneficial to the Western world. Impressed by how "both men displayed considerable knowledge of ancient history and geography," the audience gratefully acknowledged their contribution to the evening's program.[29]

Forums such as this undoubtedly helped to satisfy Louis's sincere intellectual curiosity. They certainly sharpened his public speaking skills and elevated his stature in the community. Intentionally or not, society work also appears to have afforded Louis a respectable venue to indulge his maturing "devotion to the fair sex."[30] Evidently charming, bright, and by all accounts not poorly put together or ill favored in appearance, Louis quite frankly seems to have been something of a dandy, although strong temperate habits kept him away from spirituous liquors. At first understandably awkward and lacking in confidence as an adolescent, he actually shied away from the company of ladies, preferring to secretly admire them from afar. When he became enamored with a certain Mrs. Hugh in 1861, Louis giddily waxed poetic to John Hand, romanticizing the nature of their relationship and comparing her beauty to that of the goddess Athena. Evidently immune to her charms, Hand objectively pointed out that Mrs. Hugh was twice Louis's age, and, having actually laid eyes on her himself, found Hauck's comparisons to Athena to be the product of exaggeration, intoxication, or both.

Hand continued to puzzle over his friend's misplaced affections and overall predicament. "I cannot account for your extreme bashfulness in circulating among the gentler sex," he confessed, but offered some advice on how Louis might change his romantic fortunes. He explained that after Louis left Wisconsin, several ladies in the local debating society expressed their "considerable regret" over his departure and how one in particular, Mariette, still "inquired anxiously after you." "It seems to me you have a glorious opportunity to shine in such company," Hand reasoned, "for the ladies take a natural liking to you." To Hand's way of thinking, Louis should look for "romantic attachment" among the bookish and refined

28. John E. Hand to Louis Hauck, April 30 [no year], in possession of Patrick and Cheryl Evans, Cape Girardeau, Mo.

29. *Belleville Democrat*, March 2, 1861.

30. James Park Slade to Louis Hauck, January 22, 1863, in possession of Patrick and Cheryl Evans, Cape Girardeau, Mo.

women who shared Louis's zeal for lectures, literary societies, and debating clubs. Another concerned friend, Luke Hite, concurred, reminding Louis that "intellectual young men (as we are!)" must find an educated mate in order to hold their interest.[31]

In time Hauck did in fact begin enjoying the charming company of a number of well-read "flames" before meeting his first true love, Julia, quite possibly Julia Brazeau, sometime in 1863. He confided to Barnum that he was indeed smitten and wondered if his closest, and only married, friend might offer his opinion. Barnum, who had by this time moved to Chester, Illinois, and did not know Julia personally, immediately wrote to his wise old aunt back in Belleville—who was close to the Hauck family—to get a better vantage point from which to judge the couple. "Aunty has thus become acquainted with Julia," he wrote favorably to Louis, "and thinks she is very much like you, might be your sister, talks like you, etc. 'No wonder' she tells me to write 'he was enamored of Julia at a glance and was plagued when we referred to his looking up at a window. Those whose externals are so much alike, must have corresponding internal resemblance. I fear' she says 'something serious will come of it.'"[32]

Indeed, something serious did come of it, at least for Louis. Over the next year and a half, he threw himself into courting Julia, his newfound bliss and desire to marry her apparent to all, it seems, except the reluctant Julia. Despite his persistence, at some point in late 1864 the two must have quarreled and parted company, perhaps over her relationship with a St. Louis doctor. In this regard, the best glimpse into the nature of Louis's and Julia's relationship comes from a December 1864 letter from James Slade. In it, the romantic young teacher, who had recently moved to Westerlo, New York, and also knew Julia only through Louis's correspondence, uses language he knew Hauck could appreciate to keep his friend's spirits up after what had obviously been an exhausting journey of unrequited love. "You think of the woman all the time, do you?" Slade inquired. "I should not be at all surprised, if, when the truth is ascertained, you should discover, to your great delight, that the thinking is mutual." But Louis would never know until he courageously laid siege to Julia's heart. Only then could Louis "penetrate the apparently formidable defenses, and find [himself] in the camp of a friend, who only wished to test your courage before

31. John E. Hand to Louis Hauck, September 20, December 9, 1861, January 29, 1862, Luke H. Hite to Louis Hauck, April 24, 1864, in possession of Patrick and Cheryl Evans, Cape Girardeau, Mo.
32. William H. Barnum to Louis Hauck, July 12, 1863, in possession of Patrick and Cheryl Evans, Cape Girardeau, Mo.

making (what perhaps she was all the time quite ready to make to a gallant besieger) a surrender."[33]

Six days later Louis received word from Barnum that Julia Brazeau had married Dr. Stuart Gordon in a hasty ceremony.[34]

Eighteen sixty-four proved to be a watershed year in the young life of Louis Hauck. Heartsick over Julia and perpetually uneasy over the draft, Louis saw his once bright political stock plummet. While the *Volksblatt* still faithfully carried the party standard under the watchful eye of his benefactors Morrison and Underwood, the Democrats were steadily reducing themselves to minority status in state politics, their opposition to the war rendered increasingly irrelevant with each Union victory on the battlefield. Morrison faced an uphill reelection battle for his congressional seat, and Underwood's interest in the economic development plans of the Republican Party intensified after he became one of the directors of the St. Louis, Alton and Terre Haute Railroad.

In the spring, Louis enthusiastically began gearing up for the presidential elections, keeping the editorial heat on a vulnerable Lincoln while sizing up potential Democrat challengers. Then, on May 19, a squad of armed Union soldiers laid waste to the *Volksblatt* again, this time in broad daylight before a "chuckling" and "gleeful" crowd. With guards posted at the door, the soldiers ordered the staff out at gunpoint. Louis was not in the office when the attack began, but Bartholomeaus resisted, trying in vain to protect the equipment. The "ruffians" flung the old man to the ground, injuring his hand and arm, before overturning the racks of type and strewing them across the floor. After completely demolishing the office and rendering the fixtures and presses useless, the Union soldiers defiantly marched up the street to wet their whistle at a saloon, where they decided at the last minute against attacking the *Belleville Democrat*. Summoned by his staff, Hauck and the city marshal pleaded with the gathered throng to help them apprehend the soldiers, but people "contemptuously refused, and sneeringly told the sheriff to look to his copperhead friends for assistance." The next day after a posse finally arrested six of "the rioters" in nearby Centreville, the local provost marshal conveniently intervened, informing the sheriff that the soldiers were from the Ninth Illinois Infantry and could only be held accountable to civilian authorities after their terms of military service had expired.[35]

33. James Park Slade to Louis Hauck, December 13, 1864, January 1, 1865, in possession of Patrick and Cheryl Evans, Cape Girardeau, Mo.
34. William H. Barnum to Louis Hauck, December 19, 1864, in possession of Patrick and Cheryl Evans, Cape Girardeau, Mo.
35. *Belleville Democrat*, May 21, June 4, 1864; Houck, "Reminiscences," 8.

Hauck publicly denounced the attack and the "farcical" miscarriage of justice. "The *Volksblatt*, ever since its establishment, has been a fearless defender of Democratic principles and the cause of Liberty, Justice and Truth," he indignantly proclaimed. "They cannot silence us. We will talk. We have survived the first destruction of our office—we will survive the second."[36] After moving his offices to another location, Louis had the *Volksblatt* in circulation again by midsummer, just in time to launch an all-out offensive to organize the German element for General George B. McClellan, who was nominated for president as a peace Democrat in August.[37] Before that, however, Hauck tentatively positioned himself for a run at the Illinois house. At the July Democratic state convention in Springfield, Louis secured the nomination to the position of "elector" for the Twelfth Congressional District based on his "faithful and valuable service to Democracy in St. Clair county."[38] While undoubtedly an honor, to Hauck this office was more importantly a means toward an end. If endorsed by the delegates representing the six counties of the district, he could conceivably ride the momentum and parlay their support into the coveted nomination for the state house of representatives. At the eleventh hour, however, St. Clair County party leaders stepped in to derail his strategy, reminding him that although a loyal and well-connected partisan, Hauck was after all only twenty-four and older, more established, men had seniority.[39]

Sensing his friend's extreme disappointment at this political setback, Luke Hite offered solace. "Don't worry too much Louis and fret because you can't go to Congress at 25," he wrote. "Smarter cleverer men than you have waited till 30." In an odd choice of metaphor given Hauck's temperate ways, Hite advised him to follow the example of the "saloon keepers putting their beer in an ice-chest so that it may not ferment, *Keep Cool.*" Perhaps more appropriately, Hite later correctly predicted, "As to your disappointment with election, be patient . . . honors are in store for you, your gold bearing coupons will be paid. 'cast thy bread upon the waters, and after many days it will return unto you.'"[40]

Hite's confidence fortified Louis, and he resigned himself to wait his turn and continue paying his dues. In the initial hoopla surrounding McClellan's ill-fated presidential campaign, Hauck dutifully went about his partisan

36. *Belleville Democrat,* May 21, 1864.
37. William Ralls Morrison to Louis Hauck, June 21, 1864, in possession of Patrick and Cheryl Evans, Cape Girardeau, Mo.
38. *Belleville Democrat,* June 25, 1864.
39. *Belleville Democrat,* June 25, September 24, 1864.
40. Luke Hite to Louis Hauck, April 24, July 14, 1864, in possession of Patrick and Cheryl Evans, Cape Girardeau, Mo.

work, at least outwardly never wavering in his loyalty to the Democratic ticket. His editorials—a mixture of stinging sarcasm and references to classic literature and Greek and Roman history—faithfully articulated the peace Democrat's denunciation of emancipation and demand for a cessation of hostilities. The *Volksblatt* vainly proclaimed the cause of George McClellan to be growing by the hour and called on all Democrats to settle their differences and unite behind the General's promise to seek an immediate armistice and convene a peace conference if elected.[41] In the late summer Louis undertook an exhausting "political tour," speaking extensively on behalf of Morrison, gubernatorial candidate Benjamin Edwards, and McClellan at rallies around the Twelfth Congressional District. In Chester he shared the podium with many of the old local Democratic stand-bys and helped to raise a 116-foot "McClellan pole."[42]

As summer turned to fall, however, Louis must have become increasingly aware of the futility in his labors. While canvassing and speechmaking, each day news of General William Tecumseh Sherman's military victories in Georgia further discredited his contention that the war was a failure and a victory could not be won on the battlefield. Just across the Mississippi River, Union forces were also driving General Sterling Price's Confederate cavalry out of Missouri, and thus eliminating the last legitimate Southern threat to St. Louis and that state. Coupled with Sherman's "March to the Sea," the collapse of Price's long-feared raid into Missouri strengthened the Republican case that the Confederacy was now on the run and the North should vigorously prosecute the war to its completion. Everywhere Louis traveled in southern Illinois that fall, the specter of copperheadism closely followed. What many perceived as his defeatist oratory of negotiations and voluntary reunion were increasingly out of sync with an Illinois electorate daily growing more and more intent on forcing the fading Confederacy to concede to every Union demand, including emancipation. Privately, William Barnum worried for Louis's health, scolding him for "working too hard and taking too little exercise." In particular, he fretted over his friend's safety, convinced that at best Hauck would be locked up in some Lincoln administration "Bastille" for the remainder of the war.[43]

41. *Belleville Democrat*, September 17, 1864.

42. William H. Barnum to Louis Hauck, September 18, 1864, in possession of Patrick and Cheryl Evans, Cape Girardeau, Mo.

43. William H. Barnum to Louis Hauck, March 26, May 31, June 28, September 18, 1864, in possession of Patrick and Cheryl Evans, Cape Girardeau, Mo.; *Belleville Democrat*, September 17, 24, 1864.

For all intents and purposes, the Civil War, which until this point had effectively set the parameters for Louis Hauck's young political, economic, and social life, ended with Abraham Lincoln's resounding reelection in 1864. The Republican mandate at the state and federal level marginalized Louis politically, and, like those wheels on Sesostris's chariot, turned his fortunes again by forcing him to take stock of his future as a newspaper editor and concomitantly as a resident of Belleville. Although the fighting would drag on until April 1865, Hauck's opposition to the war and Lincoln—the veritable foundation on which the *Volksblatt* was built—were now essentially non-issues with a rapidly disappearing constituency. In fact, lean years were on the horizon for Democratic politics and the newspapers that espoused them. The nearly complete triumph of the Republicans in 1864 relegated Democrats to subordinate status in postwar Illinois and left Hauck's contemporaries with the sobering possibility that the party of Jackson might now simply disintegrate into oblivion like the Whigs.

Of a more immediate concern, the election severed Louis from his primary political benefactors. William Ralls Morrison lost his congressional seat, and William Underwood bolted to the Republicans. With his party out of fashion, and out of power, even simple patronage printing jobs, let alone elected office, were a thing of the past. Making life more difficult, the bridges were thoroughly burnt between Louis and Belleville Republicans. During the election, the *Volksblatt* had skewered John Baker, the Republican who beat Morrison, and Underwood's seeming disloyalty soured the two's relationship. Of course, the *Volksblatt* had, after all, been seriously attacked twice since 1863, which understandably left palpable hard feelings between Louis and what he believed were certain inhospitable elements of the majority party still out to get him.

With every one of the original motivations behind editing and publishing the *Volksblatt* eliminated and future prospects for a Democratic newspaperman dim, a career change seemed clearly in order, and in December 1864 Louis fatefully decided to sell his interest in the *Volksblatt,* forsaking the newspaper business for the practice of law. He actually had been entertaining the idea of practicing law full-time since his admission to the bar by the Illinois Supreme Court in the summer of 1864, and since the second attack on the *Volksblatt* he also had pondered the prospect of moving off to greener, more lucrative pastures. In encouraging this decision, William Barnum perhaps unknowingly articulated the view of many Illinois Democrats when he suggested that he, Hauck, and Hite leave the Republican North for the more Democratic-friendly climate in the postwar South. Though political careers were probably out of the question for

Northerners, there would be prospects galore for ambitious young attorneys like themselves amid the fallen fortunes, abandoned plantations, and broken female hearts of the former Confederacy.[44]

Throughout the spring of 1865, Louis leaned toward taking Barnum's advice and moving to Arkansas as soon as the war ended. Yet in the midst of concluding his remaining business obligations and selling his home, Hauck received a more attractive offer from Harvey Kilpatrick Stuart O'Melveny—a prominent southern Illinois attorney and Democratic stalwart—inviting him to become a partner in the judge's newly opened Cairo, Illinois, firm. Not purely serendipitous, O'Melveny's timely partnership proposal seems more appropriately to have been an instance of what the scientist Louis Pasteur would later describe as chance favoring the prepared mind. Hauck had become acquainted with O'Melveny through party politics sometime in early 1864 and surely learned of the Irishman's intentions to retire from active political life after the election and ultimately move his family west to California. Without putting too fine a point on it, Louis recognized how the unfolding of these events might work to his advantage, especially given rumors of the Illinois Supreme Court's relocation to Cairo from Springfield. Not only could a young lawyer in O'Melveny's office confidently count on a respectable income while honing his skills against the best and brightest coming to argue at the state supreme court, but he would also be in line to possibly inherit said law office in the foreseeable future. Moreover, a young lawyer who still had not given up on his political aspirations would have access to O'Melveny's political clout in Alexander and Pulaski counties and therefore stood to also become heir to the judge's power base in one of the state's remaining Democratic outposts.

Thus Louis conspicuously endeared himself to the forty-two-year-old O'Melveny whenever possible, and when the offer finally came to become O'Melveny's partner in June 1865, Louis welcomed its generous terms. Despite any reservations he may have harbored about permanently residing in Cairo—a coarse river town he once characterized as "an awful hole"—Louis never seriously considered turning O'Melveny down. After summarily casting aside thoughts of Arkansas, if anything, the only question was over the means of travel, and since no railroad ran between Belleville and Cairo, he booked passage on a steamboat in St. Louis for the twelve-hour journey down the Mississippi.

44. Luke Hite to Louis Hauck, September 21, 1863, Robert A. Halbert to Louis Hauck, June 15, 1865, William H. Barnum to Louis Hauck, March 9, June 13, 1865, Robert A. Halbert to Louis Hauck, June 15, 1865, in possession of Patrick and Cheryl Evans, Cape Girardeau, Mo.

On the day before his departure a large gathering of friends, mostly fellow attorneys and political associates, joined Louis in the office of Judge Snyder to bid him a formal adieu. Their toasts and resultant speeches honored the didactic former editor of the *Volksblatt*—still unbent and unrepentant—for his dogged fidelity to principle that kept him steady even when, as some forlornly recalled, the storm had uprooted so many older trees in the forest. Having come to know Hauck during the last five years, many drank to his well-known "indifference" to popular passions and seemingly natural "self-forgetfulness" when focused on the given task at hand. Others commended his uncompromising nature and the almost cavalier "sort of devil-may-care" manner in which he had carried himself through the great cataclysm of the Civil War.[45]

In less serious moments of persiflage, someone surely made reference to his atrocious penmanship and the long-standing joke that it resulted from private lessons with a "Chinese writing master." Some may have offered their droll anecdotes of Louis's familiar aversion to lagers and ales—so out of step with his German heritage—and his propensity to make the ladies laugh, despite a natural boyish shyness.

Although not there to sing the songs of congratulations in person, William Barnum surely captured the sentiment of the well-wishers when he offered his sincere hope that the future would find Louis "prospering in law, love and lore." In truth, no one at the time knew Louis better than Barnum, and on this occasion of Hauck's leaving for Cairo, it was an earlier observation of Barnum's which affords the most honest insight into Hauck while at the same time perhaps the most fitting fare-thee-well to his years in Belleville. Regardless of whatever dispassionate face Hauck chose to present—which Barnum judged to be disingenuous anyway—"I catch a glimpse of you, as you have never seen yourself," he wrote in 1863, "absorbed in your books, in your quiet little retreat, profoundly studious, intent as a blood hound upon the task of learning. The glow of health lights up your face and the celestial gratifications of scholarship, paint each moment a new picture on your eye. May this, my friend, continue to be your happy, your noble lot! May it be yours to pass in grave review before you, kings and courts, philosophers, warriors and statesmen, systems, policies & laws. May you know the Past like a friend and may the Past introduce you to the Future!"[46]

45. *Belleville Democrat,* August 5, 1865, March 1, 1864.
46. William H. Barnum to Louis Hauck, July 27, 1863, April 3, 1865, in possession of Patrick and Cheryl Evans, Cape Girardeau, Mo.

CHAPTER 3

The Belle of Cape Girardeau

Before the war the "belles" of the cape were famous,
nor are they unsung since the war.

—Louis Houck

From the upper deck of a steamboat en route to Cairo, Louis Hauck unknowingly caught a glimpse of his future through the torpid haze of humidity which oppresses life along the Mississippi River on late July afternoons. Briefly interrupting his trip to transact its regular business, the packet boat taking him south tied up along the cobblestone levee of Cape Girardeau, a rough-and-tumble little river town on the Missouri side. Somewhat incuriously, Louis observed the ritual of roustabouts jumping off the gangplanks to unload merchandise stacked on the first deck and load hundreds of barrels of flour left waiting for them by the river. These roustabouts, mostly African American men hired in St. Louis, sang as they worked, and, since few of them could read, they shouted out an elaborate system of nicknames they had made for local merchants to help them remember what cargo went where. Amongst the crates and bundles, nosy townspeople milled about the levee to check out what new merchandise local stores would soon be offering and if their neighbors had made any major purchases.

The Cape Girardeau riverfront that Louis looked over may well have been the inspiration for Mark Twain's description of the fictitious Dawson's Landing, a town one day south of St. Louis, in his book *Pudd'nhead Wilson*. In the years before the Civil War, it was, Twain wrote, a "snug little collection of framehouses whose front was washed by the clear waters of the great river, and whose body stretched rearward up a gentle incline to the hills and forests on the west." Yet, Louis was not similarly inspired, or impressed, that day, remembering a Catholic church and seminary among the warehouses, but otherwise having "no other distinct recollection of the town." In fact, "never," he later freely admitted, did he entertain "any idea then that I should ever live in Cape Girardeau."[1]

Within three hours of docking, the packet boat shoved off and headed south again toward Cairo, Illinois. It would be four more years before Louis found his way back.

Arriving on August 1, 1865, Louis Napoleon Hauck commenced his law partnership with Harvey Kilpatrick Stuart O'Melveny during spirited and heady times in Cairo. Strategically located at the confluence of the Ohio and Mississippi rivers, which historically positioned the town as the central service and distribution hub of southern Illinois and southeast Missouri, Cairo boomed immediately following the Civil War. The town, which swelled in size from some two thousand to nearly twelve thousand, seemed alive with relief from the long struggle and optimism for a bright and profitable peace. From their Commercial Street office, the German and Irish law partners quickly built a reputable practice representing the multitudes of eager entrepreneurs, capitalists, and aspiring businessmen coming in from the North and in particular land speculators and maritime interests in the river town. Through O'Melveny's network of judicial and Democratic associates, Louis integrated himself into the legal community of extreme southern Illinois and began rebuilding his frayed contacts in a region whose political sensibilities were more in keeping with his own. In the area's courtrooms his practical legal education also evolved as veteran backwoods lawyers informed his developing philosophy regarding creative trial strategies and the realities of how deals were actually brokered and rural justice carried out.

It was also here in Cairo that he apparently, and unceremoniously, began using the familiar "Houck" spelling of his surname. Although it would be plausible that Louis deliberately initiated the change to distance himself from some of the unpleasantness in Belleville, this seemingly significant alteration, at least by twentieth-century standards, probably had little to

1. Houck, "Reminiscences," 9–10. Louis was referring to two icons of Cape Girardeau architecture along the riverfront: St. Vincent de Paul Church, a beautiful Gothic cathedral built in 1853, and St. Vincent's College, built between 1843 and 1853 as a preparatory school for students who would continue their seminary education at St. Mary's of the Barrens in Perryville.

do with any conscious decision on his part. Rather, it more likely occurred quite naturally because other German families with the Houck spelling were already well known in the region, and out of habit locals innocently and routinely kept misspelling the unfamiliar "Hauck." For his part, Louis looks to have accepted the change as a matter of course.

Although he *had* made the conscious decision that publishing would no longer be his livelihood, writing remained both an intellectual passion and a central feature of his professional life. Newsprint never left his blood. Not long after relocating, he regularly contributed to the *Missouri Republican* in St. Louis as a legal correspondent from the Illinois Supreme Court and occasionally wrote on other Illinois political and historical matters, curiously, often under the anonymous *nom de plume* "Ariel." What is more, in what had already emerged as a pronounced pattern that ultimately spanned nearly the entirety of his productive years, Louis mitigated against what he considered gaps in the existing professional literature— whether legal or historical—by undertaking to write the definitive texts himself. While still reading law in William Underwood's office in Belleville, Louis had discovered the lack of a standard source on the subject of Mechanic's Liens—the legal claim by workmen on real property on which they have done significant work and have not been paid—during his research for a minor case. Seeing as he had a great deal of idle time in his as yet nascent practice, Louis often filled those hours by compiling various state statutes and judicial decisions on Mechanic's Liens into a reference book on the subject.

Work continued on the manuscript once in Cairo, and in 1867 he submitted the completed text to the legal publishing house of Callaghan and Cutler, who in turn published it, his first book, *A Treatise on the Mechanics' Lien Law in the United States,* later that year. In all, during his three years in Cairo, Louis wrote two law books nearly simultaneously. In the course of fighting a bout of real estate litigation involving the laws of accretion— whereby natural deposits of soil along the shorelines of rivers or oceans actually increase the landowner's property—Louis researched and wrote *A Treatise on the Law of Navigable Rivers* that Little, Brown and Company in Boston published in 1868. Along with an accompanying essay in the *American Law Review* that same year, these two judicial tomes inaugurated a quite prolific fifty-year career as an author.[2]

Though certainly not misspent by any measure, Houck's time in Cairo proved relatively short. Despite the town's postwar flurry of activity, his

2. Ibid., 9, 10, 12, 13.

lofty expectations far outpaced actual financial rewards and chances for career advancements. Even after O'Melveny made good on his intentions to move west to Los Angeles in early 1868, Louis could not escape the fact that Cairo's boom was already tapering off and the population declining. Prominent political friends in St. Louis—in particular William Hyde, a former Belleville resident and now managing editor of the *Missouri Republican*, and Barton Able, at the time a U.S. Internal Revenue collector—coaxed Louis to take this opportunity to seek his fortune up and across the Mississippi in the Gateway City. St. Louis, and the state of Missouri in general, the men made clear, were awakening from the stupor of war ripe with commercial and entrepreneurial prospects on a scale which simply dwarfed that of Cairo. Ambitious and progressive young men of vision were reconstructing the former slaveholding state, disassociating it from the lethargic South and creating the economic conditions conducive to attracting Northern industrial development, European immigration, and national commerce.[3]

Within weeks of his opening a St. Louis law practice in July 1868 in a rented office on the corner of Chestnut and Broadway several blocks west of the river, the wheels of Sesostris's chariot turned yet again in Louis's favor. An argument between U.S. District Attorney John W. Noble and his assistant resulted in an unforeseen vacancy in the district attorney's St. Louis office. Longtime Missouri political operative Barton Able, who in his capacity as Internal Revenue collector dealt with Noble on a variety of legal issues stemming from violations of excise law, recommended Louis as a suitable replacement. From his office at the *Missouri Republican*, William Hyde, who also had Noble's ear, put in a good word for him as well. And in an apparent rush to fill the position before he left on an extended summer vacation, John Noble swiftly appointed Louis Houck, with all of five years legal experience, as assistant U.S. district attorney.

Interestingly, the nature of Missouri postwar politics, specifically the almost ironclad domination of the Republican Party, should have systematically precluded Noble from seriously considering a Democrat like Houck for the position outright.[4] Democrats had controlled Missouri politics for most of its history since statehood. But since 1864, Republicans in the state, led by a wing of the party aligning itself with the national Radi-

---

3. Ibid., 13, 14; Lawrence O. Christensen and Gary R. Kremer, *A History of Missouri, Volume IV 1875–1919*.

4. See William E. Parrish, *Missouri under Radical Rule, 1865–1870* (Columbia: University of Missouri Press, 1965).

cal Republican movement, enjoyed a virtual stranglehold on political power, charting a dichotomous course for economic progress while vindictively disfranchising the "rebel element" of Southern sympathizers thought to be infesting the Democratic Party. Missouri's 1865 constitution, referred to as "Drake's Constitution" for its primary author Charles Drake, the most powerful state political figure in the immediate postwar years, had codified the Republicans' punitive wartime treatment of the Democrats by requiring a loyalty oath for voting and participation in a variety of professions, including law. Since the oath required an individual pledge of innocence on a sweeping list of some eighty-six separate acts of disloyalty to the Union, in a painfully divided border state, even moderate Democrats had only the faintest hope of successfully qualifying. In tandem with its "purification" of the ballot, Republicans had also purged the state's judiciary system by ousting more than eight hundred judges and attorneys from positions ranging from the state supreme court all the way down to the county recorders. As a result, Missouri Democrats effectively wandered in virtual exile in the late 1860s; they were even more thoroughly marginalized in Missouri than in Houck's Illinois.

In a city he correctly gauged to be fiercely Republican, where "political feeling ran high" and "intense political antagonism prevailed," Louis once again had the good fortune—and good sense—to position himself so that he might benefit professionally from what he termed "advantageous connections" with older and better-established men who took a keen interest in his success. Given Houck's wartime experiences, Hyde and Able, both strong Republicans of some local influence, may have initially helped him navigate any sticky issues that could have potentially arisen over his own loyalty oath. Without question their ringing endorsements to Noble, another pronounced Republican and distinguished Union Army veteran, overcame what was otherwise probably an insurmountable political obstacle for someone of Louis's political background.

John Noble conducted a whirlwind two-day orientation of his office for Louis in late July before leaving his new twenty-eight-year-old assistant completely in charge until the district attorney's anticipated return in September. The storm did not end with the orientation. "I had a very important position thrust upon me on short notice," Houck recalled, "but I faithfully attended to all the business, diligently studied the law, [and] started a good many prosecutions."[5]

5. Houck, "Reminiscences," 14, 15.

Aside from simply getting a handle on the intimidating array of unfamiliar procedures, paper work, and associates, much about his new job in the district attorney general's office must have also challenged some of Louis's fundamental conceptions of practicing law and politics. Not only did Houck hastily adapt to the equally unfamiliar role of prosecutor, but the very nature of the cases that came across his desk spoke to the radical changes being wrought across the legal community by the increasingly sophisticated nature of competitive industrial capitalism. With railroads as the primary impetus, the American economy was experiencing extraordinary growth in size and scope, becoming progressively more commercial and market-driven in the generation after the Civil War. Nearly simultaneous revolutions in power, transportation, productivity, and communication were under way, resulting in the birth of the modern corporate structure with its complicated new levels of organization, bureaucratization, and professionalization. Evidence of the transformation could already be clearly seen writ large in the foundries, machine shops, breweries, mills, factories, and publishing houses that were diversifying the industrial base of St. Louis, the nation's fourth largest city by century's end.

American courtrooms were at the forefront of the struggle to maintain a sense of orderly progression amidst such rapid modernization and to negotiate the challenges to national conceptions regarding the relationship between private interest and the public good. In the cases he personally prosecuted, Louis Houck first acquainted himself with a generation of unscrupulous and ruthless Eastern businessmen, known to him all too well by the 1890s, who were mobilizing massive amounts of capital, manipulating the legal system, fleecing the consumer, and cannibalizing their competition.[6]

Louis also saw firsthand the specter of money and special interests seeping into American politics to pervert and trivialize its systems. And this more than anything rapidly soured him on St. Louis. This was the dawn of Mark Twain's and Charles Dudley Warner's "Gilded Age," an era that came to set the standard by which government corruption, bribery, and scandal are measured. Even in the years before Edward Butler became the

6. Michael Les Benedict, "Law and the Constitution in the Gilded Age," in Charles W. Calhoun, ed., *The Gilded Age: Essays on the Origins of Modern America*, 289; Alan Trachtenberg, *The Incorporation of America: Culture and Society in the Gilded Age*, 81, 84; William T. Doherty, Jr., "The Missouri Interests of Louis Houck," (Ph.D. diss., University of Missouri, 1951), 36.

recognized Democratic boss of St. Louis machine politics, disturbing trends were under way across the nation as the business of politics was increasingly being conducted outside the public forums of government, in smoky back rooms where elected officials betrayed the public trust by peddling their influence to the highest bidder. During the first year of Republican Ulysses S. Grant's sullied presidency, which marked a low point for honest government, Houck openly began to question his particular place, or lack thereof, within the federal judiciary, and the GOP's intractable monopoly on power.

Even though better situated at the time in terms of "friends and influence" than some young colleagues he knew, Louis nevertheless "began to feel that no one had any chance to wield any influence or accomplish anything unless supported with ample sums of money or a combination of political managers." "Without such aids," Houck later judged of his growing impatience with the diminishing economic and political power of the individual, "it seemed to me a man was a mere cipher." Making only $125 a month and "just barely able to make all ends meet," one thing was becoming painfully obvious: in 1869, the St. Louis he knew was more and more controlled by a well-financed Republican good-old-boy network. Louis Houck—described as small in physical organization, but massive in intellect and ambition—recognized that he was on the outside looking in. Likewise, as a man who had always been self-employed, he could not say he liked working for a salary much either. In fact, rather indicative of the nation's declining esteem for the working class in general, Louis concluded that "my experience as a salaried officer created a great prejudice in my mind against working for a salary."[7] Whether coincidentally or by design, Houck never drew another day's salary again and carefully resisted numerous temptations of elective office over the years.

"So I made up my mind that I would not remain in the city but would move to the country," Louis wrote of his resignation from the district attorney general's office after less than one year, "where individual efforts and individual exertions would have a greater influence and would accomplish more." Hyde, Able, and Noble sincerely cautioned him against what they considered a rash decision—especially his initial intention to relocate in Arkansas or Texas—but ultimately they came to support his scheme. Indeed, the men remained lifelong friends. Noble, who became a giant in the St. Louis legal community and served President Benjamin Harrison as

7. Houck, "Reminiscences," 14; *Missouri Republican* (St. Louis), May 11, 1872.

secretary of the interior, would years later represent his former assistant as lead counsel in Houck's showdown with the House of Gould. And it was William Hyde, based on his experiences at a political convention in that town, who suggested Louis consider southeast Missouri, in particular, Cape Girardeau.[8]

Primarily on this recommendation from Hyde, Louis Houck composed a letter to one of the few people he knew in Cape Girardeau, a local hardware merchant named James E. Reilly. Houck's and Reilly's friendship went back to the early 1860s, when Louis had worked for Senator Daniel Reilly, James's uncle, in the Illinois legislature. Now, through Reilly, Houck arranged to relocate for the final time in his life and establish a law practice in a modest little town he had barely given notice to on his way to Cairo.

Reilly met Louis on Cape Girardeau's cobblestone wharf when Houck's steamboat landed on April 21, 1869. He immediately introduced Louis to Leo Doyle, a friend who owned a store next to Reilly's on Main Street. From there the three removed themselves to the stately St. Charles Hotel, which stood at the southwest corner of Main and Themis streets, a block from the river, where Louis took up temporary residence. The St. Charles, with a distinctive cupola adding much-needed ornamentation to Cape's warehouse district, served for years as the social center of the town and region. Its fine accommodations and fabulous parties attracted folks from far and wide, including Ulysses S. Grant and even Mark Twain himself. In these grand surroundings, Louis opened his practice in a rented space next to the hotel office and "there," he sanguinely proclaimed, "established myself in Cape Girardeau."[9]

Louis had wanted to move to a less cosmopolitan existence, and that is just what he got. When Houck arrived, the town was languishing: it was an isolated, stagnant, and economically depressed little river community almost desperately clinging to the Mississippi. The hardships and uncertainty of war had reversed Cape's antebellum fortunes and eroded its historical position as the commercial heart of southeast Missouri. Just as Cairo had boomed across the river, Cape had declined. Guerrilla warfare and military service robbed the surrounding region of a significant portion of its population, retarding commercial and agricultural development, while a scarcity of hard money choked economic initiative. Only slowly, haltingly, did the labor force and capital return. Years of Union occupation had taken a toll on Cape Girardeau as well, giving it a grave, almost igno-

8. Houck, "Reminiscences," 14.
9. Ibid., 16.

minious, character with the added saloons, gambling, prostitution, and the arrival of the black market. Travelers to this lonely area commented on the "southern" qualities of the people: unhurried, unpretentious, difficult to impress, self-assured to a fault, fiscally conservative, but not particularly industrious.[10]

Although the city boundaries had continued to push out gradually over the years from the Mississippi, by 1870 the citizenry numbered only 3,585, primarily because of German immigration. Those businesses that survived the war still clustered primarily along Main, a partially macadamized street running parallel to the river, yet sidewalks were intermittent and numerous overgrown vacant lots blighted the downtown area. The Common Pleas Courthouse, built sometime around 1854 to handle the area's criminal, civil, and probate matters, proudly overlooked Cape Girardeau and the Mississippi from its perch high above Themis Street, but even the hill on which it stood was bare and scarred with gullies. Attorneys and other folks with business at the courthouse used a "pig path" to reach it because the stone steps for a long-proposed walkway were still piled up at the foot of the hill on Spanish Street.

Adding insult to injury, riverboat trade, around which life on the Mississippi revolved, never fully recovered from the disruption of war. While the river still connected Cape Girardeau to the larger world, the golden age of the steamboats was passing and the economic benefits of river trade diminishing with the coming of the railroads. Each year the newly constructed St. Louis and Iron Mountain Railroad to the west lured away countless tons of shipping from the town's increasingly idle wharf.

Oddly enough, despite the dismal state of affairs in these neglected backwoods, Cape Girardeau and southeast Missouri suited the determined young Houck's maturing talents and sensibilities. For the better part of the next decade the sturdy German relied on his now characteristic capacity for hard work—what associates had already identified as his "indefatigable industry"—to once more make a success of his legal practice.[11]

Again as a function of the general idleness inherent in the slow process of cultivating a sustained clientele, Louis spent a good portion of his earliest days in Cape writing another legal text. For most of 1869 and 1870

---

10. Tom Neumeyer, Frank Nickell, and Joel P. Rhodes, *Historic Cape Girardeau: An Illustrated History*, 1, 28, 31; James R. Shortridge, *The Middle West: Its Meaning in American Culture*.

11. William H. Barnum to Louis Houck, December 19, 1864, in possession of Patrick and Cheryl Evans, Cape Girardeau, Mo.

Louis laboriously edited and thoroughly annotated the first fifteen volumes of the *Missouri Reports,* a reference containing the cases argued before the state supreme court between 1835 and 1837. Much like his previous experience working on *Mechanics' Lien* and *Law of Navigable Rivers,* Louis undertook the project to keep his professional mind sharp after discovering that available copies of the *Reports* were hard to come by in outstate Missouri, especially in the south. But, never having realized much in the way of a financial benefit from the first two treatises, Louis devised a decidedly different arrangement this time in publishing his versions of the *Missouri Reports.*

In early 1870 he began traveling repeatedly to the state capital in Jefferson City, seeking to convince lawmakers that the state of Missouri should purchase in advance three hundred sets of his new and annotated *Missouri Reports* at $2.60 per book, or $39 for a complete fifteen-volume set. Since an act of the General Assembly was required for such a subscription—roughly $11,000 in total—for almost two months Houck lobbied anyone in the house or senate who would stand still about the relative necessity of his work. Eventually, after a brief bit of political intrigue on the part of the Republican leadership in the house judiciary committee, the *Missouri Reports* subscription bill passed, largely on account of Houck's persistent industriousness and moxie.[12]

Although he was sure to finally "realize a little money out of the transaction," the publishing itself was not without incident. After securing the bill from the General Assembly for three hundred sets, Louis awarded the publishing contract for five hundred sets to his friend William Hyde, who in addition to newspapers also did job and book printing. But during the process a fire at the *Missouri Republican* offices in May 1870 destroyed many of Houck's handwritten notes along with most of the manuscript for the first three volumes. The sudden and unforeseen loss of more than a year's worth of work caused considerable mental anguish, and although Louis eventually rewrote the lost material with a great deal of extra labor, the memory of the ordeal never left him. Thereafter he always went to great pains as an author to safeguard his work against fire.

The balance of Louis's professional life in those early years involved months of travel to attend the circuit courts of southeast Missouri, usually on horseback and when necessary by packet boat. To the north, Houck trekked hundreds of miles through the remote Ozark hills of Perry, Ste.

---

12. Houck, "Reminiscences," 41, 42; *Laws of the State of Missouri, passed at the adjourned Session of the 25th General Assembly,* 1870, 113.

Genevieve, Jefferson, Madison, and St. Francois counties, and to the west, through Iron, Bollinger, Wayne, Stoddard, and Butler. South of Cape Girardeau, through the wilderness of small lakes, marshes, and wetlands that made up what locals referred to as "Swampeast Missouri," he followed Crowley's Ridge, the region's only high ground extending from Cape Girardeau into Arkansas, on his way to the counties of Scott, Dunklin, Mississippi, New Madrid, and Pemiscot.

Routinely, lawyers from a given community rode together—in what Louis termed a large cavalcade—to out-of-the-way and hardscrabble villages such as Commerce, Bloomfield, Marble Hill, Clarkton, Kennett, Charleston, and New Madrid or whichever little town was hosting that term's court. Sessions usually lasted about a week, in structures that sometimes could be considered a courthouse in name only, with the colorful collection of lawyers, litigants, jurors, and spectators in attendance always giving the proceedings a festive atmosphere. At night the itinerant jurists found boarding at local homes, so-called hotels, nearby farms, or wherever they could.

For Louis, who had never ridden a horse more than a mile at any given time in his life, traveling the circuit must have sometimes seemed like a grand adventure, something akin to an expedition from southeast Missouri's not-too-far-removed frontier past. His companions on the road often included the region's foremost lawyers, men such as Colonel Solomon G. Kitchen, Major Henry H. Bedford, James H. Vail, and James W. Owens. Louis instinctively gravitated toward them and seized every opportunity to share in their accumulated knowledge of the country's oddities and peculiarities. In turn, these distinguished gentlemen seem to have graciously welcomed the affable newcomer into their casual fraternity, probably because they recognized his talent for the law and appreciated his inherently inquisitive nature. They were probably even initially somewhat empathetic to his greenhorn appearance considering that, astride a rented horse, his urbane silk hat and prominent glasses made the nearsighted and smallish Houck—just five feet, six inches tall—look much younger and by his own admission "very conspicuous" given the rugged nature of southeast Missouri.

As they made their way south into the Bootheel along Crowley's Ridge, they saw below them on each side the hundreds of thousands of acres of cypress and other hardwood forests that covered more than 90 percent of one of the largest wetlands in North America. As far as the eye could see, not so much as a single farm or clearing broke up the majesty of the immense swamp. Henry Bedford good-naturedly tutored Louis about the variety of strange new flora and fauna they encountered and in that way he familiarized himself with timber, the region's most bountiful resource, and how to tell the difference between gum, ash, hickory, or cypress. Likewise, they often passed the time reciting the names of the various topographical features such as the Gum, Taylor, and Chillitecaux sloughs that ran from the St. Francois River across the Dunklin Ridge to the Little River bottom.

Invariably, conversations turned from the natural environment to the region's political terrain. Vail or Owens might explain how Cape Girardeau, like much of Missouri, was historically a conservative Democratic town in the mold of Andrew Jackson and the esteemed Missouri Senator Thomas Hart Benton. The people, they observed, simply liked their government small, taxes low, and as little outside interference and bureaucracy from the federal government as possible; these were strict constructionist sentiments in complete harmony with Louis's own states' rights and free market orientation.

On a number of occasions companions appealed to the historian in Louis with colorful tales of the region's rich frontier and Civil War heritage. Around the dinner tables and moonlit front porches of the homes and roadhouses where they boarded, the lawyers spoke of the little-understood prehistoric mound builders, the calamitous earthquakes along the New Madrid fault in 1811 and 1812, and how in the years before statehood southeast Missouri was born of three diverse cultures: French, Spanish, and American. Kitchen and Bedford had also crisscrossed some of these trails in command of the Seventh Missouri Cavalry Regiment and a Missouri State Guard unit respectively during the war, and Kitchen in particular had fought in a number of pitched battles against Union forces in the region. It would be expected, given the veteran's proclivity to reminisce and Louis's keen interest in military history, that as they approached Cape Girardeau, Belmont, New Madrid, Hamburg, Blackwell's Station, and Fredericktown, the old officers would point out battlefields.

Whatever the course of this informal education, it seems clear that while riding the circuit courts in southeast Missouri, Houck indeed came to his lifelong devotion for southeast Missouri honestly, developing a heartfelt affection for the communities, geography, and history of this part of his adopted state. Much like his father Bartholomeaus during the 1820s, Louis had embarked on his own "wanderjahre" of sorts in 1865. From Belleville to Cairo to St. Louis and now to Cape Girardeau, Houck journeyed along the banks of the Mississippi River, completing his education and becoming a master lawyer. Still, his own years of travel had left an essential part of him unfulfilled and wanting. Since leaving his parents' home, Louis genuinely yearned to be a "permanent resident," a "fixture" in a community; to feel an authentic connectedness to its land and people with a truly vested interest in its fortunes. Now, in Cape Girardeau and southeast Missouri, Houck was discovering his own place in the world.[13]

Accordingly, in what began a lasting pursuit, within months of his arrival Louis launched an almost one-man campaign to improve the quality of life in small, subtle ways that often appealed to his own interests in horticulture. The first of these civic improvements involved agitating local businessmen, as much as a newcomer could, to get stone courthouse steps finally set. In the same way, he called for tame mulberry trees to be planted in rows along each side of the steps and for good measure some additional trees to flank Main, Independence, and Spanish streets. When he found that the town's general malaise smothered his rather progressive ideas, especially in the area of planting trees along the sidewalks, Louis enlisted the help of Charles Frederick William Shivelbine, a new friend and member of the city council from whom he was now renting an office on Main Street. Houck eventually got others interested as well, and largely through Shivelbine's efforts, left his first tangible marks on Cape's landscape.

Houck also tirelessly extolled the virtues of Cape Girardeau and southeast Missouri's untapped economic and cultural potential, generally in the form of semi-regular propaganda pieces for readers of the *Missouri Republican* and of occasional public speeches. In becoming one of the region's most consistent and outspoken enthusiasts, his overall style was fairly typical of the era's boosterism—long on shameless hyperbole and often bordering amusingly on disingenuousness. But considering southeast Missouri's natural deficiencies at the time, in order to convince others of the uncontested superiority of the Bootheel compared to the rest of the state in terms of fertility, mineral resources, climate, and health, Louis laid it on pretty thick even by late-nineteenth-century standards.

In reality, with the Ozark foothills in the north, the Benton-Commerce hills and Sikeston Ridge to the east, and Crowley's Ridge to the west, the Bootheel region of Missouri is a natural catch basin for the overflow of the Mississippi and the streams, creeks, and rivers to the north. This phenomenon left the region with rich and fertile land. But nearly impenetrable cypress and hardwood swamps covered Swampeast Missouri, making the land unsuitable for agriculture. In the late 1800s, less than 10 percent of the land in the Bootheel was actually cleared, and its overall

13. William H. Barnum to Louis Hauck, June 17, 1865, in possession of Patrick and Cheryl Evans, Cape Girardeau, Mo.

lack of productivity impeded the region's economic development. Additionally, the region was notorious, not totally undeservedly so, for being an unhealthy breeding ground for malaria and other airborne diseases, which frightened away countless would-be settlers.

In Houck's buoyant columns, though, he deftly turned the tables, accentuating the positives by asking prospective immigrants to consider instead the unique possibilities these regional foibles presented. Under the heading "News from the Southeast" Houck essentially admonished readers to not mistake *cheap* for *worthless* when it came to the value of Bootheel land. The land may well be an "elephant"—its development a substantial obstacle and challenge—but it was a "white elephant" of nearly limitless potential. Based on his extensive town-by-town canvassing of the region, Houck depicted a lumberman's paradise on some of the biggest land bargains in the state. In fact, far from useless, the magnificent alluvial soil in towns like Charleston and New Madrid actually meant that with minimal physical effort on the part of the area's virtuous yeoman farmers—many of hardy German stock—garden vegetables grew bigger, crops rarely failed, and yields approached the spectacular. And in perhaps his most accomplished bit of advertising, Houck pointed out that in perpetually soggy counties like Dunklin, farmers need never lose sleep over the prospect of drought.[14]

He continued championing southeast Missouri from the podium, eloquently articulating his own prognosis for booming the region. In one archetypal 1869 speech delivered in Fredericktown entitled "The Resources and Future of Southeast Missouri," Houck stressed the critical need for attracting labor and population, specifically through the establishment of immigration societies in all regional counties. He promoted improvements in river transportation as a means of spurring lumbering and commercial farming, as well as initiatives to further exploit the area's rich mineral deposits. Most notably, his strategies also began to prominently feature railroad development as vital to opening the area up to industrialization and modernization. Echoing this sentiment in an accompanying newspaper column, Houck chided the Bootheel counties for inexplicably lagging behind in railroad building, writing that in general "while the northern portion of the State has been pushing ahead improvements of this character, Southeast Missouri slept the sleep of Rip Van Winkle."[15]

14. Doherty, Jr., "Missouri Interests of Louis Houck," 25, 31–34; *Missouri Republican,* September 17, 1869, April 1, 1870; Houck, "Reminiscences," 48–49.

15. *Missouri Republican,* August 12, 1869; Doherty, Jr., "Missouri Interests of Louis Houck," 31–35.

That transportation in general, and railroads in particular, should begin to occupy a central place in Houck's conceptions of economic development owes a great deal to the most significant lesson he learned on the circuit. From his earliest trips in the summer of 1869, Louis had heard from the "Bloomfield crowd"—principally Kitchen, Bedford, Vail, Owens, David Hicks, and William Phelan—of the availability of hundreds of thousands of acres of public swampland for virtually nothing, and moreover, of the willingness of some southeast Missouri counties to exchange these public lands for private railroad, road, or reclamation projects.

During one session in particular of the Stoddard County Circuit Court, Louis had stayed overnight with Henry Miller, a well-known Bloomfield merchant, land owner, and former county judge. Miller's white two-story home, with a full-length front porch, looked down from a hill above the Cape Girardeau and Bloomfield Road coming into the county seat and was a favorite gathering place for the leading politicians, lawyers, and businessmen in that part of the region. It was there, over dinner in front of Miller's massive four-foot-wide fireplace, that the Bloomfield lawyers carefully detailed for Houck how in 1850 the federal government had given Missouri all the unsold public swamplands in the state and how in 1851 and 1853 Missouri had in turn conveyed these lands to the respective southeast counties to aid their development. Much of this wild and uncultivated land was meant to simply be sold by the county courts for between one dollar and a dollar and a quarter an acre. But since demand was so low for land that was underwater a good portion of the year, the enterprising lawyers agreed to show Louis just how to take advantage of their courthouse connections with various judges and sheriffs to purchase for themselves thousands of acres of land for as little as just a few cents an acre, in some cases to satisfy outstanding judicial judgments for delinquent taxes.[16]

Accustomed to having little capital and living in areas with prohibitively high land values, Louis admitted to being more than a little impressed by what he heard. He eagerly took them up on their offer and as a matter of fact not long after that accompanied Phelan and Hicks to his first of many public land sales, where he purchased 1,200 acres in Stoddard County for $150. "Nearly everybody around the courthouse," he noted with amusement, "became a big land owner in the twinkling of an eye." Yet there was more. As he savored Bellona Miller's renowned pancakes that evening in Bloomfield, he was first introduced to the concept of obtaining massive

16. "Louis Houck Memoirs," 61–63, in possession of C. A. Juden and Jeanette Juden, Cape Girardeau, Mo.

tracts of land as a form of county subsidy to finance private transportation ventures. In regard to this county aid, still legal in Missouri until 1875, Kitchen, Bedford, and Miller—all heavily involved in promoting the Missouri end of the Cairo and Fulton Railroad—described how before the war Dunklin, Stoddard, Scott, Ripley, and Butler counties all bought stock in the railroad with their swamplands; essentially trading more than 500,000 acres for some $500,000 worth of stock. Likewise, Butler County had at one time granted somewhere between 20,000 to 30,000 acres to subsidize the St. Louis and Iron Mountain Railroad just as Stoddard and New Madrid contracted to trade 20,000 and 125,000 acres respectively to build permanent roads. Often, as they also mentioned, county aid of this nature had been extended to support levee building and drainage as had previously been the case in New Madrid, Pemiscot and Mississippi.[17]

For Louis, whose resourceful and cunning legal mind was steadily growing more accustomed to scheming and working the angles of every available deal, these inspirational stories were monumentally intriguing. Through them he experienced what he termed a "revelation" in Bootheel "high finance." Fifty years later he still vividly remembered how "the world certainly looked bright and cheerful" when he awoke the next morning.[18]

Politically speaking, the Bloomfield crowd only preached to the choir. Despite his mounting distrust of Eastern speculators and monopolies, Houck quite naturally bought into the prevailing late-nineteenth-century conceptions of this American form of laissez-faire capitalism that was heavy on state aid to promote development and light on state interference. The real impact lies in how Houck intuitively grasped the notion that private interest and public good could be mutually supportive and complementary—and highly lucrative. Although in these years before a blending of age, achievement, and wealth conferred a bit of excusable egotism, Houck's unassuming manner led some casual observers in Cape Girardeau to mistakenly believe that "he [was] so modest in his pretensions that it can hardly be said that he is aspiring." In truth, he already exhibited, for better or worse, all the traits of a politician or salesman. A natural self-promoter with a magnetic handshake and real skills for writing and oration—although he spoke with a discernible German accent—

17. Edwin L. Lopata, *Local Aid to Railroads in Missouri*, 38, 57; Houck, "Reminiscences," 29–33, 45. The Cairo and Fulton, running west from the Mississippi River toward Poplar Bluff, and the St. Louis and Iron Mountain, running southwest from St. Louis through the mineral areas of southeast Missouri, were two of Missouri's early trunk lines, built between 1850 and 1866.
18. Houck, "Reminiscences," 33.

Houck could be gracious and charming when necessary, not to mention remarkably persuasive. For the rest of his life, Louis Houck's real genius lay in his ability to successfully convince southeast Missourians that the public fortunes of the region were intimately tied to his own, that, as one newspaper faithfully proclaimed years later, "a victory for Louis Houck, is a victory for southeast Missouri."[19]

Houck the regional promoter merged thoroughly with Houck the personal promoter when he met and began courting nineteen-year-old Mary Hunter Giboney in October 1869. Born nearly a full eight years after Louis on March 2, 1848, Mary, or "Mollie" to her family and friends, was the only surviving daughter of Andrew Giboney and Mary Hunter, whose marriage in 1832 had brought together two of the wealthiest and largest landowning families in southeast Missouri. Her maternal grandfather, Joseph Hunter, a Scots-Irish Revolutionary War veteran, had been appointed to an administrative position within the fledgling governing body of the Territory of Louisiana by President James Madison after establishing himself in the New Madrid area in 1805. The Giboneys had made their way from Virginia and Kentucky into the Spanish colony of Upper Louisiana after the Revolution. Mary's paternal grandfather, Alexander Giboney, married Rebecca Ramsey, a woman of Scottish nobility, and settled the family near Cape Girardeau on a sprawling twelve-hundred-acre land grant obtained from the Spanish crown's lieutenant governor of Louisiana, Don Zenon Trudeau, in 1797.

On this tract of land, designated by the Spanish as "El Bosque de los Olmos" (The Woods of the Elms), Alexander and Rebecca's youngest son, Andrew Giboney, Mary's father, eventually built the magnificent family estate Elmwood. Beginning in 1808, Giboney family slaves working alongside area bondsmen known for their skill as stone masons, carpenters, wood workers, brick makers, and craftsmen constructed Elmwood based on, some thought, the family's own recollections of the Ramsey's ancestral Scottish castle, Dalhousie. When it was finally completed in 1835, the granite, brick, and stone mansion, located about five miles southwest of the Cape on the Bloomfield Road, sat situated in the dense virgin forest, accessible only by a "winding roadway one-mile in length, adorned on either side with majestic oaks and stately elms and much dogwood that blossoms in the springtime."[20]

19. *Missouri Republican,* October 21, 1869, May 11, 1872; *Wayne County Journal* (Piedmont, Mo.), June 22, 1895.

20. *Cape Girardeau Southeast Missourian,* December 21, 1944.

Born and mostly raised in antebellum gentility at Elmwood, Mary exemplified the ideals of proud Southern womanhood common among the planter class in the region—she was a tightly laced picture of Christian virtue and Confederate honor. Although privileged and quite diminutive—no more than four feet, eleven inches tall and never weighing more than one hundred pounds—Mary, like other Hunter and Giboney women before her, was tough, intelligent, and had a certain air of authority. Her mother had died when the little girl was just over two years old, leading Andrew to send his daughter, the only one of his nine children to survive to adulthood, off to stay near the Hunter clan with her Aunt Hannah Hunter Stallcup north of New Madrid.

Mary stayed in New Madrid until her aunt's death in 1858, but the coming of the Civil War again interrupted her childhood. After Union troops took New Madrid in April 1862, the Civil War in southeast Missouri became primarily a struggle for possession of Crowley's Ridge. Occasional skirmishes, accidental encounters, and guerrilla raids along the Bloomfield Road between Cape Girardeau and Bloomfield punctuated the years 1862 and 1863. Probably fearing for his daughter's safety so near to Union-held Cape Girardeau, Andrew Giboney, himself a veteran of the War of 1812, sent Mary to Christian College in Columbia, Missouri, in 1863 and then out of state altogether to Emma Willard College in Troy, New York, for the duration of the war. While at Emma Willard, Mary took the news of the North's victory with a heavy heart and recalled that during the great calamity surrounding Lincoln's assassination, "many of the girls in attendance who had never failed to uphold the Confederacy," like herself, "had to suppress themselves and keep in the background."[21]

Upon her return to southeast Missouri in 1865, at just seventeen she assumed the daunting role of Elmwood's administrator and manager, taking care of her elderly father, a widower most of Mary's life, and helping him oversee the family's vast real estate holdings of some thirty-six hundred acres in southeast Missouri and southern Illinois.

Never considered particularly attractive, Mary nonetheless used her well-spoken charm and vibrancy to captivate those who belonged to the Cape's polite society. As the dynamic hostess of Elmwood's much celebrated and elaborate social gatherings, she was known for her merriment and how with genuine hospitality she seemingly held court over joyful throngs of visiting friends and relatives. In the ornate wood-paneled entry hall of Elmwood where "lights shone o'er fair women and brave men,"

21. Ibid.

Mary would effortlessly engage her company with a versatile knowledge of public affairs and sly, almost caustic, wit. A genuine Southern belle, it would appear she did not suffer from an empty social calendar or a lack of male suitors.[22]

Louis met Mary shortly after moving to Cape Girardeau, and over the next three years was "frequently in her society," usually visiting her at Elmwood bearing gifts of flowers and books. In no time, he too called her Mollie, perhaps even with a bit of a flirtatious lilt. Sharing a mutual affinity for fine horses, sometimes they rode along the high ground above the marshland, usually at the faster pace Mary preferred. Buggy rides into Cape Girardeau were always a spirited affair as well, especially during the fall at fair time, as it was said that no one ever passed Mary while she was at the reins. During one such trip to the old fairgrounds west of the Cape on Gordonville Road in the fall of 1872, a wayward calf spooked their horse, causing it and the buggy to plunge over the side of a bridge. The horse was killed and the buggy splintered, but luckily Louis was unhurt and Mary escaped with only a couple of broken ribs. While distressed, the two continued their courtship unabated, allowing only occasional bad weather to thwart their plans.

Both were incessant readers, and Louis appears to have been immediately drawn to Mary's intellect and honesty, delighting in their ability to share ideas about any number of current events, literature, theater, history, botany, and matters of business. Though a Northerner, he found plenty of common political ground in Mary's strong Democratic roots, still anchored firmly in the soil of the old agrarian South. They had shared a fierce critique of Lincoln's war of Northern aggression and now saw eye-to-eye on the perceived ills of Reconstruction: to them it was an insipid Republican strategy, along with the premature elevation of blacks, to ensure the subordination of the South and West to the East.

In fact, it was something about Mary's Southern carriage and demeanor that struck a deep chord in Louis. As his old friend William Barnum had observed several years before, Louis was prone to losing himself in a crowded nation within his own mind where grand heroes and scholars perpetually acted out the epic struggles of human history. In a rather quirky habit, Louis often used his unwanted books as personal homemade scrapbooks, clipping articles of interest to him from a wide variety of American newspapers and pasting them on the pages. More often than

22. Informal conversation with Jeanette Juden, January 30, 2006; *Cape Girardeau Southeast Missourian*, December 21, 1944.

not, these pages were crammed full of overlapping reports chronicling the lavish goings-on of European royal families, Old World military adventures, theater reviews, and romantic poetry. In Mary and Elmwood, Louis may well have finally touched some of these elements of chivalry, honor, and nobility of which he had only dreamed. She was a real-life feudal princess living in her own castle.[23]

Mary disappointed many of Cape Girardeau's eligible bachelors, and, it appears, her father, when she announced their engagement sometime in 1872. Andrew Giboney probably had serious reservations about granting his consent to the marriage. This landless second-generation immigrant whose social position was at least a full step below theirs would most certainly have not been Andrew's first choice for his only daughter. What, he must have wondered, perhaps aloud, did Louis Houck have to offer Mary Hunter Giboney in terms of social standing or financial gain? How disapproving the old man actually was is unknown, but Andrew's consternation was obviously not lost on Louis. If an unidentified newspaper clipping in one of Houck's scrapbooks from late 1872 is any indication, the anxious groom was expecting the worst. "A poor young man fell in love with an heiress," the anecdote reads, "and the passion being returned, it only wanted the parent's consent to make them happy. At length, meeting with the father, he asked for the daughter's hand. 'How much can you command?' asked the millionaire gruffly. 'Not much' was the reply. 'What are your expectations?' 'Well, to tell the truth, I expect, if you refuse your consent, to run away with your daughter, and marry her without it.'"[24]

On Christmas Day 1872, Louis and Mary were married by Father Timothy O'Keefe in a Catholic ceremony at Elmwood before a large gathering of friends and relatives. Because of Andrew Giboney's declining health, Louis moved into the mansion. The next year Louis's father, Bartholomeaus, died in Belleville at the age of sixty-eight, and the year after that Andrew passed away, leaving Mary the entire estate consisting of Elmwood and its acreage, thirteen lots in Cape Girardeau, another 3,632 acres in southeast Missouri and southern Illinois—essentially all the land immediately south of the Cape's city limits—in addition to a balance of $15,141.84. Custom and law dictated that the son-in-law be the executor.[25]

23. Informal conversation with Karen F. Stanley, July 28, 2005.
24. Scrapbook in possession of C. A. Juden and Jeanette Juden, Cape Girardeau, Mo.
25. Andrew Giboney, Probate Record CP-0990, Cape Girardeau County Archives, Jackson, Mo.

No doubt Louis married well, and it might appear opportunistically. All of his brothers except one married into wealthy families. But Houck seems to have taken a typically Victorian male view of marriage: he was genuinely affectionate and romantic toward his wife, and he was probably very eager to settle down. Mary, on the other hand, appears to have been more Southern in her outlook, not nearly as excited or eager to wed. She most likely saw the union as much more of a practical consideration—based on what she recognized as Louis's potential to capitalize on her already considerable wealth—and then stoically devoted herself to it. Mary unquestionably took a far more active and hands-on role in advising and counseling her husband on financial affairs than did Northern Victorian wives. In essence, they were a partnership, often of a business nature. And like any good partnership they complemented each other well; he supplied the vision, and she supplied the resources. To be sure, Mary solidified in Louis his maturing business philosophy, for he now had a vested interest in promoting any available proposal to increase property values, in particular ventures that improved transportation.[26]

Around 1874 Louis took on a law partner, Robert G. Ranney, a local attorney younger than himself who was related to the Giboney family by marriage. When not on the circuit, Houck rode into their Cape Girardeau office from the estate each day, eventually finding a horse fleet enough to make the roughly six-mile buggy ride in around forty-five minutes.[27] Back home at Elmwood, Louis and Mary welcomed their first child, Irma, an elfish little girl, on February 6, 1876. Named after the tragic heroine from Berthold Auerback's turgid 544-page double-columned German novel *On the Heights*—one of Louis's favorites, and in time required reading for all Houcks—the dark-haired charmer quickly captivated her doting Papa's heart.[28] And she enjoyed his undivided attention until her younger brother Giboney, a puckish boy himself whom many thought the spitting image of his grandfather Andrew, was born almost three years later on January 15, 1878. For the next two generations the halls of Elmwood reverberated with the sounds of practical jokes and laughter from the precocious Houck children and the nieces, nephews, cousins, and grandchildren who came to live there.

Although now a family man, the practice of law remained Louis's principal vocation for the remainder of the decade. But steadily his, and the

26. Informal conversation with Jeanette Juden, April 28, 2005.
27. Houck, "Reminiscences," 42; *Cape Girardeau Southeast Missourian*, December 21, 1944.
28. Ronald S. Reed, Jr., to Joel P. Rhodes, September 22, 2006, in possession of author.

community's, attention focused on Cape Girardeau's increasingly woeful economic conditions, each year made worse by a growing disconnection from the rail network linking the national commercial marketplace. The same year he and Mary were wed, Louis had purchased a majority of stock in the as yet still incomplete Cape Girardeau and Scott County Macadamized Road. The company had been chartered by the state in 1853 to build a hard-surface toll road approximately four miles long through the "Big Swamp" south of Cape Girardeau to connect the town with Scott and New Madrid counties. Taking over as president in 1873, a move that in due course gave him legal fits because of contentious special provisions in the original charter, Louis jump-started the stalled project and oversaw its completion. By the end of the year the primitive and treacherous mud road leading south out of Cape was replaced with a modern macadamized one running along a high levee; it became known as the Rock Levee Road.

Houck's toll road improved access to Cape Girardeau from the south, but as a catalyst to spark economic development it fell well short. Those same railroads that were further eroding the town's livelihood offered the only real hope of recovery. Cape Girardeau had let previous opportunities to build a railroad pass by. Now, like many Missouri towns faced with the literal life-or-death prospect of attracting a line of their own, Cape rushed headlong to embrace the iron horse, only to see the town's efforts meet with catastrophe.

To be sure, Houck's initial involvement in the Rock Levee Road was a crucial step along this fateful path. The same year in which the toll gate opened for the first time, he was retained as chief legal counsel for the bankrupt Cape Girardeau and State Line Railroad.

CHAPTER 4

To Cogitate and To Dream
The Coming of the Railroad

I began to cogitate and to dream a dream.

—Louis Houck

Contrary to his editorial comparisons between southeast Missouri and Rip Van Winkle in regard to the region's seemingly sleepy approach to transportation initiatives, Louis Houck actually arrived in Cape Girardeau during an era of intense railroading mania. Between 1850 and 1866, the state's "trunk" lines—the Pacific Railroad, Hannibal and St. Joseph, North Missouri, the Southwest branch of the Pacific, St. Louis and Iron Mountain, and Cairo and Fulton—had been built through fits and starts to more or less emanate out from St. Louis toward neighboring Kansas, Arkansas, and Iowa. Two of these pre–Civil War trunks—the St. Louis and Iron Mountain, and the Cairo and Fulton—in effect formed a viable triangular-shaped network across southeast Missouri. The St. Louis and Iron Mountain, the perpendicular side of the triangle, ran southwest from St. Louis through the rich iron ore deposits of the Arcadia Valley to Ironton and from there toward a proposed extension to Helena, Arkansas. The Cairo and Fulton made up the base, extending west from its Missouri terminus on the Mississippi River at Bird's Point toward Poplar Bluff. An 1868 extension of the St. Louis and Iron Mountain southeast from Bismarck, just to the north of Ironton, down to Belmont on the Mississippi, fashioned the hypotenuse by crossing the Cairo and Fulton line at Charleston. After the two roads came under the same ownership, continued westward construction by the Cairo and Fulton and simultaneous southwest advances by the St. Louis and Iron Mountain eventually formed an intersection at Poplar Bluff, thus successfully closing in the southwest corner of the triangle by 1873. The next year the whole configuration was reorganized as the St. Louis, Iron Mountain and Southern Railway.[1]

To be sure, Cape Girardeau itself had been left outside the region's rail system, and in years past, before the war, Houck's characterization of old mossbacks letting opportunity slip through their fingers may have been more apt. In 1855, his friends Solomon Kitchen and Henry Bedford, along with other organizers of the Cairo and Fulton, had in vain pitched the idea of a railroad to townspeople who passed on the idea primarily because they were still content with river traffic. Later in 1859 even after local interested parties finally moved to obtain a charter from the state for the ill-fated Pilot Knob, Cape Girardeau, and Belmont Railroad and county voters approved $900,000 in bonds, the project disintegrated without the bonds ever being issued or any track laid.

Nevertheless, in 1869, the same year Louis referenced Washington Irving's beloved fable, Cape Girardeau—by now desperate to revitalize and reverse its generation-long malaise—had become simply intoxicated by the railroad's promise of attracting vital population, capital, industry, and increased land values. Local promoters led by P. R. Van Frank came forward with an ambitious plan to construct a railroad line from Cape Girardeau toward Arkansas, feeding into the St. Louis and Iron Mountain's Belmont branch at a connection just south of Allenville, some fifteen miles southwest of Cape Girardeau. By building this "feeder" line to intersect, and eventually bisect, the triangle, these entrepreneurs reasoned that the road would supplement river traffic, establishing Cape as the region's central rail hub on the Mississippi, while concomitantly integrating local businesses, farms, and coal and iron mines into the national market economy via rail access to St. Louis. Though unassociated with the organization of this Cape Girardeau and State Line Railroad in 1869, Houck joined his fellow citizens in hearty support, applauding its intention to remake Cape Girardeau into what he called a veritable "Pittsburgh of the West."[2]

1. Lopata, *Local Aid to Railroads in Missouri*, 9–25, 63, 85, 142; Maynard Cameron Willis, "The Construction of Railroads in Southeast Missouri"; John W. Million, *State Aid to Railways in Missouri*, 155; Doherty, Jr., "Missouri Interests of Louis Houck," 38–40.

2. In actuality, the Cape Girardeau and State Line Railroad was the new name given to the old Pilot Knob, Cape Girardeau, and Belmont Railroad after its 1859 charter was amended a decade later to include the construction of this proposed new line. Louis Houck, "The Story of the Railroad Work of Louis Houck in Southeast Missouri From 1880 to 1920, Volume I," 4; *Missouri Republican*, November 26, December 2, 1869, April 1, 1870.

As was common for the time, the devil was in the details of finance. Private capital alone rarely got risky ventures like this off the ground, and eastern investors—skittish over committing their money in a state rapidly gaining a notorious reputation for lawlessness—never materialized. The Cape Girardeau and State Line Railroad needed some type of public support. Yet by 1869, Missouri law prohibited direct state aid to railroads, after that generous but horribly flawed policy fleeced taxpayers of more than $25 million during the corrupt and mismanaged development of the trunk lines.

Missouri's long, strange trip in railroad financing had begun with the basic premise that integration into the developing national railroad network was vital to the future of the state. And thus hoping to position itself as the eastern terminus of a transcontinental line, the legislature had undertaken a perilous antebellum program of public aid to fund private railroads. While never actually engaging in railroad ownership or the physical construction of rail lines, Missouri had followed a common state aid formula of the era by issuing bonds to finance the work. These bonds were loaned to the early trunk lines, which in turn could sell the bonds on the open market to generate capital while paying on a twenty-year note with annual interest. Due to a tangled web of fraud, misconduct, inconsistent development, and cost overruns, by 1860 all the railroads except one that received this state largess had defaulted on their indebtedness with fewer than one thousand total miles of track statewide to show for it. This eventually led the state legislature, faced as it was with mounting debt and taxpayer dissatisfaction, to make further state assistance to railroads illegal in the 1865 constitution. But the clear-cut fact remained that unless the troubled prewar railroads could somehow secure the necessary capital to get back on track, the lines might never get built. This had left legislators, their faith in railroad development still intact, with a truly precarious dilemma.

Accordingly, in 1868 Missouri began bailing out the railroads in a "great railroad giveaway" in which the state relinquished the indebtedness of the railroads and released them from state liens on their property in exchange for a cash settlement of pennies on the dollar and a pledge to lay a specified amount of track within fixed deadlines. The state also made provisions to foreclose on the insolvent lines and under extremely shady circumstances that smacked of conflict of interest, bribery, and collusion sold off several of them, including the St. Louis and Iron Mountain and Cairo and Fulton, at tremendous net losses. None of these policies, however, released taxpayers from their obligations to pay off the millions in bonds that the state had initially used to finance the railroads.

This entire reckless adventure meant that by the early 1870s the responsibility of funding railroads in Missouri shifted to local county and municipal subsidization when fifty or so of these small "feeder" lines, like the
Cape Girardeau and State Line, were being built across outstate Missouri
to connect those regions not yet served by the trunks. In pitching their proposals to local governments, clever railroad promoters followed the line of
reasoning that since the roads were generally locally owned and operated,
and benefited a specific local market, local governments and taxpayers
should support them. Invariably, many frantic Missouri communities,
often pitted against one another by these promoters in fierce competitions
to woo a given railroad to their town, eagerly agreed.[3]

True to their conservative political roots, a handful in Cape Girardeau
urged caution, questioning whether the town could realistically expect to
finance a railroad in the midst of such economic doldrums. Local aid to
railroads, they added, cut against the very grain of the town's preference
for small government and taxes. Nevertheless, in an unbridled enthusiasm
to get a railroad, taxpayers in Cape Girardeau threw caution and tradition
to the wind, voting overwhelmingly in 1869 to subscribe $300,000 in bonds
to the Cape Girardeau and State Line Railroad.[4]

Construction began in December 1869 to vigorous fanfare. Over the next
three years crews surveyed and graded almost forty miles of the line—
essentially clearing a wide path known as the right-of-way through the
timber—running southwest from Cape Girardeau toward the Arkansas
state line. Based on their updated surveys, the initial plan to first intersect
the St. Louis and Iron Mountain at Allenville was altered, and instead
another tiny hamlet, Delta, two miles southeast of Allenville, became the
site of the intended crossing. But cutting a railroad through the inhospitable swamps proved slow and expensive, and even though the town
issued the bonds incrementally in exchange for stock, the initial $300,000
ran out. Undaunted, the Cape Girardeau and State Line contracted with
another railroad construction company—the Illinois, Missouri, and Texas
Railroad—to complete the road. And after this new company, lead by former Missouri Governor Thomas G. Fletcher, issued an additional $1 mil-
lion in subscription bonds—similar to stock—of its own, by 1872 trestles

3. This general outline of Missouri's railroad history is based on Christensen and
Kremer, *A History of Missouri, Volume IV,* as well as Lopata, *Local Aid to Railroads in Missouri,* 6, 7, 16, 27–58, 62–63, 85, 129, 142.
    4. Lopata, *Local Aid to Railroads in Missouri,* 85, 129, 142.

were in place, a locomotive purchased, and nearly two miles of track extended out from Cape Girardeau.[5] Then construction abruptly ground to a halt.

The Panic of 1873, part of the national boom and bust cycles of the late nineteenth century, once again frustrated Cape Girardeau's hope for commercial recovery and bankrupted the Cape Girardeau and State Line railroad along with the Illinois, Missouri, and Texas. In the wake of the depression, the railroad sold off the locomotive, and within a few years thick vegetation reclaimed the roadbed, ties rotted, rails rusted, and trestles fell down. Disillusioned and angry taxpayers, saddled with $300,000 in debt and no railroad, refused to pay their taxes for services not rendered and the city defaulted on the bonds. Across Missouri, economic hard times brought overextended towns like Cape Girardeau back to this reality: in their gamble to secure a railroad, unrealistic expectations had made a bad situation worse. "All that the people of the city and township had to show for this railroad enterprise and the bonds issued was a great railroad debt made manifest by a great tax," Houck himself lamented. "The railroad construction era had passed, the dream was over."[6]

The editor of the *Cape Girardeau Democrat* later painted an even more somber and ominous picture of this "most trying period of [Cape Girardeau's] history," recalling that for the rest of the 1870s "enterprise died a natural death; property depreciated in value and went begging without a bidder; merchants were failing and bankrupt business was brisk; taxes went unpaid; people lived on credit and numbers moved away; men gazed with that faraway look that betokens stagnation, age and despair. In truth, the town was finished . . ."[7]

Even without a vested interest in the Cape Girardeau and State Line as such, the town's continued decline, now hastened by the railroad's demise, especially troubled Houck. His disappointment was all the more acute considering that the debacle coincided quite uneasily with his years riding the court circuit when he was coming to truly consider himself a Cape Girardean and southeast Missourian. Coincidentally, that March of 1873, Louis heard through the political grapevine that Governor Silas Woodson had signed the enabling legislation to create a Southeast Missouri State

5. Houck, "Story of the Railroad Work, Volume I," 7–9; *Sikeston Standard* (Sikeston, Mo.), March 6, 1936; Lopata, *Local Aid to Railroads in Missouri*, 2, 5, 71, 130.

6. Houck, "Story of the Railroad Work, Volume I," 35–37; Lopata, *Local Aid to Railroads in Missouri*, 27–58.

7. *Cape Girardeau Democrat*, March 6, 1897.

Normal School somewhere in the region. This new institution, a product of the state's Republican education system that established normal schools around Missouri in order to train teachers for the newly created public schools, was to be designated as the Third District Normal, joining District One in Kirksville and District Two in Warrensburg. Its service area would take in the twenty-six counties running south of the Missouri River and east of a line starting at the northwest corner of Gasconade County and south along the western border of Gasconade, Crawford, Dent, Shannon, and Oregon counties all the way to the Arkansas state line. And since it would be necessary to physically locate the Third District Normal in the most geographically and economically advantageous location within this broad area, the law opened up its placement to competitive bidding, stipulating that the town offering the highest incentives would be awarded the school.[8]

At once grasping what this could mean, Louis did a quick mental inventory of the seven-member board of regents—the state commission awarding the site that included Jacob H. Burrough of Cape Girardeau, Senator T. J. C. Morrison of New Madrid, and Charles Rozier of Ste. Genevieve—and was convinced that the Cape had at least "a fighting chance." Sensibly, he first consulted Robert Sturdivant, whose sage counsel Louis increasingly came to depend on in matters of business, to get his advice on the wisdom and feasibility of pursuing the school. Sturdivant had been a central feature of Cape Girardeau's business community since arriving on horseback from his native Virginia in 1835. Quiet and unassuming in manner, his varied commercial interests ranged from mercantile trade—where he had briefly partnered with Louis's father-in-law Andrew Giboney before the war—newspaper publishing, milling, and, since 1866, banking. The Sturdivant Bank, the first private bank in Cape Girardeau, had been organized out of remnants of dissolved branches of the Bank of Missouri after it became federalized in 1866. Under the Colonel's steady direction, it was on its way to becoming one of the region's most important financial institutions by the 1870s.

Though the old Virginian was initially less optimistic that the commission would be overly "friendly" to a bid from Cape Girardeau, Houck's undiluted optimism and persistence persuaded him that they would never know unless they tried. Shortly thereafter the men, along with Jacob Burrough and other like-minded community leaders, helped organize the first of several

8. Arthur H. Mattingly, *Normal to University: A Century of Service*, 3–11.

countywide meetings in Jackson, the Cape Girardeau County seat roughly fifteen miles northwest of the Cape, to plot their collective strategy.

The meeting at the Jackson courthouse in mid-April reflected early assumptions that only the combined resources of Cape Girardeau County could muster a bid well above the state's minimum requirement of $25,000 and capable of beating out challengers in Iron, St. Francois, Madison, Jefferson, and Ste. Genevieve counties. But despite a flurry of newspaper articles urging cooperation between Cape Girardeau and Jackson—not to mention speeches by Houck advocating what he thought to be the only viable proposal, a $50,000 *county* subscription to put the school in the *town* of Cape—the traditional rivalry and antagonism between the neighboring communities ultimately sabotaged their good intentions. With the two contingents unable to reach an acceptable compromise on which town would be home to the institution—Cape or Jackson—and, more importantly, on the exact amount of a subscription, Jackson citizens resoundingly defeated the bond proposal in a countywide vote.

Unwilling to see Cape Girardeau miss a good opportunity yet again, or to see Iron County—the only other serious contender left by this time—win by default, Louis tirelessly helped spearhead a campaign to convince Cape voters to go it alone without Jackson and pass a $50,000 subscription themselves. He even generously offered ten acres of Mary's prime real estate as a suitable home for the Third District Normal. Improbable as it seems, voters responded overwhelmingly in a hurriedly called citywide election, agreeing to take on another tax burden so soon after the railroad's collapse.

From there, Cape Girardeau submitted its official proposal to the board of regents, who in turn scheduled October meetings in both Ironton and the Cape for the purpose of touring the locations, reviewing the finances, and meeting with the promoters of the two leading bidders. Whatever momentum the vote had generated quickly gave way to consternation at that meeting as the regents voiced serious reservations over the virtually bankrupt town's ability to live up to the financial obligations of the bid due to poor financial health and outstanding railroad indebtedness. Issues were also raised, no doubt prompted by Iron County, surrounding the generally held perception that the farther south one traveled in southeast Missouri, the more unhealthy and prone to malaria the region became. "Naturally," Louis recalled, "we were all very anxious and uncertain as to what would be the result of our efforts."[9]

9. Houck, "Reminiscences," 60.

Ultimately, however, in late October 1873 the seven-member board of regents for the Southeast Missouri State Normal School indeed awarded the school to Cape Girardeau in a split 4–3 vote. And despite some last-minute subterfuge from some in the Arcadia Valley unwilling to concede defeat, later that same year the state legislature made the designation official. Though Houck had offered his land for free, the regents finally settled on a permanent site atop a Civil War fort north of town on land purchased from locally renowned architect Joseph Lansmon. Their reasoning was that since this land was on the highest elevation in town, the institution would be visible for miles around and could keep students well above the malaria-infested lowlands to the south. It took longer than two more years, but finally in April 1875 the first Academic Hall—a two-story red brick, eclectic mix of Victorian-era styles with a gray Mansard roof and ornamental towers—opened as the self-contained campus of what was informally known as Southeast Missouri Normal School.

Securing the Normal—one of the most important events in Cape's history—was very gratifying for Houck. His personal stake in its operations would grow profoundly, and the school would eventually pay tremendous dividends for the town and region. But it would be another generation at least before the humble little school significantly impacted the community. In the meantime, Louis, having steadfastly supported railroad subscription in 1869, never lost faith in railroad development as the real key to the economic future of this part of the state. As a matter of fact, he had been pondering the notion of getting involved in railroading himself since his days in Cairo. Shortly after his marriage he became associated with the Cape Girardeau and State Line Railroad Company, working first as its legal counsel to untangle the messy financial situation and later to help attract the outside capital thought necessary to put the project back together. As it turned out, before going bankrupt, the construction company contracted to build Cape Girardeau's line—the Illinois, Missouri, and Texas railroad—had not only raised money through more subscription bonds but also taken out a $1.5 million mortgage on the property of the Cape Girardeau and State Line Railroad. Instead of investing that money in the construction project, the company absorbed it, dividing it up among the promoters and leaving the Cape Girardeau and State Line Railroad, and ultimately the town, liable. In 1875, P. R. Van Frank, president of the Cape Girardeau and State Line, retained Houck on a contingency fee to file a suit clearing the railroad's property from the mortgage.

Meanwhile, Louis also worked closely with Cape Girardeau County state representative Robert G. Whitelaw to craft some creative legislation for allowing the city to cover its interest obligations from the railroad debt and eventually retire the principle of the bonds altogether. At a time when many Missouri counties and municipalities in similar circumstances were reconciling themselves to the hard facts that they could not legally avoid payment of their railroad debts and that a state bailout for taxpayers was out of the question, Whitelaw introduced legislation allowing Cape Girardeau to earmark two-thirds of the proceeds collected from local saloon licenses for that very purpose. This imaginative formula, clearly influenced by Houck's low opinion of liquor, allowed Cape to liquidate the $438,400 it owed in interest and principal in May 1919—a long time coming, but well ahead of the last Missouri county to retire its debt in 1934.[10]

By comparison, it only took three years of legal wrangling before Houck successfully released the Cape Girardeau and State Line Railroad from the construction company's mortgages in 1878. Yet by that time it had been more than five years since the project collapsed, and potential investors considered the forty miles of overgrown roadbed and two miles of rusty track worthless. Anxious to stimulate interest, the Cape railroad lowered its sights somewhat from the original route to Arkansas and began seeking out any potential contractor willing to build just the small fifteen-mile line to connect with the Iron Mountain at Delta. Finding no takers outside the region, even Houck fruitlessly tried to interest local investors, but as he later recalled, "the idea that the citizens of Cape Girardeau themselves could build a railroad, even if only fifteen miles long, with a roadbed already graded, after $300,000 had been spent without securing a railroad, to most people seemed chimerical." Houck puzzled over the odd lack of entrepreneurial spirit and sense of urgency in his fellow southeast Missourians. "No one seemed to value what was being offered nor what the work had cost the people," he mulled. Surely others had the vision, as he did, to see the untold potential of the region. Just fifteen miles of track separated southeast Missouri—separated Louis Houck—from tapping into the great economic, transportation, and communication revolution taking root across the nation. Slowly Louis "began to cogitate and to dream a dream": if someone needed to step up and build the road—why not him?[11]

Houck's railroad epiphany in the spring of 1880 remains a central part of the region's folklore: despite having little money, supplies, or knowledge of railroading, at forty years of age, this tenacious and sturdy little

10. Lopata, *Local Aid to Railroads in Missouri,* 7, 101, 111, 115.
11. Houck, "Story of the Railroad Work, Volume I," 11–14.

German decided to take leave of his established law practice, read some books on railroading, and start laying track out of a sense of enlightened commitment to the good of southeast Missouri. Perhaps what makes this such an enduring and charming adventure story is that there is an element of truth to it. Without question, Houck was a product of this celebrated age of "economic individualism" in the late nineteenth century when self-taught men with vision, natural genius, and entrepreneurial instincts bent modern technology to their will, building the nation while rising to great wealth and social position. What historian Alan Trachtenberg called the "practical Yankee inventor-entrepreneur," embodied by men like Thomas Edison, held out proof that despite the seemingly insurmountable challenges before him, old republican principles of rugged individualism still applied to the free market of modern industry. Even in his home state, railroad mania drove many desperate towns to entrust railroading to just about any local person willing to give it a try, leading many bankers, farmers, businessmen, and even lawyers to routinely step forward with bold plans to start a railroad.[12]

So when he initially dreamed that dream, it was probably of these popular images of the businessman-as-conquering-hero, already well established in American culture by 1880. Louis's dreams were also filled with the sound and fury of great deeds, battles, and conquests from history. Close friends knew him to be a romantic with the soul of a scholar: a historian. And like many historians, since childhood Louis Napoleon Houck, named for the French Emperor, had been losing himself in that heroic world William Barnum had earlier described where great men—kings, warriors, statesmen, philosophers, presidents, and frontiersmen—rose to do great things.

All these inspirational musings lent an almost innocent or accidental quality to Houck's beginnings in the railroad business, a perception later reinforced by how wholly Louis underestimated the increasingly sophisticated, mechanized, and systematic industry he was about to enter, especially its actual physical construction.

Although admittedly a dreamer, Louis Houck was not exactly a Pollyanna. He was an aspiring capitalist—a shrewd, sensible, and at times uncompromising businessman—so when he also cogitated, he did so over very pragmatic concerns. He can be taken at his word when later confirming that "public opinion, to a certain extent, and my own inclinations,

12. Trachtenberg, *The Incorporation of America*, 5, 54, 65, 67, 81; Lopata, *Local Aid to Railroads in Missouri*, 63.

being a large property owner in that territory, compelled me to take hold of that enterprise in order to secure and afford our town its benefits as well as develop the material resources of that section."[13] Of course in regard to his property values, a rising tide would lift all boats, and Cape Girardeau still desperately needed economic resuscitation. But for all the public-spirited rhetoric, the entirety of his subsequent railroad career suggests that Houck initially took the plunge because he clearly wanted to create a booming economic situation that he could take advantage of.

The material resources he spoke of developing were primarily timber. At the time, cypress and other hardwoods covered the vast majority of southeast Missouri, making the land unsuitable for agriculture, but an excellent source of lumber. Within a generation, huge national interests like Gideon-Anderson, C. A. Boynton, McCormick and Deering, and Himmelberger and Harrison operated some of the nation's largest sawmills in the Bootheel. Like local stave and railroad-tie giants William Brown and T. J. Moss, all these shippers needed rail access out of the bayous, and Houck felt confident he could lure them away from the St. Louis and Iron Mountain with better rates and concessions.[14]

Moreover, in looking at his myopic and suspect construction practices and lengthy bouts of litigation, it seems he based much of his decision around the fundamental reality that like the region, he was cash poor but land rich. Railroading, with all its inherent risks, afforded other obvious, and some less obvious, ways to accentuate the latter while ameliorating the former. Chief among them was still the potential for raising private subscriptions—in essence donations—from a given community aching for a railroad. The 1875 Missouri constitution had extended the ban on state funding of railroads to include counties or municipalities, due to the fallout over this dicey and by now discredited source of public support. But in the absence of public funding, a skilful promoter like Houck could still launch a successful subscription drive. Even though this process became more difficult with each passing year, all that would be necessary was to project an estimated construction cost for bringing a line to the railroad-starved town. Then create a festive air of community pride with a few animated public speeches, supplemented of course with some obligatory articles in the local newspaper booming the town or else warning of the danger and shame in letting the road go instead to a rival neighbor.

13. Christensen and Kremer, *A History of Missouri, Volume IV,* 42.
14. Houck, "Story of the Railroad Work, Volume I," 44, 45; *Sikeston Standard,* March 6, 1936; William T. Doherty, Jr., *Louis Houck, Missouri Historian and Entrepreneur,* 43.

Another equally attractive consideration was the acquisition of additional land. Houck's contemporaries on the court circuit had already convinced him that despite the prohibition of county aid to railroads, legal loopholes existed whereby southeast Missouri counties could still exchange vast tracts of public swampland for private railroad construction. The trick now was coupling the railroad work with levee building and drainage—viewed as legitimate economic development projects—and then defending the entire project as land reclamation in court: a clever ploy Houck later tried, unsuccessfully, in both Wayne and Pemiscot counties.[15]

While the promise of subsidization and land must have been alluring, perhaps the most intriguing, and ultimately decisive, aspect of railroading to Houck may well have been the potential sale of a small feeder line to a larger system.[16] By the time of his deliberations in 1880, Houck already discerned a trend across Missouri: bigger fish such as Jay Gould's Missouri Pacific Railroad were gobbling up numerous local lines and consolidating them into a small number of extensive railroad networks. With lucrative stave factories, tie companies, and sawmills along his lines, these big competitors were bound to take notice, and with a little salesmanship and legal maneuvering a small-time railroader, regardless of the physical condition of his property, could realize huge profits with relatively little investments of time or money.

Houck carefully weighed all these considerations, both from the standpoint of public good and private interest, before finally pitching the idea to Mary. Understandably "much surprised" by her husband's scheme initially, Mary also cogitated as her husband presented his case, point by point, pacing the library of Elmwood, much as he would in the courtroom. However Louis framed the argument, his sanguinity and resolve eventually sold her on the idea, and after a brief deliberation of her own, she threw her support—and, maybe more importantly, her family's resources—behind him.[17]

In what became the hallmark of his railroading career, from the outset Houck made up for his lack of practical railroad experience by playing to his strengths in promotion, journalism, and the law. Just as with the Normal School, he again approached Robert Sturdivant, a member of the orig-

15. Lopata, *Local Aid to Railroads in Missouri,* 38, 57; Doherty, Jr., *Houck,* 14; Doherty, Jr., "Louis Houck: Opponent and Imitator of Jay Gould," 54.

16. Doherty, Jr., *Houck,* 4, 15, 43; Doherty, Jr., "Opponent and Imitator of Jay Gould," 55.

17. Houck, "Story of the Railroad Work, Volume I," 14.

inal railroad's board of directors, with the proposal that the two work as partners. Though Sturdivant begged off, citing his age, sixty-three, and declining health, he exhibited an encouraging faith in the project and agreed to help arrange a $20,000 loan through his bank to get Houck off the ground. To supplement this backing, Mary sold off a sizable tract of land in southern Illinois.

With much of the necessary capital in place, in July 1880, Houck approached the firm of J. and S. Albert, who by this time held the remaining mortgages on the holdings of the defunct Cape Girardeau and State Line Railroad Company, with an ingenious business proposition. Simply put, if he, Houck, could complete the remaining fifteen—more specifically, 14.4—miles of track to connect Cape Girardeau to the Iron Mountain line at Delta, he would get clear title to all the railroad's properties along with a subscription list of potential investors and a personal bonus of $10,000. There were two catches: one, Houck would pay a nominal $6,000 for a quit claim deed on the forty miles of graded roadbed, and two, all work had to be completed by January 1, 1881, less than five months away. If he failed to comply, the properties and the $6,000, including whatever new construction Houck did manage to finish before the deadline, remained in the possession of J. and S. Albert.

While the Albert firm mulled over his proposal, a committee of boosters, organized by Houck and Sturdivant, essentially went door-to-door in Cape Girardeau wringing pledges of financial support from skeptical businessmen to cover the required $6,000. Then, to Houck's astonishment and disgust, once word of his intentions got out, other would-be railroaders complicated matters by suddenly coming forward to offer their own ingenious schemes. One particularly infuriating rival, John Cowden, the chief designer and superintendent of the Barataria Canal in New Orleans, offered to build the railroad in exchange for J. and S. Albert's help in raising one thousand barrels of Monongahela whiskey from a steamboat sunk somewhere between Osceola, Mississippi, and Memphis. Several tense days followed as J. and S. Albert evaluated their options, made more anxious by Houck's suspicion that the senior members of the firm "did not despise good whiskey." In the end, though, this and other matters were cleared away and the deal between Houck and J. and S. Albert was struck.[18]

18. Ibid., 15–18; Doherty, Jr., *Houck*, 12, 143; Doherty, Jr., "Opponent and Imitator of Jay Gould," 47.

In early August Louis took over as president and director of the newly incorporated Cape Girardeau Railway Company and set about upholding his end of the bargain. On paper, his self-confidence seemed warranted. The previous railroad had already completed some of the most labor-intensive work, clearing and grading the right-of-way from the Cape to the town of Idlewild in Stoddard County eight years before. Louis also pleased himself by quickly reaching what he thought were favorable agreements with officials from the St. Louis, Iron Mountain and Southern. From Russell Allen, vice president of that line, Houck contracted to purchase the one thousand or so tons of relaying rails and tie plates needed for construction, paying $5,000 in cash with the understanding that the balance would be paid off in monthly installments as each new delivery of rails was made to him at Delta. In a letter accompanying the contract, Louis also received in writing Allen's too-good-to-be-true promise of 25 percent of the gross earnings on all new business Houck's road sent the Iron Mountain. At the same time, Louis worked out a deal with William Kerrigan, the division superintendent of the Iron Mountain, to locate a Y-type connection to their track at Delta for him to tie into. Area tie hacks hired along the route would supply the other main ingredients by merely cutting down trees, squaring off two sides, and laying the logs in formation with the bark left on the other sides.

From what he had read in recently purchased railroading manuals such as the *Baldwin Locomotive Works Illustrated Catalogue*, and from what he had heard from those he considered to be knowledgeable railroading men, he thought his crews would be able to lay tracks and ties at a rate of about one mile per day. Once hammers began swinging, five months would be more than enough time for him to lay track from Delta to Cape Girardeau. There was no sense of urgency. No wonder that the proud Houck naturally felt taken aback when after trying his last case as an attorney, his incredulous legal associates flippantly predicted he would be back to work in his law office soon enough.

Within days, however, Louis Houck received the first of many hard lessons in his new vocation. Against the advice of the Iron Mountain railroad, Houck had already made the determination to follow the existing right-of-way, locating the crossing junction in Delta and beginning construction there, working his way east toward Cape Girardeau. The Iron Mountain preferred placing Houck's junction with their line at the original site, Allenville, roughly two miles north of Delta on higher ground. Allenville, they argued, would give the new road a downgrade run to Cape Girardeau, making it possible to pull trains with less locomotive power.

Another argument against placing the junction at Delta was that in the eight years since the existing right-of-way had been graded, the whole road had grown into what the Iron Mountain's chief engineer derisively called in the local vernacular "Nigger Wool": an almost impenetrable jungle of briars, brush, and trees.

Sure enough, upon walking down from Allenville to Delta in the sweltering heat to actually inspect the route for the first time on August 3, Houck awkwardly hacked his way through, struggling even to find the exact place where his line would tie into the Iron Mountain. That right-of-way, originally graded out to a hundred feet wide, now had oak and gum trees eight to twelve inches in diameter nearly covering "the dump." The dump itself, basically a landfill to get the ties up on high ground so they could stay dry, was riddled with a honeycomb of muskrat and beaver burrows. The old telegraph line hung in disrepair, and hunters had accidentally burned large holes in the floor of the long-abandoned little frame depot, almost completely hidden now by wilderness.[19]

Hiring local African Americans to chop through the dense brush proved much easier than finding, and keeping, suitable laborers willing to cut ties and lay track for such an uncertain venture. With the failure of the first railroad fresh in their minds, those fifteen or so laborers Houck managed to round up at any given time—men Houck described as being "of every character"—often refused to work until he personally guaranteed their wages. "Of course," he recalled about his crews, "it was taken for granted that this railroad enterprise would speedily end in my insolvency and bankruptcy," and as a result he bridled at what he considered his employees' "unreasonable demands for money at unreasonable times."[20] Never known for prompt payment of any type of debt anyway and perpetually strapped for cash, Houck faced frequent work stoppages and confrontations due to late compensation.

This general predicament actually contributed to two entertaining folktales, of which several versions developed over the years. In the first popular story, the nearsighted Houck was inspecting some recently laid track when he stepped on a branch that sprang up behind him and accidentally tapped him on the shoulder. Houck is said to have wheeled around instinctively and said, "Yes, yes, Tom, I'll have the money for you tomorrow." The

---

19. "Louis Houck Memoirs," 160.

20. Houck, "Story of the Railroad Work, Volume I," 23, 25, 26; *St. Louis Post-Dispatch*, March 1, 1925.

second anecdote, more serious, centered around Louis's version of a particularly heated exchange between a disgruntled employee seeking over-
due wages and Houck's delay in providing remuneration until "all facts
could be more fully ascertained." Finding little satisfaction in his boss's
answer, the man supposedly responded by heaving a ten-pound weight
directly at Houck's head. Louis would fondly retell how, without missing
a beat, he coolly ran a hand into his hip pocket as if to draw a revolver and,
even though he did not really have one, chased "the dastardly coward" off
by threatening to kill him.

Even on the rare occasions when wages were on time, Houck dealt with
a variety of other labor headaches. Given the soggy and isolated nature of
the area, Houck's small crew, drawn mostly from the hill country to the
north, at first boarded with families at Allenville, running a handcar down
the two miles of Iron Mountain track to Delta and then out to their work.
Later as construction progressed east past the Dutchtown road, most of the
crew, including Houck, stayed at the Philo Smith farm, the only substantial residence along the line, about ten miles west of Cape Girardeau on the
Dutchtown road. The remainder stayed at a rustic little log cabin below the
Dutchtown road that the men sardonically called the "Southern Hotel,"
after the fine St. Louis establishment. All these accommodations, including the men's propensity to get a big dose of the spirit from their hidden
stashes of liquor along the line, made it difficult to get the crew to and from
the work site in a timely manner. As summer turned to fall, shorter days
were accompanied by increasingly inclement weather, which further whittled away at productivity and encouraged frequent absenteeism.

Many of Houck's most acute problems, labor and otherwise, stemmed
primarily from his own lack of experience and the simple fact that limited
time and capital compelled him to cut costs at nearly every turn. Given his
own professed "ignorance of the first principles of railroad construction,"
it was critical that he take time to surround himself with at least some seasoned "railroad men." Yet in the interest of expedience and parsimony, he
regretfully hired men as engineers and foremen who simply lied about
their own experience. Once in the field, they quickly proved to be as unini-
tiated as he. As a result, Houck tolerated several amateurish and maddening mistakes during his learning curve that fall, leaving him "bothered
in ways no words [could] express." Basic railroad construction generally
involved first grading the right-of-way and then creating the dump. On
top of this dump ties were usually laid, with rails on top of them fastened
down with tie plates, and then rock ballast put in to facilitate drainage. But
because hauling rock would have been such a major undertaking, Louis

chose to forgo it, making the route particularly susceptible to erosion and rotting ties. What is more, the St. Louis and Iron Mountain, a competitor after all, took advantage of the tenderfoot railroader almost immediately. Contracted to supply one thousand tons of suitable rails by mid-August, the Iron Mountain disingenuously shipped him their scrap and worn-out rails, some cut down to no more than six feet in length and others twisted and battered. Though he accepted the woefully inferior rails under protest, Houck exacerbated matters by instructing his crew to use between one-half and one-fourth the standard number of ties, spacing them four to five feet apart in some spots, and fastened the rails to them using half tie plates and only one bolt. Over this unsightly line rolled, and not too cleverly, three secondhand flatcars, a homemade caboose prone to derailing, and an ancient wood-burning locomotive, named the "Andrew Giboney" for his late father-in-law, that, for reasons they only guessed was a sprung axle, would not stay on the tracks when operated in reverse.

Consequently, the autumn passed quickly, with only a couple of miles of precarious track to show for it. Working alongside his crew six days a week, Houck's involvement in the backbreaking process became considerably more hands-on than he initially envisioned. He now found himself personally "bolting rails, carrying spikes and angle plates [angle bars], and spreading and bossing the spreading of ties," and in fact, he remembered, "doing everything that I could do."[21] Mary rode out on horseback frequently from nearby Elmwood on her favorite mare Daisy to inspect their painfully slow progress, especially on Sunday when she could visit with her "Dearie"—a term of endearment she used for Louis and other close family—in private. Ahead of the main body of workers, African American men hired for their skill in cutting and hewing white oak and cypress worked alone, gradually repairing rotting trestles. Deer and turkey regularly came up on the dump to investigate. Each night, as the crew headed back to Delta, with limbs and briars scratching those hanging off the sides of their overcrowded handcar, the men heard wolves howling in the woods to the south near an area called "The Thumb" where the Whitewater River ran when it was high.

Snow and sleet suspended work intermittently throughout October before threatening to stop it altogether in November when a storm, the likes of which had not been seen in years, covered the roadbed under two to three feet of snow. Frozen hands flailed in the snow to uncover buried

---

21. Houck, "Story of the Railroad Work, Volume I," 25, 28, 29, 30, 31.

ties, angle bars, and rails, and piece them all together, sometimes laying track on top of the drifts. As the snow melted, the swamps rose, miring Houck's crew and equipment in frigid mud.

By December, Louis Houck tossed and tumbled in his bed each night, taking stock of his increasingly dire straits. "We had laid four miles of track in four months, from August 4 to December 4," he figured, confounded by his initial calculations of one mile per day, "and had twenty-six days to finish laying eight miles more of track."[22] He was worked to the point of exhaustion, but unable to sleep, and the wolves now seemed figuratively and literally at the door. Representatives from J. and S. Albert were coming out to inspect the work more regularly, each time finding it more difficult to conceal their satisfaction that he would almost certainly fail and they would retain possession of an incomplete, albeit vastly improved, railroad without so much as driving a spike.[23] What is more, if Houck missed the impending deadline, not only would he not get the railroad, but a clause in their agreement made him personally liable for the thousands in loans. For the first time since he began dreaming and cogitating, doubt and despair crept in.

But to this point in his life Louis Houck had proven that he was nothing if not a fighter, and he bore down, his naive enthusiasm giving way to grim determination. "I commenced to build that railroad and after I began to build it," he later testified, "I was like the man that caught the wolf. I had the road and it was dangerous to let go and dangerous to hold on."[24] He hired a new superintendent, a onetime California gold prospector named William Penny, to oversee the whole operation, and an experienced railroad mechanic, Dick Smith, to finish rebuilding the necessary trestles and maintain the rolling stock. Handy with tools, Smith *had* actually worked as a carpenter for the Illinois Central and impressed Houck with his ability to fix anything from a locomotive to a pocket watch. While Penny's practical knowledge of railroading was on the other hand not much better than Houck's, Louis chose him because of his intelligence and willingness to learn from his mistakes.

He also rounded up additional workers, contracting with William Tibbs, an "old railroad man" in Marble Hill, who sent enough men to enlarge his

22. Ibid., 30, 33. Houck was not counting the two miles of track the old company had already laid in Cape Girardeau eight years earlier.

23. *Cape Girardeau Southeast Missourian*, December 21, 1944.

24. *Statements and Testimony of Railroad Managers, of Shippers, Farmers and Others Taken before the Committee on Railroads and Internal Improvements of the Extra Session of the 34th General Assembly of Missouri* (Jefferson City, Missouri: Tribune Printing Company, 1887), 347.

crew to twenty-five, including, perhaps far more importantly, a veteran fore-man, Richard Berry, to keep them on task seven days a week. Neither "bois-terous" nor "loud," Berry instinctively took charge in a quiet and aggressive way the men immediately responded to. In no time, Houck found Berry's practical experience and Penny's sound judgment "invaluable."[25]

Similarly, Mary's visits became more frequent and her role more pro-nounced. Unlike her husband, who had worked indoors in some type of office setting most of his professional life, Mary had overseen a number of her father's slaves on the estate before the war and still supervised the work of some of those same African American hired hands who continued to live at Elmwood in the same cabins and small homes. In short, Mary had far more experience bossing men in the field than did Louis. And as the fre-quency of her inspections increased, the tiny woman began riding up and down the line on Daisy, encouraging the workers from her sidesaddle, at times even dismounting to offer them hot coffee or short lunches. During one of her rides to the work site, she and her husband conferred about rais-ing the crew's collective wage, presently a thrifty $90 per mile. Mary coun-seled her husband that a properly timed bonus might rally the troops more effectively than would a onetime raise. Agreeing, Houck gathered his weary crew together on December 6 and offered them this proposal: if they could make it to the Elm Swag trestle, roughly the midway point of the remaining eight miles, in ten days, he would pay them a $100 bonus in addition to their wages.[26]

Despite another bitter cold snap that froze the ground to at least a foot, Mary's idea worked liked a charm. Morale improved dramatically, with a certain rhythm and sense of urgency finally developing along the line. Rid-ing into camp at the trestle on December 16 with a sack of silver dollars from the Sturdivant Bank, an event undoubtedly staged for maximum effect, the company's auditor Thomas Wheeler distributed the bonus money among the cheering men. Reinvigorated by their progress, the gathering responded with an ambitious proposal of their own: would he pay another $100 bonus if they could lay the remaining four miles into Cape Girardeau by Christmas Day, well ahead of schedule? Though it pained him somewhat, Houck, fearing a loss of momentum, agreed.

25. *Weekly Republican* (Cape Girardeau), May 28, 1915.
26. *Cape Girardeau Southeast Missourian*, December 21, 1944; Houck, "Story of the Railroad Work, Volume I," 31, 33; informal conversation with Karen F. Stanley, July 28, 2005.

When that deadline proved unrealistic, Louis walked up and down the line telling his men not to waver, that he would still make good on the Christmas bonus if they could just finish by the end of the year. Houck further hedged his bets, and temporarily solved an acute shortage of usable rails, by instructing his men to take about half a mile of the track previously laid in Cape Girardeau years before by the old company and begin laying it west from the town out to meet his main crew building from the east. In later years, this bit of improvisation, borne out of real necessity because the Iron Mountain abruptly and inexplicably stopped its periodic shipments of rails, also took on a folk life all its own as an account supporting Houck's efficient and frugal German nature. The apocryphal version has a sneaky Houck—fast running out of rails and time—instructing his frantic crew in the eleventh hour to go back to the beginning of the line in Delta where they started and take up already laid track, haul it to the current point of construction, and re-lay it in order to allow the locomotive to roll into Cape Girardeau by the deadline. This certainly makes for a better story, but upon further review it is not particularly practical, and as it turns out, not exactly true.[27]

On the bitterly cold late afternoon of December 31, 1880, Mary rode out to the Rock Levee on the outskirts of Cape Girardeau to examine the railroad one last time. After almost five months of backbreaking and punishing labor in some of the meanest conditions around, only half a mile remained between the work crew and the connection with the old track running out from town, now clearly visible across the frozen field. As they reflected on this improbable feat, laying eight miles of track in less than four weeks, Louis allowed himself a rare pause and in a moment of self-satisfaction, confidently predicted that victory was at hand. Not so certain, Mary reminded him of the date and, out of earshot of the men, cautioned that the lure of Cape Girardeau's saloons might drain his workforce as night approached, not only leaving him short-handed during the final critical hours, but squandering the enterprise altogether if the men decided not to return at all on New Year's Day. Having come so far, perhaps it would be best, she suggested, to keep the crew on the job by paying an extra day's wage if they worked through the night.

So by the light of fires along the line and the lamp of their lone locomotive, Houck's crew joined the final rails to make a connection with the old track at 11 p.m., and at 2 a.m., January 1, 1881, they rode the Andrew

27. Houck, "Story of the Railroad Work, Volume I," 29, 31, 33, 34.

Giboney into Cape Girardeau right on schedule. William Penny, not given to the flare of railroad promotion, recalled a rather inauspicious entrance, "finding every light out [and] not even a saloon open so that the men could get a drink of Old Bourbon." The shivering and thirsty crew had to locate boarding as best they could. While granting that that may have really been the case, of course Houck, true to his nature, in later years painted the occasion in a slightly different light, remembering instead an unforgettably "cheerful and hospitable reception by the citizens of the town that had been clamoring for a railroad for many years."[28]

Perhaps the truth of the town's initial reaction to the coming of the railroad on New Year's Day lies somewhere in between Penny's and Houck's accounts. Most townspeople probably found Houck's triumphant entrance, now an iconic image memorialized in Cape Girardeau history, rather anticlimactic at first, considering that few were awake when it happened and actual daily operation of the Cape Girardeau Railway line did not commence for another three weeks. Owing to the extreme cold and the crew's haste, many of the rails, even though technically laid, had not actually been fastened together, or to the ties for that matter, and the switches were only partially installed. Moreover, the turntable, although not a necessity, took much longer to finish than predicted. Although Smith—whose own shortcomings as a railroad mechanic at times belied his competent appearance—had been working on the wooden turntable in Cape Girardeau while construction of the line was under way, to everyone's disgust the first few times they ran a locomotive on it the engine nearly keeled over into the pit.

In those hectic early weeks, Houck's attention and energies were also diverted by the first of many celebrated skirmishes with the St. Louis, Iron Mountain and Southern. Given the horribly substandard quality and insufficient number of rails the Iron Mountain had provided, Louis had been stewing for months over what he strongly considered to be the railway's violation of their contract. He boiled over completely when the Iron Mountain reneged on their agreements altogether, demanding immediate payment of the balance owed on the rails and voiding the arrangement giving him 25 percent of all new business the Cape Girardeau Railway sent their way.

Refusing to pay another cent until the Iron Mountain lived up to its word, Houck traveled to the company's regional offices in Charleston,

28. Ibid., 151–52.

Missouri, demanding satisfaction and threatening litigation. The Iron Mountain eventually conceded that they had furnished shoddy material and might be willing to supply the rest of the material at some point in the future, but made it very clear they had no intention of paying damages and in fact could make things generally unpleasant unless Houck paid up.

Houck was forced to acknowledge that he was in over his head amongst men whose "superior knowledge" of railroading far exceeded his own, and, already privately cogitating and dreaming of extending his road, he reluctantly decided to cut a deal rather than go through with a lawsuit. In exchange for the Iron Mountain's promise to finally deliver all the materials originally contracted for and someday take back the shoddy rails, Louis waived his insistence on damages and agreed to a greatly reduced earnings rate, later lamenting "so little did I know then of what really ought have been allowed me for my new business."[29] At the heart of the contract they signed in the spring of 1881, though, was an exchange of rails for bonds. Louis agreed to pay off his debt to the St. Louis, Iron Mountain and Southern, not in one immediate lump sum, but in Cape Girardeau Railway bonds at a rate of eighty cents on the dollar.

In holding on so tightly to that wolf, Houck had knowingly opened the door for the rival St. Louis, Iron Mountain and Southern—since December 1880 a part of the midwestern railroad interests of Jay Gould—to become major bondholders with leverage over his little Cape Girardeau Railway.

29. Ibid., 38–40.

CHAPTER 5

The Houck Roads

Louis Houck had a penchant for gathering rails—some old, some new, not very heavy—and making a railroad out of them.

—Henry Wollman

The unremarkable fifteen miles of track Louis Houck laid between Cape Girardeau and Delta in late 1880 launched a rather remarkable career in railroading. Upon becoming the sole owner of the Cape Girardeau Railway Company in 1881, the self-taught railroader committed mind, body, and spirit to what became an all-consuming vision of expanding feeder lines outward toward Fort Smith, Arkansas, Memphis, Tennessee, and St. Louis from the Mississippi River terminus at Cape Girardeau. Over the next twenty-odd years, during the unrivaled "golden age" of American railway history when the amount of track nationwide more than doubled to just over 193,000 miles, Houck built a provincial railroad empire of roughly five hundred miles of track across southeast Missouri that ultimately consisted of three distinct rail networks: one to the west, one to the south, and one to the north. In this same era when entire industries were being identified with a single person—Jay Gould and railroads, Cyrus McCormick and farm implements, John D. Rockefeller and oil, Andrew Carnegie and steel—these "Houck roads," as all his railroads came to be known collectively in the region, provided the first major impetus for ushering in a period of pronounced commercial, physical, and social development that transformed Cape Girardeau and southeast Missouri by the early twentieth century.[1]

1. Glenn Porter, "Industrialization and the Rise of Big Business," in Calhoun, ed., *The Gilded Age,* 9; Henry Wollman, "The Strange Story of the Cape Girardeau Railroad," 1.

The first of the Houck roads, the one heading south-southwest across the Iron Mountain triangle in the general direction of Fort Smith, was constructed in stages over the decade of the 1880s by progressively adding small sections to the original Cape Girardeau Railway line to Delta. The most obvious route was to more or less follow the old 1870 Cape Girardeau and State Line right-of-way hugging the northern edge of Crowley's Ridge toward what became the village of Idlewild, approximately forty miles away in Stoddard County, and eventually from there on to the St. Francis River. The primary advantage of this strategy was that once again Houck would only be clearing brush off an already graded roadbed and repairing a few rotten trestles. And while this had proved to be a real chore the previous year, it was still quite preferable to blazing a new trail through the morass of small lakes and marshes.

Another nifty land deal solidified his decision. It seems that in all the excitement over railroads, the good folks in northern Stoddard County had lost interest in an as yet still unfinished antebellum gravel road between Cape Girardeau and Bloomfield. At one time, the now moribund Cape Girardeau and Bloomfield Gravel Road Company had acquired around sixteen thousand acres of public land for the project, for which they had paid Stoddard County with company stock. But Louis learned, probably through his brother George—who had followed him to southeast Missouri and was by this time an established Bloomfield attorney and real estate dealer—that the county now wished to pursue a railroad instead and accordingly had brought suit to cancel their stock subscription for the gravel road and get the land back. Houck promptly orchestrated a three-way settlement. He promised both the Stoddard County Court and the Cape Girardeau and Bloomfield Gravel Road Company that if they would settle their claims by exchanging the stock and land respectively between themselves, then he would build a railroad between Delta and Lakeville through the northern portion of the county. The kicker was that Stoddard County would in turn convey those sixteen thousand acres, which included the gravel road's cleared right-of-way and a bridge over the Castor River, to Mary as a "bonus" to be put up as collateral in order to secure the necessary cash to finance the project.[2]

After the related rails-for-bonds deal was struck with the Iron Mountain, in July 1881 crews began work on the first part of Houck's extension, a roughly twelve-mile section of track through the predominantly dark cypress swamp between Delta and Lakeville. The line itself closely fol-

2. Houck, "The Story of the Railroad Work, Volume I," 41–43, 163.

lowed the Cape Girardeau and Bloomfield Road south of Hickory Ridge, across the Whitewater River, and through the lowlands locals still call the "Old" or "Big" Field, known for its thick, almost quicksandlike black soil. In spite of personal apprehensions over local predictions that a train would sink into this shaky earth, confidence again ran high.

Adding greatly to his self-assurance, Houck landed a crucial ally in the way of financial support when William Brown, the owner of the massive Pioneer Keg Works in St. Louis, agreed to relocate his stave mill on the Lakeville line. A cooper by trade, Brown for years had operated a mill in Lutesville to the north in Bollinger County that supplied sawed staves— long, thin bands of wood that are sealed together to make a barrel—for his St. Louis operation. But as of late he had become disenchanted with the shabby way in which he felt the St. Louis, Iron Mountain and Southern railroad had treated him and so was actively looking for more, and better, timberland along another railroad. This led him to Louis Houck, who, although the two men were unacquainted, Brown understood had recently acquired a sizable tract of such land in nearby Stoddard County and who also happened to be building a railroad through it. After a brief letter of introduction and a hurried meeting at Elmwood, Brown and Houck signed a mutually beneficial contract: Brown agreed to buy $10,000 of the bonds for the Lakeville line at eighty cents on the dollar—apparently their market value—and Houck sold him twenty-five hundred acres of the gravel road land for a new mill at a dollar an acre.[3]

By October, with construction of this "Lakeville division" nearing completion, a dispute over where to build the depot slightly altered the intended route and created a new town. Houck simply refused to pay $30 an acre for the Lakeville land where the depot was to be built, finding it not entirely unreasonable but far too high for land on the edge of the wilderness, and instead instructed his new college-educated civil engineer, Major James Francis Brooks, to lay out a new town about a mile west near a stand of mulberry trees where land could be had for $10 an acre. The establishment of New Lakeville, with its own depot and regular mail delivery, soon put citizens of old Lakeville into a quandary all too familiar to many midwestern towns spurned by a railroad. Some resettled to the north at Toga, while another group moved west to Houck's New Lakeville and began calling it Advance—pronounced in southeast Missouri in two distinct syllables—to show that they were "advancing."[4]

3. Ibid., 44–46, 52, 54, 165, 166.

4. Peggy Ashcraft Jensen, "Life on the Edge of the Great Dark Cypress Swamp: The Brownwood, Missouri Community History."

Houck kept advancing as well. William Brown's move to a location on the east side of the Castor River almost four miles southwest of Advance at a junction of the Hurricane Slough and Castor prompted no fewer than four other steam-powered saw and planing mills to set up shop along the same river in fairly quick succession. Each required immediate rail access, and Louis vowed to push the road through the woods to reach them as fast as he could.[5]

As he forged ahead through country that seemed to be getting progressively more treacherous, a close friendship developed between him and Brown. Although at the time not fully appreciating the real significance of their relationship, or how intertwined his fate would become with the Brown family in the coming years, Louis sincerely believed that Brown's "cooperation and generous assistance," especially the additional $10,000 of bonds he bought in the spring of 1882, was critical in continuing on to the Castor River. "He took a great interest in the enterprise and in every respect, by his means and counsel, assisted me, and always I enjoyed his undivided confidence while he lived." Louis, who it was said may well have been a noted inventor himself had he set his mind to it, also marveled at Brown's mechanical ingenuity, finding him to be a brilliant innovator whom he credited with fabricating many of the pioneering machines to saw out staves by steam power. In tribute, Houck charged Brooks with laying out the company town of Brownwood adjacent to the switch that accessed the stave mill almost three quarters of a mile away from the main line.[6]

Months later, sometime toward the end of 1882 or early 1883, James Brooks perpetuated the quaint Houck tradition of naming new railroad towns after his favorite supporters, friends, historical characters, or employees by platting the tiny community of Sturdivant, another seven miles beyond Advance across the Castor, as the temporary terminus of the Cape Girardeau Southwestern Railroad.

At this juncture, after two years in operation, the Cape Girardeau Southwestern, as it was now known, stretched nearly thirty-four miles—with an equal distance of telegraph line. The line included a couple of miles of sidetrack, three wooden bridges, six highway crossings, three cattle guards, and depots in Cape Girardeau, Delta, Advance, Brownwood, and Sturdivant. Regular twice-daily service included two used locomotives cautiously

5. Louis Houck Papers, Box 1508, Correspondence, January 1886, Folder 2, Special Collections and Archives, Southeast Missouri State University, Cape Girardeau, Mo.

6. Houck, "Story of the Railroad Work, Volume I," 52, 87–88, 157, 166, 167; Wollman, "Strange Story," 1.

pulling mixed trains of both flat cars for freight and a homemade passenger coach named the Pemanpieh, in honor of Louis Lorimier's Shawnee wife, which Dick Smith built himself in the Cape Girardeau shops.[7]

Through trial and error Louis was coming to understand the fundamental truth that given railroading's unique difficulties in the areas of organization, labor, and capital, it was one thing to build a road, and quite another to run it. Railroads were the primary force in shaping America's emerging modern corporate structure, demanding that even little ventures like Houck's adopt new levels of standardization and organization within the company between sales, legal matters, communication, record-keeping, safety oversight, and construction. "My theory," Houck concluded a few years later, "is that in order to secure the greatest economy in handling a small railroad there must be unity of management and direct responsibility to one responsible head, and who ought not to allow any expenditures to be made without fully considering the matter." "With me, on the other hand, money was always scarce, and therefore I was compelled to personally watch in detail, so to speak, expenses on the ground and see to it personally that a dollar's worth of labor or stuff was received for every dollar expended."[8]

Accordingly, William Penny supervised construction crews—now numbering forty strong and working in more efficient five- to eight-man section gangs—and Brooks, a very capable railroading man only three years Houck's junior, increasingly functioned as his right arm in the field. Back in Cape Girardeau, Thomas Wheeler and Leon J. Albert held down the fort as auditor and secretary respectively. Louis sweated over it all.

In the last half of the year Houck followed the construction train, living in a boxcar fitted as an office with a bedroom at one end and an African American youth who slept and worked in the kitchen at the other end. From his rolling headquarters, Houck, not unlike a military officer, waged a never-ending logistical battle of finding, motivating, and sheltering a sustainable labor force of men and animal teams while keeping supply lines open with a steady stream of equipment, tools, and enough food for both man and beast. Each new mile of track made these supply lines

---

7. *Poor's Manual of Railroads 1883*, 824; *Tenth Annual Report of the Railroad Commissioners for the State of Missouri Being for the Year Ending December 31st 1884*, 42, Missouri State Archives microfiche.

8. Carl Degler, *The Age of Economic Revolution: 1876–1900*, 22; Porter, "Industrialization," 9–10; Trachtenberg, *The Incorporation of America*, 58; Louis Houck to T. H. West, September 6, 1902, Houck Papers, Box 1541, Correspondence-Outgoing, September 1–8, 1902, Folder 6.

longer and more difficult to maintain. Frequently, after poring over daily status reports telegraphed in from points over the line, he labored well into the evenings, carefully fashioning his own railroading manuals by clipping material that explained the maddening lexicon of mechanical and technological innovations—load-bearing capacities, motive power, air-brakes, automatic couplers, signaling devices, etc.—and pasting them into discarded books.

A chronic lack of operating capital and increasing difficulty in finding skilled labor in the remote region, coupled with an eagerness to hurry, meant that the physical condition of the property remained suspect—all quite common traits of American railroading in this era. "Of course, our rails were old and battered, many of them, and the road was not as well tied as it should have been, nor was the track bolted in full," Louis acknowledged when assessing his railroad's progress, "but we were doing business over the railroad in a reasonably safe manner and daily gaining in more business and revenue." To sustain demand for transportation at the level necessary to support the line and pay back building costs, Louis also made time to travel around to the sparsely scattered farms, spreading his familiar refrain that people along a railroad ought to be friends of that pike, seeing as the mutual prosperity was inherently connected.[9] Indeed, in this regard, Brown's mill proved to be Houck's ace in the hole, and with other mills up and running, he could reasonably expect gross earnings in both freight and passenger service to continue to climb exponentially with the addition of the twelve-mile "Lakeville division"—technically a seven-mile "Zalma division"—and seven-mile "Sturdivant division." The latter two, incidentally, Houck had been able to finish in around nine months each; not quite the one mile a day he once naively fancied, but a noticeable improvement over the first days on the "Delta division."

All the same, apart from a number of unexpected mishaps—including a section boss dying in a freak hunting accident and drunken workers encouraging unpaid crews to tear up track in protest—Louis faced real fiscal concerns. No matter what the century, financing railroads is a very problematic enterprise. For one, construction does not lend itself particularly well to being done piecemeal, as it was done under Houck. In other

9. Houck Papers, Box 1508, Correspondence, January 1886–April 1888, Folder 2; *Seventh Annual Report of the Railroad Commissioners for the State of Missouri Being for the Year Ending December 31st 1881*, 32–33, Missouri State Archives microfiche; Doherty, Jr., "Missouri Interests of Louis Houck," 64; John H. Armstrong, *The Railroad—What It Is, What It Does* (Omaha, Neb.: Simmons-Bordman Publishing Corp., 1978), 7.

words, all construction normally must be completed before trains can run, and this often means no return on capital for long periods of time. Additionally, once completed, railroads are extremely expensive to maintain and operate, taking into account equipment, maintenance, and facilities, and these costs continue regardless of a line's productivity. For Houck, these harsh realities manifested themselves primarily in a mounting debt of some $198,000.

If there was a bright side to this potentially worrisome state of affairs, it lay in another truism Louis figured out: that the business of railroading rarely involved the actual flow of your own liquid capital. In this day and age "you don't build railroads with money," a fellow railroader later revealed of the increasingly sophisticated nature of American finance. "You build them with bonds and pieces of paper and by bookkeeping."[10] Hence, it could be considered encouraging that the majority of the Cape Girardeau Southwestern's debt was in friendly hands. Houck's personal liability to Sturdivant had grown to $30,000, Brown controlled $20,000 in bonds, and Mary remained the largest bondholder with around $76,000 in her name.

But on the other hand, the most disconcerting feature was the other nearly $76,000 in bonded indebtedness to the Iron Mountain, which was under Missouri Pacific management and ultimately in Jay Gould's unfriendly hands. As another direct consequence of his lack of capital and haste, Louis had gotten in deeper by purchasing another five hundred tons of rails from the Iron Mountain in exchange for an additional $8,000 in railroad bonds on the Lakeville division. By again trading the cost-conscious Houck those discount rails for bonds, and thus becoming increasingly vested in each of these early divisions of his railroad, effectively, in a phrase familiar to southeast Missourians, the Missouri Pacific was giving him enough rope to hang himself. In this era of tension between national interests like Gould who saw the big picture of connecting transcontinental commerce and the more insular regional railroaders like Houck, this was actually a tried and true method of predatory railroad consolidation: leverage the local guy and let him do the hard physical labor of actually building his little road, wait for him to go bankrupt in the process, and then swoop in with foreclosure and swallow him up.[11] It seems Louis

10. James Irvine to Louis Houck, March 2, 1896, Houck Papers, 1896, Box 1518, Correspondence, March H–Z, Folder 16.
11. Houck, "Story of the Railroad Work, Volume I," 79, 89–91.

understood this phenomenon of consolidation in general, and in fact was probably banking on getting bought out on his own terms at some financially advantageous point; he was just a little slow to see the scenario unfold the way it did.

His mind was instead focused on timber and, increasingly, iron ore. Sometimes, in the jungles between Brownwood and Sturdivant, Louis sought relaxation by indulging his historical inquisitiveness exploring the sprawling remains and relics of what he judged to be extensive mound-builder fortifications from the prehistoric Mississippian culture. Perhaps here he pondered for a moment the wisdom of pausing to catch his breath, maybe going back and greatly improving the route's physical condition by upgrading from iron to superior steel rails or reorganizing its financial condition by reducing bonded indebtedness and rates of interest. But no matter, Houck had a real taste for railroading now, and the lure of striking great mineral wealth, in particular alleged deposits of hematite iron ore, farther west in the Ozark Hills of south central Missouri obsessed him. Since first suspecting that the original Cape Girardeau and State Line had cleared their right-of-way out as far as they did for this purpose, he began leading a series of scouting expeditions up and down the St. Francis and Current rivers through the unspoiled, rolling pine-crowned hills of Wayne and Carter counties in search of iron. And even though hired experts came away with discouraging news, Louis came back from his travels sufficiently impressed, seeing only a blank bucolic canvas awaiting modern extractive industry and his railroad.[12]

Standing directly in his way, though, was the daunting St. Francis River, and even before that a particularly ornery stretch of swamp known as the Mingo Bottom. Some four miles wide and twenty miles long, the Mingo Bottom runs northeast from the St. Francis between Wayne and Stoddard counties to the basin of the Castor and other streams draining the Ozark Hills. Mingo Creek ran through the bayou before emptying into the St. Francis. But since the Mingo Bottom is in effect a great depressed bowl, seasonal flooding routinely caused the marsh to fill with anywhere from between two to ten feet of water until the St. Francis and Castor seemingly merged into one huge lake.

A self-described "rose-colored optimist" by nature, Louis bore in mind the lessons of the old Bloomfield crowd when plotting his course, considering especially how by combining railroad work with levee building and

12. Ibid., 56, 169, 170, 177.

drainage Missouri counties could still exchange public wetlands for private railroad construction. After one of his earlier scouting trips, he had actually approached the Wayne County Court with just such a mutually beneficial scheme. At this March 1882 meeting in Greenville, the county seat, Houck detailed for the judges how the Cape Girardeau Southwestern might be willing to drain and undertake other reclamation work in the Mingo Bottom swamp if in return the court agreed to deed more than ten thousand acres of public land over which to build a railroad from Sturdivant to the St. Francis. His simple plan hinged on raising the embankment of his railroad high and wide enough through a twelve-mile stretch of Mingo from the Stoddard County hills to the Wayne County hills that the embankment could serve double duty as a levee. A system of drainage ditches and culverts built into this levee and a floodgate where the line crossed Mingo Creek would then protect the surrounding areas when the St. Francis overflowed. The court readily accepted, giving Houck until March 1884 to finish the job.[13]

The push west to the river began in earnest in the spring of 1883, after Houck again convinced Brown, recently appointed as his vice president of the Cape Girardeau Southwestern, to buy additional bonds, this time offering as a "bonus" the Wayne County land. Making the task all the more daunting was the additional consideration that the old right-of-way he had been so closely following since Cape ended before reaching the Mingo Bottom. This meant a whole new ball game in regard to construction, and after reaching Idlewild that summer, Houck found himself for the first time carving out his own right-of-way, leveling grades, constructing trestles from scratch, blasting through ridges, driving piles, and erecting cribbing. Houck's boys consisted of a lead right-of-way crew of primarily African American laborers forging a good half mile ahead of the main workforce, hacking out the right-of-way through this "malarial district." Since a roadbed must be made as level and straight as possible so as to not make a locomotive labor too hard, predominantly Irish grading teams followed, building up some areas and leveling others. Another three-quarters of a mile behind them came the tie hacks and layers. Again Houck gave this construction his entire personal attention and from his private boxcar personally oversaw every rail laid to the St. Francis River, only returning to Elmwood once or twice a month. "Knew every contractor and almost every laboring man on the job," he noted with pride, "white or black."[14]

13. Ibid., 92, 93, 94, 179.
14. "Louis Houck Memoirs," 126.

They reached Puxico by November before an unseasonably rainy spell unleashed flooding that stopped them in their tracks. Mingo Swamp was overnight transformed into a sea, submerging their partially completed embankments and driving out the contractors. The embankment, east of Puxico across the area of Flat Mingo, became so saturated and soft at one point that the track slipped when a locomotive pushing a train of rails tried to cross, sending the engine down into five feet of water and stranding the construction train. With his trusty walking stick in hand, Houck directed the difficult rescue of his crews from the waist high water. Yet sitting idly by for several weeks while the water receded to the point that they could haul out the engine and resume work temporarily broke his momentum and shook his confidence.

Though outwardly stoic and eternally buoyant, Louis was given to periods of introspection and may well have turned over in his mind during the excruciating wait the strain of constantly advancing the line forward. Maybe he thought about how he missed Mary, Irma, Giboney, and Elmwood, or again experienced the frustration at the prospect of not making a deadline. Perhaps too he even paused to consider his young "negro cook" who had taken "a congestive chill and died there." All these burdens certainly were made more acute by the cold and damp. Once more Louis momentarily despaired, later confessing that "at times I was much discouraged and walked out in the woods standing untouched around and was overcome by my emotions."[15]

By the time work got under way again in January, it was clear that the March deadline could not be met, leaving Houck with the unsavory task of ingratiating himself before the county court to ask for an extension. On his way to Greenville, Louis thought through his approach, basing his argument chiefly on the premise that his progress thus far warranted more time. But he also anticipated the need to maybe grease the wheels of county politics a bit so he hired Newt Morrison, a local attorney well versed in the powers that be in these parts, to guide his request successfully through. As they rode together, Morrison confirmed Houck's reading of the situation. To the local man's similar way of thinking, a little politicking and a relatively small sum of money would in fact do the trick, since the presiding judge, C. F. Bruihl, was already inclined to grant an extension, judge John Raney was undecided, and he, Morrison, was a good friend of sheriff James Hatton who in turn was related to judge E. C. Rubottom.

At the courthouse, a curious drama played out over the course of one long afternoon, almost, Louis suspected, as if scripted. After Morrison met

15. Houck, "Story of the Railroad Work, Volume I," 85, 97, 98, 180.

with the court in private, he returned to Houck with the judge's demand of $2,000 in "judicial" costs for the extension. The request for money was not unexpected, but the amount was outrageous. Incredulous and incensed, Louis likened it to simple extortion. He pointedly refused to pay and even threatened to walk away from the project all together, at a personal loss, rather than be robbed in broad daylight on the courthouse steps.

In conversation Houck usually spoke like a lawyer, in the measured, deliberate, and eloquent fashion of a well-read individual who keenly appreciates the power of words and carefully chooses each one for its desired effect. Except, that is, when he got angry or excited. Then his fierce temper—not always under firm control in the best of circumstances—burst forth, heralded, almost as a rule, by steady profanity. When in the presence of Mary—who vigorously scolded him for using his irreverent language—Louis routinely composed himself in a hurry and apologized, especially to ladies, for not having meant exactly what he said.[16] But in his wife's absence, Louis no doubt unloaded on Morrison, sending the apologetic attorney scurrying back to the judges, including Rubottom, who was sick in bed, to arrange a compromise.

While waiting for Morrison's return, Louis was cogitating as he paced around the courthouse when he happened to see Morrison and Hatton leaning over the courthouse fence discussing matters in hushed tones. Putting all the pieces of the plot together, he quickly deduced that a scheme was afoot to squeeze some cash out of him, and the ring embraced the whole Wayne County crowd. The figure Morrison next presented was $1,000, which Houck countered would be acceptable as long as he could pay it in railroad bonds. No deal—the judges wanted cash, leaving Louis, in the interest of his overall operations, to finally settle on $900. Almost immediately, the judges, including the heretofore bedridden Rubottom, materialized to hear Morrison's formal request and then unanimously granted the perfunctory extension to August 1884. Louis begrudgingly made a draft on the Sturdivant Bank for the $900 and on the ride back to camp stewed over the prospect, even though he could not prove it, that Newt Morrison at that very moment was probably splitting the money with Hatton and the judges.[17]

16. Christine Wheeler Heil, "Recollections," privately printed manuscript [no page number], Box 1034, Folder 5, Christina Wheeler Heil Papers, Special Collections and Archives, Southeast Missouri State University.

17. Houck, "Story of the Railroad Work, Volume I," 102; Madison R. Smith to Louis Houck, February 10, 1893, Houck Papers, 1893, Box 1513, Correspondence, Folder 16.

Even this five-month extension proved extremely challenging to meet. Persistent spring rains bogged the crews down yet again, and further complicating matters, much to his chagrin Houck soon discovered that with so much water and mud, no grading could be done on this section of the road until late in the fall, and moreover that nearly half a mile of crib work would be necessary. In railroad engineering terms, cribbing is the labor-intensive process of building a type of lattice-work structure to reinforce embankments in swampy regions such as the Mingo Bottom. Usually logs are driven into the embankment horizontally for support and then the lattice of wooden beams—similar to what a corn crib looks like—are constructed on the outside of the embankment to guard against erosion and washouts. Ox teams tediously dragged the logs out of Mingo for crews of contractors to fashion into cribbing, an ordeal that was still being finished months after the road was in operation. In certain locations men cribbed the approaches to pile bridges, another staple of swamp railroading where surfaces are not adequate to support the weight of a train. Here again logs were driven by machine, vertically this time, into the ground as piles and then a bridge laid horizontally across. The pile bridges workers drove for Houck were not especially high, just enough to get the track out of the water. In fact, gum tree stumps technically served this engineering function too, and in a pinch Houck was not above hastily cutting them down to satisfy his piling needs.

In a scene reminiscent of the last frantic weeks of December 1880, as the August deadline loomed, Houck's boys scrambled to lay the last track over the partially erected cribbing and bridges, both of whose completion had been further hindered by troubles renting a decent pile driver. Bitter cold was not the problem this time; instead, true to the region's radical weather extremes, intense, almost tropical heat bedeviled crews as the eleventh hour approached. But again, like his first line to Delta, a final surge down the stretch brought the tracks to within a mile of the St. Francis River as required by the contract, with even a couple of days to spare.

Houck swiftly headed north to Greenville to notify the county court of his success, leaving behind instructions to plat the town of Wappapello, a name, as legend has it, he chose either for the friendly Shawnee Chief Wapepileese or Fox Chief Wapello, who had willingly moved his people west of the Mississippi into Iowa.[18]

18. Houck, "Story of the Railroad Work, Volume I," 103, 104; Doherty, Jr., "Missouri Interests of Louis Houck," 69.

Act two of the Wayne County land saga opened when the court found that the Cape Girardeau Southwestern had indeed fulfilled its contractual obligations and therefore authorized Sheriff Hatton, who had been holding the ten thousand acres in escrow, to release the title to Houck. Yet the title was not forthcoming, even after Louis demanded it. In time he was informed, by none other than Newt Morrison, that Hatton had no intention of turning over the land unless Louis came up with the apparently customary "judicial" fee of $2,000. Louis rebuked Morrison for such a "bare faced attempt to levy blackmail" and promptly filed a lawsuit to gain possession of the deed. This moved the prickly dilemma back into the courtroom, an arena Louis never really walked away from when he retired from actively practicing law any more than he had quit writing when he sold the *Volksblatt*.[19]

As it turns out, by 1884 this ill-fated deal was not altogether unfamiliar to the Wayne County Circuit Court or the Supreme Court of Missouri. Shortly after Houck signed the original contract with Wayne County, the state board of education brought a suit of their own to invalidate the deal, primarily on the grounds that swampland proceeds were supposed to go to aid county schools, not railroads. Both the circuit court and later the state supreme court had upheld the legality of Houck's contract. These victories were no accident, nor were they based on any misunderstanding of the law. Since 1875 Missouri categorically forbade county aid of this kind to railroads. Houck knew that, of course. He simply had done his homework and had come up with ways to beat the law by defending the overall venture as land reclamation in court.

Nonetheless, his legal strategy was soon tested after the Mississippi County Circuit Court, the venue where Louis prudently moved the case, dismissed his claims that he had lived up to a contract previously deemed valid by two courts. If this "effrontery" was not "remarkable" enough, in next appealing to the Missouri Supreme Court, his claim to the ten thousand acres, like the justice's earlier decision, was thoroughly reversed. The high court now ruled that regardless of the board of education's case, Wayne County had exceeded its authority and that this land deal was in direct violation of state law regarding railroads. Not only, as it was pointed out in the hearing, did William Penny simultaneously work for both the county as its commissioner entrusted with supervising the reclamation *and* for Houck as his railroad superintendent, but the agreement itself

19. Doherty, Jr., "Missouri Interests of Louis Houck," 50.

amounted to "merely a donation of the lands to the company in consideration of building and operating its road, and not a contract to deed swamp lands as repayment for reclaiming them." In no uncertain terms, the court concluded that Houck had simply built an ordinary railroad embankment—required of all lines by state law—to drain water from alongside his road; no more, no less. Calling it a levee, the judges told him, did not make it so. Therefore the contract was voided.[20]

This verdict should well have put the matter to rest under the appropriate heading of fair-is-fair, but Houck launched a protracted counterattack of unsuccessful litigation over the next few years trying to get the Missouri Supreme Court to see things his way: that the law ought not to protect a county from its obligations to fulfill a contract after it had enjoyed the benefits of said contract. To be sure, he was in fact out of a lot of time and money—more to the point, Brown was out of a lot of land—due to this turn of events. Still, it was Houck's first real legal and railroading defeat, and he found it hateful to be bested, especially in the courtroom. Hence, in reality it was probably the untenable nature of his original claim that he was unwilling to concede. From his perspective, the defeat amounted to a clear-cut case of conspiracy, seeing as he did the fingerprints of not only the Missouri Pacific all over the decisions, but also of the man he considered that railroad's longtime judiciary friend and coconspirator, Missouri Supreme Court Justice Thomas A. Sherwood, who Louis believed still held a grudge because of Houck's failure to support his candidacy for U.S. senator.[21]

With plans for further extensions temporarily shelved pending the outcome of the legal showdown with Wayne County, by 1884 construction on the line slowed to only sporadic projects. One such project resulted from Brown's insatiable need to secure additional supplies of white oak timber and an itch to try his own hand at railroading. To scratch the itch, Brown and Houck scouted a prime location seven miles north of Brown's existing operation near the settlement known as Bollinger's Mills along the Castor River. In the middle of magnificent stands of oak and pine cover-

20. *The State* ex rel. *Board of Education, Appellant, vs. County Court of Wayne County,* Missouri Reports 98 (1889): 362–68; *Cape Girardeau Southwestern Railway Company, Appellant, vs. Hatton, et al.,* Missouri Reports 102 (October 1890), 55; Houck, "Story of the Railroad Work, Volume I," 105–10.

21. See *William Brown Estate Company, Appellant, vs. Wayne County,* Missouri Reports 123 (June 25, 1894), 464–79; *St. Louis, Cape Girardeau and Fort Smith Railway, Appellant, vs. Wayne County,* Missouri Reports 125 (4 December 1894): 351–58; Doherty, Jr., "Opponent and Imitator of Jay Gould," 54; Houck, "Story of the Railroad Work, Volume I," 110.

ing the surrounding foothills, they chose one particular water mill, believed to be among the first operated by pioneer George Fredrick Bollinger, as a logical terminus of the proposed line. In warmly recalling the site, Louis remembered his amusement at the nearly eight hundred geese penned up in Bollinger's Mills by local merchants and being instantly taken by the Castor's crystal-clear waters and extensive gravel bars. He imagined how he could use the gravel to improve and ballast his road if he ever got around to it.

The construction of this Brownwood City and Northwestern Railway, known to railroaders as a temporary "tap road" and mistakenly called a tram by Houck, took somewhere around a year, including the building of a small bridge over the Castor. Upon its eventual completion sometime around 1886, Brooks renamed Bollinger's Mill Zalma in honor of Zalma Block, the operator of Cape's St. Charles Hotel. And while ostensibly a separate entity, the little tap railroad was hardly distinguishable from the Houck roads: Brown furnished all the necessary capital, Brooks surveyed it, Louis personally oversaw some of his own crews building it, and on paper Brown and Houck simply swapped places with the former serving as president this time and the latter as vice president.[22]

Aside from this "Zalma division," Houck occupied most of his productive *leisure* time at mid-decade in Cape Girardeau in the opportunistic pursuit of three unforeseen diversions from railroading. The first two were of a decidedly unfortunate sort. Sometime in 1884, Louis crossed paths with an energetic newcomer, James Pass, who intrigued him with the notion of starting a pottery factory in the Cape. Pass's logic appeared to be quite sound, pointing out as he did that the region's ridges were home to an excellent variety of clays, including large beds of kaolin, or China Clay, which were already being mined and shipped up the Ohio River to the

22. Sometime in early 1898 the Brown estate sold Houck the Brownwood City and Northwestern Railway Company along with its still unfinished southern extension through Bloomfield. Since its inception, the Browns had dabbled on and off with this addition into neighboring Stoddard County, showing as little enthusiasm as success. At one point, they had even purchased the rickety little Missouri Southeastern line running a short distance south from Bloomfield to a connection on the Cotton Belt at Zeta. Yet within months of consolidating the several companies into the new Cape Girardeau, Bloomfield and Southern (still nominally within the Cape Girardeau Southwestern system), Houck rebuilt the ramshackle line, completing the perpendicular road from Zalma to Zeta through Bloomfield. H. N. Holliday to Louis Houck, February 1888, Houck Papers, Box 1508, Correspondence, 1888 Correspondence Feb A-H, Folder 26; "Louis Houck Memoirs," 181–87; *Cape Girardeau Democrat*, February 19, 1898.

large pottery factories of "Crockery City": East Liverpool, Ohio. Would it not be more profitable to establish operations near the source, Pass inquired, especially when taking into account that tiny Commerce to the south of Cape had supported pottery operations since the 1830s?

Pass, the son of an accomplished English potter with some degree of experience himself, "talked so plausibly and seemed to have such good reason for urging the establishment of a pottery" that he convinced Louis to embrace his scheme. Houck in turn recruited other hopeful investors, including Henry Hunze, and together with Pass founded the Cape Pottery Company on the corner of Fountain and William streets in an area of town known as "The Happy Hollow" for its whiskey distillery. Several thousand dollars of up-front capital got the kiln built, and using Pass's molds, along with coal bought largely on credit to fire them, the plant turned out simple stone china ware they sold in bulk to the St. Louis Glass Company. Houck knew even less about the pottery business, however, than he had about railroading, and their little pottery concern perpetually operated in the red. To boost sales, Pass oversaw the addition of a second kiln to increase production and, after some initial miscalculations, experimented with the addition of other materials like feldspar to mix with the kaolin to improve the china's glaze. Likewise, they began decorating the faint ivory-colored china with the company's new elephant trademark on the bottom of all pieces—perhaps an intentionally ironic choice given that the heavy beast would have been understood in the nineteenth century as a euphemism for something burdensome.

Still, the business sputtered. Sales were steady, but production costs, including the expense of importing feldspar from back east, erased any hope of profits. Pass was the first to abandon ship after just over a year, heading off to an award-winning career at the helm of the renowned Onondaga Pottery Company in Syracuse, New York. Soon thereafter the Cape Pottery Company factory closed its doors for good, with Hunze and Houck probably each out between $4,000 and $5,000 over the failed venture. Poorer but wiser, Houck rode past the idle pottery and its dead kilns for years afterward, wryly acknowledging them as a potent "object lesson" in folly.[23]

---

23. Houck, "Reminiscences," 72. The failed Cape Girardeau Pottery Factory was the first step in a quite satisfying career for James Pass. After leaving the Cape in 1885, Pass became the superintendent and later president of the Onondaga Pottery Company. For twenty-eight years he led the company to national prominence in ceramic research. His pioneering work with vitreous china, today known as Syracuse China, won him a medal at the 1893 World's Fair.

This bumpy commercial detour, however, paled in comparison to the fiasco surrounding Houck's contentious role in the political squabble that broke out over the location of the state's branch penitentiary. The drawn-out ordeal began innocuously enough in January 1885 when outgoing Governor Thomas J. Crittenden recommended that the legislature "maturely" consider the legitimate need for a second state prison to relieve dangerous overcrowding at the lone facility in Jefferson City. Soon after, the General Assembly passed, and new Governor John Sappington Marmaduke signed, legislation authorizing the creation of this Missouri Penitentiary No. 2 contingent on a suitable location being found that afforded rail access, a relatively healthy environment, and ready opportunities for the employment of convict labor. A three-man board of prison inspectors made up of state auditor John Walker, state treasurer James Seibert, and attorney general Banton G. Boone were entrusted to select such a site and given a budget of $20,000 to do so.

That the prison sweepstakes would entail fierce competition between Missouri communities, unabashed boosterism, sectional animosity, a little Gilded Age political trickery, and inevitably some resultant sour grapes before all was said and done was to be expected. Also to be expected, it seems, was Louis Houck's keen appreciation for the potential in attracting yet another state institution. At the time Houck's Cape Girardeau land holdings had ballooned to include 400 acres and various properties within the city limits in addition to approximately 12,000 acres within a nine-mile radius of town, most of it immediately to the south. Houck and his wife also owned between 8,000 to 10,000 acres in adjacent Scott County. Given these circumstances, Houck instinctively envisioned this branch penitentiary on a tract of land he owned south of Cape on the river—part of the same acreage he originally offered to the Normal School in 1873—situated as it was along his railroad *and* his blue limestone quarries.[24]

For all of the interest Houck managed to generate locally, Cape Girardeau faced stiff competition for the branch penitentiary from early frontrunner Kansas City and a host of other communities including Louisiana, Hannibal, and Moberly. To effectively make the town's case, Louis led a contingent of eager citizens to Jefferson City who in essence set

24. *Report of Committee on Charges Preferred Against Honorable John Walker, State Auditor, Together with the Testimony of Witnesses, 34th General Assembly of the State of Missouri* (Jefferson City, 1887), 175, Box 1, Folder 1, RG: 561-Joint Interim and Special, SG: 34th General Assembly, Regular Session, 1887, Series: House Committees, Missouri State Archives; Doherty, Jr., *Houck, Missouri Historian and Entrepreneur*, 73.

up residence in the capital for several weeks during the summer of 1885, diligently lobbying legislators and the prison board. And, according to capital scuttlebutt, Louis capably cultivated an ever-growing network of Democratic officials with the understanding that Cape would be willing to offer various other inducements as might be required. As a result, the determined Cape crowd ended up bucking the prevailing wisdom that had the prison going to Kansas City: the inspectors agreed on an option to purchase one hundred acres of Houck's riverfront land for $200 an acre, the maximum price allotted by the state. Per capital custom, Houck celebrated the victory by hosting a champagne reception at the Madison Hotel.

Indeed, up until this point the brief history of the branch penitentiary had followed a trajectory rather routine in awarding political prizes of this sort: special interests with connections in the government had reinforced sectional loyalties. In this case Houck worked in collaboration with political ally and confidant James Seibert—himself a personal friend of Governor Marmaduke and a native of Cape Girardeau County—to sway the other inspectors Boone and Walker for a unanimous decision. But now Houck's heretofore uneventful bid to get Cape Girardeau its prison, not to mention cheap convict labor to quarry his stone, collided with the far more sweeping political battle then under way in the nation and state over, of all things, railroad regulation.

By the 1880s, mounting anxiety over the seemingly limitless size and power of the railroads, an industry not consistently governed by market forces of supply and demand, had convinced many ordinary Americans that the preservation of the public good required some type of state regulation of this private interest. Across the Midwest, states had been responding to mounting pressure from voters by establishing regulatory agencies and passing laws to fix railroad rates while making it illegal to unfairly overcharge small shippers for short hauls. In Missouri, where the Democrats had regained a tenuous hold on power, farmers led this strident chorus calling for tighter state control of railroads and less collusion between legislators and railroad lobbyists that eventually obliged the normally low-tax, low-service oriented state government to follow suit. Within two years of becoming governor in 1885, John Marmaduke, a Democrat and former state railroad commissioner himself, successfully guided the state's own set of regulatory legislation through the General Assembly, which standardized rates, eliminated short-haul versus long-haul discrimination, and curbed a corporation's ability to create monopolies with intent to restrict competition. The same year that Missouri passed its legislation, 1887, the cause reached all the way to Washington, D.C., where state oversight gave way to national supervision of interstate railroads with the creation of the Interstate Commerce Commission.[25]

Houck and the untimely penitentiary deal became embroiled in this larger, ostensibly unrelated, fight primarily through the person of John Walker. Almost immediately upon Cape Girardeau being awarded the prison in the summer of 1885, newspapers from around the state began strongly scrutinizing the excessive price Houck charged the state for the land, and by implication the overall legitimacy of the selection process. The *Moberly Monitor* first contended that Houck's flood-prone land was worth at most three dollars an acre and its community had been offering a much better plot for a mere $5,000. Fanning these flames, the *St. Louis Post-Dispatch* then revealed a more suspicious element of the story: that as state auditor, Walker, as well as Seibert, served as members of the Board of Equalization, where they had previously assessed Houck's land in Cape Girardeau at five dollars per acre. Now in their capacity on the Board of Prison Inspectors they had authorized the purchase of the same property for forty times as much. Even more damning, Walker also acted as a railroad assessor and once valued all of Missouri's railroad properties at $38 million for the purposes of taxation when the state Railroad Commission had set the figure closer to $103 million. Houck's own line, it was made clear, while stretching fifty-one miles, had been illegally assessed for taxes in 1885 at only forty and then for a mere $2,500 a mile. Critics claimed the line to be in actuality "stocked, bonded, and watered at $25,000" per mile.[26]

At a moment when public perceptions of state government suffered and Missourians inherently distrusted railroads and politicians, the paper went several steps further in casting aspersion on what folks came to believe was a "shady arrangement" between Houck and Walker. Walker, who owned an interest in a shoe company that made use of convict labor, seemed to inadvertently imply at one point that the convicts at the branch

25. Christensen and Kremer, *A History of Missouri, Volume IV,* 17–20; Porter, "Industrialization," 13; Steven L. Piott, *The Anti-Monopoly Persuasion: Popular Resistance to the Rise of Big Business in the Midwest,* 12, 18, 30. The law of supply and demand allowed railroads to routinely offer much cheaper freight rates and rebates for shippers sending their goods longer distances, usually between cities, while making up their profits gouging "short haul" shippers, usually farmers located along a single isolated line.

26. *St. Louis Post-Dispatch,* June 16–19, 22, 1885; *Missouri Republican,* March 15, June 18, 1885; Doherty, Jr., "Missouri Interests of Louis Houck," 295. The Missouri Board of Equalization consisted at the time of Governor Marmaduke, Auditor Walker, Attorney General Boone, Secretary of State McGrath, and Treasurer Seibert.

penitentiary would be hired out to work not only in the quarries of Cape Girardeau but also in the region's railroads and sawmills.[27] Perhaps, some speculated, this beneficial labor arrangement hinged on Houck's support of Walker in the auditor's expected quest for the gubernatorial nomination in 1888. Other critics across the state saw a transparent case of "boodle," or bribery, a charge made more plausible when Louis admitted to paying J. R. Willis, a former warden appointed to head the branch penitentiary, a commission of around 15 percent of the $20,000 land price in exchange for Willis's help in securing the prison for Cape. And although no evidence ever came to light directly linking Walker to this money, the simple fact that Houck's payment came just two days prior to the inspector's favorable decision looked mighty suspicious.[28]

In the political fallout over this increasingly embarrassing scandal being played out chiefly in the St. Louis press, the state abruptly scotched the notion of a Cape Girardeau branch penitentiary in July 1885 in favor of just expanding the existing prison at Jefferson City. The prison inspector's official repudiation of the deal with the Cape cited recent flooding on Houck's land—derisively described as "a frog pond"—and the lingering disagreement as to its relative worth. Regardless, in the minds of many Missourians, the sordid linkage between Houck and Walker became proof positive of the incestuous nature of railroaders and politicians while at the same time providing invaluable ammunition for the proponents of stronger regulation. Louis's outspoken commitment to the free market and denunciation of all forms of regulation outright as a matter of principle played directly into the hands of those seeking to discredit this embattled way of thinking and all who adhered to it. Over the next two years, as Houck vainly worked through state Senator Madison R. Smith and Representative Robert Whitelaw to revive the branch prison idea, and in particular after the Missouri legislature launched a full investigation of Walker, even those publishers friendly to Houck like William Hyde at the *Missouri Republican* took their shots. In the course of the Walker investigation the *St. Louis Post-Dispatch* called on Governor Marmaduke to "strike a telling blow in the interests of honesty, decency, reform and political purity" by "punishing the rascals who raised a fund" to bribe state officers on behalf of Cape Girardeau's prison initiative. And although this editor did not

27. *St. Louis Post-Dispatch*, June 13, 17, 29, 1885.
28. *Report of Committee on Charges Preferred Against Honorable John Walker*, 178; *Missouri Republican*, March 15, 1887; Doherty, Jr., *Houck, Missouri Historian and Entrepreneur*, 74–76.

mention anyone by name, Houck had already testified to that effect. Itself crusading for railroad regulation in that atmosphere of reform in 1887, the *Missouri Republican* editorialized that "the Mr. Louis Houck mentioned as a party to the above bargain was the same Mr. Louis Houck who had been actively interested against railroad regulation." Comparing the manner in which Houck went about obtaining the prison with his business practices in railroading, the newspaper concluded that his conduct in this particular scheme "gives a very fair idea of his methods."[29]

Without a doubt, all this stung Louis. Not as thick-skinned as one might imagine, he could be, in fact, quite sensitive to criticism and acutely attentive to perceived wrongs against him. But while he smarted over the negative editorials, he also learned a great deal from them. Although Houck carefully monitored the regulation movement in the state house, he would never share the reformers' sentiments, rebuking legislators in 1887 with his acerbic allegation that standardized railroad rates amounted to a flawed socialistic attempt to "make myself and the Iron Mountain one road."[30] Neither did he fancy attracting their ire; it made bad business sense. To counterbalance mounting unfavorable impressions of himself amongst reformers in Missouri, Louis became markedly more image-conscious, especially in regard to how he was portrayed by newspapers in the region and around the state. He redoubled efforts to spell out in newsprint the compatibility and mutual benefits between the public good of southeast Missouri and the private interests of Louis Houck. He also began distancing himself as much as possible from the tainted image of avarice surrounding railroad barons in favor of promoting his more folksy man-of-the-people qualities. By the 1890s this emphasis on the popular perception of rugged individualism, not entirely disingenuous by any means, reached its full expression as Louis cast himself as a regional David to Jay Gould's national Goliath during their illustrious receivership clash. Likewise, in time, Houck complemented this strategy in the regional press with a great many philanthropic endeavors, practicing in his own localized way what Andrew Carnegie later articulated as a "Gospel of Wealth."[31]

---

29. *St. Louis Post-Dispatch*, March 15, 1887; *Missouri Republican*, March 29, 1887; Robert Whitelaw to Louis Houck, January 17, 1887, Houck Papers, Box 1508, Correspondence, 1887 Jan-M-Z Feb A-F, Folder 3.

30. James Brooks to Louis Houck, December 6, 1887, Houck Papers, Box 1508, Correspondence, 1887 December A-H, Folder 21; *Missouri Republican*, June 2, 1887; John O'Day to Louis Houck, March 1, 1887, Houck Papers, Box 1508, Correspondence, 1887 March A-Z, Folder 5.

31. Doherty, Jr., "Opponent and Imitator of Jay Gould," 46–56; Trachtenberg, *The Incorporation of America*, 143, 231.

The emphasis on improved public perception notwithstanding, Louis's maneuvering within the furtive machinery of Missouri's Democratic Party continued unabated. Since arriving in southeast Missouri almost twenty years before, Louis had drawn on his life's political experience to carefully and systematically integrate himself within a network of regional lawmakers, lobbyists, and influential political friends where favors and reciprocity were the coin of the realm. His detailed knowledge of the political topography of Jefferson City—down to each new bill and committee meeting—persuasive character, and money steadily solidified his influence over the years with senators and representatives from the southeast such as Robert Whitelaw, Madison R. Smith, and Robert B. Oliver. During election season, candidates for statewide office also offered their assistance to Houck as a matter of course, seeking not only his endorsement but often free railroad passes, just as Governor Marmaduke's eventual successor David Rowland Francis would do within a year. And though the spanking Houck took in the press reinforced an inclination to conduct important political business behind closed doors, his valuable service to the Democratic Party and the importance attached to his opinion by those residing in the governor's mansion soon informally bestowed on him the very public title of "Colonel," one of several powerful "political colonels" around the state.[32]

Quite naturally, in the midst of the penitentiary affair, Louis's first substantive step toward living a gospel of wealth came via this route, apparently as a sort of political consolation prize from Governor Marmaduke. In January 1887, the same year Marmaduke died in office, the governor—under whose watch the entire prison hullabaloo played out—officially appointed Houck to the board of regents of the Southeast Missouri Normal School.[33] After the disappointments and setbacks at mid-decade, this was a welcome victory, a public service Louis would come to revel in over the next thirty-eight years as he led the humble little college—for thirty-six years he would serve as board president—during one of the most dynamic periods in the institution's history.

Another heartening and hopeful occasion in an otherwise gloomy couple of years—which had also included the death of his mother, Anna, in 1884—was the birth in February 1886 of the Houcks' last child, Rebecca,

32. John Franklin Eddy, "Former Pioneer Traces Early History of County in Writing His Memoirs," *Democrat-Argus* (Caruthersville, Mo.), June 21, 1946.
33. In 1887 the Normal School Board of Regents consisted of W. B. Wilson, Louis Houck, C. C. Rozier, Lewis W. Danforth, George T. Bartlett, J. R. McKinney, and W. E. Coleman the state superintendent of schools.

named for the heroine of Sir Walter Scott's *Ivanhoe*.[34] Yet while perhaps not completely rivaling his daughter's joyful arrival or the regent's appointment in terms of significance or satisfaction, Louis's encounter with Thomas Jefferson Moss would provide a much-needed spark to his railroad enterprise.

Louis never forgot that balmy Sunday afternoon back in September 1884, when, as he later mused, "who should come sailing out of the clouds but Mr. T. J. Moss?"[35] In truth, at the time, Moss was merely a relatively small-time railroad-tie contractor from Higbee, Missouri, who had paid an unannounced visit to Elmwood in the hopes of talking urgent timber business. Upon finding Louis still bedridden from a bilious attack contracted while superintending the construction work in Mingo a month earlier and in no position to talk to anyone, Moss simply would not take no for an answer and finally obliged Mary to let him meet with her convalescing husband in the sick room. Mary probably relented because the Houcks had heard of young T. J. Moss, as the twenty-six-year-old orphan from Tennessee was already fairly infamous in southeast Missouri for buying white and burr oak timber from local farmers at what was considered foolhardy and outlandish prices by regional standards. Before Moss's arrival in the region in the early 1880s, a time when large-scale lumbering was in its infancy and farmers found the virgin forest little more than a nuisance, many still attempted to clear land by "deadening" timber, typically cutting a ring around the trees one year, and then burning them off the next. But now locals "flocked" to Moss to sell their timber "for a song," often with Moss taking bills of sale on the timber and writing checks for it on the stumps of fallen trees. "Generally," Louis thought, "it was considered that a fool had come into the country, ready to spend money for timber, and that it was good policy to sell quick before he discovered the worthlessness of the stuff he was buying."[36]

But Moss was anything but a rube. Here was a man with vision seeking out a kindred spirit. Between 1870 and 1890, more than 110,000 miles of railroad track were laid nationally, and "with the rapidity of judgment and action that characterized all his business life," Moss prophetically detailed for Louis "the magnificent possibilities for his business" in southeast Missouri furnishing the requisite ties and bridge timbers. Confidently he made it clear that he fully expected to ship two thousand flatcar loads of

34. Ronald S. Reed, Jr., to Joel P. Rhodes, September 22, 2006, in possession of author.
35. Houck, "Story of the Railroad Work, Volume II," 158.
36. "Louis Houck Memoirs," 111.

railroad ties a year from several proposed sawmills around Puxico. For his part, Houck confessed to being "fairly overwhelmed" by these audacious figures and "full of doubt as to his ability to do what he proposed to do." Nevertheless, he listened as another discontented lumber man, not unlike William Brown, privately censured the Iron Mountain, detailing how that railroad sometimes promptly furnished the immense numbers of cars he needed, and sometimes not. At the conclusion, Moss eagerly expressed his desire to defect to the Cape Girardeau Southwestern if the price was right.

Whatever apprehensions Louis may have harbored about Moss that day, he was savvy enough to recognize talent when he saw it. Within a week of settling on a favorable shipping rate and almost immediately after Moss fired up his new Stoddard County mills, what Louis described as indeed "an enormous tie business" began operations on his road.[37]

If anything, Moss's bold early predictions erred on the side of modesty. While Louis had gotten sidetracked tending to pottery and prison matters, Moss had deftly exploited the region's principal resource, and by the time Houck took his place on the board of regents in 1887, more than 700,000 of T.J. Moss's ties had moved over the Houck roads. Within a decade Moss employed nearly three thousand men at his various mills and had become a millionaire credited with being one of the largest tie contractors in America. That the addition of this second invaluable customer "wonderfully benefited" the line in the profit and loss columns should be an obvious understatement, but equally significant are the other ways in which the presence of T. J. Moss impacted the Houck roads. The tremendous strain of these previously unimaginable loads mandated radical changes in terms of volume and speed. To accommodate Moss, Houck continuously sought to acquire more locomotives and rolling stock—first thirty, sixty, then one hundred additional cars—usually, over Moss's strenuous objections, from inexpensive secondhand sources. Similarly, Moss demanded faster turnaround times to get his freight trains to and from Puxico, which meant that in order to keep pace Houck often unintentionally neglected smaller shippers along the line—a number of whom were also tie makers that followed Moss's lead—due to a scarcity of cars and tighter schedules.[38]

The relationship between Houck and Moss, almost two decades his junior, also paralleled in many respects Louis's association with William

37. Ibid., 111–13.
38. T. J. Moss to Louis Houck, January 13, 1886, Houck Papers, Box 1508, Correspondence, January 1886–April 1888, Folder 1; T. J. Moss to R. H. Whitelaw, January 19, 1887, Houck Papers, Box 1508, Correspondence, January 1886–April 1888, Folder 2.

Brown. Easily Houck's two biggest customers, Brown and Moss were disgruntled Iron Mountain shippers who came to Houck looking for a better deal. Like Brown, Moss and Louis also over the years worked in an atmosphere of perpetual business tension, mainly over issues constantly arising from customer service, or the lack thereof. Matters of money, more specifically fairness and profitability, were omnipresent between the three men. This appeared particularly true after Brown and Moss, who both took a keen interest in the railroad industry, became financially vested in the Cape Girardeau Southwestern: Brown by investing his money and Moss by purchasing brand-new rolling stock himself and renting it to the short-handed line in exchange for divisional bonds.

Still, even when Moss and Louis disagreed—which occasionally happened, as when Houck's crews would pilfer ties for new construction projects—the two maintained a healthy business and candid personal respect for each other. They shared a rapport that allowed for ample sarcasm and good-natured teasing. Both seemed to appreciate the symbiotic nature of not only their business arrangements but also their bond in the larger context of regional development. When it came to booming the region, Houck and Moss saw themselves as benefactors; "however," as Thomas once reiterated of Louis's own sentiment, "I don't think either of us object very much to a 'small compensation for our labors.'"[39]

Ultimately, T. J. Moss's untimely death in 1893, also comparable to that of Brown's, would deal a serious blow to Houck personally and professionally. But in 1887 Moss was a catalyst, just as Brown had earlier been, refocusing Louis on railroad expansion with a sense of immediacy and urgency that distinguished their friendship. In doing so, Moss used Houck's own words to remind him that "it is important to move ahead in some way, when the Whole World about you is moving."[40]

Several intriguing options presented themselves for extending the railway toward new outlets in the West and the East without ever straying too far from the security of a major through line or the Mississippi River. In 1887 the western terminus of the Cape Girardeau Southwestern abutted the St. Francis River after crews completed the remaining one-mile addition from Wappapello in late 1885. On one hand Houck could now move south along the eastern bank of the St. Francis to a Dunklin County link with the St. Louis

39. T. J. Moss to Louis Houck, June 26, 1887, Houck Papers, Box 1508, Correspondence, 1887 June M-Z, Folder 12; *Cape Girardeau Democrat*, August 12, 1893.

40. T. J. Moss to Louis Houck, August 11, 1887, Houck Papers, Box 1508, Correspondence, 1887 August M-Z, Folder 16.

Southwestern. Known as the Cotton Belt, this railway formed a sideways Y-shaped pattern across the region by running southwest from the Mississippi at New Madrid below and roughly parallel to the base of the Iron Mountain triangle and also northeast to another river terminus at Bird's Point.[41] The practical reasoning behind this alternative centered on giving the oft-reorganized Cotton Belt, which until 1896 was not affiliated with the Gould interests, a competitive access to St. Louis via the Houck roads. Or Houck might bridge the river before heading south to bisect the Iron Mountain triangle completely with another crossing, this time at Poplar Bluff. Either connection with the Cotton Belt or the Iron Mountain, Louis trusted, would position the Cape Girardeau Southwestern to fully occupy the St. Francois Valley. On the other hand, he might go north into Wayne County by bridging the St. Francis and crossing the Iron Mountain again at Williamsville. For good measure, James Brooks completed reconnaissance surveys—done by eye without any instruments—for all these proposed routes.

Cape Girardeau remained the eastern terminus, yet its landlocked geographic location made maintenance of the status quo increasingly problematic. Louis understood that without access to eastern markets, the earnings potential of the Houck roads would be forever restricted to only what he could bring in regionally. Since the beginning the obvious connection to the East had been St. Louis by way of the St. Louis, Iron Mountain and Southern. But this left Houck beholden and ultimately dependent on a cantankerous rival that had not exactly been doing him any favors either in supplying substandard material or charging excessive "trackage" rates, or tolls, to run Cape Girardeau Southwestern trains up to St. Louis. Just to keep his head above water against the Iron Mountain's cheaper rates and unfettered rail service to Missouri's premier city, let alone maintain any competitiveness, Louis would have to gain a measure of control over his own eastern connections. For that reason, the Mississippi River would have to be factored into the equation, either using barge traffic to reach St. Louis or a transfer boat to ferry trains over to Illinois on their way to Chicago.[42]

In consultation with Brown and Moss, Houck followed a two-prong strategy: simultaneously building toward Williamsville, with the long-term intention of someday making it all the way across southern Missouri,

41. *Ninth Annual Report of the Railroad Commissioners for the State of Missouri Being for the Year Ending December 31st 1883,* Missouri State Archives microfiche. By 1888 the Cotton Belt also ran from Malden to Delta, where it connected with both Houck and the Iron Mountain.
42. Houck, "Reminiscences," 52.

while supporting Moss's organization of a barge line with an eye toward eventually operating a transfer boat. Thereafter, events began to take on a momentum of their own. All the earnings of the railroad, above the day-to-day operating budget, were put toward the new western construction in an attempt to "defray the cost." But since this alone would be inadequate, Houck cobbled together an effective finance package. He and Brown acquired a huge tract of Bollinger County land for $30,000 in railroad bonds, which they in turn sold to Moss "for cash and ties." One million dollars in bonds were also issued, which meant that after paying off the nearly $300,000 of the road's entire underlying bonded debt—most held by Brown and Mary—more than $500,000 was left to underwrite the extension. In commemoration, Louis had the bonds steel-engraved in New York with Giboney's picture, along with his nine-year-old son's favorite crossbow and "old battered straw hat," adorning each "just to satisfy a little family vanity."[43]

Following the St. Francis to Otter Creek and "westward along the valley of that creek in the most direct line," Houck's boys resumed laying iron. With picks, shovels, and animal-powered scrapers they graded hilly and timbered Ozark land considerably different from the swampy flat terrain to which they were accustomed. By the fall of 1887, the sounds of their sledgehammer pings rang out in the village of Chaonia, seven miles from where crews wrestled with bridging the St. Francis. In Cape Girardeau, Moss and Houck worked together to "handle the business by river." Initially, Moss contracted with William and Henry Leyhe's storied Eagle Packet Company to ship his ties by barge to St. Louis; Keokuk, Iowa; Peoria, Illinois; and other points north. Soon thereafter, to facilitate his own business as well as ship merchandise for other companies along the Houck roads, he incorporated the Cape Girardeau Transportation Company that by the 1890s boasted a fleet of twenty barges and three steamboats. One of these steamers, the *Louis Houck,* could carry upwards of 100,000 ties at a time and was considered to be one of the largest and most powerful vessels on the river. With thirty to forty carloads of ties rolling into Cape every day, it would not be uncommon in warmer months to see more than half a mile of Mississippi shoreline below St. Vincent's College entirely covered with ties awaiting shipment.[44]

43. "Louis Houck Memoirs," 121, 123, 124, 154–55.
44. T. J. Moss to Louis Houck, February 1887, Houck Papers, Box 1508, Correspondence, 1887 Jan-M-Z Feb A-F, Folder 3; T. J. Moss to Louis Houck, February 11, 1889, Houck Papers, Box 1509, Correspondence, Feb M-Z 1889, Folder 16; "Louis Houck Memoirs," 136–38.

Impatiently thinking several moves ahead, Houck and Brooks headed west again on horseback through what is today the Clark National Forest to resume their exploration of a possible route to Springfield.[45] During their adventures, Louis marveled at the timber and erroneously documented what he took to be vast iron deposits in the rock formations. Besides their "native" guide, one of the few living souls they happened upon in the pines among other assorted black bear, mountain lions, bobcats, and wild hogs was Timothy Canty, whom oddly enough Louis had once known as a boy back in Belleville. Another was John Barber White, an agent working on behalf of the Grandin family from Tideute, Pennsylvania, to oversee their immense timber holdings in Carter, Butler, and Shannon counties. From White, Houck heard the enticing news that the Grandins' Missouri Lumber and Mining Company was at that very moment building a huge sawmill in southern Carter County and that a Current River branch of the Kansas City, Fort Scott and Memphis railroad was already on its way to reach it. Back at the camp site, Louis performed some hasty calculations regarding potential freight tonnage and the serendipitous fulfillment of his dream of an east-west line running through southern Missouri. A slight change of course was in order. Instead of a now unnecessary west, slightly northwest run to Springfield, he announced to Brooks, they would point the road in a southwesterly direction after reaching Williamsville the next year, aiming toward the company town of Grandin and a connection with this Current River railroad.[46]

Leaving Brooks behind with a team of men to survey the new route, Houck caught up with his boys along Otter Creek somewhere east of Williamsville, to supervise the fabrication of the seven bridges crossing Otter Creek, an engineering necessity to maintain a sufficiently low-grade line. Into 1888, progress to Williamsville grew tougher and more expensive. Another sizable bridge had to span the Black River, leaving Louis with much trepidation and sleepless nights, especially after he received unnerving safety reports concerning the first bridge they had rebuilt over the Whitewater seven years before. Apparently it had become so dangerous that the section boss, fearing it would no longer support a locomotive's weight, instructed all engineers to push, not pull, the cars across the bridge

45. James Brooks to Louis Houck, May 31, 1888, Houck Papers, Box 1509, Correspondence, May 1888, Folder 1.
46. "Louis Houck Memoirs," 115, 121, 122, 173, 174; James Brooks to Louis Houck, December 8, 1889, Houck Papers, Box 1510, Correspondence, December A-G, Folder 5. The Current River Railroad connected with the Kansas City, Fort Scott, and Memphis at Willow Springs, Missouri, in central Howell County.

where another locomotive on the other side would hook them up and take them on from there.

In conjunction with this new bridge, there was also a thousand-foot-long trestle over the Black River bottom under way. Yet the granddaddy of all Houck's worries was the eight-hundred-foot tunnel being blasted to assure a satisfactory grade from Otter Creek across the Black River valley. Like a proud papa, Louis camped along the creek near the tunnel, his first, for most of 1888, lovingly attending to every detail of its creation. And while he knew in his heart and mind that it should be lined with brick to avoid slides, he could not see his way clear to spending that extra money and instead timbered the walls from one end to the other. The first locomotive rolled through Houck's masterpiece in November, inaugurating a concise twelve-year run that ended with the tunnel's eventual collapse and condemnation.[47]

Then out of the blue, in November William Brown died suddenly while riding a Cape Girardeau Southwestern train, leaving Louis grieving over "a great loss just at a time when I needed not only his financial aid, but more than ever his wise counsel and advice." In offering his condolences over the unexpected death of "our very best friend," T. J. Moss conceded that "his demise is no doubt a severe blow to your property temporarily at least." Nevertheless, Moss concluded, there was no time to feel sorry for themselves. The railroad needed at least a seventh locomotive, maybe more, to pull the endless string of trains from Puxico to Cape Girardeau, and even though roundtrip rail service on the Cape Girardeau Southwestern had been whittled to just eight hours, Moss's business suffered because the Houck roads simply could not keep up with the huge volume of ties pouring out of the mill. Then, of course, with work substantially completed to Williamsville, the next challenge of linking up with the Current River Branch of the Kansas City, Fort Scott and Memphis was staring them in the face. Still, Moss refused to worry, confident that "of course you have energy and vim to overcome almost any obstacle."[48]

Fortunately, for the time being, Daniel S. Brown, William's oldest son who assumed control of the Pioneer Keg Works, and the other heirs of the estate came through for Houck, carrying out their father's contractual

47. James Brooks to Louis Houck, June 19, 1888, Houck Papers, Box 1509, Correspondence, June 1888 A-M, Folder 3; M. S. Carter to Louis Houck, January 7, 1889, Houck Papers, Box 1509, Correspondence, Jan A-R 1889, Folder 13.
48. T. J. Moss to Louis Houck, November 7, 1888, Houck Papers, Box 1509, Correspondence, Oct-Nov 1888 A-Z, Folder 10; Missouri Pacific to Louis Houck, July 17, 1888, Houck Papers, Box 1509, Correspondence, July 1888, Folder 5.

agreements "to the letter" and advancing "much additional money" for the expected rendezvous with the Current River line some twenty miles away in Carter County.[49] After laying the crossing over the Iron Mountain at Williamsville in January 1889, crews graded west, putting up a long trestle over the Black River bottom in a matter of weeks. Men, animals, and machinery gradually inclined the roadbed for miles at a time through what by southeast Missouri standards are mountains. Up and down the grade, Louis paced with his walking stick, praising the swiftness and symmetry of the axe men hauling in logs to waiting crews who fashioned them into a series of trestles, and how neither crew interfered with track laying. "Every rail almost on this line of track was laid down under my supervision," Louis boasted of their three-mile-a-day pace, "bolted and spiked, and lay in a perfect line." At their depot in Upalika a flatcar loaded with ties got loose and raced down the steady grade toward the Black River at no less than a forty-mile-an-hour clip, but although ties scattered everywhere, the runaway car never jumped the track as it was laid with such precision. Surely, Louis thought, it was the best work they had ever done.

Still following the ridge flanked on one side by Brushy Creek and on the other side by Cane Creek, Brooks laid out the town of Elsinore, and by October 1889, construction crossed the state road heading south to Little Rock, Arkansas. Finally, in late November 1889 at a point nearly ten miles southwest of Elsinore on the rolling hills over the crystal-clear Current River, the Cape Girardeau Southwestern reached the newly completed Current River railroad at a junction the Kansas City, Fort Scott and Memphis platted as Hunter, for one of the principal Pennsylvania investors of the Missouri Lumber and Mining Company.

Though a lingering desire to penetrate into Arkansas infatuated Louis for many years, Hunter marked the last extension of the first Houck road, now totaling 103 miles. Relatively speaking, conquering this little chunk of the Ozark Hills had been physically easier than slogging through the swamps, but still very costly. Houck discovered too that predictions on the profitability of this last twenty-mile "Current River division" had been overly optimistic, and this discontinuity between expectations and reality drove home another harsh railroading lesson. Geographically, railroads could be built to go virtually anywhere, therefore the salient questions in deciding where to locate them had to be honestly answered by straight-

49. The heirs consisted of Daniel S. Brown, Martha L. Brown, Lydia U. Brown, and William C. Brown. Jensen, "Life on the Edge of the Great Cypress Swamp," 32; "Louis Houck Memoirs," 130.

forward economics. Successful roads were those built through areas where there already was, or could reasonably expect to be, sufficient demand for transportation to not only cover initial construction costs but also sustain support for the line. Sometimes faith and luck were not enough, and, as Houck belatedly came to realize, the road from Williamsville to Hunter had been a financial mistake because quite frankly "the country was not worth a railroad."[50]

Exacerbating matters, despite the Cape Girardeau Transportation Company's river traffic, Houck's railroad still labored under its dependency on the Iron Mountain for links to bigger markets. For all of his boasting and advertising of the Cape Girardeau Southwestern as a "through line" to St. Louis by way of Moss's barges, that assertion was simply not truthful; it was another disingenuous and amusing promotional instance of Houck being Houck. In reality, Louis acknowledged that "I soon learned to understand that the small rate of my railroad, added to the Iron Mountain rate or through rate, shut out the business men of my road." As long as shippers had to transfer from the Houck roads to the Iron Mountain to reach St. Louis, Houck would be "at the mercy of the big concern" and always handicapped as far as profits.

"As it was, however, I got along as best I could," Louis noted with disappointment of the Iron Mountain's "Might makes Right" position, "and gradually developed a purely local business from the river west in connection with the boats." Nevertheless, he confided, "financial matters began greatly to worry me."[51] The fiscal pinch of operating the road, so disconcerting and seemingly endless, dictated that Louis ratchet up his hunt for new investors wherever they may be: Cape Girardeau, St. Louis, Chicago, New York, or London.[52] Since as early as 1885, Louis had been corresponding and periodically visiting with several banking and brokerage firms in New York to secure additional capital. Just as it was transforming modern corporate structure, so too was railroading changing the face of American finance, the industry's unquenchable appetite for unprecedented amounts of capital fueling the rise of modern investment banking and the stock market. Some of the agents Houck dealt with in New York were legitimate, but increasingly by 1889 the risky nature of

50. Armstrong, *The Railroad*, 7; "Louis Houck Memoirs," 174.

51. "Louis Houck Memoirs," 126, 135–36; Missouri Pacific to Louis Houck, July 19, 1888, Houck Papers, Box 1509, Correspondence, July 1888 A-M, Folder 5.

52. W. J. Alt to Louis Houck, June 5, 1888, Houck Papers, Box 1509, Correspondence, June 1888 A-M, Folder 3; Louis Houck to Arthur W. Soper, November 28, 1889, Houck Papers, Box 1510, Correspondence, November A-C, Folder 3.

bankrolling railroad ventures had spooked off many bona fide business-men, only to have them replaced with speculators and outright crooks.[53] In swimming with these sharks, Louis encountered a colorful collection of New York's most conspicuous financial characters, ranging all the way up to J. P. Morgan himself.

In 1887 Houck hired the New York brokerage firm of Coffin and Stanton as financial agents of the Cape Girardeau Southwestern and entrusted them with handling the sale of the railway's recently issued consolidation bonds. At the time, it did not seem to overly bother him that up until then William Edward Coffin and Walter Stanton mainly marketed municipal and water work securities, but had recently become very desirous of expanding into the field of corporate railroads as well. Yet even with Coffin and Stanton advancing money from time to time, Houck still found himself in an uphill battle because his New York brokers repeatedly lagged behind in selling enough bonds in the East to pay for the completion of the Cape Girardeau Southwestern. At the same time, with construction of the "Current River division" hemorrhaging money, Louis barely scraped together just enough to cover the semiannual interest on the bonds Coffin and Stanton did manage to sell.[54]

With a national depression on the horizon, the economic situation reached critical mass in the fall of 1889, leaving Louis to fall back on an old standby, Robert Sturdivant. And although it made Moss, Brown, and him equally uneasy, they borrowed significant sums of cash from the Cape banker. "For all this money so advanced by Col. Sturdivant," Louis conceded, "I made the notes of the company, endorsed by me personally, and some of them were also endorsed by Mr. Brown."[55] For another day at least they kept the wolf from the door, but in doing so they plunged deeper into the dangerous spiral of debt.

53. Porter, "Industrialization," 9–10; Trachtenberg, *The Incorporation of America*, 58; telegram to Louis Houck, May 21, 1888, Houck Papers, Box 1509, Correspondence, May 1888, Folder 1.

54. A. E. Godeffroy to Louis Houck, June 5, 13, 1888, Houck Papers, Box 1509, Correspondence, June 1888 A-M, Folder 3; Walter Stanton to Louis Houck, March 19, 1889, Houck Papers, Box 1509, Correspondence, March A-G 1889, Folder 17; "Louis Houck Memoirs," 189–90.

55. "Louis Houck Memoirs," 155, 189, 190; T. J. Moss to Louis Houck, June 13, 1889, Houck Papers, Box 1509, Correspondence, June K-Z, Folder 24; Walter Stanton to Louis Houck, March 19, 1889, Houck Papers, Box 1509, Correspondence, March A-G 1889, Folder 17.

"So late in December, 1889," Houck recalled, "I went to New York to confer with Coffin and Stanton to arrange to stave off financial disaster and also to ascertain whether or not I could not dispose of the road and thus get out of the railroad business without loss." This particular trip proved short and fruitless, and after finding no satisfaction in the East, on New Year's Day 1890 the soon to be fifty-year-old Houck wearily boarded a west-bound train for Cape Girardeau. Unquestionably, over the past ten years the legal, monetary, and logistical trials and tribulations and the ceaseless anxiety of railroading had, in his words, "disturbed my mind." And it was upon his return from New York at the close of the decade—separated again from his family, which was gathering at that very moment in Belleville for Christmas—that those distressing doubts of overreaching himself were revisited. Staring out the window of a passenger coach, he reflected on his depressing circumstances, noting that "along the shore of Lake Erie it began to rain and rained all the way home, the rainstorm beating heavily against the car windows; but I did not dream then that this same rain extended from the lakes down to Southeast Missouri and was swamping my newly built railroad."[56]

56. "Louis Houck Memoirs," 191; P. B. Walker to Louis Houck, December 30, 1889, Houck Papers, Box 1510, Correspondence, December H-Z, Folder 6.

The unremarkable fifteen miles of track Louis Houck laid between Cape Girardeau and Delta in late 1880 launched a rather remarkable career in railroading. Courtesy of the Southeast Missouri State University Special Collections.

Louis Napoleon Houck, circa 1910. Courtesy of
C. A. and Jeanette Juden, Cape Girardeau, Missouri.

Mary Hunter Giboney Houck. Used by permission, State Historical Society of Missouri

Irma Houck. Courtesy
of Ronald S. Reed, Jr.

Giboney Houck. Courtesy
of Ronald S. Reed, Jr.

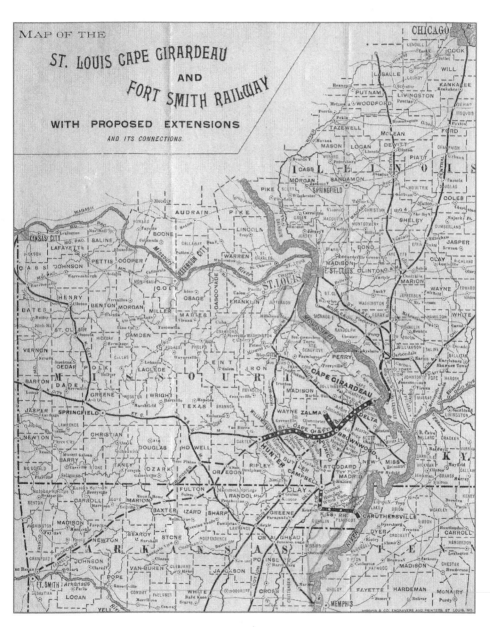

The St. Louis, Cape Girardeau, and Fort Smith: the first "Houck road."
Courtesy of the Southeast Missouri State University Special Collections.

Along the St. Louis, Cape Girardeau, and Fort Smith near Blomeyer, circa 1880s. Courtesy of C. A. and Jeanette Juden, Cape Girardeau, Missouri.

Early lumber operations near Delta, circa 1880s. Courtesy of C. A. and Jeanette Juden, Cape Girardeau, Missouri.

Houck depot in Advance, circa 1880s. Courtesy of C. A. and Jeanette Juden, Cape Girardeau, Missouri.

Brownwood, circa 1880s. Courtesy of C. A.
and Jeanette Juden, Cape Girardeau, Missouri.

Trestle work across the Mingo Bottom, circa 1880s. Courtesy
of C. A. and Jeanette Juden, Cape Girardeau, Missouri.

Part of the original fifteen-mile section of the Cape Girardeau Railway approaching St. Vincent's College in Cape Girardeau, circa 1880s. Courtesy of C. A. and Jeanette Juden, Cape Girardeau, Missouri.

African American laborers on an unidentified stretch of
Houck road. Courtesy of the Cape River Heritage Museum.

In both Wayne and Pemiscot counties, Houck unsuccessfully tried to
couple railroad work with drainage in order to sidestep Missouri law
that forbade county aid to railroad development. Courtesy of the
Southeast Missouri State University Special Collections.

Derailments were frequent on the Houck roads, leading the Missouri Railroad Commissioners to the conclusion "that lives are not lost or persons injured thereby, is due more to luck than management." Courtesy of the Southeast Missourian.

Academic Hall under construction on the campus of Southeast
Missouri Normal School. Courtesy of the Southeast Missouri
State University Special Collections.

Missouri's foremost historian. Courtesy of C. A.
and Jeanette Juden, Cape Girardeau, Missouri.

"Southeast Missouri stands as a monument to the vision of Louis Houck—a dream realized," lauded a Federal Writer's Project historian. Considering him "The Father of Southeast Missouri," the biographer concluded that to Houck, "more than any one man, the alluvial valley of Southeast Missouri owes an unpaid debt of gratitude for the place it holds in the civilized world today." Courtesy of C. A. and Jeanette Juden, Cape Girardeau, Missouri.

CHAPTER 6

Zwei Meinungen
Of Two Minds

Before I got to the Bayou, I sat down on a log, and overcome by fatigue, as well as the thought of the work I had undertaken to build through this swamp, involuntarily the tears came to my eyes. But this weakness passed off.

—Louis Houck

Louis Houck's expressed intention to walk away from the Cape Girardeau Southwestern in New York was not simply an impulsive epiphany born of frustration in the gray months of early 1890. Indeed, the potential sale of his small feeder line to a larger system through consolidation had been on his mind more or less since the beginning. But for four years, roughly 1887 to 1891, an unmistakable ambivalence concerning railroading bedeviled him. When his business and the national economic forecasts were sound, as had been the case in 1887 when the first line enjoyed its highest gross earnings, Louis burned to expand into Arkansas, Illinois, and Tennessee, chasing independent access to the national rail networks. Another clear case in point was 1891, likewise a profitable year, when he assumed control of the second of the Houck roads, the St. Louis, Kennett and Southern, heading south into the Missouri Bootheel toward Memphis. In fact, that same year he accelerated an unsuccessful promotion of the Grand Tower and Cape Girardeau Railroad Company to transfer trains into southern Illinois en route to Chicago. Yet, by contrast, when commercial prospects soured, as they had in 1890, he felt—not always incorrectly—as though he were beset on all sides by natural and human forces aligning and conspiring against him.[1] During these dark times he carried

1. Jno. A Talty to Louis Houck, June 23, 1891, Houck Papers, Box 1511, Correspondence, 1891 June K-Z, Folder 9.

on a troubled and agonizing courtship with the notion of selling out at almost any price. One of the most fascinating features of this wavering between expansion and liquidation is how intimately the two impulses coexisted together; there was virtually never one without the other. Even in the darkest days of 1890, when he would lose a night of sleep over making his payroll payments, breakfast conversation the next day invariably included casual musings about laying more track.

Houck's first personal encounter with Jay Gould in October 1887 offers a fairly pronounced starting point to this four-year pattern of vacillation. By the mid-1880s, Gould's relentless appetite for railroad expansion and genius for ruthless stock speculation had placed him in control of four western railroads, including the mighty Missouri Pacific and its affiliated St. Louis, Iron Mountain and Southern. By preying on his weaker competition, either driving them out or buying them out—the latter usually accomplished through hostile takeovers on the stock market—Gould represented, in terms of sheer track mileage, the controlling interest for more than ten thousand miles, or, more impressively, 15 percent, of the nation's railways. Together with his Western Union telegraph monopoly, Gould's rail empire spread out like a great treacherous spider web, earning the tycoon a reputation as the most unethical and unscrupulous of all the Gilded Age "robber barons."[2]

It appears that the Missouri Pacific's strategy toward the Cape Girardeau Southwestern encompassed both of these techniques Gould helped pioneer. While sinking their hooks deeper into Houck through the attrition of bonded indebtedness, Gould initially tendered a friendly offer to buy the Houck roads in October 1887. The first overture came through Missouri Pacific Superintendent William Kerrigan, who in a presumably "disinterested" manner quietly suggested to Louis that as a friend he thought it safer in the long run for Houck to quit while he was ahead and get out of the railroad business while his lines were still solvent. Without specifically mentioning his employer by name as a potential buyer, Kerrigan made another personal gesture by promising Louis that the next time Jay Gould came west to inspect his properties, he would arrange a purely social meeting between the two.[3]

---

2. The dismissive stereotype of Jay Gould as simply a ruthless robber baron and railroad wrecker, advanced by the contemporary press and thereafter perpetuated in the popular imagination, has been credibly challenged by revisionist scholars Julius Grodinsky, *Jay Gould: His Business Career, 1867–1892*, and Maury Klein, *The Life and Legend of Jay Gould*, who offer a more nuanced and complex appraisal.

3. "Louis Houck Memoirs," 116.

True to his word, Kerrigan soon dispatched a spur-of-the-moment Western Union telegram inviting Houck to meet with a junket of Missouri Pacific dignitaries, including the big man himself, at the depot in Delta for a ride on the Iron Mountain to Belmont. Despite the short notice, Louis eagerly agreed, joining Kerrigan, Amos Lawrence Hopkins, S. H. H. Clark, Gould, and others on the short trip, probably in Gould's new Pullman car the *Bedford Penola*. Immediately upon being introduced, Louis tried to take the measure of Gould, judging him to be "over fifty years of age and in personal appearance decidedly Jewish." This was actually a common misperception given the surname, but it was nonetheless one of many Gould stereotypes that may have been reinforced in Houck's mind when Gould abruptly began their conversation by asking how much Louis wanted for his railroad. Momentarily caught off guard by the bluntness of his host, Houck stalled, bending the truth a bit in replying that he had never "considered the subject in detail." When Gould further surprised Louis with an impressive grasp of the details surrounding the Houck roads, Louis countered with the observation that since William Brown owned a sizable interest in the line, no serious discussion involving its sale could take place without him. "After this answer," Louis remembered, "he seemed to lose interest in the subject, and after a few remarks about other matters," perhaps their mutual interests as amateur historians, Gould turned his attention elsewhere.[4]

For more than an hour, Hopkins, a close associate of Gould's and a veteran railroad man, and Kerrigan took Louis aside, admonishing him to seize the day before Gould changed his mind. When again in Gould's company, the railroad mogul placed a specific figure on the table: $100,000 in cash and $500,000 in Iron Mountain consolidated bonds for Houck's roughly fifty miles of track. Louis hesitated. Figures from recent Cape Girardeau Southwestern company ledgers were undoubtedly responsible for his indecisiveness. Passenger earnings were projected to be nearly triple what they had been in 1881, with freight revenue increasing a whopping twenty-five fold. Net earnings for 1887 would near $54,000, and with Moss's business, Louis foresaw nearly unlimited potential for future enterprise. Accordingly confident, and justifiably so, Louis stalled instead of promptly accepting the offer and thereby realizing more than $200,000. As he later regretted, "I asked for time, and so lost my opportunity."[5]

4. Ibid., 116–17.

5. Ibid., 118–19; *Poor's Manual of Railroads 1888*, 749; Doherty, Jr., "Missouri Interests of Louis Houck," 77.

As they sat down to dine, Gould tellingly declared "that a man might as well be killed for stealing a sheep as a lamb," a remark not lost on Louis, who believed at the time that it "furnished a pretty good insight into his character." "We had waffles for supper and Mr. Gould took more than his doctors advised," Houck remembered, "and that was the consolation he gave himself. In his business transactions he seems to have followed this maxim."[6] In a more superficial way, Houck appears to have understood Gould to mean that in regard to his overeating that night, if he was going to die someday anyway, he might as well eat his fill. More ominously, perhaps Louis also detected in this analogy a harbinger of things to come— that if a man is going to be guilty of a crime, better for it to be a big one than a small one. Having tried to buy Houck out, Gould now seemed content to resume patiently harassing him out of business.

Three years later, in May 1890, when Louis next met the Goulds—this time including George, Jay's oldest son, who would eventually replace his ailing father—much had changed in regard to his financial circumstances and outlook, and thus his attitudes toward selling out.

Throughout 1890, Houck stayed constantly on the move, never lingering in one place, including Elmwood, for more than a day or two. He was a Teutonic blur of motion up and down his roads, supervising the extensive rebuilding of embankments at Mingo—at times under thirty-one inches of water—tending to a morass of sundry wrecks, derailments, employee drunkenness, and creditors, all the while meeting with a parade of prospective financiers from the Missouri River to the Atlantic Ocean.

By March of that year Houck was back in New York for another go-around with Coffin and Stanton. The awesome Brooklyn Bridge over the East River and magnificent Manhattan skyline of steel and stone towered above the small Missourian in testament to the nation's technological revolution and rapid urbanization. So too did the veritable sea of immigrants whose babbling tongues and rich cultural traditions gave parts of Manhattan the vibrancy of a great swirling ethnic kaleidoscope. Yet it was instead the rain and snow that cast the dreary, cheerless backdrop to a series of uneasy negotiations between a railroader and investment bankers involving cold statistics of mounting floating debts and diminishing earnings potential. More than once, Louis made it known that as a way of getting out from under the debt—$1.2 million by this time—he would be willing to entertain the prospect of selling out to them for $675,000:

---

6. "Louis Houck Memoirs," 119.

$300,000 for the stock, $200,000 for his controlling interest, and around $100,000 to buy out Daniel Brown's share of the bonds.[7]

Even if investors took to the idea in principle, time and again Houck nevertheless met with long, humiliating waits, maddening stalling, and uncomfortably cool receptions. Most would-be buyers eventually balked at the $300,000 asking price for the bonds or were frightened off by uncertain monetary conditions in the former Confederacy, of which southeast Missouri was still considered part. Since much of his time was spent waiting or riding the rails, to pass the hours and sort out his thoughts during this trying period, he diligently kept the only known journal in his life. Of the wear and tear of this odyssey, and of working on his fiftieth birthday, he poignantly noted, "Ought to be at home but cannot be there." "It seems to me as if I am not as sanguine as buoyant and combative as I was. Getting old, I suppose." And while business consumed his days, Louis took what solace he could from the arts, attending the New York theater often and losing himself in literature whenever possible. On the trains he devoured *The Confessions of Jean-Jacques Rousseau*—"It would have been a pity to have gone through life and not read this book"—and the debates of the Virginia Convention on the adoption of the Constitution. "Wonderfully interesting," he concluded. "Forget railroads when read about great men."[8]

After another particularly heated morning exchange with Coffin and Stanton in late spring of 1890, Louis left their office extremely inflamed, only to have an agent of the firm attempt to ply him with alcohol. On this rare occasion, Houck let down his guard enough to share a little drink of whiskey—the strongest he had ever tasted—at a Broadway saloon, but soon suspected the man's generous offer for additional rounds was only a scheme to extract tactical information from a drunken railroader.

"When will the tide turn?" Louis caught himself asking after this latest frustration. "I still stand up and do not feel cast down, but it is pretty hard." It was at this time in May 1890 that Houck, on the advice of his friend Solon Humphreys, went back to see the Goulds. Louis probably met Solon Humphreys at some point in St. Louis, where this associate of Gould and J. P. Morgan had at various times finagled legal control of the Eads Bridge and the Wabash, St. Louis and Pacific Railway Company. By 1890 the savvy businessman, whom Houck greatly admired, was Louis's first

7. T. J. Moss to Louis Houck, March 7, 1890, E. F. Blomeyer to Louis Houck, March 12, 1890, James Brooks to Louis Houck, March 30, 1890, Houck Papers, Box 1510, Correspondence, 1890 March G-Z, Folder 11; "Louis Houck Memoirs," 192, 194, 195, 198.
    8. "Louis Houck Memoirs," 203, 207, 209.

unofficial New York adviser and only real East Coast confidant. When in New York, Houck enjoyed dropping in on Humphreys at his Broad Street office to regale the delighted easterner with colorful tales of how railroads were built southeast Missouri–style. And so it was that Houck listened when Humphreys suggested that since word on the street had the Missouri Pacific intent on building a line into Cape Girardeau, the time might be ripe to approach the Goulds, not with an offer to sell at first, but with a proposal for some type of more favorable joint track arrangements between their respective lines.

The meeting at the Gould offices in the Western Union building got off to a bad start. Houck had never met George, and when the younger Gould opened by curtly informing Louis that the Missouri Pacific's proposed new line into Cape "ended the matter" between them, Houck recalled, "I took this coolly, very." Still, George kept the door open just a bit by continuing to quiz Louis about the Cape Girardeau Southwestern and in fact invited him back the next day so that his father might sit in on their chat as well. Jay Gould remembered Houck, which made for a more pleasant atmosphere, and their conversation soon took on the feel of a negotiation, played out almost in an elaborate, not quite spontaneous, fencing match. Without being specific, Louis thrust first by generally expressing the unsolicited opinion that he fully expected to get a couple hundred thousand dollars for the road. Jay parried with the more precise observation that with $1.2 million in debt, that figure represented the entire value of the company. Louis quickly countered—having been coached by Humphreys—by asserting that the sheer market value of the iron in the railroad had to be considered in its overall worth. Even so, the Goulds argued, the Missouri Pacific had recently acquired a short line off the Belmont Branch of their Iron Mountain to Jackson, Missouri, a road that nearly paralleled Houck's Delta division. Why, Jay rhetorically inquired in a bit of trademark trickery well known in railroad circles, would they want to buy a line brokers estimated to be worth no more than $6,000 or $7,000 a mile, when their own Missouri Pacific could complete the remaining nine miles into Cape Girardeau for $9,000 a mile and by those much cheaper means effectively achieve the same ends? Buying the Houck roads would be akin to buying water. Nevertheless, knowing good and well the multitude of predicaments the Houck roads faced and more significantly of Louis's recent New York visits—it was almost as if he had come hat-in-hand to put the troubled railway up for sale—Jay concluded with a request for another meeting the following day as well and for the submission of a written proposal from Houck.

Undoubtedly for effect, this meeting was postponed twice, for a total of almost six days, before Louis—by now nervous, unable to sleep, and suffering from headaches—finally received word that no sale would be forthcoming. Composed and nonplussed, outwardly at least, Louis—without hesitating—changed tactics to ascertain the true nature of the Goulds' bargaining position. Bluffing a bit himself, again almost certainly under Humphreys' tutelage, Houck reminded the Goulds of how he had not come to peddle the road, but merely to discuss harmonizing their lines with mutually advantageous trackage rights. Accordingly, he put forward a new deal whereby the Missouri Pacific would pay the Cape Girardeau Southwestern a small trackage fee for the right to enter Cape Girardeau via the Delta division. To this Jay Gould conceded that perhaps instead of building into Cape themselves, Houck's plan might be acceptable, and he nonchalantly instructed Louis to take up the matter with local Missouri Pacific management in St. Louis on his way home. Shrewdly, and with an air of detachment, Houck jumped at the small opening, replying how utterly self-defeating it would be to waste his time in St. Louis if Jay and George truly intended the Missouri Pacific to enter Cape Girardeau anyway. When Jay gave his assurance that he personally endorsed the trackage deal—thereby belying the Goulds' extension scheme altogether—the advantage, for the moment, apparently had gone to Houck.

Without delay Louis rushed this news of Gould tipping his hand to Humphreys. "They want your road," Humphreys confirmed, seeing reason for optimism. "You go home. All this is merely done to depreciate your property. You don't have to sell. You rest easy."[9]

Alas, Humphreys' prognostication, while comforting to hear in an ephemeral sort of way, was actually a long time in coming to fruition. In the absence of any immediate relief, Louis returned to Cape Girardeau only to pick up the burdens of railroading in southeast Missouri right where he had left them, and for the remainder of 1890 he swam mightily upstream against wave after wave of hardship. The absence of ballast in the construction of the lines finally caught up to them. Initially cutting this fairly important corner saved money, but over the next decade ties lying on the exposed ground had rotted, causing an epidemic of derailments by 1890. Similarly, bad joints between rails, resulting from improper bolting and lack of careful maintenance, meant rough track, which in turn meant further wear and tear on the rails and unnecessary stress on locomotives

9. Ibid., 211–15, 251.

and rolling stock—all of which equated to escalating expenses. There was also a real art in running a locomotive for eighty miles a day without sending it disabled to the maintenance shop for a broken axle, ruptured valves, burst cylinders, or complete seizure from being run without enough water; some of Houck's engineers could do it, but others could not.

Workmen were killed—a line repairer and brakemen—depots and rolling stock burned, an expensive pile driver plunged into a canal, and water tanks sprang leaks. All this misfortune spelled slow service, late trains, and diminished earnings. Public opinion and the state Railroad and Warehouse Commissioners demanded costly physical improvements— permanent trestles and bridge approaches, surfaced rails, the correct number and proportion of ties, and safer speeds—at the same time creditors lined up for their money as well. "This trouble about paying every month, this being short all the time, makes me feel that I want to lay down and quit, no matter what happens," Houck fretted. "Always in hot water. Always imposing on your friends is pretty hard on a fellow." After one train derailed from hitting a cow, Louis, almost with bemused melancholy, scribbled in his journal, "Another instance of our bad luck in 1890. We are undoubtedly hoodoed, as the darkies would say. Such continued ill luck as we have had this year stands alone . . ." Pondering matters further, Louis internalized the misfortune: "I guess I am ready to quit and give it up. I am not fit to run a railroad. It's terrible . . ."[10]

The lone bright spot, far outshining the daydreams of a potential buyer's salvation, was a "romantic trip up the mountains" of Colorado in the early summer with Mary and the children. Louis missed them all terribly, and was always diligent in returning from his travels with gifts of candy for the girls and books for Giboney. The Colorado holiday seems to have been an occasion for the Houcks to reward, as a family, Irma's commencement from Christian College in Columbia. Just fourteen, diminutive—a Houck family trait—and bright, Irma was a strong personality like her parents and by all accounts provided a great deal of the sparkle in the family. Before matriculating to Christian College, she had attended Almira College in Greenville, Illinois, a small Christian liberal arts school for women whose president was none other than Houck's old boyhood pal James Park Slade. By Mary's estimation a good student with a reputation as a brilliant conversationalist and a tendency to spout off in Latin or

10. E. F. Blomeyer to Louis Houck, August 23, 1890, W. H. Brown to Louis Houck, August 25, 1890, Houck Papers, Box 1510, Correspondence, 1890 August A–G, Folder 18; "Louis Houck Memoirs," 222.

Greek, Irma most assuredly gave her father a deep satisfaction and pride in how she favored him.[11]

Beautiful weather, spectacular mountain vistas, and Fourth of July fireworks pleased Giboney, now twelve, and baby "Rea," just four, to no end—but "not so much Irma"—and in a small way helped to momentarily mend Louis's body and spirit. As bouts of "Neuralgia"—fierce headaches—and stomach pain more frequently overtook him, his overall health had noticeably declined at the very time several friends and family members—including Mary's aunt Susan Giboney and his youngest brother, John—passed away. Louis was apparently taking arsenic—a popular nineteenth-century curative known as a "therapeutic mule"—for this condition, which they regretfully forgot to pack. "I made a mistake in not bringing the arsenic along," Mary confided to cousins back in New Madrid, and without the influence of medication "he looks very thin in the face and weak." Still, after arriving in Colorado "completely exhausted," in time the peaceful mountains and Mary's orders for several days of bed rest left Louis looking "much improved."[12]

Nonetheless, the welcome respite proved short-lived, and with telegrams arriving daily reporting the latest calamity along the railroad, Louis cut short his stay, leaving the family to enjoy the rest of the summer without him. Mary and Rebecca accompanied him to the depot to say good-bye. "Rea almost cried," he noted, "and I came very near it."[13]

The year 1890 eventually, and mercifully, drew to a close, marked only by more bad news and pessimism. In preparing for their annual Christmas holiday fete in Elmwood's recently added ballroom, Louis bade a fitting adieu to the year that was—a year, he remarked to friends, that would have killed any other man. "Santa Claus is costing me some money, as usual," he managed to joke, but "It seems to me that the end of the year is always hard on me of late . . . Gives me the blues. This railroad is getting to be a big burden. Am going in deeper and deeper. Can't tell where I will land . . . I lost my time to make money when Mr. Gould offered me $100,000 and $500,000 I.M. bonds. Well, the best thing to do is to hold on, keep a clear head, not worry, and do the best possible to be done. It is worth all

11. Mary Hunter Giboney Houck to "Dearie," April 20, 1890, Houck Papers, Box 1510, Correspondence, 1890 April A-Z, Folder 12; Ronald S. Reed, Jr., to Joel P. Rhodes, September 22, 2006, in possession of author.

12. Mary Hunter Giboney Houck to "Dearie," April 20, 1890, Houck Papers, Box 1510, Correspondence, 1890 April A-Z, Folder 12.

13. Houck, "Story of the Railroad Work, Volume I," 213, 215.

the money in it, and more, and somebody will make a big thing out of it."
"I hope that 1891 will be more promising than this year."[14]

Indeed it was. Having weathered the storm, business along the Cape
Girardeau Southwestern modestly improved in the new calendar year, setting a promising pace for more than $80,000 in net returns that would
make 1891 the high-water mark for the first Houck road in this regard.[15]
With revenues on the increase, Louis felt sufficiently emboldened to carry
out the business of expansion with a new spring in his step. Selling out
increasingly slipped in relevance. While entertaining thoughts of further
extending the Cape Girardeau Southwestern to Mammoth Springs,
Arkansas—a notion that actually necessitated changing the name to the
new St. Louis, Cape Girardeau and Fort Smith Railroad—Louis caught
wind of a largely "unfinished and deplorable" little stretch of track for sale
in the Missouri Bootheel.

This line, the St. Louis, Kennett and Southern, all twenty miles of it in
Dunklin County, stretched south from a connection with the Cotton Belt
in Campbell to Kennett, and had recently become operational, if only in
the strictest sense of the word. On the positive side, the railroad's first-
time promoters—Eugene S. McCarty, a former conductor on the Chicago
and Alton, and Andrew J. Kerfoot, a brakeman by trade—enjoyed the
enthusiastic financial backing of a wealthy St. Louis investor, Melvin L.
Gray, who had endorsed the note of the company to the St. Louis Trust
Company. And in fairness, in its first year of existence, the road operated
well in the black.

But on the other hand, the physical condition of the line, which made even
Louis cringe, seriously undermined its long-term viability. Owing to the
extreme haste of the builders, who were chasing a temporal monetary bonus
just as Houck had been in 1880, the St. Louis, Kennett and Southern was not,
in industry terms, "lined up to centers," which meant that even though surveyors had fixed a center line to locate the exact path, work crews had
instead laid the track "by the eye," leaving it to meander and wobble from
side to side. Outside of Kennett the tracks actually weaved around stumps
and larger trees. What is more, ties—only half the number required—and
track rested on the natural contour of the sandy ground without any grading, dumping, ditching, or even elevated trestles over the sloughs. In some

14. "Louis Houck Memoirs," 229, 232, 238; O. L. Garrison to Louis Houck, July 17,
1890, Houck Papers, Box 1510, Correspondence, 1890 July G-Z, Folder 17.
15. Houck Papers, Box 1616, Giboney Houck, Oversized, Ledger, 1891–1895, 152,
154.

places grades were so prohibitively steep that in the absence of trestles the lone wood-burning engine would routinely sink down into the sloughs when it tried to cross and stall itself out trying to climb back up.[16]

Still, as it stood, even with major rehabilitation expenses just to get the line up to Houck's standards, let alone to meet the increasingly stringent state specifications, rail access to hundreds of thousands of acres of prime timber and arguably the most prolific cotton-producing region in Missouri was just too good to pass up. Consequently, in the early months of 1891 Louis brokered a deal with McCarty and Kerfoot, buying out their interest in a capital-friendly move that involved no cash. Having graduated to that point in a railroader's career when even purchases of other railroads could be made with stock from his existing lines, Louis paid $10,000 in bonds of the St. Louis, Cape Girardeau and Fort Smith Railroad with the agreement to also assume the $100,000 note in the hands of the St. Louis Trust Company. The arrangement also called for Melvin L. Gray to extend payment on the note for one year, a courtesy for which he received $180,000 worth of the St. Louis, Kennett and Southern as collateral and Houck's personal guarantee to rebuild the road in a timely fashion. For good measure, Louis retained McCarty to serve as general manager and Kerfoot superintendent.[17] The foundation of the second Houck road, the southern system, was now in place.

Simultaneous to initiating his ambitious venture into the Bootheel, Louis aggressively shed himself of the last lingering vestiges of an ongoing scheme to bypass the Iron Mountain system and St. Louis market altogether with a transfer boat across the Mississippi River and direct rail access to Chicago. Like most of his railroading aspirations during this era, this transfer boat project had ebbed and flowed with the prevailing economic tide. Beginning in 1887, just as construction began to Williamsville and Moss's Cape Girardeau Transportation Company was picking up steam, Houck first shopped around the idea to both the Illinois Central and the Mobile and Ohio Railroad of building a branch line in southern Illinois to a point on the river opposite Cape Girardeau. After both proposals died from neglect, in the late 1880s he approached Ethan A. Hitchcock and William O. Garrison of the small Grand Tower and Carbondale Railroad, a predominantly coal shipping line running between those two Illinois locations. The beauty of

16. Louis Houck, "Story of the Railroad Work, Volume II," 1–3; *Dunklin Democrat* (Kennett, Mo.), April 19, 1938.

17. *Cape Girardeau Democrat*, July 18, 1892; Houck, "Story of the Railroad Work, Volume II," 2–4; Doherty, Jr., "Missouri Interests of Louis Houck," 134–35.

transferring cars at the Cape, Houck had explained, was in the way such an enterprise brought their respective interests into harmony. For the Grand Tower he was offering an outlet from the Illinois coal fields into southeast Missouri with connections to the Iron Mountain, Cotton Belt, and parts beyond; for himself, there would be a piece of the Illinois coal action and a foothold in his native state from which to branch out to the more expansive Illinois Central or Mobile and Ohio.

Their agreement commenced the Grand Tower and Cape Girardeau Railroad Company of Illinois, a partnership ostensibly between the three men to locate a roughly thirty-mile extension down the eastern shoreline of the Mississippi from Grand Tower to East Cape Girardeau, Illinois. Silent New York investors with interests in the Mount Carbon coal fields in Illinois backed the railway, contracting with Houck to build the road for $300,000: $150,000 paid in a cash advance and $150,000 in forthcoming bonds.[18] The necessary funds would be raised through two sources: stocks and bonds. Generally speaking, stocks are a capital-raising tool whereby corporations sell shares on the market entitling investors—stockholders— to any potential dividends. Likewise, bonds are another form of economic development, but one in which a corporation actually guarantees to the purchasers—bondholders—payment of their original investment plus interest by some specified future date. In this particular instance, the capital stock value of the corporation was set at $1 million, with the amount to be raised through the sale of shares on the stock market.

The investors then subscribed $180,000 in bonds to get the ball rolling with the stipulation that Hitchcock, Garrison, and Houck raise the remaining $120,000 to cover Houck's construction costs. But to Louis's chagrin, this arrangement inconveniently complicated matters by technically running afoul of a complex Illinois law which clearly stated that capital stock could be fixed at any amount the incorporating body deemed proper, but bonds could not be issued until all the capital stock was subscribed. More simply, the scheme was effectively doomed because the partners could not legally sell the bonds required to pay Louis's entire $300,000 construction fee until someone stepped up to the plate and bought up the outstanding balance of $950,000 in stock. The problem was that due to cold feet on the East Coast, additional investors turned out to be as scarce, as they would say in Missouri, as hen's teeth—leaving the project hopelessly snagged.

18. Houck, "Reminiscences," 53–55; "Louis Houck Memoirs," 143–45; Surveyors report, January 12, 1887, Houck Papers, Box 1508, Correspondence, January 1886–April 1888, Folder 2.

In serious jeopardy of seeing the whole business slip through his fingers, Louis, in a daring moment of late 1880s confidence, "astonished" his partners—probably himself too—by waiving his contract as the builder and boldly putting up the requisite $950,000 in his and Mary's money to become almost the sole stockholder in the Grand Tower and Cape Girardeau Railroad. Already hailed by fellow investors as having risked "a good deal of sand," Houck also threw in ten acres of Giboney family land in Illinois to serve as the eastern terminal. From there, construction went forward, and by November 1889 the first trains rolled down the incline on the Cape side where a four-car transfer boat, the *Vice-President*, ferried rolling stock across the Mississippi and unloaded them onto an eight-hundred-foot rock pier in Illinois on their way to Grand Tower.[19]

Yet in near perfect symmetry, 1890 brought a familiar host of difficulties. It soon became painfully evident during periods of low water on the Mississippi that the incline Houck had fashioned in Cape Girardeau would have to be extended progressively out into the river in order to give the transfer boat, which had to land up against the incline, deep enough water. The same proved true in East Cape Girardeau. And then there were the sandbars that ensnared the *Vice-President*, which lacked an ordinary headlight for reasons of economy, on foggy nights. The question too of who should actually control the transfer business also remained perpetually sticky. In order to efficiently coordinate transfers, Houck, Hitchcock, and Garrison needed to work and play well together. But Louis found the Illinois men "rather overbearing" and troublesome to deal with, chiefly because they physically operated the Grand Tower and Cape Girardeau, leaving the Houck road, he believed, to labor, in regard to rights and profits, not as master but as servant.[20]

The bottom line was that the Grand Tower and Cape Girardeau along with the transfer business generated considerably less earnings than Houck initially envisioned; as a matter of fact, at only a puny two dollars for a four-car transfer, he never made any money from it at all. The earnings of the road fell well short of paying operating expenses and interest, and thus twice in 1890 the Grand Tower and Cape Girardeau defaulted on interest payments, leaving its primary stockholder, Houck, on the hook for around

---

19. "Louis Houck Memoirs," 146–48; Theo Chase to Louis Houck, February 17, 1888, Houck Papers, Box 1508, Correspondence, 1888 Correspondence Feb A–H, Folder 26.

20. H. Martin Williams to Louis Houck, April 2, 1891, Houck Papers, Box 1511, Correspondence, 1891 April J–Z, Folder 5; O. L. Garrison to Louis Houck, January 22, 1892, Houck Papers, Box 1512, Correspondence, Feb A–H, Folder 3.

$39,000 in compounded interest due on the matured bonds. Worse, his Cape Girardeau Southwestern Railroad had been named as guarantor on these outstanding bonds.[21] In protesting the financial load now squarely on his shoulders alone, Louis followed a line that ran right back to Hitchcock and Garrison, recognizing their conspiracy, he thought, to run the road and keep all the profits for themselves while unlawfully sticking him with the indebtedness. Predictably, matters wound up in federal court in St. Louis.

After suits and countersuits between the owners of the Grand Tower and Cape Girardeau road bogged down from amendments and postponements, Garrison and Houck reached a private out-of-court settlement in early 1891 in front of the courthouse on Fifth Street. Completely by chance, and no doubt uncomfortably, the two men bumped into each other in St. Louis, and to Houck's surprise—given the frosty nature of the relationship—Garrison wearily released him from any liability in exchange for all his stock in the Cape Girardeau and Grand Tower. The railroad even paid all court costs, and just like that Houck's troubled affiliation with the Grand Tower came to a relatively satisfactory, or at least acceptable, end. But the transfer boat continued to bind the two rancorous entities inescapably together for years to come. As Houck recalled of the ill will, "Hitchcock and Garrison never ceased to abuse me personally because they were unable to overreach me in this transaction, and frequently in St. Louis I heard they cautioned everybody not to have any dealings with me. In that way, they did me no little injury."[22] All the same, with this latest elephant off his back by May 1891, Louis paid his attorneys' fees off in Pemiscot County land worth perhaps two to three dollars an acre and caught another train for New York.

With his financial conditions fairly stabilized and in some semblance of order, Louis deliberately took a much different tack in New York than he had the previous year, playing it cool as to not seem so desperate, and pledging to "go very slow and watch corners. Concede nothing without a quid pro quo."[23] Good thing, because deceit and treachery were as common as the homeless and unemployed he distastefully observed sleeping in the streets of New York that spring. The first hint of trouble came from Walter Stanton, who for months had been reassuring Louis that his firm

21. "Louis Houck Memoirs," 148–49, 152, 156–58, 196; E. A. Hitchcock to Louis Houck, January 21, 1889, O. L. Garrison to Louis Houck, January 22, 1889, January 23, 1889, Houck Papers, Box 1509, Correspondence, Jan S–Z 1889, Folder 14.
22. "Louis Houck Memoirs," 148, 149, 150, 151, 196.
23. Ibid., 245.

still held out interest in buying the St. Louis, Cape Girardeau and Fort Smith Railroad; even if that deal never materialized, Stanton maintained that the only way to sell the line to Gould would be through Coffin and him. Now back in New York, William Coffin advanced yet another method. What if, since they had it on good authority that Gould would never pay more than an insulting $750,000 for the road, Louis gave them a one-year option on all the railroad's stock—meaning basically that he could not sell his stock to anyone except them for a one-year period—so that they might have more time to enlist serious investors in a partnership group that would ultimately purchase the road outright? There would be, of course, a small payment of earnest money to cement the option, with the balance then coming in a year. Even though financial matters were in such "flattering shape" at the moment, to protect the option Coffin insisted that Houck would also be required to take up the income and all prior bonds from the St. Louis, Cape Girardeau and Fort Smith and replace them with one large consolidation mortgage at $15,000 per mile through the friendly firm of Coffin and Stanton.

In essence this was the quintessential wolf in sheep's clothing, nothing more than an elaborate takeover scheme that differed in degree of complexity, but not in kind, from that of Gould's Missouri Pacific. Both pirates were motivated by an inherent belief that after the previous year's flailing and gasping, Houck would certainly turn belly-up soon and his pitiful railroad, as it was said, would "give up the ghost." In anticipation of that day, the slippery Coffin and Stanton were positioning themselves in the coming year to squash Houck's ability to shop around his sure-to-be-plummeting stock for a fair market price. And after another disastrous year like 1890, they would have him between the proverbial rock and a hard place—facing foreclosure from defaulting on his mortgage and powerless to sell out at anything but their bargain-basement terms. The plan was beautiful in its ruthless efficiency.[24]

Wisely, however, Louis did not take the bait, balking first at their refusal to guarantee that no matter what happened, as the foremost priority, his personal debt to Robert Sturdivant would be paid back in full, and later because, as he tersely spelled out to Coffin, he could not give an option on the stock while the personal liability on the notes of the company remained with him. Though his stomach hurt and he often could not join business

24. B. St. John Hoyt to Louis Houck, November 18, 1891, Houck Papers, Box 1511, Correspondence, 1891 November A-L, Folder 18; W. J. Thompson to Louis Houck, September 21, 1892, Houck Papers, Box 1512, Correspondence, Sept M-Z, Folder 23.

associates for lunch breaks due to what was most certainly an ulcer, Houck squarely declined the option with an insightful observation that speaks directly to the fortification of his fragile psyche over the tortuous year just past. "You never can sell a road as long as you want to sell and are hawking it about . . . That has been my trouble in this business all along. A fellow that hawks his ware about never gets a good price."[25]

In a series of subsequent meetings Louis scheduled primarily to cultivate interest in his dream to run a line to Memphis, he persisted in holding his ground when the inevitable topic of a buyout came up. For whatever reasons he does not seem to have connected with Solon Humphreys, but one new acquaintance from these conferences, Newman Erb, an expert railroader of "practical character" most recently at the helm of the Kansas City, Wyandotte and Northwestern, befriended Houck and essentially took over Humphreys' earlier role as de facto New York guide. The two traveled socially together, attending the theater and public lectures while Louis was introduced around the exclusive Manhattan Club in the Stewart Mansion, a landmark of high society. Though slightly suspicious, Louis also seemed to be awed by the German-born Erb's intellect and appears to have taken it as a courteous favor when his new companion—the same man who by decade's end would finally wrest ownership of the St. Louis, Cape Girardeau and Fort Smith from him—helped navigate the financial waters of the city. Through Erb, Houck learned of nefarious schemes then under way in which some smaller financial sharks had surreptitiously purchased St. Louis, Cape Girardeau and Fort Smith bonds through Coffin and Stanton, just as Erb had, with the sole intention of selling them to Gould. Erb also confided that as a Coffin and Stanton client himself, he too had initially favored the stock option initiative. However, despite those past transgressions and any misgivings Louis might have about his role in them, Erb confidentially revealed that he now harbored a personal interest in the success of the Houck roads and ultimately broached the subject of a potential partnership between the two men.[26]

Through Erb and William Coffin, Louis sat down for one of his last meetings during this East Coast trip with notable financier Russell Sage, a

25. "Louis Houck Memoirs," 242, 243, 244, 245, 250, 255; Louis Houck to Coffin and Stanton, April 20, 1891, Houck Papers, Box 1541, 1886–1897, Correspondence-Outgoing, Folder 2; Robert Sturdivant to Louis Houck, March 12, 1891, Houck Papers, Box 1511, Correspondence, 1891 March L-Z, Folder 3.

26. "Louis Houck Memoirs," 247, 248, 252, 253; Cape Girardeau Democrat, May 6, 1899; B. St. John Hoyt to Louis Houck, September 21, 1892, Houck Papers, Box 1512, Correspondence, Sept H-M, Folder 22.

close associate in Jay Gould's incestuous business directorates with a seat on the New York Stock Exchange and more than a passing interest in western railroads. Although nothing came from their brief conversation, Houck's own account almost perfectly encapsulates all the shifty characters and sordid dealings he encountered in New York during the spring of 1891. "To be sure, he is very affable and plain and unassuming and looks very kindly apparently," Louis noted of Russell Sage in his journal. "But all the same he reminds me in his appearance and behavior, as much as a man can, of a tiger. He has the same kind of a smile and the same look about the eye and mouth and his hands move constantly and his feet also move backward and forward and he slides back and forth in his chair, smiling all the time, like the tiger moving up and down in a cage and switching its tail, looking very peaceful all the while, but nevertheless a terror. Think Sage is a very dangerous man for those he has in his power."[27]

Before leaving the city altogether, Houck agreed to touch base with Jay Gould at his Western Union office on May 4. Coffin sat in on the discussions, which irritated Louis, and apparently Gould as well, because from the onset the two railroaders somehow seemed to be more firmly on the same page. Per usual, Gould commenced the proceedings with a blunt question of price. "$1,300,000 at the very least," Houck responded. Gould offered an even million. After Coffin's unwelcome interruption that they would take $1,200,000, Louis took the bull by horns, forsaking all matters of sale and instead frankly informing Gould that he would rather "make an alliance with you, offensive and defensive." The dying businessman looked Houck squarely in the eyes and with body language that bolstered Louis's self-assurance arranged for the two to meet in private the next morning—when Gould would be fresh and Coffin would be gone—to hammer out the form of this proposed alliance.

A succession of interruptions and cancelled follow-ups stalled these talks and left the fragile possibility of cooperation up in the air for several days. Disheartened, yet still convinced that Gould was acting in good faith, on the afternoon of May 8 Houck left the Astor House, where the staff now knew him by name, to call on Jay Gould a final time. After initially being told by Gould's "boy" that the boss would gladly see him soon, a long wait ended with news that Gould had unexpectedly gone uptown and would not be available. Louis grinned, and then laughed, knowing

---

27. "Louis Houck Memoirs," 255. Interestingly, later that year in December, a man carrying a dynamite bomb walked into Sage's office, conceivably the same where he met Louis, and blew up himself and a secretary in a failed assassination attempt.

this to be a blatant lie. With no sale and a partnership with Gould stillborn, Houck was heading back to Cape Girardeau, presumably "as the saying is 'A sadder and wiser man.'" Then again, given time to reflect, he reconsidered: "Do not know, however, that I am sad. Rather, I am glad."[28]

Amid swirling, unfounded Cape Girardeau rumors of an impending Gould and Houck alliance, Louis took possession of the St. Louis, Kennett and Southern in September 1891 and began in earnest the tremendous task of putting the road into operating shape. In his grand scheme, this precarious stretch of land-locked iron, whose only outlet was the Cotton Belt, never represented an end in and of itself. Rather, Houck always envisioned it would be—as the "Southern" portion of the name implied—the first necessary foothold in a larger expansion across the Bootheel that would someday reach into Arkansas and ultimately to Memphis. Accordingly, fresh sources of capital would need to be tapped, and toward that end Louis invited Newman Erb to southeast Missouri in order that the two might make good on Erb's interest in collaboration. Erb and Houck conferred at Elmwood for several days over funding possibilities, finally deciding to concurrently explore European options, step up earlier efforts to entice George H. Nettleton of the Kansas City, Fort Scott and Memphis into a partnership, and make contact with some capitalists Erb knew in Memphis.[29]

To facilitate the rehabilitation of the St. Louis, Kennett and Southern, Houck dispatched James Brooks, signaling something of a milestone in the business evolution of the Houck roads. For more than a decade, as the miles of track had physically multiplied, their overall management continued to keep pace, naturally becoming exponentially more sophisticated and complex. Now, however, unlike the first railway, headquartered in Cape Girardeau, this second system would be run primarily out of Kennett, the Dunklin County seat. This dictated a delegation of authority and diffusion of daily decision-making power away from the home office that was unprecedented by earlier standards. Unmistakably, the buck still stopped with Louis in regard to the big picture of strategy, and exhaustive daily reports still kept him well versed with virtually every detail along his roads: from conductors enumerating each car handled by their train to every station agent accounting for all the cars in their yard, and, of course, all construction.

28. Ibid., 257–59; George Houck to Louis Houck, December 15, 1891, Houck Papers, Box 1511, Correspondence, 1891 December A–H, Folder 20.

29. George Nettleton to Louis Houck, December 8, 1890, Houck Papers, Box 1510, Correspondence, 1890 December A–M, Folder 24; J. B. White to Louis Houck, September 23, 1891, Houck Papers, Box 1511, Correspondence, 1891 September A–M, Folder 14.

But necessity compelled Houck to adopt a fairly standard hierarchy of railroad management whereby a rather autonomous "general manager" oversaw various subordinate "superintendents" who in turn fulfilled the requisite responsibilities of physically caring for the properties, making schedules and monitoring all traffic, setting rates and soliciting business, and collecting revenue and keeping statistics.

To his eventual dismay, in the short term he was stuck with McCarty and Kerfoot in these capacities down in Kennett. In time, experience and an inherent respect for the bonds of family compelled Louis to place personal and familial loyalty as the ultimate benchmark by which qualifications for management were measured. Put simply, as his railroad enterprises continued to stretch out, Louis increasingly leaned on a tight circle of men he could trust to superintend the lines. Edward F. Blomeyer emerged as the key lieutenant in the Cape Girardeau office, effectively conducting most of the railroad's daily business as auditor and secretary. James Brooks acted as Louis's proxy in the remote reaches of southeast Missouri and for many locals was the visible face of the Houck roads. And since railroads were popular targets of litigation—especially loss and damage claims for missing freight and dead livestock—Houck also retained a stable of regional attorneys such as Madison Smith, Moses Whybark, and John Hope to act as an informal legal department. Similarly, both Blomeyer and Brooks, along with Louis, also groomed Houck's young nephews Louis Bartholomew and Julius, his brother Julius's boys, as they worked their way up through the ranks to one day take over leadership of the new Houck family trade.

In the fall of 1891, Brooks arrived in Kennett with a St. Louis, Cape Girardeau and Fort Smith locomotive to fix a grade line for the road in order to straighten out its winding ways. Once the line was established, a pile driver arrived to put in trestles over the sloughs along with a steam shovel and many cars to haul in sand for a dump. Since the track had been initially laid without any prepared roadbed, Brooks loaded countless tons of sand, quite plentiful in the region, onto cars and spread it evenly over the tracks. Crews then mechanically jacked up the rails and rough-hewn log ties to allow the sand to settle underneath them, while other gangs replaced the logs with actual ties before lowering the tracks back down and tamping the sand into place.[30]

---

30. "Louis Houck Memoirs," 260; Houck, "Story of the Railroad Work, Volume II," 4; Hal H. McHaney, "The History of the McHaney Family in Dunklin County, Missouri," *Dunklin County Historical Society* (May 24, 1948), 324–25, in Doherty, Jr., "Missouri Interests of Louis Houck," 134.

For his part, November found Houck back on the East Coast for "one last visit of endeavor to financially arrange matters in New York for the road." Without informing Coffin and Stanton of his arrival, Louis saw Gould alone and was instantly taken by his physical deterioration. "He seemed to be pleased to see me," Houck commented, "but he was very pale and seemed to suffer from something." Still, Louis noted, "his eye had the same searching look I noticed formerly." As the two chatted, Houck sensed an uncharacteristic "air of benevolence" about Gould, who appeared to "talk sympathetically" regarding the Houck roads, sincerely inquiring, it appeared, about the condition of the road, its business, present terminals, and the productivity of the land south of Cape Girardeau. Without making any mention of a sale, Gould at some point abruptly, but very casually, rose from his chair and without a word left the room, leaving Louis to politely wait for his return. Soon a secretary entered to inform Louis that Gould had gone to a board meeting and that Houck was free to call again tomorrow. But he never revisited Jay Gould, who died of tuberculosis the next year with an estimated fortune of $72 million.[31]

With substantive progress along the Kennett line and a gratifying bottom line on the St. Louis, Cape Girardeau and Fort Smith, Louis rang in 1892 with Irma on his arm at a gala leap-year costume ball. In dazzling attire, father and daughter celebrated with Cape Girardeau's elite at the Opera House: she as Empress Josephine and he, of course, due to his middle name and height, as Napoleon Bonaparte.[32] By spring the St. Louis, Kennett and Southern was turning a profit, and to keep the momentum going, Houck single-mindedly hounded Melvin L. Gray into personally buying $140,000 of the railway bonds. This move retired the $100,000 note from the St. Louis Trust Company due that fall and positioned a "warm personal friend" as the sole bondholder of the road with interest personally guaranteed by Houck for three years.[33]

Now poised to commence the long-anticipated extension to Memphis, circumstances dictated Houck instead alter his long-range plans and for the immediate future veer east to Caruthersville on the Mississippi. Evidently the annexation of the St. Louis, Kennett and Southern had set off a chain reaction that prompted Brooks to fix a roughly north-south survey line from Kennett through the Bootheel. This included Pemiscot County, the area sandwiched between Dunklin County and the Mississippi River.

31. "Louis Houck Memoirs," 263–65.
32. *Cape Girardeau Democrat*, January 2, 1892.
33. Houck, "Story of the Railroad Work, Volume II," 4–8.

In conjunction, Houck had brokered a questionable land-for-reclamation-and-railroad deal with the Pemiscot County Court reminiscent of his doomed arrangement with Wayne County. When the time came to actually begin construction in 1892, however, Louis found little monetary backing in extreme southeast Missouri and northeast Arkansas. What is more, the "general cussedness" of the Farmers' Alliance—a local manifestation of a fledgling political movement gaining strength across the Midwest—had frightened the Pemiscot County Court regarding railroads in general and Houck's schemes in particular. Thus faced with an increasingly unfavorable political climate in the region, a skittish county court, and uncomfortable recollections of the Wayne County land disaster, Houck reconsidered his plans in favor of a rather ingenious new approach.[34]

By mutual agreement with the Pemiscot County Court, the first contract was cancelled. In its place, the two entities agreed to retain the basic core of the original deal: the county would still exchange 40,000 acres of land for a railroad and accompanying drainage ditch along the road to divert water if both projects were completed within five years. Yet here is where the new wrinkles from Houck's learning curve came into play. First, the line would not be north-south, but instead east-west, from Kennett to Caruthersville, thus affording more immediate river access to help the new road become a paying concern months before a longer Memphis route could hope to do so. Second, Houck and his new partner John Eddy Franklin would actually purchase the land for a mere $1.25 an acre, around $56,000 in total, using bonds of the railroad as collateral to secure a loan from the county. The third, and most revealing, provision was that contractually the deal was struck between the individual Louis Houck and the county court, not between the St. Louis, Kennett and Southern and the county, thereby outflanking legal impediments to government aid to railroads.[35]

For attorneys and other aficionados of jurisprudence, Houck's "litigious temperament" and pronounced legal skills are perhaps most spectacularly illustrated in land deals such as this one. One of his great-grandsons—himself a former U.S. attorney and Missouri legislator—judged Louis to be "a superb legal draftsman" whose "deeds and other conveyances are masterpieces of the lawyers' art." His great belief in "entailment"—tying up

34. George Crumb to Louis Houck, May 20, 1891, Houck Papers, Box 1511, Correspondence, 1891 May G-Z, Folder 7; George W. Carleton to Louis Houck, October 2, 1892, October 13, 1892, October 29, 1892, Houck Papers, 1892 Box 1513, Correspondence, October A-H, Folder 1.

35. St. Louis Globe Democrat, September 15, 1891; "The Lumber World," May 19, 1892, Houck Papers, Box 1512, Correspondence, May H-Z, Folder 13.

the title to real estate for several generations to come—confounded creditors, and his creativity in using land as economic development is truly
impressive.[36] Although Franklin conceded that this land deal plainly
looked like an evasion of the law, in this particular case in Pemiscot
County, Houck nonetheless had manipulated the legal distinction
between person and corporation to thwart Missouri's regulations. As a
matter of fact, it appears Louis had been perfecting this particularly clever
technique for some time. Routinely, he purposely, and often fondly,
blurred the differentiation between Houck and the Houck roads, attaching
personal pronouns when referring to the railroad so that it came out as
"my rates, my railroad, my depots, and my trains" almost as if naturally.
The semantic merger became so securely fastened that Houck eventually
followed the corporation-as-person paradigm to its logical—or illogical, as
the case may be—conclusion in claiming during his celebrated receivership trials that the Fourteenth Amendment's protection of property rights
applied equally to citizens and to his railroads.[37]

When the land deal became an accomplished fact, Houck incorporated
the Pemiscot Railroad to construct a permanent levee system over which
the railroad would run. As a bit of a sideshow, almost concurrently, at the
request of local melon farmers—and with their financial backing—he also
formed "Houck's Missouri and Arkansas Railroad" to connect Cape
Girardeau to Morley, the watermelon capital of southeast Missouri. The
first thirteen miles of Houck's Missouri and Arkansas railroad between
Commerce and Morley were "rapidly and defectively constructed"
between April and August 1893. An incline at Commerce to connect the
road to the Illinois Central across the Mississippi took slightly longer, but
at a time when construction gangs on the Pemiscot line were still hacking
their way through a quagmire just to clear a path, almost five hundred carloads of watermelons a month were already arriving at the river bank.[38]

Though obviously shorter, the simple reason the relatively painless Missouri and Arkansas became operational so much quicker than the Pemiscot is that the physical construction of the latter line returned Houck's boys
to the unique perils and toil of swamp railroading. Pemiscot is after all

36. Ronald S. Reed, Jr., to Joel P. Rhodes, July 26, 2006, in possession of author.

37. Eddy, "Former Pioneer Traces Early History of County in Writing His Memoirs";
Doherty, Jr., *Houck, Missouri Historian and Entrepreneur*, 107; Wollman, "Strange Story,"
1; *Missouri Republican*, June 2, 1887.

38. Houck, "Story of the Railroad Work, Volume II," 61–63; *Cape Girardeau Democrat*,
April 15, 1893, May 26, 1894. Business and profits on this thirteen-mile line from Commerce to Morley were directly tied to the warm watermelon season and during the rest
of the year the line made just enough money to stay open.

thought to be a Native American word for "liquid mud," and Kennett and Caruthersville were separated by the nearly impenetrable Nacormy Swamp, an overgrown lake so thick and inhospitable that few humans ever traversed it. Even the normally steady Brooks, a veteran of southeast Missouri's howling wildernesses, occasionally got disoriented and lost in the "gumbo" while surveying the grade. The only commercial access between Dunklin and Pemiscot counties at the time was the risky Hickory Landing plank road, but then only in drier years, which 1892 and 1893 were certainly not. Before work began, Houck recalled, the two towns were about as isolated from each other, and travel between them as problematic, as "between Africa and South America." "It took about as much time to go from Caruthersville to Kennett," he maintained, only partially in jest, "as from Kennett to New York."[39]

Crews tore into the swamp from both sides, simultaneously working inward from the Kennett depot heading east and from Caruthersville moving west. In no time, what had been one of the most desolate areas in the state—considered to be "outside the world"—became "alive with people." Houck's gangs were never known for being "kid-glove, buggy-riding, afraid-to-face-the-weather [men]," and all through 1893 and 1894 more than two hundred of them—now almost all Irish and under the direction of Brooks's assistant A. R. Ponder—cleared, graded, and drove piles at various points along Brooks's survey line in some of the most horrendous conditions in North America.[40] The men, of course, worked in teams, and each team lived in its own camp behind "the Front," the most recent point of impact between construction and jungle. At night the camps were primitive communities of hard-working and hard-drinking men dining on bear steak, roast raccoon, or fish. Those near Brooks's headquarters under the big oaks on the Little River came to appreciate the chief engineer—himself born on a Missouri River steamboat—as an accomplished storyteller. So too, did laborers come to know their boss, A. R. Ponder—a recent graduate of the Missouri School of Mines referred to affectionately with his own southern enunciation of "Pon-dah"—as a marvelous mimic of their voices and expressions.[41]

39. Houck, "Story of the Railroad Work, Volume II," 15, 22.
40. Ross to Louis Houck, December 28, 1892, Houck Papers, 1892 Box 1513, Correspondence, Dec P-Z, Folder 8.
41. Eddy, "Former Pioneer Traces Early History of County in Writing His Memoirs"; A. J. Kerfoot to Louis Houck, August 27, 1894, A. R. Ponder to Louis Houck, August 28, 1894, Houck Papers, 1894 Box 1516, Correspondence, August S-Z, Folder 7; A. J. Kerfoot to Louis Houck, June 11, 1895, Houck Papers, 1895 Box 1517, Correspondence, June P-Z, Folder 18.

Each morning the crews would come up from their camps in the rear to "the Front" with the twenty-man right-of-way team chopping through grass far taller than their heads and felling hundreds of cypress and oak to painstakingly carve out the line. Ox teams wrenched stumps from the ground, and behind them tie hacks stacked lumber along the developing right-of-way to easily supply all the ties and piles for the forthcoming construction gangs. A steam shovel and pile driver moved up and down the grade, the latter forcing many of these logs into the marsh to build almost two miles of pile trestles and bridges. In accordance with the contract, and complemented by other drainage projects commenced by local farmers, a four-foot levee began to rise from the marshes, in places the product of untold thousands of grueling wheelbarrow loads of dirt.[42]

During the winter, the same freezing overflow waters and mud that had hamstrung previous Houck construction in Delta and Mingo meant that progress would be measured by yards. In the summer, stifling heat and swarms of apparently man-eating mosquitoes tortured crews while each step in the stagnant bayous sent snakes slithering and boots sinking. After almost fifteen years in railroading, Louis no longer lived in the field with his men and in fact ventured down from Cape only a handful of times. On one of these outings to get a firsthand feel for the challenge and exhaustive physical cost of moving this enterprise ahead, he hiked from Kennett to a construction camp at the Clay Root Bayou nearly seven miles away. "How I managed to get through," he noted, "I can hardly say." Just months before he had mingled with thousands of awestruck spectators at the Columbian Exhibition in Chicago, reveling in the cosmopolitan splendor of the White City and even taking the podium at the Missouri exhibit to deliver a glowing speech on his beloved southeast section.

But here, utterly alone, slightly disoriented and soaked through with sweat, as he searched for his men thought to be clearing across Ingram's Ridge, Louis was yet again briefly overcome by emotion. Already a messy receivership proceeding threatened the first Houck road. He had also buried his friend Thomas J. Moss in St. Louis and perhaps with him his magnificent tie business. Before reaching the bayou, Louis solemnly reflected on this stretch of road he increasingly felt certain was leading straight into the "jaws of death." "I sat down on a log, and overcome by fatigue, as well as the thought of the work I had undertaken to build

42. *Cape Girardeau Democrat*, August 4, 18, 1894; A. J. Kerfoot to Louis Houck, August 5, 1891, Houck Papers, Box 1511, Correspondence, 1891 August M-Z, Folder 13; Eddy, "Former Pioneer Traces Early History of County in Writing His Memoirs."

through this swamp, involuntarily the tears came to my eyes. But this weakness passed off."[43]

The entire process of clearing and preparing the roadbed took well over a year.

When men began laying track from the Kennett end in August 1894, the toughest stretch across the Nacormy Swamp was finally behind them, and for the remainder of the year crews "spiked," so to speak, downhill. In a stroke of good luck, even the oldest pioneers could not remember a drier fall, which allowed gangs to sustain their rather brisk pace. After laying out the town of Hayti the men worked through Christmas and New Year's Day, with the first snow-covered construction trains completing the entire run from Campbell to Kennett to Caruthersville on January 24, 1895. Within days ox teams retrieved a derailed locomotive with a broken drive wheel and crews scrambled to replace the first washout near Hayti. "The road was rough, half built, you might say," Louis concluded with detectable relief, "but for all that was a railroad."[44]

43. Houck, "Story of the Railroad Work, Volume II," 18–19; *Cape Girardeau Democrat,* August 12, 1893; Mary Houck to Louis Houck, September 8, 1892, Houck Papers, Box 1512, Correspondence, Sept M-Z, Folder 23; George Houck to Louis Houck, August 5, 1893, Houck Papers, 1893 Box 1514, Correspondence, August A-H, Folder 10.
44. Houck, "Story of the Railroad Work, Volume II," 21–25.

CHAPTER 7

A Damn Fine Lawyer

You are the first man that ever beat me in a railroad fight. I have seen your railroad at Delta, and I have heard you conduct your case here, and I want to say, sir, that you are a damn poor railroad man, but a damn fine lawyer.

—Attributed to Jay Gould in southeast Missouri folklore

While the townspeople of Caruthersville generally rejoiced in the arrival of the Pemiscot Railroad in 1895—having waited for the iron horse "awful anxious" and "as impatient as the school-boy is for recess to come"— Houck still felt obliged to vigilantly defend himself against the slings and arrows of mounting negative public sentiment in southeast Missouri.[1] As a hard-bargaining and high-profile capitalist with substantial and diversified interests in commercial and residential real estate, farming, and the railroad, over the years Houck—who frankly could be quite prickly in his personal business dealings—drew more and more the ire of state officials, business associates, and fickle locals. What is more, his restless energy made him elusive and remote, and while he had many friends, precious few people professed to know him well. In truth, the realities of assuming nearly sole responsibility for such radical change in the region—while according occasional well-deserved accolades—conversely positioned him as a lightning rod for much of the blame when things went awry.

Since the prison humiliation a decade before, Houck had been consciously stewarding popular perceptions of himself, especially in newsprint.

1. Hina C. Schult to Louis Houck, July 15, 1892, Houck Papers, Box 1512, Correspondence, July L-Z, Folder 18.

This typically entailed balancing any repudiations in the court of public opinion with affirmations of his numerous contributions to southeast Missouri. "Some people misjudge Mr. Houck and call him selfish and grasping. Concede it," the friendly *Cape Girardeau Democrat* editorialized as an excellent illustration. "Yet, you are bound to admit he has been the means of bringing large sums of money to this city and in working hard to increase the inflow. Yet, unwittingly, you dam up the millrace that drives your gristmill . . . still you find fault with him and try to paralyze the hand that feeds us." Another emblematic editorial avowed, "Louis Houck has done more for the city of Cape Girardeau in the last ten years" than the "anti-Houck element" could do in one thousand.[2]

Nevertheless, by the mid-1890s, Houck found it progressively more difficult to effectively answer his many contemporary detractors who dismissed him as a self-interested "pusher," who "most of the time [is] thinking of Mr. Houck," and who was "best kept aloof from" when handling business.[3] In Cape Girardeau, citizens railed before the city council over the latest something or other Houck was doing, or not doing, with his various properties, be it the high rental prices he charged for homes and businesses he owned or the potential fire hazard of storing empty oil barrels in wooden buildings near his downtown depot.

As a matter of philosophy, Louis and his subordinates infamously would not pay bills, either promptly or in full, and this applied equally to magazine subscriptions and locomotives. The matter of maintaining good credit with punctual repayment seemed to him a damned waste of good capital that only limited his financial range of motion. Merchants, brokers, attorneys, tailors, dance teachers, horse breeders, inn keepers, and tax collectors begged to differ, and what had been uneasily tolerated, even taken in good humor, at the onset of his career eventually wore thin.[4]

Despite opening southeast Missouri to railroading, that industry did not always win Houck many friends either. He constantly squabbled with aggrieved parties over inconsistent shipping rates, damaged merchandise, inexplicable delays that rotted produce, payroll trains arriving two months behind, and perpetually late mail service (a common complaint which spawned the local joke that mail on the Houck roads was like the tail of a cow—always behind). Perturbed passengers howled at the regularity with

2. *Cape Girardeau Democrat,* March 6, 1897, April 11, 1891.
3. B. St. John Hoyt to Louis Houck, May 5, 1892, Houck Papers, Box 1512, Correspondence, May A–H, Folder 12.
4. Franklin, "Former Pioneer Traces Early History."

which broken-down locomotives compelled ticket holders to finish their journey by foot with no refund. And many exasperated landowners loudly complained that on principle, railroad construction crews should not grade or harvest ties on their property until *after* legal contracts purchasing the rights-of-way were concluded.[5]

Apparently even when Houck was right, he was still often deemed wrong. For instance, on the issue of race, Houck was very much a product of the racial sensibilities of his time—if anything, by southeast Missouri standards, he was slightly out in front. Fundamentally paternalistic in outlook, he and Mary kept a number of good and faithful "negro" servants and tenants at Elmwood over the years, one of which, Thomas Higginbotham, was put through school at Lincoln Institute in Jefferson City by the couple. The words "Sambo" and "nigger" did casually appear in Houck's correspondence and no doubt conversation—as was, regrettably, common at the time—and when it came to labor, Louis considered southeast Missouri blacks oftentimes unreliable, even publicly criticizing the "American citizen of African descent who prefers coon hunting in the Little River swamp to other forms of endeavor."[6] Even so, as an old free-soiler and free market advocate, he frequently employed African American labor, which ran him afoul of many "old moss backs" in the Bootheel whose prejudicial ordinances often prohibited such contracts. More than once, Houck found his black crews driven off and his good name sullied.[7]

Then of course there were issues surrounding the notoriously poor physical condition of the Houck roads, sometimes derisively mocked as small-time "Jim Crow" roads locally.[8] Over time, though the quantity of track increased and construction times got considerably faster, the quality of his roads did not appreciably improve; according to state regulators, it actually declined in some instances. Even his most fierce critics acknowledged the natural obstacles in operating a railroad through Swampeast Missouri, and in comparison to some other abysmally constructed railroads in the region—for instance McCarty and Kerfoot's St. Louis, Kennett and Southern—the Houck roads could not be considered exactly atypical for rural Missouri during the era.

5. Leon J. Albert to Louis Houck, January 2, 1887, Houck Papers, Box 1508, Correspondence, 1887, Folder 3; *Cape Girardeau Democrat*, February 4, 1893.

6. *Missouri Republican*, November 2, 1869.

7. *Cape Girardeau Democrat*, May 13, 1897; 1880 Cape Girardeau County Census; 1900 Cape Girardeau County Census.

8. *St. Louis Republic*, June 10, 1896.

Yet it is likewise clear that Houck never truly transcended his own per-sonal limitations as a railroader, whether in regard to practical mechanical know-how, attention to detail, operating efficiency, or laissez-faire distaste for state oversight, taxes, and regulatory standards.[9] Throughout the 1890s, Missouri railroad commissioners found frequent complaints about the St. Louis, Cape Girardeau and Southern to be well-founded, in some places finding the railway "little more than two streaks of rust and the right of way." These sections of the first Houck road were judged by the state to be in "shaky condition" with sixty of the nearly one hundred miles of track consisting of shattered, splintered, twisted, old, and worn-out rails. At a time when more than 85 percent of Missouri railroads had been upgraded to steel rails, many miles of the Houck roads were still in iron. Only a few miles were ballasted, and nearly 50 percent of all bridges and trestles—some with apt nicknames like the "Crazy trestle"—along with the accompanying ditching and cattleguards were determined officially unfit.[10]

Houck's crews earned a dubious notoriety in the Bootheel for taking certain engineering liberties, such as piling downed trees in the deep swamps to hastily fashion roadbeds with all the stability, it seemed to pas-sengers, of a house of cards. One southeast Missourian would remember the almost amusement-park log-ride experience on the road from More-house to Morley, "known locally as the 'peavine' because it was so crooked." "At one place just south of Benton," the old-timer recollected, "Houck had felled two trees and laid them across a small creek, building his track on this structure instead of the regulation trestle. This caused the track to rise up in order to get on the trestle, and we recall the warning which the conductor always gave the passengers: 'Look out, she's going to jump!' in order that they might prepare themselves for the sudden change in the roadbed" and oncoming splash of water.[11]

Others frequently accused Houck of callously ignoring basic safety requirements in running his trains. On one particular occasion state inspectors reported that a Houck "freight train carrying passengers, the

9. Doherty, Jr., *Houck, Missouri Historian and Entrepreneur*, 39–41.

10. *Seventeenth Annual Report of the Railroad and Warehouse Commissioners of the State of Missouri for the Year Ending December 31, 1891* (Jefferson City, Mo.: Tribune Printing Company, 1892), 280; *Twelfth Annual Report of the Railroad Commissioners for the State of Missouri Being for the Year Ending December 31st 1886* (Jefferson City, Mo.: Tribune Print-ing Company, State Printers and Binders, 1887), 15.

11. *Charleston Enterprise Courier* (Charleston, Mo.), February 26, 1925; Bonnie Ste-penoff, "'The Last Tree Cut Down': The End of the Bootheel Frontier," 65; *Cape Girardeau Democrat*, March 24, 1900.

train consisting of about 18 cars, and with the locomotive in the center of the train, passed us at a speed of not less than 35 miles per hour. We are free to say that in all our railroad experience of many years, we never witnessed a more reckless disregard of reasonable precautions than was shown in this instance." Over this same stretch of track, officials took note that "in many places from two to five ties consecutively were found broken or completely rotten, intervals of from two to nine feet occurring without any support for the rail except the ground. In many places the rail is not spike[d] to the ties and is from one to two inches clear of them, the consequences being bad low joints, bent and warped rails, and the track utterly out of line and surface." Their conclusions leveled a fairly informative, and in regard to many locals a representative, indictment: "Derailments at these points are frequent, and that lives are not lost or persons injured thereby, is due more to luck than management."[12]

Precisely during these years when Houck's reputation appeared most under assault and his legacy most in jeopardy, the inimical series of small skirmishes with the Goulds finally erupted into an almost guerrilla-like war over possession of both the St. Louis, Cape Girardeau and Fort Smith and St. Louis, Kennett and Southern. In the defining moments of his professional career, Houck's adroit legal and extralegal maneuvering through the protracted receivership battles with the House of Gould, as well as equally deft narration, afforded an unprecedented opportunity to recast the public discourse surrounding his tarnishing image. While locked in mortal combat over the ownership of the railways he had virtually willed and finagled into existence, Houck advantageously reaped a veritable public relations bonanza by carefully crafting and zealously maintaining a "David vs. Goliath" biblical imagery that permanently solidified his legacy and larger-than-life folk hero status in southeast Missouri.

Southeast Missouri circled the wagons around him, celebrating his clear-eyed practical horse sense and straightforward resiliency in the face of an army of Wall Street capitalists and lawyers: traits his friend Willard Vandiver would one day express as the state's distinctive "Show-Me" character. For all of Louis Houck's commercial shortcomings—and there were indeed many—at the end of the day he was, after all, the devil that they knew. Put a slightly different way, "Jesus Christ," as an editor would

12. *Twenty-Third Annual Report of the Railroad and Warehouse Commissioners of the State of Missouri, Year Ending June 30, 1898* (Jefferson City, Mo.: Tribune Printing Company, State Printers and Binders, 1898), 38–40, quoted in Doherty, Jr., *Houck, Missouri Historian and Entrepreneur*, 38–39.

write after the great receivership fights, "made the way clear for the way-ward sinner and Louis Houck opened the gates of prosperity for Cape Girardeau and Southeast Missouri."[13]

Considering that the Houck roads ran parallel to, and intertwined with, both the Missouri Pacific's affiliated St. Louis, Iron Mountain and Southern and the Cotton Belt, competition and resultant friction between the roads was virtually assured. The first conflict between Houck and the Missouri Pacific had flared almost immediately after the road to Delta opened back in early 1881, with charges that the Iron Mountain was supplying inferior materials and breaking trackage agreements. After Houck avoided litigation by agreeing to a rails-for-bonds deal with the Iron Mountain, it was almost like prying the first olive out of a jar; other similar contracts soon followed in succession until Gould interests controlled roughly $80,000 of some of the first line's divisional bonds. What is more, while Houck and the Goulds were conducting their uneasy repartee in the late 1880s and early 1890s, the Mercantile Trust of New York was quietly becoming the trustee for $650,000 worth of the St. Louis, Cape Girardeau and Fort Smith's $1 million out-standing divisional bond debt. The Mercantile Trust was also under the directorate of the House of Gould.[14]

The year 1893 brought another economic panic to the United States, the last in a cycle of serious late-nineteenth-century depressions that left in its wake bankruptcies, foreclosures, and unemployment. Since the 1870s, innovative American businessmen had responded to these periodic finan-cial downturns by developing larger and more consolidated corporations in an effort to control production and hold competition in check. These spectacular monopolies, led by the likes of John D. Rockefeller's Standard Oil, took advantage of hard times by making use of their considerable advantages in sheer size, ability to offer cheaper rates, and political influ-ence to buy out financially unhealthy smaller firms. In this way they became at once vertically integrated—combining all the functions of a given industry within a single centralized company—and horizontally integrated through corporate mergers.

Thus was the case in 1893 when a "Great Merger Wave"—lasting until the economy fully recovered by 1904—broke over the country and threat-ened to engulf the St. Louis, Cape Girardeau and Fort Smith. The exact level

13. *Cape Girardeau Democrat*, June 28, 1902, June 13, 1903.
14. Wollman, "Strange Story," 2; Doherty, Jr., *Houck, Missouri Historian and Entrepre-neur*, 24.

of premeditation on the part of the Goulds, or a precise timetable for their strategy, is unknown, but it nonetheless appears fairly certain that like their colossal corporate brethren, they seized the day to finally horizontally integrate Houck's rival little feeder line into the Missouri Pacific fold.

Since his peak year in 1891, Houck had watched his St. Louis, Cape Girardeau and Fort Smith's earnings plummet. By 1893 passenger earnings were down $16,000 and freight earnings down $30,000. Recession, operating expenses, and what he perceived to be unfair state interference were partly to blame. New state taxes of between 8 to 13 percent on smaller railroads—a rate Houck considered discriminatory and "little better than highway robbery"—along with additional directives to reinvest earnings toward the improvement of deplorable conditions on the line had swollen the cost of running the road by some $25,000. This left the one-hundred-mile railway's net earnings at approximately $17 per mile or $17,000 a year. Consequently, interest payment on the million-dollar bonded indebtedness lapsed for more than twenty-four months. Houck was certainly ripe for the picking. As Gould attorney Henry Wollman later concluded, the St. Louis, Cape Girardeau and Fort Smith "was about a hundred miles long, but if it had been ten thousand miles long, it could not have been the subject or object of more or bitterer litigation than it was."[15]

Round one opened on March 1, 1893, with the Mercantile Trust bringing a suit of foreclosure on the allegedly insolvent Houck road. Two days later, George Gould, having assumed control of his father's interests, expedited the process by dispatching Missouri Pacific attorney E. G. Merriam to Bloomfield, Missouri, to formally initiate receivership proceedings. Since a railroad could sue, or be sued, in any county in which it operated, in choosing Bloomfield, the Missouri Pacific obviously engaged in what lawyers today would call "forum shopping"; that is, they searched for a judge thought to be antagonistic to Houck.[16] And sure enough, once Merriam entered his petition in the Stoddard County Circuit Court, Judge John G. Wear granted the provisional appointment of Eli Klotz as receiver of the St. Louis, Cape Girardeau and Fort Smith.

A receiver is a court-appointed custodian to oversee a bankrupt company's financial reorganization. In the grand scheme of things, a receivership seeks to nurse the ailing corporation along until reorganization can

15. H. Martin Williams to Louis Houck, April 2, 1891, Houck Papers, Box 1511, Correspondence, 1891 April J-Z, Folder 5; Doherty, Jr., *Houck, Missouri Historian and Entrepreneur*, 24; Wollman, "Strange Story," 2; *St. Louis Republic*, March 15, 1893.
16. Ronald S. Reed, Jr., to Joel P. Rhodes, July 26, 2006, in possession of author.

cure its fiscal ills.[17] Considering that Klotz was ostensibly a disinterested Piedmont, Missouri, man with only a passing interest in railroading, this appears to be another cunning legal move because it introduced a local, nonthreatening character—someone or something not named Gould or the Missouri Pacific—as a central protagonist in an otherwise therapeutic process. Merriam's unconvincing sentiments before the court gave voice to the ruse: ". . . all I want is simply for them to pay their honest debts," the plaintiff maintained. "I have applied for a receiver so that I and the rest of the bondholders can get what is due them. . . . This is not an attempt of the Missouri Pacific to seize the road."[18]

No doubt aware of the impending likelihood of a receivership for his faltering road, Louis still heard no advance notification of the Klotz appointment and in fact first learned of it via a hasty telegraph from his brother George in Bloomfield. Although the timing seems to have caught him off guard, he instantly put two and two together: a Gould lawyer representing investors who held bonds on only a few of the railroad's divisions had secured a receiver for the entire railway. As Moses Whybark, one of Louis's long-time attorneys from Marble Hill, extrapolated, "the Merriam case is simply the old Fisk [Jay Gould's partner in crime James "Jubilee Jim" Fisk] and Gould game played by them for years in New York, to get possession of a railroad, and then wreck it, and buy it for a song. They are trying the same game in Mo. with this road. They had Judge [corrupt Tammany Hall adjudicator Albert] Cardozo in N.Y. and they have his duplicate [Wear] here."[19]

Within forty-eight hours, Houck orchestrated an ingenious counterattack to forestall what he perceived to be an obvious preemptive assault. Since Judge Wear's appointment of Klotz was temporary, or provisional, and would not become permanent until a required bond could be posted on March 13, Louis rousted Judge Alexander Ross of the Cape Girardeau Common Pleas Court out of bed to petition for the appointment of a permanent receiver.[20] In a nifty legal move years ahead of its time, he asked the common pleas court for a "friendly receivership," someone sympathetic to his railroad who would help conserve the property. Who would

17. William Z. Ripley, *Railroads: Finance and Organization,* 372.

18. *St. Louis Post-Dispatch,* March 11, 1893; James Irvine to Louis Houck, March 8, 1893, Houck Papers, 1893 Box 1513, Correspondence, March H-R, Folder 18.

19. Moses Whybark to Louis Houck, November 27, 1893, Houck Papers, 1893 Box 1514, Correspondence, November N-Z, Folder 21; Houck, "Some Reminiscences," 40.

20. Franklin, "Former Pioneer Traces Early History."

be more congenial than the president of the line, Louis Houck? Ross agreed with this line of reasoning, and, muddying the waters dramatically, named Houck as permanent receiver of his own railroad.[21]

The St. Louis, Cape Girardeau and Fort Smith now had two receivers, one appointed provisionally by a circuit court and one permanently by a common pleas court. But the plot only continued to thicken. While Houck's hastily assembled legal counsel of Madison R. Smith, William H. Miller, Moses Whybark, and Robert B. Oliver acquainted themselves with the case, over in Bloomfield Judge Wear serendipitously became extremely ill the week before he was to make Klotz's appointment permanent on the thirteenth. Since Wear could not hear the large docket scheduled in his court room, members of the local bar attending this term of the circuit court—in accordance with Missouri law and apparently with Wear's naive blessing—elected a "Special Judge," with all the same powers as the regular judge, to transact the remaining judicial business; their choice was a local Stoddard County attorney, George Houck. George faithfully took the bench and efficiently disposed of all the matters that came before him during the week, some three hundred cases in all.

On Sunday, March 12, the day before Wear was scheduled to return from convalescing at his Poplar Bluff home, Louis summoned George to an emergency palaver with his attorneys at the depot in Delta. The brothers were close—perhaps more so than any other of Bartholomeaus's and Anna's children—and they had grown increasingly reliant on each other, it appears, after George's wife, Mary, passed away in 1892. George handled the bulk of Louis's real estate and legal matters in the Bootheel and his adolescent sons George, Jr., and Rudolph lived a large portion of the year at Elmwood. Just six years younger than Louis and now a well-established commercial lawyer and banker in his own right, George most likely balked at what his older brother asked of him on the platform that evening. But as he later made clear, "his brother's private fortune was in it (the litigation) and . . . all he had was at stake." Therefore it was "natural" for George to do whatever it took.[22]

21. Houck based his strategy on what he believed to be a recent precedent set by his friend Solon Humphreys's receivership of the Wabash, St. Louis and Pacific. Even though the Missouri Supreme Court eventually ruled against him on this particular point of law in the 1890s, within a generation the appointment of the former president of a road to be a "friendly receivership" actually became fairly common. See Bradley Hansen, "The People's Welfare and the Origins of Corporate Reorganization: The Wabash Receivership Reconsidered," 374–405; Wollman, "Strange Story," 5–6.

22. *The State* ex rel. *Klotz vs. Ross, et al.*, Missouri Reports 118 (November 9, 1893): 67.

At just past eight o'clock on the morning of March 13, George opened the Stoddard County Circuit Court. After sentencing two men to the penitentiary, he turned to M. R. Smith and William Miller, who had spent the night in his Bloomfield office, and went through the pretense of asking them if they had any motions to file. In no more than thirty minutes he considered their lengthy petitions to vacate Wear's appointment, which he had also already read the previous night, before granting a perfunctory annulment of Klotz's temporary receivership. After bringing the gavel down and promptly adjourning the court for the rest of the term at nine o'clock, Judge Houck excused himself from Bloomfield to attend to personal business in the northern part of Stoddard County.[23]

When Wear returned that same morning aboard the 8:15 train to Dexter, following the roughly hour-long hack ride into Bloomfield, he and Merriam's recently arrived counsel recognized that they had been bamboozled. Indignantly, Wear immediately expunged Judge Houck's orders. And seeing that Louis's lawyers had likewise skedaddled from Stoddard County and could mount no objections, he in turn reestablished Klotz's appointment and empowered him to immediately take physical possession of the railroad. The judge also granted a motion for a change of venue from Houck's southeast Missouri to the Iron County Circuit Court in Ironton, widely considered to be "an Iron Mountain R.R. company town" well within the Missouri Pacific's sphere of influence.[24]

In preparation for the inevitable showdown, Houck immediately obtained a restraining injunction from Judge Ross at the Common Pleas Court to block Klotz when he arrived in Cape Girardeau. Besides this delaying action, Louis also began, on the advice of James Irvine, a supportive New York bondholder, to gird his loins for the long haul. "Though your move was well conceived and well carried out . . . I am sure you will find that the battle is not over," Irvine had warned. Nor, the two men agreed, would this contest likely be won by any one skirmish alone; conceivably it could be

23. A good deal of the narrative regarding the receivership is quoted and paraphrased directly from "Louis Houck Memoirs," much like many passages of William Doherty's *Louis Houck: Missouri Historian and Entrepreneur.* Therefore, often our narratives are very similar, both remaining faithful to Houck's original unpublished manuscript. "Louis Houck Memoirs," 266–70; Wollman, "Strange Story," 2–3; *St. Louis Republic,* March 15, 1893; George Houck to Louis Houck, March 7, 1893, Houck Papers, 1893 Box 1513, Correspondence, March A–H, Folder 17; Doherty, Jr., *Houck, Missouri Historian and Entrepreneur,* 25; Doherty, Jr., "Opponent and Imitator of Jay Gould," 50.

24. *The State* ex rel. *Klotz vs. Ross, et al.,* 68–69; *Cape Girardeau Democrat,* September 16, 1893; George Reynolds to Louis Houck, September 7, 1893, Houck Papers, Box 1514, Correspondence, September, Folder 14.

expected to run for several years.[25] Hence, Houck rallied friendly bondholders into two committees, one in the Midwest and another in the East, to
stand by him in a defensive alliance against Gould's strike. In like manner
he started keeping a confidential notebook under lock and key to maintain
an official record of all spending outside of ordinary operating expenses. In
particular he carefully logged all payments of principal or interest on the
bonded debt in case Coffin and Stanton—by now considered "Wreckers"
firmly on "the other side"—doctored the books. Against the recommendations of his lawyers, he also fired off the first of many letters to the editors of
the *St. Louis Republic* and *Cape Girardeau Democrat* to carry the fight into the
newspapers.

When Eli Klotz reached Cape Girardeau on March 15 with Missouri
Pacific lawyers to seize the St. Louis, Cape Girardeau and Fort Smith, they
were abruptly met at the depot by deputy sheriff Henry Kopper, who in
his imperfect German-English served the paperwork barring Klotz from
interfering in any way with the operation of the road or its receiver, Louis
Houck, in managing it. From there the group, escorted by a very friendly
and accommodating Kopper, marched directly up the steep sandstone
steps of the Common Pleas Court House—by this time remodeled with its
present wings and portico—to lodge their request that Judge Ross vacate
Houck's receiver appointment. Finding Ross "irascible," the interlopers
eventually beat a hasty retreat after the judge "rudely and emphatically"
slammed his fist on his desk to announce the matter settled. Back on their
Missouri Pacific train bound for Jefferson City, Gould's legal team prepared a *writ of mandamus* for the state supreme court, a legal device to force
Ross into surrendering the road to Klotz.[26]

For the next three years, as a common pleas court, three circuit courts,
the Missouri Supreme Court, and the U.S. Supreme Court eventually considered the unglamorous legal details involved in this case, local citizens
read "with no little interest" wildly hyperbolic newspaper accounts
depicting the epic struggle between the great Missouri Pacific and Louis
Houck over the very fate of railroading in southeast Missouri. The *St. Louis
Republic* correctly billed the conflict as "one of the most interesting and
sensational railroad fights ever inaugurated in Missouri."[27] Indeed, from

---

25. James Irvine to Louis Houck, March 13, 1893, Houck Papers, 1893 Box 1513, Correspondence, March H-R, Folder 18.
26. "Louis Houck Memoirs," 270–72.
27. *Cape Girardeau Democrat*, March 18, May 6, 1893; J. M. Seibert to Louis Houck,
April 11, 1893, Houck Papers, 1893 Box 1513, Correspondence, April R-Z, Folder 22;
Doherty, Jr., *Houck, Missouri Historian and Entrepreneur*, 26.

a strictly legal perspective, Houck's receivership points up the dynamic role of American legal institutions in sorting through the problematic nature of rapid industrialization and adjusting law to commercial changes of the late nineteenth century. At a time when corporate cases were eclipsing personal cases on court dockets, a certain "laissez-faire constitutionalism" prevailed reflecting the general public's conservative anxiety that undue government intervention in the economy would deprive businessmen of their personal property and retard continued expansion. In this regard, the fundamental questions before the courts kept hinging primarily on whether duly elected Judge Wear in Stoddard County had the legal authority to set aside temporary Judge Houck's order. But in reaching their respective verdicts, the Missouri Supreme Court in particular helped break ground in examining more substantive legal implications such as the appointment of a friendly receiver or the graceful pirouette Louis and George employed in defining the corporation-as-person.[28]

When also considering the conflict of interest between the Houck brothers and other fertile grounds for collusion, the inseparable public outpouring of support perhaps likewise reveals what historian David Thelen identified as the typical Missourian's fiercely independent resistance to modernizing influences invading the state. "Interest is once again revived in the energetic little gentleman (for Mr. Houck is large only in brain and bank account)," the *Charleston Democrat* crowed at the onset of what the *St. Louis Republic* cast as a referendum "as to whether the small road can resist the boa constrictor proclivities of [Vice President] George Gould, who is said to crave the small road with the whetted appetite of a mighty serpent of the tropics."[29]

In celebrating Louis's opening victories against such a predator, the *Cape Girardeau Democrat* delighted its readers by borrowing symbolism recognizable in the African American community as the "trickster" Brer Rabbit outwitting Brer Fox. Klotz "imagined that our lawyers and court officers were a lot of numskulls who would tremble at the sight of a couple of big railroad lawyers," the editor chortled, "but they were greatly surprised." The Missouri Pacific attorneys were in fact heavyweights, including Henry S. Priest, in time a U.S. district judge, former Pennsylvania Congressman

28. Benedict, "Law and the Constitution in the Gilded Age," 289–303.
29. David Thelen, *Paths of Resistance: Tradition and Dignity in Industrializing Missouri; Cape Girardeau Democrat*, reprinted from *Perryville Sun*, January 28, 1893; *Cape Girardeau Democrat*, reprinted from *Charleston Democrat*, March 4, 1893; *Cape Girardeau Democrat*, reprinted from *St. Louis Republic*, March 18, 1893.

Alexander G. Cochran, and onetime Congressman Martin L. Clardy. But as the *Democrat* warned, just "because our lawyers"—now actually including George Reynolds and Houck's old boss John W. Noble—"reside in the backwoods and live on bacon and turnip greens is no indication that they are not versed in the law."[30]

When the Missouri Supreme Court heard the *mandamus* case in June 1893, Houck's counsel ably argued that the powers of a special judge were as complete as a regular judge, and the latter had no power to reopen a term of court after it had been properly closed by the former. To cover all possible objections, they also reasoned that George Houck's order presented no violation of state statutes preventing a judge from ruling when he was related to either litigant because George was after all kin to Louis, not the St. Louis, Cape Girardeau and Fort Smith.[31] All but one of the state's highest judges agreed, upholding Judge Houck's actions. The lone dissenter was Thomas A. Sherwood, a thorn in Louis's side during the Wayne County land case and brother-in-law of Judge Wear with long-rumored connections to the Missouri Pacific.

The triumph sustained, temporarily at least, Houck's position as receiver, and accompanying newspaper accounts continued to elevate him into one of the most compelling figures in the state. The time had come and passed for the Missouri Pacific to "put up or hush up," the *Cape Girardeau Democrat* rejoiced. "It was a case of brains against money and brains won." Hopefully now the "Gould combination" had "given up Southeast Missouri to our own railroad king." By the end of the year local Democrats, believing the victory had overcome the political liability of being known as a railroad baron, began calling for Houck to run for Congress.[32]

In spite of this first Supreme Court victory, Houck later recalled, "the main litigation then started." Now, Madison Smith soberly declared, "we have war against the Goulds."[33] Inside of a month, Missouri Pacific attorneys filed another suit with the Missouri Supreme Court, this time a *writ of*

30. *Cape Girardeau Democrat,* March 11, 15, 1893; Wollman, "Strange Story," 4.

31. *The State* ex rel. *Klotz vs. Ross, et al.,* 23–79; Wollman, "Strange Story," 4; "Louis Houck Memoirs," 273; George Reynolds to Louis Houck, April 27, 1893, Houck Papers, 1893 Box 1513, Correspondence, April R-Z, Folder 22.

32. *Cape Girardeau Democrat,* July 1, November 25, 1893; A. J. Kerfoot to Louis Houck, February 3, 1894, Houck Papers, 1894 Box 1515, Correspondence, February R-Z, Folder 8.

33. Henry L. Lamb to Louis Houck, May 11, 1893, Houck Papers, 1893 Box 1514, Correspondence, May G-M, Folder 2; "Louis Houck Memoirs," 273; M. R. Smith to Louis Houck, June 30, 1893, Houck Papers, 1893 Box 1514, Correspondence, Folder 6.

prohibition against Judge Ross on the grounds that the Cape Girardeau Common Pleas had no jurisdiction to appoint Houck as receiver and, moreover, that by law a corporation could not apply for a friendly receiver.[34]

The second round of the receivership fight revolved around these two legal questions, which Louis admitted to be "serious and important." "The case," Moses Whybark concurred, "will necessarily be a lengthy opinion, as the subject is all new, and the authorities not systemetized [*sic*], and it will take time to classify, and anylize [*sic*] them." Any decision would undoubtedly be "learned and scholarly," "intricate, and important."[35] Still Houck's lawyers arrived for the proceedings fairly confident. Public opinion was mobilizing in their favor, and they figured precedent to be on their side given that in a previous case involving the Wabash railroad, the legality of that line's friendly receiver had not been directly sanctioned, but neither had it been attacked by the supreme court of Missouri.

Their firm legal ground eroded, however, toward the end of the 1893 term of the court, when Louis began correctly sensing that the seven justices on the bench were increasingly divided and the tide was turning against them. So to once again "provide against every contingency"—that is, to keep physical possession of the road as long as possible while the supreme court deliberated and also hedge his bets in the eventuality that the court ruled against him—Houck nimbly instructed R. B. Oliver to break off from the main battle and outflank the Goulds. Even before round two concluded in Jefferson City, 235 miles away Houck and Oliver brought forward Leo Doyle, a heretofore obscure local trustee for the bondholders, to file an independent suit in the Cape Girardeau County Circuit Court to begin a totally new foreclosure proceeding on the railroad and yet again appoint Louis Houck as receiver.[36]

In the meantime, Louis of course continued his coordinated campaign, principally in the press, to ensure that Missourians appreciated the depths of the "evil" conspiracy being waged against him by this "'gang' of desperados, headed," as it was, "by that hybrid outlaw, the 'sporting'

34. To provide a legal forum that was not dependent on a circuit riding judge, Common Pleas Courts were established in Missouri river communities such as Cape Girardeau, Hannibal, and Louisiana, where the county seats were already set in towns farther inland.

35. Moses Whybark to Louis Houck, February 9, 1894, Houck Papers, 1894 Box 1515, Correspondence, February R-Z, Folder 8.

36. "Louis Houck Memoirs," 268, 273, 274, 275, 276. In this case the railroad had effectively mortgaged its property to the trustee who held it, as their agent, as security for the bondholders in case of default. Ronald S. Reed, Jr., to Joel P. Rhodes, August 31, 2006, in possession of author.

Judge."[37] Houck had it on good authority that the "usurper" Judge Wear, rumored to be a drunkard, was "after blood" and with a "malicious thirst" sought to "disfigure" all those in the Houck camp, in particular the legal practice of George Houck, whom it was said he now watched "as does a vulture his prey."[38] More damning, it turns out that not only was Wear related to Supreme Court Justice Sherwood by marriage but also the Stoddard County judge had been a former attorney and agent for the Missouri Pacific as well as a personal friend of that "Missouri Pacific tool" Eli Klotz. Perhaps this fiendish lineage helped shed light on why some unscrupulous state official authorized a surprise State Railroad and Warehouse Commission inspection of the Houck road, knowing full well that the unfortunate receivership difficulties had disrupted service and delayed employee payroll for months?[39] Yet even those connivances paled in comparison to the pièce de résistance: Wear's son Charles was currently facing murder charges in the death of Charles Leal . . . an Iron Mountain railroad employee. Even if Louis did not need to spell it out for the people, he did anyway. Forget impartiality, Houck postulated. To protect his son, Wear might sell his soul to the devil, or at least to George Gould.[40]

All of Houck's maneuvering notwithstanding, the Missouri Supreme Court granted Merriam's prohibition request by a split 4–3 decision in April 1894. The state's high court declared that in fact a corporation on its own motion could not ask for the appointment of a receiver and that a common pleas court had no equity jurisdiction to appoint such a receiver. Consequently, Ross's appointment was declared void and thus Houck

37. C. W. Dunifer to Louis Houck, July 7, 1893, Houck Papers, 1893 Box 1514, Correspondence, July A-K, Folder 7; O. L. Garrison to Louis Houck, May 27, 1895, Houck Papers, 1895 Box 1517, Correspondence, May A-H, Folder 13.

38. George Houck to Louis Houck, May 22, 1893, Houck Papers, 1893 Box 1514, Correspondence, May G-M, Folder 2; George Houck to Louis Houck, June 27, 1893, Houck Papers, 1893 Box 1514, Correspondence, June G-M, Folder 5.

39. H. W. Hickman to Louis Houck, May 3, 1893, Houck Papers, 1893 Box 1514, Correspondence, May N-Z, Folder 3; Cape Girardeau Democrat, August 5, 1893.

40. Indeed, a tangled web of overlapping receiverships, murder, questionable jurisdiction, partiality, and conflict of interest bound together many of the principals involved in these cases. In particular, Charles Wear had been indicted by a Butler County grand jury on first-degree murder charges for the death of Charles Leal in 1893. Despite using Missouri Pacific attorneys for his defense, Wear was convicted of second-degree murder and sentenced to thirty-five years in the penitentiary. In 1898 the Missouri Supreme Court, with Justice Sherwood still on the bench, overturned Wear's conviction on a legal technicality and he was finally acquitted. R. F. Walker to Louis Houck, November 4, 1893, Houck Papers, 1893 Box 1514, Correspondence, Folder 20; St. Louis Republic, March 15, 1893, June 20, 1896; Cape Girardeau Democrat, January 25, February 1, 1896.

was ordered to turn over the St. Louis, Cape Girardeau and Fort Smith to Eli Klotz.[41]

In appearance, Houck remained undaunted by the disappointing verdict, except perhaps for his hair, which he sometimes unconsciously rumpled when thinking. Swiftly regrouping his lawyers, Louis laid down simple marching orders: he refused to recognize Klotz and under no circumstances intended to surrender the railroad. Only months after he openly wept in the Dunklin County swamp, Louis coolly commenced round three in 1894 with superb field of vision, anticipating his enemies' next moves and taking the fight to them in several theaters of battle at once with a coordinated litigious flurry of retooled motions, appeals, and statutes.

Their immediate concern focused on tangible control of the road. Here Houck held the high ground, firmly entrenched as the physical custodian of the line. All along the St. Louis, Cape Girardeau and Fort Smith, telegraphs went out to agents cautioning them to be on guard "against surprises and [to] repel efforts to obtain forcible possession."[42] The situation back in New York posed other serious problems that begged their own quick retort. Eastern bondholders were naturally extremely confused by the twisting and turning receivership saga west of the Mississippi. It was primarily for this reason that Houck had initiated the "Reorganization Committee" to shore up support there and to streamline communication. But lo and behold, Louis's allies had already detected a scheme hatched within that committee involving William Edward Coffin, Walter Stanton, and Newman Erb—working "hand and glove together"—to take advantage of the situation by bullying investors into turning over all their Houck road bonds to the brokerage firm. Making matters worse, it appeared that "the Gould people [had] joined forces with the Erb crowd" in a consolidated plan to then corner the market on the St. Louis, Cape Girardeau and Fort Smith's bonded debt. If this came to pass, the Erb and Gould alliance would certainly move to trump any future Missouri legal impasses by asking a federal court to step in and assign a new receiver.[43] Time was of the essence.

---

41. *State* ex rel. *Merriam, Petitioner, vs. Ross, Judge, et al.,* Missouri Reports 122 (June 4, 1894): 435–78; Wollman, "Strange Story," 5, 6; George Reynolds to Louis Houck, March 24, 1894, Houck Papers, 1894 Box 1515, Correspondence, March M-S, Folder 11; *Cape Girardeau Democrat,* June 16, 1894.

42. Moses Whybark to Louis Houck, March 9, 1894, Houck Papers, 1894 Box 1515, Correspondence, March S-Z, Folder 12; George Reynolds and John Noble to Louis Houck, June 27, 1893, Houck Papers, 1893 Box 1514, Correspondence, June M-Z, Folder 6; Wollman, "Strange Story," 6.

43. Henry L. Lamb to Louis Houck, May 19, 1893, Houck Papers, 1893 Box 1514, Correspondence, May G-M, Folder 2; George Reynolds to Louis Houck, April 27, 1894, Houck Papers, 1894 Box 1515, Correspondence, April R-Z, Folder 15.

Facing the possibility of hefty contempt of court charges, Houck—evidently "in a contemptuous frame of mind"—directed R. B. Oliver to fight the Missouri Supreme Court through the circuit court by pressing the Leo Doyle lawsuit.[44] In order to address the issues just called into question by the higher court, he maintained that the litigation this time should explicitly stress the facts that, one, unlike previous petitions for a receiver this revised suit originated with the trustee representing aggrieved bondholders, not the corporation itself, and, two, it had been entered in the Cape Girardeau County Circuit Court, not the common pleas court.

Madison Roswell Smith, like Oliver a former state senator who had also aligned himself with Houck on the branch penitentiary deal, traveled north to personally oversee a motion still pending in the Iron County Circuit Court, the original Wear appointment of Klotz since removed from Stoddard County. The objective here, to vacate Klotz's designation as receiver, relied heavily on Houck's premise that a court ought not allow bondholders with investments in only comparatively small divisions of a larger railroad to procure a receiver for the whole because it would effectively, in his words, "segregate a line of road, and to do so, would be to break it up, and render it practically useless."[45]

Noble and Reynolds—facing their own contempt-of-court penalties—headed to Jefferson City to appeal the writ of prohibition verdict back to the Missouri Supreme Court. Finding no satisfaction there, they pushed the matter all the way to the U.S. Supreme Court. When friction over egos and payment—too much of one and too little of the other—eventually led to Reynolds being replaced, the feisty Smith enthusiastically put his "war paint on" and joined Noble in Washington.[46]

Yet despite Louis's handcrafted brief that sought redress from what he perceived to be the Missouri court's violation of his railroad's Fourteenth Amendment rights—that no state shall deprive any person of life, liberty, or property without due process of law—the highest court in the land declined to hear the appeal, finding there to be no constitutional questions

44. M. R. Smith to Louis Houck, March 23, 1895, Houck Papers, 1895 Box 1517, Correspondence, March R-Z, Folder 8; *Cape Girardeau Democrat*, January 29, 1896.

45. M. R. Smith to Louis Houck, July 10, 1894, Houck Papers, 1894 Box 1516, Correspondence, July N-S, Folder 3; George Reynolds to Louis Houck, April 7, 1894, Houck Papers, 1894 Box 1515, Correspondence, April H-R, Folder 14; Wollman, "Strange Story," 7; Doherty, Jr., *Houck, Missouri Historian and Entrepreneur*, 29.

46. George Reynolds to Louis Houck, December 1, 1894, Houck Papers, 1894 Box 1516, Correspondence, December M-Z, Folder 18; M. R. Smith to Louis Houck, December 20, 1894, George Reynolds to Louis Houck, January 15, 1895, Houck Papers, 1895 Box 1516, Correspondence, January L-R, Folder 21.

involved. In short order the Iron County Circuit Court overruled his motion there as well. So too did the Missouri Supreme Court dismiss that ensuing appeal on the grounds that a receivership appeal could not be carried from a circuit court to the supreme court.[47]

Like their client, the forceful men who made up Houck's legal counsel did not take very kindly to these damaging reversals. They felt reasonably sure that Judge Henry C. Riley of the Cape Girardeau County Circuit Court would rule favorably in the Doyle suit. Still, in the best-case scenario, if Riley once again appointed Houck receiver as expected, this would waste valuable time by only landing them back at square one—two receivers appointed by two courts—with access to the state supreme court now legally closed off. Even Noble, whose "pride [had been] considerably aroused" by facing off against Gould's men, and who relished the fight, considered this the end of the line and refused to pursue litigation any further.[48]

For his part, Louis stubbornly would not stay beaten. With all eyes on Riley's court, he, Oliver, and Smith "silently" went back to the drawing board for one final end-around. In Smith's words, they intended to "make out of this, not only a legal fight, but . . . [to] carry it into the politics of the State." With the assistance of state senator Robert G. Madison of Festus and state auditor James M. Seibert—good Democrats all—they worked behind the scenes throughout late 1894 to secure a new statute in the state legislature that opened a pathway of appeal from a circuit court to the supreme court on legal questions regarding the appointment of a receiver.[49]

When Riley indeed named Houck as receiver in February 1895, the ambitious combination of plans came together and dominos then began falling Louis's way in rapid succession. Having satisfactorily strengthened the weak portions of his cases from the first two rounds and restored access to

47. John Noble to Louis Houck, March 5, 1895, Houck Papers, 1895 Box 1517, Correspondence, March A- F, Folder 5; Wollman, "Strange Story," 6, 7; Doherty, Jr., *Houck, Missouri Historian and Entrepreneur*, 29; *Missouri ex rel. Merriam vs. St. Louis, Cape Girardeau and Fort Smith Railway Company*, U.S. Reports 126 (January 22, 1895): 478; *Merriam vs. the St. Louis, Cape Girardeau and Fort Smith Railway Company*, Missouri Reports 2 (January 22, 1895): 445–48.

48. "Louis Houck Memoirs," 277; M. R. Smith to Louis Houck, December 20, 1894, Houck Papers, 1895 Box 1516, Correspondence, January L-R, Folder 21.

49. M. R. Smith to Louis Houck, April 16, 1894, Houck Papers, James M. Seibert to Louis Houck, April 11, 1894, Houck Papers, Box 1515, Correspondence, April R-Z, Folder 15; "Louis Houck Memoirs," 279. The law was Senate Bill 211, which Governor William Stone signed on April 11, 1895. See *Journal of the Senate of 38th General Assembly of Missouri* (1895), 437, 853; Doherty, Jr., "Missouri Interests of Louis Houck," 118n39.

the state supreme court, Louis immediately petitioned the high court again that on the wishes of his bondholders Klotz's appointment should be permanently vacated. Missouri Pacific attorneys, conceivably sneering, objected that such appeals had already been disallowed. Only then did Madison Smith call the courtroom's attention to the new Missouri statute on the books. "Very greatly astonished" was how Louis acerbically remembered their reaction. "Their whole plan of war was destroyed."[50]

The Missouri Supreme Court ruled a final time on the convoluted matter of *Merriam vs. St. Louis, Cape Girardeau and Fort Smith Railway* in 1896. In legal terms, the court held that contrary to Merriam's original intention, a receiver could not be appointed for an entire railroad line on the petition of plaintiffs that controlled only a portion of the divisional bonds on just two sections of the line. In other words, since the Mercantile Trust held bonds on roughly twenty-six of the one hundred miles of track, they were not legally entitled to appoint Eli Klotz to oversee the other seventy-four. Further, the supreme court upheld the Cape Girardeau Circuit Court's appointment of Louis Houck as receiver on the grounds that Leo Doyle, the trustee who petitioned the court, represented a mix of bondholders with interests in the whole road.[51]

The court, the *Cape Girardeau Democrat* announced to the eager public, "redeemed itself from the odium cast upon it by some of the people of the great state of Missouri—to wit: that it belonged body and soul to the big railroad corporations. It has decided that George Gould—big as he is—cannot legally in the grand state of Missouri swallow up one of our citizens." Similar to Jay Gould himself, Houck had brilliantly manipulated the legal system to score a major victory almost at the eleventh hour.[52] His definitive appointment as receiver of his own railroad assured for the foreseeable future the integrity of the St. Louis, Cape Girardeau and Fort Smith, finally freeing up valuable resources and paving the way for a new start.

For all intents and purposes, after the Pemiscot railroad had been completed in early 1895 and officially absorbed into the St. Louis, Kennett and Southern system that same year, Louis deferred most concrete expansion plans for the Houck roads until after dispensing of the Klotz threat. James Brooks continued to survey from Hunter, Missouri, to Mammoth Springs

50. "Louis Houck Memoirs," 278, 279.
51. *Merriam vs. St. Louis, Cape Girardeau and Fort Smith Railway*, Missouri Reports 136 (December 1, 1896): 145–69; *Cape Girardeau Democrat*, June 27, 1896; Wollman, "Strange Story," 8.
52. *Cape Girardeau Democrat*, June 22, 1896; Doherty, Jr., "Opponent and Imitator of Jay Gould," 46–56.

and then on to Harrison in northwest Arkansas in the summer of 1895, but nothing ultimately came of it. For several years, Houck had also been corresponding with lumber titans Himmelberger and Harrison along with C. A. Boynton regarding an anticipated southern extension to their substantial sawmills in the Bootheel.[53] But considering he stood a real chance of losing the St. Louis, Cape Girardeau and Fort Smith, these ventures would have been foolhardy at the time. Not so in 1896, and upon learning of the Missouri Supreme Court's decisive verdict, Louis once again looked forward to concentrating on laying more iron.

Incredibly, though, even before the court's decision officially came down, another acrimonious and involved receivership contest erupted, this time over possession of the one-hundred-mile St. Louis, Kennett and Southern. When this second showdown began, southeast Missourians immediately understood the matter to be a renewed offensive in the same running battle; newspaper headlines announced yet "another move of the Gould people to break down Louis Houck . . . and intimidate all others from attempting to build any other railroad in this section."[54] To be sure, Louis, as a matter of strategy, did nothing to dispel this particular rendering. And in truth, the name Gould was nominally attached.

For this go-around, the St. Louis Southwestern, or "Cotton Belt," now emerged as the buccaneer in the public's eyes. By 1896 this oft-reorganized railroad operated well within the Gould directorate with both sons George and Edwin exercising palpable influence in its management, the latter as vice-president. Since building the Pemiscot road, Houck's people felt sure the Cotton Belt had been "aching for trouble": it had hired locals to tear up St. Louis, Kennett and Southern track, refused to transfer rolling stock, threatened to build into Cape, and generally harassed the smaller railway whenever possible.[55]

Still, despite the Goulds' direct or indirect association—and the promotional hay Houck made from it—this second receivership episode appears more likely to have had its origins not so much in the context of the Great Merger Wave as in local sour grapes and a personal vendetta.

On April 13, 1896, A. J. Kerfoot, the erstwhile superintendent of the St. Louis, Kennett and Southern whom Houck had essentially inherited as

53. "Louis Houck Memoirs," 280; Isaac Himmelberger to Louis Houck, September 15, 1893, Houck Papers, 1893 Box 1514, Correspondence, September A-H, Folder 13.
54. *Cape Girardeau Democrat*, April 18, 1896.
55. A. J. Kerfoot to Louis Houck, October 6, 1894, Houck Papers, 1894 Box 1516, Correspondence, October S-Z, Folder 13; James P. Forbess to Louis Houck, March 21, 1895, Houck Papers, 1895 Box 1517, Correspondence, March F-K, Folder 6.

part of the purchase of that road, filed suit in the Dunklin County Circuit Court requesting that a receiver be appointed for the railway. While seeking the same outcome—the removal of Houck—Kerfoot's petition differed materially from Merriam's, where a bondholder had sought a receiver for nonpayment of interest. The St. Louis, Kennett and Southern admittedly had no matured outstanding indebtedness and if anything continued to be "a splendid paying property." Instead, Kerfoot was a former employee who still owned stock in the railroad and claimed that for reasons of mismanagement, not insolvency, the company would have to be placed in receivership to untangle the mess. In presenting his case—to none other than presiding judge John G. Wear—Kerfoot enumerated a litany of Houck shortcomings as president of the road, including terms that amounted to breach of contract, fraud, embezzlement, misappropriation of company funds, and wrongful termination.[56]

This last charge, the most sensitive and central, stemmed from Kerfoot's abrupt firing and the subsequent elevation of Houck's young nephew Louis B.—or L. B.—to the position of superintendent. The working relationship between Louis Houck and A. J. Kerfoot had never been a satisfying one for either party. For one thing, employees complained of Kerfoot's abusive management style and several valuable men resigned rather than continue under his watch. Moreover, James Brooks did not trust the manner in which Kerfoot took advantage of his position as superintendent to establish a string of general merchandise stores along the St. Louis, Kennett and Southern. These ventures not only distracted the superintendent from his full-time railroad duties, but also his exorbitant prices for goods and questionable business practices alienated other merchants and patrons of the road.

Then too there was Kerfoot's heavy-handed treatment of Julius Houck, who, at his uncle's direction, had come south to essentially apprentice as a general agent on the St. Louis, Kennett and Southern. Kerfoot resented the twenty-year-old Julius's presence, dismissing him as an unqualified "informer" sent to snitch on him after Brooks became increasingly convinced the superintendent was out to "rob" the railroad in some way.[57]

These simmering hard feelings had boiled over when Houck replaced A. J. Kerfoot with L. B., up until that time the auditor and freight agent of

56. *St. Louis, Kennett and Southern Railroad Company et al. vs. Wear, Judge, et al.*, Missouri Reports 135, 232–38; Doherty, Jr., "Missouri Interests of Louis Houck," 147.
57. Julius Houck to Louis Houck, August 20, 1894, A. J. Kerfoot to Louis Houck, August 24, 1894, Houck Papers, 1894 Box 1516, Correspondence, August S-Z, Folder 7.

the St. Louis, Cape Girardeau, and Fort Smith. Louis maintained he made the change "for the best interest of the company," but acknowledged that Kerfoot left on exceedingly bad terms—"disgruntled, disappointed and offended."

Presumably, in Houck's opinion, lawyers retained by Kerfoot after the firing first planted the idea in his head that "he might put the road into the hands of a receiver" as a sort of retaliation.[58] If this view was accurate, then it would have been in Wear's Dunklin County courtroom that the specter of Gould entered the picture. After granting Kerfoot's request, the judge once more quietly designated a receiver for a Houck property—understandable given the enmity that existed between the two. His choice of Samuel W. Fordyce, the rival Cotton Belt's president, made less sense from a purely legal standpoint considering both men realistically should have been disqualified from the case. Regardless, it certainly opened up the entire proceedings to shrill accusations from the Houck camp that Fordyce vigorously pursued the receivership of the St. Louis, Kennett and Southern as "an effective champion of the Gould interests" "using Kerfoot merely as a tool."[59]

Lending instant credibility to the notion of corporate conspiracy, Wear's appointment of Fordyce—like that of Klotz—came without any prior notification. Further, the subsequent disingenuous manner—Louis later described it as "guarded" and secretive—in which the Cotton Belt chief attempted to physically assume control in turn gave all the appearances of another deliberate plot hatched to steal the Houck roads. The day after Wear's designation, Samuel Fordyce contacted superintendent L. B. Houck, not to serve notice of the receivership in good faith, but to innocuously ask only for permission to run a special Cotton Belt excursion from Campbell to Kennett, the headquarters of Houck's southern system. When this Trojan Horse arrived, only then did Fordyce and his attorneys announce the true purpose of their trip.[60]

The sly ploy, probably reflecting a justifiable concern that the Houcks might respond to the news of a receivership with some chicanery of their own, indeed caught Louis completely by surprise again.[61] Yet, sure enough,

58. *Cape Girardeau Democrat,* December 30, 1893; Houck, "Story of the Railroad Work, Volume II," 27.

59. *Cape Girardeau Democrat,* June 27, 1896; *St. Louis Republic,* June 10, 1896.

60. Houck, "Story of the Railroad Work, Volume II," 27–28; *St. Louis Republic,* June 10, 1896.

61. George Houck to E. F. Blomeyer, April 13, 1896, Houck Papers, 1896 Box 1518, Correspondence, April A-H, Folder 17.

just as his brother George had earlier stepped into the breech to stave off disaster, L. B. now mounted a no less audacious defense. In consultation with his namesake back in Cape Girardeau, the twenty-nine-year-old L. B. unequivocally denied the surrender demand and, to protect the integrity of the railroad's physical assets until forces could be mustered to execute a proper legal strategy, effectively immobilized Fordyce. After first securing the Dunklin County sheriff's tacit agreement to momentarily turn a blind eye to the court order of transfer, L. B. dispatched his attorney T. R. R. Ely to the Kennett railroad yard where Fordyce, Kerfoot, and a contingent of Cotton Belt lawyers had retired to the sleeping car of their private train. On Ely's orders—admittedly given "perhaps in an unethical way"—the conductor of a nearby freight train loaded with ties opened the switch just north of where the sleeper was side-tracked and gave his locomotive "the high-ball," slamming headlong into the open switch with a thunderous roar. Although the Cotton Belt crowd emerged unhurt—albeit dazed, dusty, and confused—the impact obliterated the switch, mangling the track beyond immediate repair and scattering ties and debris everywhere.[62]

With Fordyce's train left hemmed in on the siding by the wreckage, in the ensuing chaos Houck's men scrambled to cut their own locomotive loose and hastily couple together a motley collection of the railroad's available coaches and freight cars. L. B. directed the whole evacuation before climbing aboard this fugitive train and stealing away down the track to Caruthersville in Pemiscot County, safely out of Judge Wear's Dunklin jurisdiction. Behind them loyal crews assured the retreat's success with additional derailments, severed telegraph lines, and sabotaged timbers on the Little River trestle bridge separating the adjacent counties.

It took Fordyce and Kerfoot some time to free themselves in Kennett, but when they finally did they were left with no choice but to travel north to Cape Girardeau and confront the senior Houck directly with their demand for possession of the company's paperwork and ledgers. By this time, the battle-tested old attorney greeted his antagonists with a characteristic "pig-headed" obstinacy and one-two punch.[63] After a couple of days of flatly rebuffing their exhortations, Louis, with all the faux earnestness he could muster—given his delightfully ironic retelling in the newspaper of

62. *Cape Girardeau Democrat,* April 18, 1896; T. R. R. Ely's account from an unidentified newspaper in Kent Library, quoted in Doherty, Jr., *Houck, Missouri Historian and Entrepreneur,* 32; *Dunklin Democrat,* April 19, 1938; Houck, "Story of the Railroad Work, Volume II," 27–28.

63. *Cape Girardeau Democrat,* January 21, 1893, March 7, August 22, 1896.

how Fordyce had already come into possession of a small bit of track "by force"—instructed his auditor to go ahead and turn over any and all material the lawyers requested. The catch: for security reasons the attorneys would have to write out a "detailed and specific receipt" for "each article, one at time." Each of the several thousand documents would have to be, with "painstaking care," "elaborately described, even to the minutest particular." At his boss's insistence, the auditor started with the most trivial bills and other similar ephemera first, leaving the important ledgers for last. "To use Houck's expression," the Cotton Belt men "turned white around the gills" and loudly protested that this lunacy could take months. Instead they demanded just one lump receipt for all the papers, which Louis politely declined, explaining that while cumbersome, the railroad's investors were legally entitled to these receipts as legal surety before giving possession of the line to a receiver. In fact, the process might well consume at least three months before Fordyce could officially take control.[64]

In the interim, while guile and quick thinking obstructed Fordyce's efforts to seize the physical and documentary assets of the St. Louis, Kennett and Southern, Madison Smith dutifully journeyed again to Jefferson City, where the state supreme court granted first a temporary, and later a permanent, writ of prohibition to legally restore the property to Houck's control.

"The attempt to steal his Kennett railroad will go through the courts," the Cape Girardeau Democrat rejoiced, "and in the court room Mr. Houck is a giant. The bigger the lawsuit the happier is Mr. Houck."[65] And naturally, the litigation did get bigger. Kerfoot moved across the Arkansas state line and "without explaining matters of the former suit in the state supreme court," "surreptitiously" obtained from U.S. Judge Elmer B. Adams in St. Louis another order that again appointed Fordyce receiver.

"Because it was not prudent to defy the United States court, although apparently deceived," Louis momentarily yielded to the decision. Within days, however, John Noble was sent out to file a thorough and comprehensive "answer" to Adams's order spelling out for the judge all the pertinent facts, including Kerfoot's previous attempts to have Fordyce appointed receiver, the impropriety of appointing a competitor as receiver, and the state supreme court's writ of prohibition.

After several more anxious weeks of deliberation in the federal court—during which time it appeared Fordyce gallingly absorbed all the earnings

64. St. Louis Republic, June 10, 16, 1896; St. Louis Post-Dispatch, March 1, 1925; Houck, "Story of the Railroad Work, Volume II," 28–29.
65. Cape Girardeau Democrat, April 18, 25, 1896.

of the railroad—Judge Adams reversed himself and once and for all returned the St. Louis, Kennett and Southern to its rightful owner.[66]

At last vindicated in what combatants for both sides came to call the "Cape Girardeau Railroad war between Houck and Gould," Louis breathed a tremendous sigh of relief after three years that surpassed even the previous ones as the most taxing of his life. Nevertheless, although Louis was "much elated at having whipped out the gang," in actuality, this "clean sweep" in both receivership cases did not bring peace in his running fight with the Missouri Pacific, Cotton Belt, and other predatory creditors.[67] Nor did it mitigate the manifest financial difficulties of the Houck roads. It was estimated that approximately half of the existing railroads in the United States during this era had at some time been reorganized, with nearly one thousand sold at foreclosure. The depression of the 1890s made receiverships and foreclosures especially acute, with some thirty thousand miles of track caught up in these types of proceedings during 1893 alone. For the remaining years of the century, Louis maintained only a tenuous grip on the St. Louis, Cape Girardeau and Fort Smith as receiver before ultimately seeing it pass from his control with relatively little fanfare during a less celebrated foreclosure sale in 1899. Three years later the southern system was sold off as well.

But in the summer of 1896 his stature as the region's premier railroad empire builder and champion appeared at its zenith.

"Louis Houck is a lion over in Southeast Missouri," the newspapers proclaimed for his fearless defense against "the barefaced attempt of the Missouri Pacific to steal the Cape Girardeau road."[68] In blurring the cases and characters together somewhat, the *Cape Girardeau Democrat* reiterated that "the decision is not only a victory for Louis Houck. It is a victory for Southeast Missouri. . . . It is a victory for the City of Cape Girardeau, for it goes abroad that we have a citizen—a man who is one of us, who out generals the best lawyers that a big corporation with its millions of dollars can employ."[69] "If David was entitled to Biblical mention for having killed Goliath with a single rock, we think Louis Houck deserves the national

66. Houck, "Story of the Railroad Work, Volume II," 30–32; *St. Louis Republic,* June 7, 1896.

67. Houck, "Story of the Railroad Work, Volume II," 32; Wollman, "Strange Story," 9, 11.

68. *Cape Girardeau Democrat,* reprinted from *Cairo Daily Argus,* July 11, 1896.

69. *Cape Girardeau Democrat,* June 22, 1896.

reputation which he has earned for opposing so long and so well the Gould octopus with only a few rocks."[70]

Everywhere he traveled across the region, men, women, and children approached him to offer their congratulations and thanks. Often spontaneous parades marched with him from the depot to the public square when his train arrived in the towns of Dunklin County. Earlier in the year officers and employees of the Houck roads had presented Louis and Mary with a handsome oil painting of Elmwood. In June the Cape Girardeau City Band and Captain Hunze's Light Artillery serenaded the family at the estate. Before a crowd of nearly seventy townspeople, cannons boomed—frightening neighbors for miles—and martial music filled the summer night air as the Houcks watched from the doors and windows. At the insistence of the revelers, Mr. and Mrs. Houck greeted well-wishers at the front door and after an impromptu speech, Louis graciously thanked everyone, apologizing for not having something good to eat on the occasion of their surprise visit. To this the crowd heartily responded that "we brought the refreshments along," after which all were invited into the castle. Older citizens sought Houck out personally to express their admiration. Younger folks gravitated toward Irma, already adopting the look of a twentieth-century "new woman," as she led dancing in the ballroom until midnight.[71]

Long after the colorful editorials and delightful memories of that evening faded, one story in particular survived, and over the years came to symbolize Houck's improbable triumph over the Goulds in the region's popular imagination. Intriguingly, the obscure initial showdown in early 1881, and not the receivership conflict, seems to be the genesis of this engaging legend. As the story goes, Jay Gould was to have been present for the entire week in that Charleston courtroom—having arrived via a special train of five coaches—where Houck acted as his own counsel to defend against a lawsuit over his refusal to pay the Iron Mountain for the substandard rails they supplied him. After the trial Gould supposedly approached Louis to congratulate him on his victory, snidely offering the backhanded compliment that "You are the first man that ever beat me in a railroad fight. I have seen your railroad at Delta, and I have heard you conduct your case here, and I want to say, sir, that you are a damn poor railroad man, but a damn fine lawyer."[72] This would have been high praise

---

70. Ibid., July 18, 1896, November 6, 1897.
71. Ibid., January 4, June 27, 1896.
72. *Charleston Enterprise Courier* (Charleston, Mo.), February 26, 1925.

from the genius who first made a name for himself snatching victory from the jaws of defeat by outwitting Cornelius Vanderbilt in the courtroom to wrest ownership of the Erie Railroad. It was indeed high praise considering John David Rockefeller once called Gould the most skilled businessman he ever encountered—had it been true.

Alas, this wonderful anecdote and magnificent quote is a cherished myth analogous to the last-minute rail switcheroo on New Year's Eve 1880. For one, it could not have taken place at any point during the receivership struggle between 1893 and 1896. Jay Gould died in 1892. Neither could it have realistically occurred in 1881. The Iron Mountain's lawsuit against Houck never went to trial, and what is more Louis claimed to have met Jay Gould for the first time in October 1887. The story first seems to have appeared in late 1895 in anticipation of the state supreme court's final verdict. The *Cape Girardeau Democrat* reprinted an account which maintained that "the late Jay Gould on a certain occasion in speaking of Hon. Louis Houck is said to have made this statement: 'He may not be much of a railroad man, but I'll be d—d if he isn't the best lawyer in the world.'"[73] The later version that bestowed on Louis the distinction of being "a damn fine lawyer" probably evolved from this through word of mouth and eventually found its way back into newsprint as an epitaph to Houck in 1925. While apocryphal, the story's implausible origins and tall-tale qualities do not diminish its sentiment; it is a fitting tribute to a determined man at the top of his craft.

73. *Cape Girardeau Democrat*, reprinted from *Iron County Register*, November 2, 1895.

CHAPTER 8

St. Louis, Kennett and
Southern and Allied Lines

I often wonder when your hard work will be completed,
it seems to increase day by day.[1]

The real challenge to understanding, or even taking the full measure, of
Louis Napoleon Houck lies in the futility of trying to describe any one specific endeavor or experience. Like all truly remarkable characters, the man
simply moved too quickly—so fast in fact that a running joke spoke of the
impossibility of ever photographing him—and his interests were too
diverse to truly do them justice separately. In keeping with his pronounced
determination to lead the "strenuous life"—a pursuit gleaned from his
admiration of Theodore Roosevelt—virtually no activities were undertaken in isolation. Indeed, perhaps the true essence of Houck is that most
unfolded simultaneously.

The years immediately preceding and following the turn of the twentieth century—really from 1892 to 1908—were a period of considerable productivity for Houck. In the first decade of the new century alone the
rebuilding of Academic Hall at Southeast Missouri Normal School was lay-
ered and compressed in historical time with the publishing of a five-
volume history of colonial Missouri, and does not even take into account
his livelihood: railroading. In regard to his railroads, for a while between
1895 and 1899 in particular, Louis juggled three balls in the air at once, operating all three of the Houck roads simultaneously. From their epicenter in

---

1. George Harp to Louis Houck, October 18, 1898, Houck Papers, 1898 Box 1521,
Correspondence, October P-Z, Folder 15.

Cape Girardeau, the St. Louis, Cape Girardeau and Fort Smith staggered westward, the St. Louis, Kennett and Southern and Allied Lines pressed south into the Bootheel, and the fledgling Chester, Perryville, Ste. Genevieve and Farmington managed to secure a tenuous foothold in the north. And while none would ever reach the intended destinations of Fort Smith, Memphis, or St. Louis, that would not be for lack of trying.[2]

Critics thought they saw weakness in Houck's propensity to overextend. Admirers and friends, such as associate Albert Allen, conceived of it differently. When expressing his wonderment at Houck's Sisyphean labors and penchant for tending to so many irons in the fire, Allen believed that given the "multiplicity of demands" upon Houck's time, the hardest working man in the world was "an idler and loafer as compared to you."[3]

While the receivership clash unquestionably slowed railroad construction severely, it did not entirely suspend it, the most significant example being the first elements of what became the third Houck road: the Cape Girardeau Northern. An extension to St. Louis and the rich mineral deposits of the Pilot Knob mines around Ironton, Missouri, had been on Louis's mind more or less since his first railroad cogitations in the 1870s. In fact, the antebellum plan to build from the Cape to Ironton had actually been the genesis of the old Cape Girardeau and State Line Railroad that Houck took over in 1881. Still, other bold ventures and unforeseen crises over the intervening years had a way of repeatedly arising to take precedence and push such plans to the backburner. That is, until 1894, when conditions began to congeal in such a way that Louis revisited the northern route—more precisely, a line from Cape Girardeau through Perryville to the Mississippi River—with newfound determination.

The scheme captured the imagination of folks in Ste. Genevieve, Perry, and northern Cape Girardeau counties as well and generated so much talk that soon Gould interests caught wind of it and announced their own preparations to extend the Jackson Branch of their Iron Mountain railroad north. This ultimately proved to be nothing more than a bluff, just another irritant in the ongoing feud, but it had the unintended positive result of heightening interest in the proposed enterprise to the point that residents along the line began beseeching Houck to undertake the project and making promises of generous financial support. Competition between towns and, moreover, what they were willing to offer in the way of financial

2. Doherty, Jr., "Missouri Interests of Louis Houck," 185.

3. Albert Allen to Louis Houck, August 10, 1895, Houck Papers, 1895 Box 1517, Correspondence, August M-Z, Folder 23.

inducement to build a railroad to them was a central factor in determining the course of most railways in Missouri, and the Houck roads were certainly no exception, especially the northern one.

So in January 1894, with James Brooks by his side, Louis traveled by buggy to Perryville—as no railroad yet reached it—where he delivered a formal speech at the courthouse laying out his plans. Experience taught him that if he tipped his hand and began building north from Cape Girardeau, the Iron Mountain would likely unveil another spurious parallel plan, if for no other reason than to prevent potential investors from putting their money behind his road in the face of direct competition from Gould. Accordingly, he deferred mentioning anything about Cape Girardeau, offering instead to build the first twenty miles of this proposed route from a Mississippi River landing at West Chester, known in Missouri as Claryville, almost due south to Perryville. In that way a transfer boat across the river would connect them with the nearest rail outlet, the Wabash, Chester and Western railroad at Chester, Illinois. At the same time, Houck also promised an ancillary ten-mile branch west from Claryville that would hug the river to St. Mary's—today known as St. Mary—on its way eventually to Ste. Genevieve. Civic leaders in the various towns along the route enthusiastically accepted, pledging more than $70,000 of the subscription bonds and the necessary rights-of-way so that the work might begin within a year.[4]

Events delayed construction until April 1895, but after that the Chester, Perryville, Ste. Genevieve and Farmington Railroad moved forward in impressive fashion. Given the inherent difficulties in undertaking a railroad from scratch with no physical connection to another road, workmen first fabricated a temporary incline at Claryville and operated it as the chief point of entry for all men, equipment, and materials. Rails, spikes, and angle bars came down from St. Louis on barges while T. J. Moss ties came upriver. From Grand Tower came boats loaded with two used locomotives and rolling stock: two coaches, a baggage car, and five boxcars. All were unloaded on the high sandbar across the river in Chester with Houck's very capable nephew, L. B., then skillfully managing the tricky transfers across the Mississippi.

Once L. B. established efficient supply lines, Brooks brought A. R. Ponder up from his duties in the Bootheel to help direct construction out across the roughly twenty-six-thousand-acre Bois Brule, a vast agricultural

4. Houck, "Story of the Railroad Work, Volume II," 98–100; *Cape Girardeau Democrat,* January 20, February 3, 1894.

region since the time of the French that was set in a natural flood basin. By July, methodical crews—now including seventeen-year-old Giboney—reached Lithium, named for its natural spring containing the mood-enhancing lithium carbonate, and from there the crews built earthworks and a roughly three-hundred-foot trestle at a place called the "Blue Spring opening." As they neared the home stretch, curious folks from Perryville came out to witness this trestle being built "from the stump"—that is, with the timber and stringers cut from the surrounding woods and hewn on site, a process that took a mere ten days from the first axe swing until the construction train ran across it.

In October 1895, trains pulled into the newly completed Perryville yards and depot. But although the actual physical construction went swimmingly, Houck experienced numerous financial problems with the line—indicative of many of the troubles persistently facing all his roads—which postponed the planned link with Cape for another four years. First, of course, there was debt. In the midst of the critical moments of the receivership litigation, Louis only had some $500 cash to his name when he built the Chester, Perryville, Ste. Genevieve and Farmington and thus the $70,000-plus in subscription bonds formed the basis of the new line's financial backing. This quickly went for construction costs, materials, and rolling stock that he purchased on the "car trust plan" for one-quarter down and monthly installment payments. Ultimately the subscriptions did not come close to covering the necessary capital, leaving Louis to piece together additional sources, including digging deeper into his own pockets. After putting up all the rents collected from the various Houck farmlands, he also pitched in his monthly salary as receiver of the Cape Girardeau Railroad. Still it was not enough, and after flooding in 1896 destroyed the first permanent incline at Claryville—built at a cost of $6,000—the next year a more expensive one replaced it.[5]

Second, the earnings were disappointing. Despite initial preconstruction projections that estimated the gross earnings of this line, including the St. Mary's branch, at roughly $2,500 per month, during the first year of the Chester, Perryville, Ste. Genevieve and Farmington's existence the actual figures did not exceed $1,300 total: a 96 percent shortfall.[6] Most busi-

5. Louis Houck to F. Wade, December 5, 1899, Houck Papers, Box 1909, Folder 4.

6. Houck, "Story of the Railroad Work, Volume II," 112; *Twenty-Second Annual Report of the Railroad and Warehouse Commissioners of the State of Missouri, Year Ending June 30, 1897.* (Jefferson City, Mo.: Tribune Printing Company, State Printers and Binders, 1898).

nesses in the region still preferred the packet-boat trade up to St. Louis, and so what business came Houck's way usually came when the river was down and packet-boat service not as regular. Consequently, even under the steady leadership of L. B. and E. F. Blomeyer, during the last years of the century the northern line struggled to break even after paying operating expenses and creditors. This of course did not even take into account the interest on the $300,000 of bonds coming due regularly, and with nervous bondholders crowding him for their money, Louis resorted to accepting the interest coupons of the bonds as payment for hauling freight. Once again a Houck railroad rolled down the somber line toward receivership and foreclosure.

Perhaps fittingly, money mixed uneasily with politics in the fall of 1896 during another critical election in American history, as Houck passionately took up the banner of "Free Silver!" Since the late 1860s, a political movement among the nation's farmers had been unfolding in the Midwest borne of agrarian discontent that the United States was industrializing largely at their expense. By 1892 a "People's" or "Populist" party united this activism into a national third party to confront the disproportionate economic power of corporate America and the corrupt and unresponsive two-party system. The Populist platform, based in some measure on the influence of delegates from Missouri, included a number of sweeping initiatives for recasting the country's political and economic life, including what became their signature issue: government expansion of currencies to include the unlimited coinage of silver dollars. This controversial and often misunderstood plank rested on the premise that the primary way to help break the downward spiral of low prices, debt, and foreclosure devastating family farmers was to expand the nation's currency supply by loosening the federal government's strict fiscal reliance on the gold standard as the sole basis for determining the value of the American dollar. Populists argued that silver, then being mined in large quantities in the West, could be minted into cheaper silver dollars as a supplement to gold in a more democratized "bi-metal" formula. In this way, the government could increase the supply of currency in circulation and thus create an artificially induced inflation, making it easier for debt-strapped farmers to obtain credit and pay off mortgages.

Seeking to gain an edge in the razor-thin Gilded Age presidential elections by harnessing Populist support, in 1896 astute Democrats skillfully absorbed portions of the Populist platform and some of its leadership, most notably by taking up the cause of "free silver" and nominating William Jennings Bryan to head the Democratic ticket for president that year. In Missouri, where farmers still accounted for the majority of population, the perplexing free silver issue generated considerable enthusiasm, and debate over its eventual adoption by the Democrats dominated party politics during the election season. Oddly enough, one of the strongest "Silver Democrats" to emerge in the state was Louis Houck.

Louis certainly had no use for the radical political agenda of the Populists; like future president Theodore Roosevelt, he considered the Populists to be a dangerously socialistic lunatic fringe. As a Democrat, his advocacy of free silver stemmed from a partisan desire to steal the thunder of this potential third-party menace that was threatening to supplant his own party in Cape Girardeau County and southeast Missouri. With other leading local "silver men" such as attorneys Jefferson W. Limbaugh and R. B. Oliver, Houck admonished fellow Democrats that unless they stood up as champions of the common man against the wrongs of corporations on issues like silver, "we shall create a Populistic movement in Missouri which will wreck our party here as the Republican party was destroyed in Kansas."[7] As a businessman, however, his interest in silver took a more pragmatic turn, in that like farmers his operations were almost completely dependent on credit and he perpetually struggled upstream against torrents of debt. Artificial inflation would serve him well, and on this matter he joined Missouri Congressman Richard "Silver Dick" Bland and lame-duck Governor William Stone in staunchly promoting the party's silver platform. At the 1896 Democratic National Convention in Chicago, he even relented to have an artist draw a picture of him—a rarity—to be included among a gallery of top Missouri supporters of Bryan for president.

Diligently, Houck canvassed southeast Missouri in the fall of 1896, giving speeches and debating, in both English and German, the detractors who warned that free silver would drive down wages and purchasing power amongst the working class.[8] This crusade on behalf of free silver soon spilled over into the confines of the Third District Normal, where the college's president and fellow "silverite" Willard Vandiver was running a controversial campaign for Congress that cast Houck in the rather delicate partisan position of running interference for his candidacy.[9]

Houck was completing his tenth year on the board of regents, after having been recently reappointed by Governor Stone in 1895. Since 1889, he

7. *St. Louis Globe-Democrat*, May 15, 1894; *Cape Girardeau Democrat*, February 24, 1894, June 29, August 3, 1895.
8. *Cape Girardeau Democrat*, July 11, October 10, 31, 1896.
9. Mattingly, *Normal to University*, 19, 49–50, 61.

had served as president of the board, presiding over a key transitional period as the school sought to establish its own identity as an institution of higher education and its overall place in the educational scheme of Missouri, all in the midst of a national depression. Vandiver's hiring in June 1893—the school's first president to be drawn from the faculty—facilitated the stability and direction Louis's steady leadership helped foster at the Normal. But as president of the Normal, Vandiver was required to travel the region to promote the institution, and within a couple of years the politically ambitious administrator had begun informally campaigning for the Fourteenth District congressional seat while on these college trips.

Before officially throwing his hat in the ring, Vandiver had sought Houck's private counsel regarding the wisdom and propriety of running while still employed by the Normal. As to the wisdom of the plan, the top regent initially responded negatively, admonishing Vandiver that "no man ought to go into politics unless he is rich enough to pay the bills without missing the money, or has nothing and can't lose it." And although Louis eventually gave his sanction, on the issue of propriety he most certainly reminded Vandiver that since the establishment of the normal system in Missouri, governors had appointed members of the board of regents with an eye toward at least ostensibly keeping a political balance between Republican and Democrat, unprejudiced by partisanship. Yet as they both knew, politics were a dynamic feature of the board, and Vandiver's candidacy was sure to create serious political incongruity between the regents and the president. For that reason, Houck explained, his endorsement would remain rather staid, at least publicly. "I can't take much part in the fight," he instructed, "but I am for you."[10]

Indeed, Vandiver's political activity swiftly stirred up ample trouble on the board, which, as expected, split along clear party lines over this unprecedented problem: did his candidacy necessitate his immediate resignation? The Republican wing of the regents led by Edward Rozier and John H. Rainey assumed so and were aghast when, instead of Vandiver either resigning or dropping out of the race as they wished, Houck stepped outside his authority to unilaterally grant Vandiver a leave of absence until

---

10. Ernest Kent Farmer, "Southeast Missouri State Normal, 1873–1921," 155; *Cape Girardeau Democrat*, August 1, 1896, June 26, 1897; Paul B. Moore to Louis Houck, Houck Papers, 1897 Box 1519, Correspondence, June C–I, Folder 15. In 1896 the Southeast Missouri State Normal Board of Regents consisted of three Democrats—Louis Houck, Leon J. Albert, and J. L. Haw—and three Republicans—Moses Whybark, Edward Rozier, and John H. Rainey. However, State Superintendent of Public Schools J. R. Kirk was the ex-officio chairman of the board and a Republican.

the November election.[11] Rozier thinly accused Louis of assuming "sovereign authority" over the school and stridently, and repeatedly, called on Houck to convene a special meeting of the regents to remove Vandiver. For his part Louis sandbagged, and after stalling as long as he could—during which time Vandiver campaigned forcefully—the president of the board finally called this special meeting to order in October. But by this time, of course, it was effectively too late. Vandiver was elected to Congress within weeks and resigned on his own terms before the legislative session began in 1897.[12]

Willard Vandiver went on to serve four consecutive terms in Washington, where perhaps his most noteworthy accomplishment was to be credited with coining the iconic phrase, "I come from a state that raises corn and cotton and cockleburs and Democrats, and frothy eloquence neither convinces nor satisfies me. I am from Missouri. You have got to show me." He also remained an influential and well-positioned friend of Houck's who over the years continued to take a deep interest in the welfare of the Normal and southeast Missouri.

Nevertheless, Vandiver's victory in 1896 was really one of the few triumphs for Louis and the cause of free silver in that otherwise dismal election year. Despite Democrat Lon Stephens's successful gubernatorial run and to a lesser extent the fact that William Jennings Bryan actually carried Missouri over the Republican William McKinley, the free silver issue was a loser. Bryan's lopsided defeat in the presidential election drove home the hard truth that most Americans outside of the agrarian Midwest and South neither understood nor supported the measure. Moreover, the fallout over silver's demise resonated most immediately with Louis because it threatened to taint him in the eyes of eastern investors whose support was critical to his respective railroading enterprises. Although Houck detested the Populists, from the perspective of East Coast business associates—in particular railroaders and financiers—his Missouri locale and silver stance amounted to guilt by association. If word got out around New York of Houck's active association with silver it would present a liability certain to injure the struggling Chester, Perryville, Ste. Genevieve and

11. Willard Vandiver to Louis Houck, September 15, 1896, Houck Papers, 1896–1897 Box 1519, Correspondence, Sept-Oct A-Z, Folder 1; Mattingly, *Normal to University*, 54–56.

12. Board of Regents Minutes, vol. I, 1873–1925, 168; *Cape Girardeau Democrat*, December 19, 1896; Farmer, "Southeast Missouri State Normal," 158. When Vandiver returned to Missouri in 1904 he worked as campaign manager for Joseph Folk's successful gubernatorial run. In turn Folk appointed Vandiver state insurance commissioner in 1905, and he became a nationally recognized state insurance superintendent.

Farmington, or, more importantly, the ongoing reorganization of the St. Louis, Cape Girardeau and Fort Smith.

Victory in the receivership battle with the Goulds over this first Houck road had been just half of the same walnut so to speak. Houck's ultimate court appointment as receiver in 1896 merely confirmed him as the legal custodian to administer the second phase of the process, which was the complicated untangling of his bankrupt railroad's knots of floating debt, colliding claims, and conflicting accounts of liability for accrued interest. This sticky ordeal, while not nearly as spectacular or celebrated as the Cape Girardeau railroad war between Houck and Gould, turned out to be an equally intriguing and somewhat fitting end to the whole sordid affair.

As early as 1893, when the various bondholders of the St. Louis, Cape Girardeau and Fort Smith first began banding together into two reorganization committees to keep the property out of Gould's hostile hands, Newman Erb reemerged as chairman of the eastern group. With Houck's consent and cooperation, Erb started the ball rolling toward eventual reorganization by convincing the majority of bondholders in the East to deposit all their securities with the committee so that they might be held strategically in a more manageable block. Thus, at the same time Louis was outmaneuvering Eli Klotz in the Missouri courts, Erb was effectively gaining control of virtually all the railroad's East Coast bonds outside of those held by the Goulds.

Immediately upon the conclusion of the receivership proceedings, Erb ostensibly continued to collaborate with Houck to craft a viable strategy that would give the St. Louis, Cape Girardeau and Fort Smith a brand-new start under its founder's continued leadership. This changed when Erb abruptly abandoned plans of reorganizing the line under its present ownership in favor of foreclosing and starting over from scratch with himself as president. Erb seems to have been operating with his own agenda from the start, discreetly handicapping Houck while at the same time plotting behind his back with Missouri Pacific attorney Henry Wollman to pursue foreclosure. In fact, in yet more railroading sleight-of-hand, Erb used Wollman to strike a deal with George Gould whereby Erb and his associates clandestinely acquired the Gould bonds as well. As Wollman later admitted, when it came to Houck, as of 1896 "Mr. Gould's and Mr. Erb's interests up to a point were identical."[13]

Houck only slowly came to grips with the depth of Erb's "devilment"— although his attorney Madison R. Smith seems to have figured it out much quicker. But when he did, instead of promptly confronting the usurper

13. Wollman, "Strange Story," 9, 14.

directly and candidly in a public showdown—which was his style—Louis appears to have wearily resigned himself to the St. Louis, Cape Girardeau and Fort Smith's fate.[14] Once Wollman filed the motion to foreclose in the Cape Girardeau Circuit Court in late 1896, Houck uncharacteristically cooperated fully with the court, and over the next years as foreclosure became increasingly imminent, Louis negotiated closely with Erb—although now handling him "like a live coal of fire"—not over possession, but in order to ensure that whatever form the railroad's new management took, he and local bondholders such as Sturdivant would be treated equitably.[15]

The end itself, on May 2, 1899, was almost anticlimactic. Based on Wollman's legal work, the circuit court foreclosed on the railway Houck had operated for nearly twenty years and sold it on the county courthouse steps in Jackson to Erb's proxy Albert S. Bard. Immediately following the purchase of the St. Louis, Cape Girardeau and Fort Smith for $425,000, or not even one-third of the line's value, Newman Erb took over as president and renamed it the Southern Missouri and Arkansas. Within a few years he put the railroad in better condition and sold it to the St. Louis and San Francisco—or Frisco—railway for a tremendous profit.

While all creditors were eventually paid in full and all bondholders duly compensated, Louis walked away from his first railroad venture without receiving any cash whatsoever, a disappointment all the more acute given the recollections of Jay Gould's original $100,000 cash offer to buy him out back in October 1887. He did receive a substantial chunk of Southern Missouri and Arkansas Railroad bonds in the transaction, which his friend Sturdivant advised him to sell outright to pay off his personal debts and retire from railroading altogether. Instead, Houck solemnly put them up as collateral to push construction ahead on his troublesome northern and southern routes. If he privately ached over losing the St. Louis, Cape Girardeau and Fort Smith he never let on, perhaps taking some consolation in the fact that regardless of what Erb called the railway, it would always be known in southeast Missouri as a Houck road.[16]

---

14. "Louis Houck Memoirs," 291, 292; Henry Lamb to Louis Houck, June 26, 1896, Houck Papers, 1896 Box 1518, Correspondence, June A-J, Folder 21.

15. M. R. Smith to Louis Houck, January 24, 1898, Houck Papers, 1898 Box 1520, Correspondence, January M-Z, Folder 21; To all Bondholders of the SL, CG & FS, January 8, 1896, Houck Papers, 1896 Box 1518, Correspondence, January G-Z, Folder 12.

16. *Cape Girardeau Democrat,* May 6, 1899; Newman Erb to Louis Houck, April 14, 1899, Houck Papers, 1899 Box 1522, Correspondence, April A-F, Folder 1; Robert Sturdivant to Louis Houck, August 31, 1899, Houck Papers, 1899 Box 1522, Correspondence, August A-G, Folder 16; Wollman, "Strange Story," 14–16; "Louis Houck Memoirs," 291–94.

Years later, in observing one of the hallmarks of Houck's railroading career, the *St. Louis Post-Dispatch* concluded that "his restlessness never allowed him to wait until one road had paid out or had laid up a surplus. He must always start another without sufficient finances to finish it . . . the law allowed him to bond each five miles of laid track. He would use the money from the first five miles to build another five miles and so on."[17] Indeed, this tendency to repeatedly fund future construction by borrowing against the collateral of previous railroad securities may never have been more evident than in the midst of the foreclosure in the late 1890s.

In tandem with the Chester, Perryville, Ste. Genevieve and Farmington Railroad then running in the north, Louis penetrated deeper south into the Missouri Bootheel and Arkansas with his second rail system, collectively referred to as the St. Louis, Kennett and Southern and Allied Lines. Since the opening of the St. Louis, Kennett and Southern between Campbell and Kennett in 1891 and his Missouri and Arkansas line from Commerce to Morley in 1893, Louis doggedly continued to pursue the business of the region's large landowners and lumber companies, all the while seeking that elusive connection to a through line to Memphis. The triumphant conclusion of the receivership battle with A. J. Kerfoot reignited the ventures and earned Houck local accolades for being the only man in America who kept on building railroads during the Grover Cleveland panic years. "They say," he would sometimes tell Blomeyer and whoever else happened be around the offices, "that Louis Houck builds his railroads on a nickel." Then plunging a hand into his pocket and drawing out a coin, with a hearty laugh he would exclaim, "here's the nickel."[18]

The receivership struggles—and the lessons drawn from them—also guided the creation of the legal identity of the southern system. At least on paper the organization of these "allied" lines to the south of Cape Girardeau was a noteworthy departure from the first Houck road as all extensions west had been "divisions" within the St. Louis, Cape Girardeau and Fort Smith, not a collection of semi-independent railways under a single Houck directorate as would become the case in the southern system. It seems likely Louis followed this course of not consolidating his various railroads in the Bootheel into one large corporation because the second system was not always contiguous and moreover because it would be more difficult for a receiver to capture his entire system. By dividing up his railroads into a

17. *St. Louis Post-Dispatch,* March 1, 1925.
18. Ibid.; *Cape Girardeau Democrat,* January 22, 1898.

dozen or so different corporations, Houck believed that a dishonest judge might appoint a receiver for one of his lines, but not for all of them. In other words, Louis divided so that he would not be conquered.

In 1897 the St. Louis, Kennett and Southern railroad formed an irregular right angle in Dunklin and Pemiscot counties with Kennett as the vertex and rays running north to Campbell and east to Caruthersville. Yet farther to the south and east a lumberman's paradise still awaited the railroad, and so with his eyes never completely losing sight of Memphis, Houck once more slogged his way into the swamps. At the urging of Abe R. Byrd, who owned a sizable tract of land south of Senath, Missouri, and in part with Byrd's financial backing, Louis incorporated the Kennett and Osceola Railroad to extend south from Kennett toward Osceola, Arkansas, running roughly parallel to the St. Francis River in the Bootheel's most remote corner. Inside of a year, crews painstakingly carved out a line nearly fifteen miles long through Senath to a junction point with the Paragould and Eastern Railroad that Louis simply called Arbyrd.[19]

While scouting future Arkansas routes in 1898, Louis crossed paths with C. A. Boynton, a lively Illinois land speculator whose family controlled some sixty thousand acres along the Missouri-Arkansas border. The two forged an instant and sustained friendship, and soon the Boyntons largely underwrote the further extension of the Kennett and Osceola down to Leachville, Arkansas, to service their massive saw and planning mills.

When a bungled deal to purchase the small Tyronza Central line stymied yet another scheme to finally gain a competitive outlet to Memphis, Houck next concluded that it increase the value of the Kennett road to instead secure a connection with the Iron Mountain at Poplar Bluff. Accordingly, he purchased a short sawmill railway already under construction from Campbell northwest over Crowley's Ridge to the depot of Caligoa on the Butler County line and incorporated his St. Francois Valley Railroad in January 1898 to finish and operate the new road. By June his trains reached Caligoa—now completely intersecting Dunklin County north to south—and preparations were made to cross the St. Francis River and finish the extension north to Poplar Bluff. But the lure of big lumber money back below Crowley's Ridge eventually sidetracked this connec-

19. Houck, "Story of the Railroad Work, Volume II," 34–37; *Cape Girardeau Democrat*, December 8, 1896; J. E. Franklin to Louis Houck, October 26, 1897, Houck Papers, 1897 Box 1520, Correspondence, October D-H, Folder 5; James Brooks to Louis Houck, August 22, 1899, Houck Papers, 1899 Box 1522, Correspondence, August S-Z, Folder 19.

tion as well and left tiny Caligoa as the terminus of the ten-mile St. Francois Valley railway.[20]

Nearing his sixtieth birthday and becoming more prone to periods of poor health, Houck continued to recede from the daily minutiae of the business—an ongoing process years in the making. After 1896 the remainder of his railroading career was relatively free of major litigation, at least by 1890s standards. Aside from pesky minor lawsuits brought by landowners over rights-of-way disputes, confusion over titles, and livestock run over by trains, the legal front remained fairly quiet and was largely handled by M. R. Smith and later Giboney, who graduated from law school at the University of Missouri. In the north, John Tlapek and Julius Houck for the most part now saw to the Chester, Perryville, Ste. Genevieve and Farmington, and his other nephew, L. B.—the titular president of Houck's Missouri and Arkansas line—steadily assumed more responsibility overseeing operations across the entire provincial network, especially during his uncle's and aunt's extended winter vacations in San Marcos and San Antonio, Texas.

Having worked his way up as a general agent and then traffic manager, L. B. Houck gained a practical education in railroading, as well as in real estate, from his uncle. In fact, many of his eventual real estate holdings in downtown Cape Girardeau have been erroneously attributed to the elder Houck for years. But while their overall business philosophy and savvy may have been similar, L. B. seems to have been in many ways the more colorful and "modern" of the two. He was, for instance, one of the first two men in Cape to own an automobile, a gadget Houck disdained for years, warning friends that "if a horse falls on you, he will get up. If a car falls on you, it will crush you to death."[21]

A new telephone line run out to Elmwood also helped Louis become less physically bound to his general railroad office, which, amusingly, moved temporarily into the old Baptist church building on Lorimier Street in 1899. Houck bought the structure from the departing congregation and with no other interested tenants refurbished it for his own use. Inside of a few years, however, he sold what townspeople made fun of as "Houck's railroad church" and moved his headquarters to the stone depot on Independence

20. Houck, "Story of the Railroad Work, Volume II," 43–44; *Cape Girardeau Democrat,* January 22, 1898; S. S. Miller to Louis Houck, August 20, 1899, Houck Papers, 1899 Box 1522, Correspondence, August S-Z, Folder 19.

21. Heil, "Recollections."

Street, primarily because he grew irritated at the constant jokes around Cape about moneychangers having taken up residence in the temple.[22]

So too did Louis find himself called away to other diversions for increasingly longer periods of time. For one, he rekindled his life-long love of history, and his voracious reading habits—especially in regard to the colonial era of the Louisiana Territory—accelerated. He spent more time in his own library at Elmwood and also in the library of Academic Hall. Except during business hours or meals, rarely did one find him without a book in his hand.[23] Already widely regarded as an amateur historian of some note, Houck, also a member of the State Historical Society of Missouri, routinely received many requests for information of a historical nature concerning Missouri and regional genealogy.

In addition to historical research and thankless duties on the Cape Girardeau Fair Association Board of Directors, Houck also followed the brief Spanish-American War in 1898 with particularly keen interest. Like many impassioned young college men, Giboney enlisted as a private in the U.S. Army shortly after war was declared in April to free Cuba from the clutches of Spain. Although an isolationist by nature and therefore philosophically opposed to what people of his mind-set considered a naked quest for empire, Louis nevertheless proudly supported his son's determination to be a soldier. He took issue, though, with a young man accustomed to "the pleasures and comforts of an elegant home [and] the association and influence of splendid parentage" doing so as an enlisted man and instead arranged with Governor Lon Stephens to have Giboney named battalion adjutant with the rank of first lieutenant in the Fifth Regiment of Missouri Volunteers.[24] As a lieutenant in what was effectively the Missouri National Guard, Giboney trained in Georgia before sailing for Cuba, while his father purchased a wall map of the island from the War Department to follow the fighting and his mother booked passage on a steamer for her son's favorite horse.

A messy and embarrassing flap over the legitimacy of Giboney's rank delayed his departure; given that this "Splendid Little War" lasted but four months, by the time the young Houck went ashore in Cuba in December it was for occupation duty only. Thus freed from the worry of their only son's safety, Louis and Mary celebrated by taking Irma for a three-week

22. Franklin, "Former Pioneer Traces Early History."
23. Heil, "Recollections."
24. J. M. Seibert to James Brooks, May 17, 1898, Houck Papers, 1898 Box 1521, Correspondence, May S-Z, Folder 3.

vacation to Havana in February 1899. While the ladies socialized, Houck reveled in the tropical climate to the point that he appears to have rethought his feelings regarding America's first war on behalf of other peoples. "Houck left here about three weeks ago a rampant contractionist," the *Cape Girardeau Democrat* informed. "He returns home after looking over a portion of Cuba a rampant expansionist"—so much so it seems that he may well have purchased a few thousand acres of orange and pineapple land in Cuba's Santiago Province.[25]

On New Year's Day 1900, Louis marked the anniversary of his first train pulling into Cape Girardeau by hosting a maiden excursion of prominent citizens down the long-awaited extension from the Cape to Commerce on his Missouri and Arkansas railway, a trip that was of course cut short because of an accident. More to the point, the twentieth century dawned on two attractive deals with the Deering Harvester Company and the firm of Gideon and Anderson Lumber and Mercantile that further influenced the timing and direction of the southern allied Houck roads. Sometime in 1900 the Chicago-based Deering—just two years shy of a merger with the McCormick Harvesting Machine Company that would create the colossal International Harvester—commenced operations at a new Pemiscot County sawmill about seven miles south of Pascola. Surrounded by nearly fifty thousand acres of the most magnificent and dense growth of virgin black and white oak likely to be seen in the United States, this mill demanded immediate rail access for the enormous volume of raw lumber soon to be shipped north and manufactured into agricultural machinery. Advantageously for Houck, with a depot already in remote Pascola, or, as some called it, Seldom Seen, the St. Louis, Kennett and Southern was uniquely positioned to expediently oblige.

Working through friend and fellow land speculator John E. Franklin as an intermediary, Louis formed the Pemiscot Southern in September 1900 to reach the mill and company town of Deering by building down the Elk Chute creek from Pascola. By February, a steady stream of flatcars loaded with Deering lumber rolled up the short Pemiscot Southern to the Kennett road and over to Campbell, where they transferred to the Cotton Belt en route to Chicago. The arrangement proved profitable, but troubled for both parties, as Houck and the Deering corporation bickered perpetually over rates and the mill's habit of overloading the cars to the point of giving the

25. *Cape Girardeau Democrat*, February 18, March 18, 1899; P. Nickel to Louis Houck, January 1901, Houck Papers, 1901 Box 1525, Correspondence, Folder 5.

railroad fits when making connections. Although Louis later felt vindicated when the Frisco took over his roads and Deering continued to be a headache for the new owners, his maxim in dealing with this enormous client remained simply that "it [was] not good policy to antagonize a local manufacturing concern supported by ample capital."[26]

That same year two Ohio sawmill promoters, Eugene Gideon and William P. Anderson, bought several thousand acres east of Clarkton from A. J. Matthews on the stipulation that the deal hinged on securing a rail outlet for their proposed mills. Matthews in turn introduced Gideon and Anderson to Houck, who readily agreed to run a branch line from Gibson, a station on his Kennett road, out a few miles to Clarkton in exchange for the lumbermen subscribing the money. The physical construction of this minor Clarkton Branch progressed uneventfully over level, sandy, and dry country that required little in the way of filling, embankments, trestles, or bridges.

Yet what started out to be a relatively short line venture soon grew exponentially. The Gideon mills were actually about two miles beyond Clarkton to the east, and even though the initial agreement only called for an extension to that little hamlet, once Houck got there the company changed its mind and insisted he continue on to Gideon. This impulsive revision perturbed Louis, but the size of the giant mills with their company store and housing—and expansive yards swollen with huge stockpiles of lumber—tempered his irritation, and he adjusted his plans accordingly. Although only two miles long, construction of this particular extension—which closely followed the old Clarkton pole road—took a little more work, requiring crews to bring in a steam shovel to haul in hundreds of carloads of sand from nearby hills to create a few embankments over the sloughs. Still, by 1902 yet another local manufacturing concern supported by ample capital was sending great shipments of lumber rolling across the line toward Campbell.

Just as it seemed work on the Clarkton Branch was wrapping up, the folks in nearby Malden—through which the Cotton Belt already ran—decided they needed a connection to Houck's St. Louis, Kennett and Southern road to accommodate their thriving cotton factories as well. So, after the necessary rights-of-way were hastily arranged, track went down,

---

26. Houck, "Story of the Railroad Work, Volume II," 45–49; J. E. Franklin to Louis Houck, August 17, 1901, Houck Papers, 1901 Box 1525, Correspondence, August F-P, Folder 22.

telegraphs went up, and a rail connection was secured from Malden, Clarkton, and Gideon to Gibson on the main line of the Kennett road; it provided a second link to the Cotton Belt as well.

With one more short extension from Gibson over to Tallapoosa, in 1901 Houck put what would be the finishing touches on his southern system. The final two pieces of the network that tied the various allied lines radiating out from the Kennett road together were Houck's Missouri and Arkansas and the St. Louis, Morehouse and Southern. These last railways—forming a rough north-south axis through the Bootheel—were constructed more or less simultaneously to the aforementioned allied roads throughout 1899 and 1900 and upon their completion provided the system with its only direct link to Cape Girardeau.

Before the receivership battles in 1893, Houck had begun operating the first section of his Missouri and Arkansas Railroad between Commerce and Morley to satisfy local watermelon traffic. However, large timber interests once again intervened, and in 1897, at the behest of the Himmelberger-Luce Land and Lumber Company, he extended the line farther south into New Madrid County along a new Morley and Morehouse Railroad.[27] Himmelberger-Luce had recently moved their extensive milling operations to Morehouse along the Iron Mountain railway, virtually revolutionizing that section of southeast Missouri with an unprecedented influx of men and material. With more than two hundred thousand acres in the region and soon to be the nation's biggest hardwood sawmill, Himmelberger-Luce—later Himmelberger-Harrison—transformed Morehouse into the most important shipping point on the Poplar Bluff branch of Iron Mountain almost overnight. Even so, Himmelberger-Luce was wholly dependent on the Iron Mountain for shipping, and knowing that, the Iron Mountain served them accordingly.

Houck's Morley and Morehouse road gave Himmelberger-Luce a competitive alternative with rail access from Morehouse to Commerce and then over the Mississippi River by transfer boat to the Illinois Central. The lumber company advanced the money, which Houck attempted to repay with freight rebates, and with A. R. Ponder and John H. Crowder surveying and superintending respectively, the road pushed south along the Sikeston ridge in Scott County. Crews steam-shoveled out more sand to fill in the low areas. And given the dynamic growth of the area, hickory axe handle manufacturers and other mills—including branch facilities of the

27. *Cape Girardeau Democrat*, September 8, 1900.

T. J. Moss Tie Company now under the leadership of John Wallace Fristoe—eagerly set up operations right along the construction sites so they would be ready to go when the line opened. To keep abreast, stations were hurriedly built at Vanduser, Crowder, and Salcedo.[28]

This unassuming stretch of steel became the notoriously crooked "peavine" line, scorned as one of the worst of the Houck roads. But the only real drama in the otherwise routine extension came courtesy of the lingering antagonism between Houck and the Goulds. To reach Morehouse, Louis had to first cross the Belmont Branch of the Iron Mountain railway at Morley, which his rivals deliberately blocked by hastily building a sidetrack and keeping it completely filled with empty freight cars around the clock. Apparently still flushed from his receivership victory, Houck calmly appeared before town officials in Morley with an offer to return the right-of-way through town that they had given him—and which ran perpendicular to the Iron Mountain line—if the good people of Morley would use it instead as a street. His only request: that his railroad be granted the right to run its tracks through the street. The town agreed and promptly served notice to the Iron Mountain to remove any and all obstructions to this new municipal thoroughfare.[29]

This heretofore loose assortment of railroads began coming together into a coherent shape, which Louis plotted carefully on his large blueprint map of southeast Missouri that hung for years in the general offices. In 1900 Houck took over the St. Louis, Morehouse and Southern to link Morehouse to the Kennett road in the south at Pascola and thus totally secured for himself all the timber business throughout Scott, New Madrid, and Pemiscot counties. Himmelberger-Luce originally incorporated the St. Louis, Morehouse and Southern themselves, but after realizing they had bitten off more than they could chew in the almost impassable marshes, they gladly turned over the project to Louis along with a $100,000 loan and a completion deadline.[30]

28. T. E. Jackson to Louis Houck, May 23, 1899, Houck Papers, 1899 Box 1522, Correspondence, May I–S, Folder 6;

29. *Charleston Enterprise Courier* (Charleston, Mo.), February 26, 1925; Houck, "Story of the Railroad Work, Volume II," 60–71; J. H. Friant to Louis Houck, May 11, 1899, Houck Papers, 1899 Box 1522, Correspondence, May C–I, Folder 5.

30. Memorandum of Agreements, Himmelberger-Luce Land and Lumber Company and Houck's Missouri and Arkansas Railroad, July 1, 1897, August 31, 1900, Houck Papers Accretion, Box 1903, Folder 5; Clarence Brown to Louis Houck, April 30, 1900, Houck Papers, 1900 Box 1523, Correspondence, April M–Z, Folder 23.

For the last time in his life Houck gave railroad building in Swampeast Missouri his full and undivided personal attention, returning to live with his men in the construction trains and camps. Almost symbolically, the construction of the St. Louis, Morehouse and Southern was really a microcosm of all his railroading experiences in the region's wetlands. For one, just as with the original Cape Girardeau Railway Company, he raced against an arbitrary deadline that along with a shortage of rails held his feet to the fire with the omnipresent threat of impending financial ruin. As they had with the St. Louis, Kennett and Southern, his crews worked inward from both ends to expedite the construction, building down from Morehouse and up from Pascola. In between these two points, the all-too-familiar hardships of the Bootheel's extreme weather and unpredictable terrain tormented his men.

Severe flooding and freezing temperatures by the end of the year hampered progress through the lowlands near Lotta, a station Louis renamed Parma after the Italian city of that name. When his African American laborers refused to work in the cold—a seasonal dilemma that ironically exasperated Houck because the Irish would not leave the comfort of camp and the liquor bottle when it was hot—hundreds of Greeks, Italians, and their interpreters were brought in from St. Louis. To further build momentum and stretch resources, Houck directed A. R. Ponder to cut down trees and stretch them lengthwise across the right-of-way. Over these felled trees, ties went down and rails were laid before a parade of sand cars came along to build a sand dump on this timber foundation.[31]

When spring came, crews had a devil of a time with ties, not because of scarcity—the dense woods always afforded plentiful raw materials—but because once axmen cut them and left them lying along the route, tall grasses and reeds made it quite difficult to find them again. So exotic was the lush vegetation that Louis personally sent particularly unusual specimens to the Missouri Botanical Garden to be identified and catalogued.

Nonetheless, after erecting a mile-long trestle over one particularly problematic lake, by July 1901 the northern and southern crews converged in New Madrid County in a remote stretch of jungle Louis christened Tallapoosa, probably for the town in Georgia where Robert Sturdivant then lived in retirement.

---

31. J. B. Bobby to Louis Houck, September 1, 1900, Houck Papers, 1900 Box 1524, Correspondence, September A-F, Folder 13; A. R. Ponder to Louis Houck, February 12, 1901, Houck Papers, 1901 Box 1525, Correspondence, February S-Z, Folder 8; *Cape Girardeau Democrat*, April 21, 1900.

On a summer day so hot that track layers lost consciousness, Houck brought an excursion train down from Cape filled with friends and well-wishers to witness the joining of the rails of the Clarkton Branch and the St. Louis, Morehouse and Southern. To commemorate the momentous finale of the past two years' "grand rush," Louis triumphantly drove the ritual last spike to a host of cheers and the click of a photographer's shutter. Aside from the routine maintenance, this spike the master of ceremonies drove in 1901 effectively marked the end of new construction on the second Houck road south of Cape. Locals now claimed that because of Louis Houck, all of southeast Missouri was within six miles of a railroad. While this was a bit of an overstatement, the St. Louis, Kennett and Southern and Allied Lines—interlaced as they were with the Iron Mountain and Cotton Belt—were in fact now approximately 250 miles long.[32]

With "great relief and satisfaction," friends and associates congratulated him on the triumphant conclusion of his "herculean enterprise" and pronounced role in positioning Cape Girardeau and southeast Missouri on the verge of "substantial growth." "I think that you and what you have done are already a part of the history of the State of Missouri," Edward Hidden assured Houck, "and the story will make very interesting reading."[33]

Conversely, they also again expressed a vain desire that Louis take advantage of the occasion to sell off the lines and walk away from railroading for good. In wishing this was "the end of all your difficult railroad undertakings," Robert Sturdivant spoke for many who believed that "it would be well for you to retire to the Farm, and spend your last days with Mrs. Houck and the 'children,' enjoy sleep, rest and your good library." Facing his own mortality, the elderly banker concluded that "I would not have undergone your labors, worry and exposures for all the Railroads west of the Mississippi."[34]

32. Jensen, "Life on the Edge of the Great Cypress Swamp," 14; Houck, "Story of the Railroad Work, Volume II," 73–81; *Cape Girardeau Democrat,* August 13, 1904; J. E. Franklin to Louis Houck, July 29, 1901, Houck Papers, 1901 Box 1525, Correspondence, July A–G, Folder 19. However, at the time of the St. Louis and Gulf sale to the Frisco, Houck's crews were still finishing portions of the St. Louis, Morehouse and Southern per his original deal with Himmelberger and Luce. Because Himmelberger and Luce had put some of the Houck railroad bonds the corporation owned into an escrow account to finance completion of this road from Tallapoosa to Pascola, they would not release the bonds until all work was done. Thus in order to finalize the transaction with the Frisco, Houck was actually engaged in minor construction along this particular route after 1901.

33. Edward Hidden to Louis Houck, February 6, 1902, Houck Papers, 1902 Box 1526, Correspondence, February G–R, Folder 13.

34. Robert Sturdivant to Louis Houck, July 30, 1901, Houck Papers, 1901 Box 1525, Correspondence, July G–Z, Folder 20.

Without a doubt, Louis took these opinions to heart, and for the first time in many years even paused as if to catch his breath. After celebrating his daughter Irma's wedding to Charles Guild Juden, Jr., Houck sent out feelers to both the Cotton Belt and Frisco to gauge their level of interest in purchasing the southern system. He also started negotiating in a preliminary way with Newman Erb to explore the possibilities of organizing a mutually beneficial combination that would buy him out.[35] And while entertaining these comforting thoughts of ridding himself of the "mental worry" and "physical labor" of railroading, Houck also "exalted" in what Sturdivant referred to as the "cheerful exercise" of his "intellectual machinery."[36]

On the eve of the centennial of the Louisiana Purchase, Houck delved even deeper into historical research and writing as his broad and general interest in Missouri's heritage became an increasingly more focused agenda to tell its colonial history. Late in 1901, he published the first fruits of his self-professed labor of love, the brief ode to the genius of Thomas Jefferson and manifest destiny entitled *The Boundaries of the Louisiana Purchase: A Historical Study*. It was his third book. Fellow historians recognized it for what it was, a fairly orthodox commemoration of the landmark event *and* the tentative prologue of his magnum opus. "I am glad you have taken the first step in the right direction," his friend L. H. Davis encouraged, "and hope you will keep up the steps."[37]

The following spring, as he continued to immerse himself in the historical literature, a deal to sell the St. Louis, Kennett and Southern and Allied Lines to the Frisco actually began to solidify. Even so, as the time approached to pull the trigger, those close to him recognized his familiar restlessness and his reluctance to finally let go of the wolf after twenty-one years: in essence, selling would be a surrender to the region's larger railroads, which in the wartime atmosphere he had taken to calling "Spaniards." "I guess this is however as bad as talking to the wind," Sturdivant grumbled over Louis's apparent cold feet, "but remember you are a lone man, actually, as to your RR enterprises and that the other party is

35. Newman Erb to Louis Houck, June 22, 1900, Houck Papers, 1900 Box 1524, Correspondence, June R-Z, Folder 4; Newman Erb to Louis Houck, December 13, 1901, Houck Papers, 1901 Box 1526, Correspondence, December S-Z, Folder 6.

36. Robert Sturdivant to Louis Houck, April 29, 1901, Houck Papers, 1901 Box 1525, Correspondence, April M-Z, Folder 14.

37. L. H. Davis to Louis Houck, March 29, 1902, Houck Papers, 1902 Box 1526, Correspondence, March A-D, Folder 15. See Louis Houck, *The Boundaries of the Louisiana Purchase: A Historical Study* (St. Louis: Phillip Roeder's, 1901) and Frederick Moore, review of *The Boundaries of the Louisiana Purchase*, in *American Historical Review*, vol. 7 (1902): 608.

a 'continuing corporation,' in the hands of those who never die; or suspend their efforts to reach their ends." Edward Hidden's prognosis was
equally apt. "If you do conclude to sell and get out with a basket full of
money I believe you would before long be building some more railroads.
You have iron in your blood."[38]

Nevertheless, while Houck wrestled with the notion of retirement miles
away at Elmwood, on the night of April 7, 1902, Cape Girardeans were
roused from their slumber just before midnight by the Presbyterian
Church bell and the calamity of Fritz Tierkauff riding a horse down Broadway frantically shouting "Fire!" A blaze completely engulfing Academic
Hall illuminated Normal Hill high above town for miles and soon left little doubt as to what was burning. When firemen finally reached the campus from the courthouse grounds with a hand-drawn fire engine, little
remained for them to do other than join the crowd of one hundred or so
disheveled onlookers in stunned disbelief and sorrow. The few hoses volunteers managed to direct at the inferno only cooled the searing air. By
sunrise, all that seemingly remained of the Southeast Missouri Normal
School was the smoldering rubble of an empty, burned out, naked shell.[39]

38. Edward Hidden to Louis Houck, February 6, 1902, Houck Papers, 1902 Box 1526,
Correspondence, February G-R, Folder 13; Robert Sturdivant to Louis Houck, July 1,
1901, Houck Papers, 1901 Box 1525, Correspondence, July G-Z, Folder 20.
39. Heil, "Recollections"; Louis Houck to W. T. Carrington, August 1, 1902, Houck
Papers, Box 1541, Correspondence-Outgoing, January–August 1902, Folder 4.

CHAPTER 9

Academic Hall

So let me plead with you to not build any more railroads or write books or history but come up here to the capital peacefully, but bring your 'war paint' along if it has to be put on.

—R. B. Oliver to Louis Houck

Professor Harry L. Albert, a dedicated faculty member of the Third District Normal, wept openly at the sight of what remained of the school's ornamental towers before joining other stunned colleagues and students at the Common Pleas Court House for a hastily convened public meeting. Even while the building smoldered in the early twilight of Monday, April 8, 1902, word began spontaneously spreading among bystanders that all were to gather at ten o'clock to hear the administration's response to this unprecedented catastrophe. Though shaken, the institution's president, Washington Strother Dearmont, now in the third year of his tenure, addressed the crowd first. To reassure anxious minds, Dearmont earnestly reminded everyone that the Normal was not just a building, but a community that still resided in all students, faculty, and townspeople. Louis Houck spoke next, urging students to complete the year's school work and resolutely promising that the regents and town were already working to provide the necessary space and equipment to do so. Admitting that it would take a great deal of effort and sacrifice on everyone's part—especially the faculty—Dearmont then announced that classes would be temporarily held in the courthouse, the Baptist, Lutheran, Episcopal, and Methodist churches, Armory Hall, and several vacant commercial buildings owned by Houck. Students were to return to the courthouse the next morning to receive programs listing where and when classes would be conducted and then would immediately be dismissed to attend them. Classes at the Southeast Missouri Normal School would be suspended because of the fire, it was concluded, for just one day.[1]

The destruction of the Normal's main building, as university historian Arthur Mattingly pointed out, came at a critical time in the institution's history because "more was at stake than the loss of the building and its contents."[2] The immediate logistical concerns of temporarily relocating the actual daily functions of the school paled in comparison to the very significant strategic decisions Houck and the regents faced regarding the long-term future, and even the continued existence, of the Normal.

On the one hand, the viability of the normal-system philosophy was perpetually under attack in Missouri toward the end of the nineteenth and beginning of the twentieth centuries. Like clockwork, each new session of the General Assembly witnessed a showdown between "pro-normal" supporters and "anti-normals" who thought it more efficient—more cost-effective—to train teachers at either the high school or college and university levels. On the other hand, a sense of anxiety prevailed because the fire reignited controversy in the region over the state's original designation of Cape Girardeau as the home of the Third District Normal in 1873. The competition between Cape and rivals in Iron County had never really cooled after nearly thirty years, and the demise of old Academic Hall convinced some to the north that the time was finally ripe to relocate the school to a more central place in the district.

Hence, with a real sense of urgency—as any perceived delay or outward signs of indecision could jeopardize the school's future in Cape—the regents had to chart a course that would get the institution back on its feet in the quickest amount of time, and as cheaply as possible. Yet they differed on exactly how to do that: should they take the roughly $34,000 in insurance money from Academic, knowing full well it would have to be greatly supplemented by the state, and rebuild a substantial—read *permanent*—main building on the original site? Or should they instead use the insurance money to construct another smaller and cheaper building to tide them over?

At the time of the fire, work was under way on what was to be a second campus building, a new $20,000 Science Hall just a few hundred feet to the

1. W. S. Dearmont to Louis Houck, December 4, 1902, Houck Papers, 1902 Box 1527, Correspondence, December C-M, Folder 24. The general outline of the events surrounding the rebuilding of Academic Hall is based on Mattingly, *Normal to University,* Farmer, "Southeast Missouri State Normal," and Heil, "Recollections."

2. Mattingly, *Normal to University,* 87; *Cape Girardeau Democrat,* April 12, 1902.

east of Academic to accommodate the recently created Department of Chemistry and Agriculture and Department of Manual Training. Since all campus activities would conceivably now have to be consolidated into this much smaller structure for the foreseeable future, the notion of speeding up its completion while at the same time constructing a similar building nearby so that both would be open within a year or so made sense to Dearmont and every regent—except Houck. For Louis, the idea of saving time, money, and prestige in the long run by rebuilding Academic on its own ruins and reconstituting as much of the original material as possible appeared much wiser.

Skeptical of his apparently penny-wise-but-pound-foolish stance, but reluctant to oppose Houck outright, the regents demanded proof that the foundation and walls of burned-out Academic could even safely support the weight of new construction. To prove that they would not—and thus in effect overrule Louis without a fight—local contractor Edward F. Regenhardt was brought over from his work on Science Hall to test the older structure. As they assembled at the ruins in late May, Houck insistently lectured the 6'6", 270-pound Regenhardt on the virtues of his stance. Yet even when Regenhardt's thunderous sledgehammer blows against the foundation shook the walls and brought bricks raining down on the regents, Louis stubbornly stood by his case for rebuilding on the old substructure. The others, however, had seen enough, and under a shade tree on the terraces of Normal Hill, they decided, over Houck's lone dissenting vote, to immediately construct a Manual Training building on another site just northwest of the ruins. After razing the old foundation, the regents would then at some point ask the state for an appropriation for a completely new Academic Hall.[3]

Noticeably exasperated over having his judgment questioned on such a fundamental issue, Louis announced that after years of serving the school it now appeared to him that the regents had lost faith in his leadership. If that was the case, he said, and the decision to abandon the old walls was a vote of no confidence for his presidency, then he was prepared to leave the board if his colleagues saw fit. With that he abruptly walked down the hill and rode away in his buggy.[4]

Regenhardt broke ground on the Manual Training School—today the Arts Building—in late summer 1902. To stretch the insurance money, the

3. Benjamin W. Simmons, "Washington S. Dearmont and His Impact upon Southeast Missouri State University," 29.

4. W. S. Dearmont to Floyd Shoemaker, April 16, 1940, Dearmont folder, Special Collections and Archives, Southeast Missouri State University, Cape Girardeau, Mo.

regents briefly considered constructing it of brick, but Houck strenuously maintained that in the interest of aesthetic continuity Regenhardt must use the same exterior dimensions of the Science Hall—presently A. S. J. Carnahan Hall—and the same white limestone, or Cape Girardeau "marble." As with Science Hall, the respected St. Louis architect Jerome Bibb Legg again worked with Dearmont to design the interior of the Training School, and upon Louis's further recommendations four Missouri coats of arms were cast in bronze, instead of carved into the stone, and positioned in the pediments above each building's two front doors. Thus upon their opening in 1903, the two "sister" halls established the model for future campus buildings in regard to material and color.[5]

While both Science Hall and Manual Training were under way in 1902, Louis overcame those earlier trepidations about selling the St. Louis, Kennett, and Southern. Since 1897 the St. Louis and San Francisco railroad—Frisco—had been pursuing a concerted policy of expansion throughout Missouri, Oklahoma, Kansas, Texas, and Arkansas. Most of the railway's new mileage in this era—some 2,375 miles by 1907—came via an unscrupulous strategy of buying up preexisting railroads at grossly inflated prices from various syndicates and construction companies that were indirectly controlled by Frisco president Benjamin F. Yoakum or other officials. The nine railroads the Frisco eventually absorbed in this manner before bankrupting itself included Houck's southern system and, incidentally, Newman Erb's Southern Missouri and Arkansas road—the first Houck road.[6]

Louis first approached the Frisco the year before through Thomas H. West, an executive with that line and the president of the St. Louis Trust Company, which owned much of the paper on his railroad debts. West put Houck in contact with Yoakum and B. L. Winchell in the Frisco's St. Louis headquarters, and the three negotiated on and off for months. At one point, as legend has it, Houck became so desirous of concluding favorable terms that in order to make the roads look more prosperous than they were to Frisco representatives visiting Cape Girardeau, he intentionally disrupted normal operations in favor of loading several trains to their freight-hauling capacity. These same few trains were then cunningly run back and

5. Mattingly, *Normal to University*, 90; Farmer, "Southeast Missouri State Normal," 179; J. B. Legg to Louis Houck, November 19, 1902, Houck Papers, 1902 Box 1527, Correspondence, November H-P, Folder 21.

6. Ripley, *Railroads*, 41–42; *Cape Girardeau Democrat*, January 18, 1902. The Frisco eventually acquired the Southern Missouri and Arkansas indirectly when it took over the St. Louis, Memphis, and Southeastern, which had absorbed Erb's line in 1902.

forth all day to the Cape Girardeau depot to give the illusion of a bustling freight business up and down the road.[7]

Eventually, the deal he reached called for a smooth four-step progression in what was evidently quintessential B. F. Yoakum fashion. Houck first suspended his practice of no longer consolidating the roads, and instead combined all the St. Louis, Kennett, and Southern and Allied lines into one St. Louis and Gulf. In actuality, the newly organized St. Louis and Gulf railway was a syndicate, still nominally under Houck's direction but now financed primarily by West's St. Louis Trust Company with a capital stock of $5 million and heavily under the influence of the Frisco's Yoakum and Winchell. Once organized, the St. Louis and Gulf purchased the southern system from Houck for $1.33 million; more specifically, this huge divestiture of seven railroads amounted to $558,000 in cash and bonds and the assumption of $775,000 of existing and outstanding bonded indebtedness. Since the St. Louis and Gulf's maintenance shops and terminals in Cape Girardeau were on property owned by Mary—and in fact Louis's railroads had been leasing the land from his wife for $2,000 annually—the Frisco had to pick up the lease with an option to buy that real estate as well. In due course, Houck resigned as president of the St. Louis and Gulf that September 1902, and within two years the company sold to the Frisco for $2.7 million, or another tidy profit of more than $1.3 million.[8]

Although the Interstate Commerce Commission would one day take issue with Yoakum and the Frisco's business practices, seemingly everyone walked away from the St. Louis and Gulf a big winner. Not only did the lucrative sale to a national railroad interest vindicate, in the eyes of many, the original vision of the man lauded as "the Pontifex Maximus of Southeast Missouri development," but also the windfall afforded new opportunities in both time and money for Houck to pursue what some capitalists of his generation would have recognized as a "Gospel of Wealth."[9] Louis had always been a philanthropist—giving generously to churches, civic organizations, and education—but the sale of the southern

7. *The Tiger* (Cape Girardeau Central High School), March 28, 1941; B. F. Yoakum to Louis Houck, October 7, 1902, Houck Papers, 1902 Box 1527, Correspondence, October R–Z, Folder 19.

8. *Cape Girardeau Democrat,* May 24, September 6, 1902; *Poor's Manual of Railroads 1903* (New York: H. V. and H. W. Poor, 1903), 545, John W. Barriger III National Railroad Library; Louis Houck to George Houck, September 27, 1902, Houck Papers, Box 1541, Correspondence–Outgoing, September 22–30 1902; Houck, "Story of the Railroad Work, Volume II," 89–90; Ripley, *Railroads,* 41.

9. *Cape Girardeau Democrat,* December 6, 1902; A. O. Phalen to Louis Houck, December 22, 1902, Houck Papers, 1902 Box 1527, Correspondence, December, Folder 23.

system in 1902 clearly marks a pronounced increase in his commitment to make art, culture, libraries, and formal education available to all social classes in southeast Missouri.

These pursuits were at the core of celebrated industrialist Andrew Carnegie's notion of a "Gospel of Wealth." In arguing against growing popular demands for the government to check the increasingly unbalanced distribution of wealth in the nation—particularly some type of effective income tax system—Carnegie posited that huge private fortunes created by industrialization were actually being held in a sort of public trust by the wealthy. To Carnegie and other like-minded philanthropists, the rich made their money fair and square because healthy capitalist competition was allowed to flourish in America's laissez-faire free market system without government interference. Yet ultimately, being rich carried with it an obligation to reinvest that wealth for the overall benefit of the public good. Based on an abiding twentieth-century faith in science and education to facilitate social progress, this school of thought considered cultural refinement and learning to be among the best avenues for elevating the poor and working classes. Accordingly, men, and women, of means across the country followed Carnegie's lead by investing their millions in the creation of institutions such as private universities, municipal museums, concert halls, and public libraries.[10]

In the immediate weeks and months around the sale of his railroad, Louis and Mary indulged in an extended vacation of health resorts and Caribbean cruises to mend, as he said, his impaired constitution, first visiting Rea at school in Pittsburgh, then traveling on to New York before spending almost two months in Jamaica and Cuba with L. B. and his new wife, Virginia.[11] Between some of these sojourns, in August 1902, the Houcks approached Cape Girardeau with an offer to establish what they called the Giboney-Houck Free Library. They would donate to the town $30,000 for a building, equipment, furnishings, and books. In return the couple asked that the citizens of the Cape make a firm commitment to the library by furnishing the land—a roughly $2,000 property just north of Houck's railroad church on Lorimier Street—as well as free lighting, water, and fuel. Moreover, they asked for a commitment to perpetually support the institution with an annual tax of two mills on the dollar upon all the taxable property within in the city limits.

10. Trachtenberg, *The Incorporation of America*, 143, 231.
11. *Cape Girardeau Democrat*, June 14, July 26, December 20, 1902; John Shepley to Louis Houck, September 12, 1902, Houck Papers, 1902 Box 1527, Correspondence, September R-Z, Folder 16.

As Louis explained in the initial proposal before the Commercial Club—the direct forerunner of today's Chamber of Commerce—with Cape Girardeau entering a period of economic, commercial, and cultural prosperity, a public library was a necessary element in continuing this march forward. The city council and townspeople immediately concurred, passing with little opposition an ordinance to accept the magnanimous gift and voting overwhelmingly to approve the library tax that would make it a reality. The support delighted the Houcks, who announced plans to break ground by the end of the year on a modern Italian Renaissance building "intended to be architecturally an ornament to this city." As stipulated in the ordinance, the Giboney-Houck Free Library was to be governed by a ten-member board, and Louis also took the liberty of submitting to the town a list of men he considered suitably civic-minded and exhibiting the requisite scholarly, literary, and educational qualifications. Houck also reminded the city council that another provision of the endowment called for two rooms in the library—one for adults and the other for children—"to be set aside for the exclusive use of the colored people of Cape Girardeau."[12]

Here, however, what should have been a festive occasion for Cape Girardeau began going sour. The Missouri Supreme Court abruptly stopped the proposed library in its tracks when the justices overturned a lower court's decision and found the tax supporting the institution illegal based on the fact that Cape citizens were already taxed at the maximum rate allowed by the state constitution for cities of fewer than ten thousand people. In the absence of this tax, the donation of the library effectively became a moot point because the town would never be able to employ librarians and staff, buy additional books, or generally sustain it in the manner in which the Houcks had specified.

Not one accustomed to take no for an answer from any judicial body, Louis launched a statewide campaign to get all the library boards in Missouri—in particular Kirksville, Jefferson City, and Springfield—to join him in submitting a constitutional amendment to the General Assembly allowing cities to levy a special tax dedicated to the support of public libraries. As a show of good faith and confidence in this proposed amendment's passage, the Houcks also deposited the promised $30,000 with the St. Louis Union Trust in the form of railroad bonds. The bonds were to remain for a period of five years. If and when the amendment passed and Cape could adequately support the library through taxation, the funds would be made available immediately. If not, the Houcks would take back the bonds

12. *Cape Girardeau Democrat*, September 13, October 4, 1902.

at the end of the five years including all interest accrued during that time. The five years elapsed and the amendment never passed.[13]

Besides the library campaign, Mary Houck also pursued her own charitable interests as a charter member of two other prominent women's organizations. The first, the Daughters of the Confederacy, was founded probably in the 1890s in St. Louis largely as a result of Mary's crusade to raise money for the struggling home for disabled Confederate veterans in the "Little Dixie" town of Higginsville, Missouri. In 1901 she formed the Cape Girardeau chapter, only the third one in the state, and devoted herself to putting on annual fund-raising and social events, including serving as hostess at lavish Christmas parties at Elmwood until she was well into her seventies. That same year Mrs. Houck also helped organize a Cape chapter of the Daughters of the American Revolution, presiding as president of the eleven-member group, which they christened the Nancy Hunter Chapter because all were descendants of the Hunter family. Through her active membership in the Daughters of the American Revolution and also the Colonial Dames, Mary sponsored yearly contests with prizes for students and citizens who wrote the best historical essays on Missouri.[14]

Though other initiatives to benefit their beloved community would be forthcoming, the pièce de résistance of Louis Houck's reinvestment in Cape Girardeau was clearly his service on the board of regents of the Southeast Missouri Normal School and perhaps more specifically his unflagging dedication to the erection of Academic Hall.

Much of Houck's tenure as president of the regents coincided with the administration of Washington Dearmont, arguably, as Arthur Mattingly contends, "one of the most successful in the history of the institution." Despite the two men not always seeing eye-to-eye and ultimately undergoing a nasty "divorce," their stable and firm leadership in the early twentieth century provided the primary impetus for remarkable intellectual and physical growth. They fostered the guiding philosophy at the institution that education should be accessible to everyone who sought it, and not just academic book learning, but cultural enrichment as well. This meant keeping education affordable and increasing the scope of the school's role as a service institution in a still relatively impoverished quarter of the state that stretched roughly from St. Louis to Arkansas, and from the Mississippi River westward to Springfield.

13. Ibid., December 19, 1903, January 23, 1904; Doherty, Jr., *Houck, Missouri Historian and Entrepreneur*, 93.
14. *Cape Girardeau Southeast Missourian*, December 21, 1944.

Embracing the school's role as the educational center of this region, Dearmont and Houck directed the critical maturation from a Normal that simply trained elementary and high school teachers to a four-year college centered on a traditional liberal arts curriculum and more rigorous academic standards. As the official name change to Southeast Missouri State Teachers College in 1919 suggests, the expanded mission embraced the demands the president and head regent placed on the institution, offering students a breadth and depth of learning by acquainting them with the best writing and thought in the fields of language, mathematics, literature, history, business, music and art, physical science, and the social sciences.[15]

Much of this eventual progress and growth was, however, still predicated on rebuilding Academic Hall. By the end of 1902, work was under way on Science Hall and the Manual Training building, yet the school still had no main building and no money to build it. Since the fire, Louis had been pushing the board of regents to focus on replacing the old Normal with a substantial new main building, and now, with Dearmont's help, Houck put any lingering hard feelings aside and set about doing just that. Dearmont and the regents came to the consensus that state money constituted the only viable means of carrying off such an ambitious undertaking. First, and most logically, only the state had the economic resources necessary to come up with enough money to cover such a huge price tag. Second—and apparently Dearmont voiced this insightful consideration—was that a substantial state appropriation would force Missouri to go on record once and for all as both supporting the normal system in general and Cape Girardeau as the permanent home of the Third District school in particular. Dearmont understood that while the state commonly supported building projects at the University of Missouri—in particular the oddly similar rebuilding of "Old Main" on the Columbia campus in 1892—the General Assembly had been less inclined to do so at the normals. This convinced him that until lawmakers put their money where their mouth was, the status and future of the normal system would remain in question.[16]

Where the regents differed was on the issue of exactly how much to ask for. By his logic, the president of the school and several board members favored the whopping figure of $250,000. The president of the regents,

15. Mattingly, *Normal to University*, 70, 72, 77–78.

16. Ibid., 91; Farmer, "Southeast Missouri State Normal," 179; A. O. Phalen to Louis Houck, November 28, 1902, Houck Papers, 1902 Box 1527, Correspondence, November A-H, Folder 20; A. O. Phalen to Louis Houck, December 5, 1902, Houck Papers, 1902 Box 1527, Correspondence, December A-C, Folder 23.

however, found a quarter of a million dollars imprudent and simply fool-hardy, no doubt reminding his colleagues that the extravagant sum repre-sented two-and-a-half times more than the value of all the buildings of any given normal school in the state, and moreover that the entire sum appropriated to the institution for building and support in its twenty-eight years of existence had amounted to only $352,312.[17]

During his time on the board, Houck seems to have been known pri-marily for several things: his willingness to delegate tasks coupled with a natural tendency to at times micro-manage, his penchant for being a real stickler for attendance, and perhaps most of all his habit of translating his thrifty railroading philosophy to the business administration of the school. According to historian William Doherty, perhaps Louis's greatest contri-bution to the overall prosperity of the college was his ability to change the mind-set of the regents toward being more "economical with state appro-priations." Previous boards had routinely underspent in order to main-tain a budget surplus, a practice Houck found inexcusable because it only undermined future appropriation requests. Louis, while always aggres-sive in pursuing state money and never afraid to deficit-spend to fund cap-ital improvements, preferred to religiously follow the maxim of "asking only things that we actually need and that we can demonstrate almost to a mathematical certainty ought to be granted" and then resourcefully spending every penny granted by the state.[18]

Houck preferred requesting $100,000 for Academic, although he pri-vately doubted whether the state would even appropriate this more mod-est amount. But in time, through a little diplomacy and deft administrative politicking—garnering the vocal support of the Alumni Association—Dearmont gently swayed Louis to his way of thinking, and together they lined up the rest of the board behind the plan to request $250,000. Although a late convert to this figure, once the decision was made Houck took up the cause enthusiastically, and he and Dearmont, likewise a trained lawyer, worked closely to craft the strategy necessary to land such a huge fish. Louis enjoyed impressive access to several levers of power in Jefferson City, but such an improbably large allocation of state funds would take even more pull and more favors than he could muster. They needed someone in the General Assembly—a politician known to advocate the normal school philosophy in general, one well respected outside of Cape County who

17. *Cape Girardeau Democrat,* March 28, 1903.

18. Doherty, Jr., *Houck, Missouri Historian and Entrepreneur,* 82, 83; Farmer, "Southeast Missouri State Normal," 133, 180, 222; Houck, "Some Reminiscences," 61–62.

could skillfully shepherd the appropriation through the legislature. And with 1902 being an election year, they needed him now.

To their credit, Houck, Dearmont, and the regents found their ideal "instrument" in attorney Robert Burett Oliver, and with all of their political acumen combined got him elected to the Missouri House of Representatives in November. Perhaps owing to Houck's connections, Speaker of the House James H. Whitecotton promptly appointed the newly seated representative as the chairman of the Committee on Normal Schools for the 1903 session, a move that positioned him wonderfully to introduce the appropriation as soon as the session got under way in January.

In addition to his legal service to Houck in the Gould wars, R. B. Oliver was also a seasoned politician and veteran of many legislative battles. A former Cape County prosecutor and Democratic state senator, he correctly judged the house to be more resistant than the senate to the $250,000 request, and so he concentrated the majority of his behind-the-scenes lobbying efforts there. Oliver also rallied all the regents to Jefferson City for a diplomatic offensive, imploring them to "organize our friends throughout the state" and exhaust every political contact at their disposal. "I have put my whole soul in this matter," he wrote Houck, "so let me plead with you to not build any more railroads or write books or history, but come up here to the capital peacefully, but bring your 'war paint' along if it has to be put on."[19]

Houck did indeed reach out to Governor Alexander Dockery, appealing to the chief executive's well-known suspicion of the burgeoning reform impulses that would soon become associated with the Progressive movement. In this regard, the paramount importance of rebuilding the Third District Normal better than before lay in the institution's unmatched capacity to impose proper industrial work values in the region, or, in Houck's words, to "educate teachers in Missouri schools in order to propagate Missouri ideas," meaning limited government and fiscal conservatism. "It is because western and southern people allowed the education of the children to fall into the hands of New England teachers," he warned the governor, "that so many 'isms'"—in particular the political threats of lingering Populism and creeping Socialism in the Bootheel—"are flourishing through the South and West."[20]

19. R. B. Oliver to Louis Houck, February 21, 1903, February 27, 1903, Houck Papers, 1903 Box 1528, Correspondence, February M-Z, Folder 5; Farmer, "Southeast Missouri State Normal," 180; Mattingly, *Normal to University*, 92–93.

20. Louis Houck to A. M. Dockery, December 16, 1902, Houck Papers, Box 1541, Correspondence–Outgoing, December 13–31, 1902, Folder 14.

As part of the broader general appropriations bill for educational institutions, in March 1903 the Missouri House of Representatives authorized $246,300 for the District Three Normal, or $200,000 for construction and $46,300 for salaries and maintenance.[21] For the remainder of the spring Houck and the regents set to work hiring an architect, selecting plans, and deciding on the right building contractor for Academic Hall, a truly mammoth public building as they envisioned it, unprecedented by southeast Missouri standards. Each of these steps, Louis insisted, would be done carefully and deliberately, not in haste. For weeks a delegation consisting variously of regents Houck and Leon Albert, State Superintendent of Public Schools W. T. Carrington, Dearmont, and J. B. Legg toured other normal campuses in Iowa and Illinois, as well as Washington University in St. Louis, where they also inspected the spectacular pavilions and palaces being constructed in Forest Park for the upcoming Louisiana Purchase Exposition.

As they traveled, a general conception of the form and function they wanted began to solidify, and upon their return to Cape Girardeau they decided to start with only a general list of recommendations and allow interested architects to competitively submit plans based on these.[22] Architecturally, Houck had always derisively considered the old Normal building as an "excrescence," and now as he, Dearmont, and Albert conceived of it, Academic Hall would have to be in harmony with Science Hall and Training Hall, which meant blue limestone for the basement and white limestone for the two upper floors. That frontage was to be nearly 260 feet with a grand main entrance leading into an auditorium with a stage and gallery. The main floor must also contain a library along with reading and reference rooms. The basement should house a gymnasium, divided for male and female, while the third floor would be broken up into classrooms and society rooms.

Fellow regent Moses Whybark may well have spoken for the whole board when he gave Houck his vote of confidence on these provisions. Go ahead and build Academic Hall the way you see fit, Whybark told Louis. "Pay no attention to the criticisms of the few who look more to the cost of a thing than its utility." After all, "it is a state institution, and permanent, and the future is all ahead of us."[23]

21. Mattingly, *Normal to University*, 121; *Cape Girardeau Democrat*, January 16, 24, 1903.
22. J. B. Legg to Louis Houck, April 8, May 20, 1903, Houck Papers, 1903 Box 1528, Correspondence, April E-S, Folder 10.
23. Moses Whybark to Louis Houck, September 6, 1903, Houck Papers, 1903 Box 1528, Correspondence, September K-S, Folder 23.

Based primarily on the desire for continuity with Science Hall and Train-ing Hall, the regents retained J. B. Legg as architect. Legg's daring neo-classical design, which estimated construction costs at no more than $175,000, exceeded each of the regent's requirements, and did so using imposing elements of Greek and Roman architecture with four Ionic columns dominating the facade and a magnificent copper dome. Again sustaining Houck's determination that they maintain a "unity of pur-pose," they awarded the contractor's job to Regenhardt and Maule, the only southeast Missouri company that bid on it.[24]

From virtually the minute work began in 1903, the same year the other campus buildings opened, Louis shifted the bulk of his professional atten-tion and energies to the pursuit of completing Academic Hall. When he first arrived in town from Elmwood each morning he went straight to the site to monitor the operation, and sometimes made another visit before returning home in the evening. In Regenhardt's quarry near what is today Memorial Hall, he observed the formation of the walls from start to finish, first as laborers extracted the white limestone and sawed the rock into appropriately sized slabs, and later as stone cutters chipped and shaped the stone into the correct form.

In his railroad office, Houck and Legg, or often Legg's partner Charles Holloway, pored over blueprints and photographs—including Andrew Carnegie's just completed mansion—hammering out details ranging from the use of galvanized iron instead of terra cotta in the main cornice to the type of doors leading into the water closets. Some regents, like Moses Whybark, ventured up the hill only periodically to see the edifice under construction, but owing to their lack of building experience chose to take Job's biblical advice that it was folly for them to "darken counsel by words without knowledge, and so do more harm than good."[25] Not so with Houck. He delighted in having a say in even the minutest details of the project, submitting hand-drawn sketches, walking the grounds with sub-contractors to locate water and sewer pipes, directing electricians on the placement of fixtures, and calculating with engineers the load-bearing capacity of beams to support heavy classroom equipment. He even felt free to offer his original ideas on fire proofing—including a wholly imprac-

24. Henry Van Brunt to Louis Houck, May 16, 1903, Houck Papers, 1903 Box 1528, Correspondence, May R-Z, Folder 14.

25. Moses Whybark to Louis Houck, August 16, 1903, Houck Papers, 1903 Box 1528, Correspondence, August H-Z, Folder 21.

tical twenty-five-thousand-gallon iron tank in the dome that would "flood" any part of the building with water within a minute's notice.[26]

Much of his involvement required alternatively stroking, scolding, and mediating between the very strong personalities who made up the principals, especially Legg and Regenhardt, whose tense working relationship stretched even tauter over the next couple of years. In truth, Legg, the St. Louis architect, never considered the local Regenhardt "big enough" to conquer "the magnitude of his contract"—ironic given Regenhardt's robust physical dimensions—and he fretted endlessly throughout 1904 and 1905 over the inadequacy of the contractor's progress, or, more irritatingly, Regenhardt's perceived lack of a sense of urgency.[27] The first of these quarrels arose in the summer of 1904 just as construction progressed above the ground level of Academic's acre-wide foundation. As stone cutters laid the first rows—or courses—of white limestone blocks, quarrymen began running out of suitable stone at their on-site pit, which not only threw off Legg's tight schedule but also potentially compromised the continuity of the campus.

Houck provided stone from one of his quarries as a stopgap measure and then began smoothing ruffled feathers. First he calmed Regenhardt—who, like Louis, had a propensity for "cursing and raging"—predicting that plenty of good stone still remained buried in the ground. "No man could expect to get all meat and no bone," Louis assured, it was just a simple fact of quarrying that sometimes inferior stone got hauled up. When blasters indeed began uncovering another layer of better stone some twenty feet below just as Louis forecast, apprehension grew that any defects or variations in the color of the limestone would ruin the overall look of the building, making it appear striped or spotted. Here, Houck and Dearmont worked to build a consensus that the overall beauty of the structure would lie in its "massive appearance" and any flaws in the stone would be rendered unnoticeable by its sheer size.[28]

By the end of 1904 as construction fell further behind schedule, it became apparent that Academic Hall would not be completed for the fall

26. Louis Houck to J. B. Legg, April 10, 1905, Houck Papers, Box 1543, Correspondence–Outgoing, April 1–17 1905, Folder 7.

27. Jerome B. Legg to Louis Houck, October 4, 1904, Houck Papers, 1904 Box 1530, Correspondence, October K-J, Folder 28.

28. Louis Houck to J. B. Legg, June 17, 1904, Houck Papers, Box 1542, Correspondence–Outgoing, June 17–30 1904, Folder 22; W. S. Dearmont to Louis Houck, November 12, 1904, Houck Papers, 1904 Box 1530, Correspondence, November S-Z, Folder 32.

term in 1905 as contracted, and Houck increasingly came to agree with Legg that Regenhardt was largely to blame. In accordance with Dearmont, the regents did grant the builder an extension, albeit with the caveat that as a united front they deal with Regenhardt's tardiness with a firmer hand. To avoid any misunderstanding, Houck personally explained to Regenhardt that up until this point the regents had in their mind been "very indulgent" regarding the contracted schedule primarily because of unforeseen work stoppages resulting from the weather, the quarry, and delays in the shipment of steel beams. However, all those problems had largely been ameliorated and still the regents observed no appreciable quickening of the pace. "You seem to look upon this as a century job," content to let it take years, Houck told Regenhardt, but this attitude would no longer suffice. Thereafter any holdups caused by the contractor's "own neglect and want of foresight" would hereafter result in the contractor being docked with economic penalties.[29]

"Am urging the construction of that building all I can because I want to see it finished while I live," Louis confided to Robert Sturdivant. "[K]now that I won't take any interest in things after I am dead."[30] But before that day of reckoning came, he busied himself with ancillary ventures to complement the anticipated opening of Academic. For many years, the inaccessibility of the campus had been a real impediment to enrollment. While Houck's railroads may have allowed more students to come to Cape from neighboring counties, there just were not any good paved roads or convenient walkways up to the campus. Since the 1890s, the regents had been spending money to improve accessibility, mainly in the form of lowering and grading Normal Avenue, which runs east and west over Normal Hill in front of Academic Hall, and filling in that washed-out ravine. Finally, in 1904 the regents requested, and a year later the city built, a modern granitoid sidewalk complete with gutters and curbs on both sides of Pacific Street connecting the major thoroughfare of Broadway to Normal Avenue.

True to his horticultural sensibilities, Louis seems to have amended these sidewalk plans with the stipulation that the elm trees he had earlier furnished along the streets leading up to the Normal be protected. Houck took a large measure of pride in personally handling projects that beautified the school, and here his abiding interest in tree planting and care is

29. Louis Houck to Edward Regenhardt, October 3, 1904, Houck Papers, Box 1542, Correspondence–Outgoing, October 1–31 1904, Folder 29.
30. Louis Houck to Robert Sturdivant, August 17, 1903, Houck Papers, Box 1542, Correspondence–Outgoing, August 15–29 1903, Folder 4.

clear. During daily tours of the construction site, Louis commonly strolled along in the company of his walking stick and a professor in the Chemistry and Agriculture Department to determine the placement of the many varieties of new trees that were part of the comprehensive landscaping plan he initiated for the campus. Often he might stop to chastise the janitors for not keeping the fences whitewashed or the elms pruned and safe from the insects that attacked them. Indeed, so concerned was he for preserving the natural pastoral beauty of the school, and reducing water runoff, that over the previous decade he had also hired James Brooks to terrace the east side of Normal Hill and build a two-foot-high sandstone retaining wall along Normal Avenue, although admittedly this last project was more to stop wayward farm animals from straying onto the grounds.[31]

By the same token, Houck saw to the beautification and advancement of Academic Hall's interior sanctuaries as well. The plans for Academic called for a modern library to occupy the entire eastern wing of the first floor. To facilitate this physical expansion of the school's library, Louis lent his hand to increasing the holdings to nearly four thousand volumes in total, including around a thousand books on history and the Civil War with a special collection for Missouri and the West. Soon, his own significant writings would constitute the centerpiece of the collection. Together with the history section, the library also acquired another thousand volumes of American and classical literature and around eight hundred volumes of science, pedagogy, music, manual training, and philosophy. Through Louis's connections with Congressman Joseph J. Russell, the Normal eventually became the official repository of government documents of the Fourteenth Congressional District, and for good measure Willard Vandiver donated another substantial collection of federal papers. And with equally obvious Houck influence, the new reading room began receiving more than one hundred periodicals as well as all local newspapers and the major dailies from around the country.[32]

During his visits to the World's Fair in 1904, Louis also kept his eyes open for opportunities to bring some of the exhibition's wonders back to southeast Missouri. Houck spent at least ten days in October marveling at the spectacle of the fair's layout, then the largest such event in history. He and Mary roamed a good deal of the seventy-five miles of walkways

31. Farmer, "Southeast Missouri State Normal," 142–43; Mattingly, *Normal to University*, 19, 98–99, 101; Houck, "Some Reminiscences," 63, 66–67.
32. Farmer, "Southeast Missouri State Normal," 203; Mattingly, *Normal to University*, 79.

throughout the twelve-hundred-acre Forest Park site, much of it designed by famed landscape architect George Kessler. Louis lamented that this awesome celebration of the Louisiana Purchase's centennial—including some fifteen hundred buildings in total—was "too big for me and as for that too big for anybody. It is discouraging to walk around trying to see things and in the evening quit foot sore and weary and feeling that after all you can only casually glance at things . . . one can walk around day in and day out and not see a soul you know." But for all that, he loved the "big Fair," believing it an "extraordinary" event for St. Louis, Missouri, and the West.[33]

Upon learning that the fine furnishings in the Missouri State Building would be sold to interested state agencies after the exposition closed at the end of the year, Houck proposed that instead they simply be given to "impoverished" little institutions like the Normal. Following a little negotiating with the state's Board of Equalization, and after a fire in the Missouri Building that damaged many of the pieces, a boxcar ultimately arrived in Cape Girardeau filled to the ceiling with several hundred yards of fine carpet, two leather divans, the grand chandeliers still hanging in Academic's corridors, two large oil paintings, assorted ornaments, and a mahogany mantle and table Louis specifically coveted for the new regents' room.[34]

What he could not secure gratis from the fair, he purchased. In addition to the glassware, jewelry, and furniture from around the globe that Louis bought for Elmwood, he also bought a collection of ancient, medieval, and modern works of art reproduced by German artist August Gerber and donated them to the school with the wish that a room be made available in Academic Hall so that the statuary would be permanently displayed. The fifty-eight reproductions, which were displayed at the German Educational Exhibit, had been crafted by Gerber using his "special and secret substance" composed in part of alabaster. Being of the same dimensions and finished in either bronze or marble, they appeared in every respect to be exact replicas of the original masterpieces, so much so that their well-respected Cologne-born sculptor received a "Grand Prize" from fair judges.[35]

33. Louis Houck to Robert Sturdivant, October 27, 1904, Houck Papers, Box 1542, Correspondence–Outgoing, October 1–31 1904, Folder 29.
34. Heil, "Recollections"; Louis Houck to J. B. Legg, November 22, 1904, Houck Papers, Box 1542, Correspondence–Outgoing, November 18–30 1904, Folder 31; Louis Houck to Alex M. Dockery, December 5, 1904, Houck Papers, Box 1543, Correspondence–Outgoing, December 1–13 1904, Folder 1.
35. *Cape Girardeau Democrat*, December 24, 1904; Louis Houck to W. S. Dearmont, October 22, 1904, Houck Papers, Box 1542, Correspondence, October 1904, Folder 29.

During the last months of the World's Fair, M. E. Leming and his wife, Thelma, accompanied Dearmont's wife, Julia, to St. Louis for another round of state requisitions, this time picking out surplus furniture for yet one more Houck-inspired improvement project: dormitories. Intertwined with the nagging inaccessibility issues, the Normal also suffered from a lack of appropriate student housing, a problem made more acute by the school's historically female population and physical distance from the community. The trouble was that due to a lack of dormitories on campus, "scholars" were compelled to make arrangements to room in town far away from Normal Hill, which left the administration with little oversight as to whether the accommodations in Cape's boardinghouses were sufficient to protect the delicate female virtues of the student body. On-campus dormitories were an obvious solution, but one that the state intractably refused to fund. Thus, in 1904 regents Houck, M. E. Leming, and Leon J. Albert took matters into their own hands and formed the Normal Dormitory Association to privately build and operate that very thing.

Finding few citizens willing to subscribe money for bonds to finance what townspeople considered a risky venture, Houck, Leming, and Albert took out loans to acquire land on the south side of Normal Avenue where today stands the University Center. With J. B. Legg already at work on campus, and again in the interest of symmetry, the Dormitory Association employed the architect to design Albert Hall, which began going up across the street from Academic in September. Built and equipped—with electricity and steam heat—for around $40,000, the three-story limestone dormitory for men contained its own kitchen, pantry, dining hall, laundry room, and gymnasium in the basement while its top two levels were divided among parlors and reception rooms, bath and toilet rooms, and forty-four student rooms.

While Albert Hall welcomed its first residents in March 1905, Houck, Leming, and Albert—the latter two a lumberman and banker respectively—contracted to build a second dormitory, Leming Hall, nearby. Their decision was driven by the considerable demand for female housing, which in fact had compelled the Normal Dormitory Association to open Albert Hall temporarily as a women's dorm. The roughly $50,000 Leming Hall closely followed the same blueprint as Albert Hall, although it was slightly larger to accommodate more students, and, because the structure rested in an exhausted thirty-foot quarry, the foundation was almost as deep as the building was high. Upon its completion in March 1906, the female scholars moved into Leming and the men took up residence in

Albert; these were the only dormitories on the campus of a Missouri normal school at the time.

To maintain that proper Victorian gender demarcation, Dearmont proposed, and the board enacted, a rule that hereafter students were prohibited from living in private co-ed boardinghouses and in like measure prospective students would not be admitted unless they resided in either the dormitories or some form of faculty-approved arrangement. Besides banning co-ed habitation, Louis also sought an injunction to prohibit the sale of intoxicating liquor at the district fair, which at the time was held just two blocks from campus where Capaha Park is today, to likewise thwart the demoralizing effects of alcohol on the student body.[36]

By December 1905, Regenhardt's crews in and around Academic Hall were wrapping up, with only a handful of jobs left to be completed. As work progressed throughout 1905, the strain and pressure of the enormous undertaking never really subsided, but although hard feelings persisted between Dearmont and Regenhardt, probably resulting in the builder only receiving his due credit and full compensation belatedly, the president entered Academic Hall on December 2 with some five thousand people who toured the structure during its first opening to the public.[37] Nearly a month later, J. B. Legg gave notice to the regents that construction was now finally finished, and on January 24, 1906, the state formally accepted what was at the time the largest public building in Missouri.[38]

The official dedication of Academic Hall actually came in May to coincide with graduation. In an atmosphere of jubilation, Houck served as the master of ceremonies in Academic's grand auditorium. At Dearmont's invitation, Willard Vandiver gave the commencement address, and various

36. Houck and his partners always intended to sell the dormitories to the state so that they might officially become part of Southeast Missouri Normal School, but that did not come to pass until after 1911 when the General Assembly finally made them state property with an $85,000 appropriation. *Daily Republican,* October 9, 1905.

37. The violent encounter between Washington Dearmont's jaw and the fist of Regenhardt's night watchman Logier Lowe in July 1905 attested to this. Under specific orders from Regenhardt to keep all unauthorized persons off the site after hours, Lowe denied Dearmont's entrance to the unfinished building and when the president persisted, Lowe broke his jaw. Simmons, "Dearmont and His Impact," 39–41.

38. Due to some $5,600 in penalties invoked by the Board of Regents for missed deadlines, it took years before Regenhardt finally received thousands of dollars still owed to him by the state for building Academic Hall. N. O. Nelson Manufacturing to Louis Houck, March 29, 1907, Houck Papers, 1907 Box 1533, Correspondence, March M-Z, Folder 12.

dignitaries ascended the rostrum to extend well-deserved congratulations on this occasion, which in fact marked the dedication of Academic Hall, Science Hall, Training School, and the Manual Training and Power Plant all together. While their sentiments were not recorded as such, perhaps they voiced as J. B. Legg had earlier that although Regenhardt came in nearly a year behind schedule, Academic Hall was obviously very well put together and structurally quite sound. In truth, Legg had even publicly praised Regenhardt, maintaining that the overall construction could be considered the finest he had seen in thirty-seven years as an architect. Surely someone recognized Houck as "the leading spirit in behalf of the board in all things with reference to the erection of these buildings," or maybe echoed a resolution submitted to the board of regents by R. B. Oliver that gave singular credit to Louis Houck and Washington Dearmont for each "hav[ing] given, if possible, more of their time to the erection of the buildings than their own private property." Despite his occasional vulgar language, Louis was known to speak beautifully in public, and on this occasion, as he often did, he talked at length while only rarely looking at his notes.[39]

Just as it does today, Academic Hall dominated Cape Girardeau's landscape in 1906. Four years earlier the institution's darkest hour had threatened its continuation in Cape Girardeau. Now, hereafter its superlative dome would stand as a beacon of higher education across all of southeast Missouri. Below Normal Hill, Academic's completion converged with two other critical elements—railroads and the Little River Drainage District—to form a trifecta of catalysts which opened an era of revitalization that finally reversed the Cape's generation-long malaise. Louis Houck's fingerprints were all over two of the three.

Inasmuch as the pioneering Houck roads brought the Iron Horse to southeast Missouri, the eventual acquisition of all three lines by the larger Frisco system truly situated Cape Girardeau as the transportation, distribution, and service hub connecting the entire region to the growing national market. From roughly 1906, when the boom began in earnest, until the opening years of the Great Depression in 1931, Cape Girardeau's reemergence as a regional center fueled the most dramatic period of growth, expansion, and development in the city's long history. "Think the Cape has been permanently 'yanked' out of its ancient ways," Louis noted with hard-earned

39. Farmer, "Southeast Missouri State Normal," 186; *Cape Girardeau Democrat*, January 27, 1906; Board of Regents Minutes, Volume I, 1873–1925, 223, Special Collections and Archives, Southeast Missouri State University; Charles Davis to Louis Houck, April 23, 1909, Houck Papers, 1909 Box 1535, Correspondence, April K–Z, Folder 10.

pride. "The time that we have all been looking for for so many years seems finally to have come, and Southeast Missouri, instead of being off on one side, will actually be on the main line of travel and business."[40]

Nearly realizing Houck's bold predictions that Cape's ascendance as a very important point on the Frisco system would necessarily lead to 10,000 new residents, the population surged from 4,815 in 1900 to 10,252 by 1920. The city limits also stretched outward from the river as many of the construction projects between 1906 and 1931 gave Cape Girardeau much of its modern commercial and residential architecture. "The town is, so to speak, waking up and expanding in every direction," Louis wrote to Sturdivant in Alabama. "Hardly know half the people on the streets now when I go up Main Street. Almost everyone seems a stranger to me." In this regard, observers credited Houck's railroads specifically for allowing prominent capitalists throughout the region such as Himmelberger and Boynton to relocate their business headquarters and family residences to Cape Girardeau and effectively commute back to their mills in the swamps.[41]

Besides the railroad, the second, often overlooked, ingredient in Cape Girardeau's economic revolution was in fact the resurrection of Academic Hall, primarily because it finally silenced talk about moving the normal school away from town. The Dearmont and Houck era at the school lasted until the early 1920s, but it was during these earliest years of the century that the number of campus buildings increased from one to six, four of which still form the basic core of the university's modern built environment. Consequently, the student body at the soon-to-be-designated Southeast Missouri State Teachers College, or, as some informally called it, "Cape State" or "the Houck school," increased nearly eightfold, likewise permanently fixing Cape Girardeau as the educational center of the region.

"The former graveyard has developed into a lively commercial city which is well and favorably known in the great trade centers of the Mississippi Valley," the *Cape Girardeau Democrat* proclaimed with its customary hyperbole decorating what was more than just a kernel of truth. "To say that Louis Houck is largely responsible for this change would be merely stating a fact that is well known to all citizens who are posted as to

40. Neumeyer, Nickell, and Rhodes, *Historic Cape Girardeau,* 31–36; Louis Houck to Robert Sturdivant, January 5, 1904, Houck Papers, Box 1542, Correspondence–Outgoing, Folder 13.

41. *Cape Girardeau Democrat,* September 8, 1900; Louis Houck to Robert Sturdivant, August 17, 1903, Houck Papers, Box 1542, Correspondence–Outgoing, August 15–29 1903, Folder 4; Louis Houck to Robert Sturdivant, November 10, 1902, Houck Papers, Box 1541, Correspondence–Outgoing, November 1–15 1902, Folder 11.

the history of their city." "It was the brain, the ability and the energy of Mr. Houck which has wrought these changes and it would be no exaggeration to assert that he has done more for the progress and development of Southeast Missouri than any other one hundred men in that section . . . He goes ahead with his different business enterprises, does more work than any ten men, and people look on and simply wonder how he accomplishes so much."[42]

42. *Cape Girardeau Democrat,* January 5, 1906.

CHAPTER 10

The Histories

During a somewhat busy and active life, by no means devoted to literary pursuits, the interesting material embodied in this work has been
collected. For me it has been a labor of love, absorbing for a long time
nearly all my leisure hours—diverting my mind from business cares.

—Preface to Louis Houck's *A History of Missouri*

Louis Houck never set out to author a seminal work on Missouri before
the Louisiana Purchase. The books he knew as simply "the histories" grew
naturally out of an enduring passion for the historical discipline, a
"remarkable memory," and the almost compulsive compilation of material, artifacts, and genealogies of his adopted state. "During my life I
always took a great interest in the growth and development of the country in which I lived but also in its history generally," he reflected in retirement. "In me it was so to speak, a compelling instinct. It was impossible
for me to live in a country and become identified in its business or its people living in it without taking an interest in its early settlement and growth
and the development of its agricultural, industrial, and social life."[1]

Much of his early interest revolved around this vague aspiration to famil-
iarize himself with the secondary literature on these topics, a pastime that
filled Elmwood's library with the scholarship of the world's principal colonial historians such as B. F. French, Charles Etienne Arthur Gayarre, and
Elliott Coues. Supplementing these green cloth-bound volumes was a generation's worth of periodicals, scientific studies, conference proceedings,

---

1. Houck, "Some Reminiscences," 79; John Snider to Louis Houck, June 10, 1903,
Houck Papers, 1903 Box 1528, Correspondence, June A-K, Folder 15.

historical journals, and speeches. In the same manner, Louis also collected state histories to acquaint himself with that genre of the historian's craft.[2]

From reading such general treatments, often in his favorite leather-backed chair, Louis progressed, as historians do, to the pursuit of more fulfilling primary accounts from any early explorers, travelers, and missionaries along the Mississippi River who could throw light on the subject. Over time, his elegant wooden bookshelves bulged with sundry centuries-old foreign documents, military records, archeological surveys, local county records, contemporary travel accounts, reminiscences, and his own written memories of rambling through the backwoods of Missouri and engaging its peoples. So overcrowded did the library become, in fact, that Houck squirreled away materials and books throughout every room of the mansion, even stacking them upon the ballroom's stage. Dinner guests recalled that when casual conversations turned controversial, the host would sometimes scurry from room to room in search of the correct volume to definitively answer the question at hand.[3]

Then, at some point in his informal studies, Louis came to the realization that no comprehensive story of colonial and territorial Missouri had ever been written. In his estimation, this amounted to a serious gap in the historical literature, and since this was just prior to the wholesale professionalization of the historical discipline, amateurs such as himself could still make significant contributions to the body of historical literature by filling in those gaps with their own untrained scholarship—the academic equivalent of a lawyer audaciously deciding to build a railroad.

"So in an inarticulate way," he modestly concluded of the erudite epiphany, "as my own knowledge of the subject increased and expanded, the idea took possession of my mind that at any rate a feeble effort should be made to write this neglected period." He "resolved to undertake the work." "For twenty years or more during the busiest part of my life, when engaged in building railroads and looking after landed interests, I employed my leisure hours to put what I thought was valuable that I had collected, into my colonial and territorial history of Missouri, incorporating with it such personal recollections as I could secure from persons still living when I began to collect my material."[4]

2. Jasper Blines to Louis Houck, September 7, 1899, Houck Papers, 1899 Box 1522, Correspondence, September A-D, Folder 20; Minnesota Historical Society to Louis Houck, October 7, 1899, Houck Papers, 1899 Box 1522, Correspondence, Folder 25.

3. Doherty, Jr., *Houck, Missouri Historian and Entrepreneur,* 97–112.

4. Houck, "Some Reminiscences," 79; Louis Houck, *A History of Missouri from the Earliest Explorations and Settlements until the Admission of the State into the Union,* vol. 1, v; Louis Houck to D. A. Ball, June 12, 1903, Houck Papers, Box 1541, Correspondence–Outgoing, June 12–20 1903, Folder 28.

Writing *The Boundaries of the Louisiana Purchase: A Historical Study* in 1901 gave focus to his research agenda, while the sale of his second railroad the next year subsidized it. What had heretofore been an irregular hobby, something relegated to evenings, Sundays, or whenever the mood seized him or he needed to relax, increasingly crowded into his already dense daily workload. Around Elmwood began revolving a vast, and ever expanding, orbit of librarians, archivists, research assistants, translators, and professional historians to lend their particular expertise. A great many were actually informal contacts whom Louis approached regarding a specific query or a facet of his investigations temporarily at a snag. For instance, finding it initially difficult to obtain reliable information regarding Native American tribes, Louis consulted with Henry H. Bedford to see if his elderly friend from those circuit-court riding days remembered seeing any Indian trails or highways in the antebellum years. Likewise, knowing that W. T. Carrington traversed Missouri in his job as state superintendent of education anyway, Houck asked him, at the same time the two were conferring over Academic Hall, to visit with locals about any firsthand recollections still out there concerning native settlements or culture. Willard Vandiver became the retriever of all materials from the Congressional Information Bureau and the Smithsonian Institution. And Joseph Vaeth, an unsuspecting member of the Normal faculty, took a leave of absence to enroll as a student at the Sorbonne, but not before Louis presented him with a list of research needs in Paris.

Marie Louise Dalton, in her capacity as librarian for the Missouri Historical Society, became a much-relied-upon associate as Louis delved deeper into the society's collection, and indeed began loaning the organization some of his most rare materials. Through Duncan, and the Chouteau family, Louis came into possession of the letters of the pioneering Frenchmen Auguste Chouteau and the censuses taken in the late 1700s by Upper Louisiana Commandant Charles Delassus, which in turn the society contracted to have translated at half a cent per word. Similarly, Houck began making research requests at the new State Historical Society in Columbia, of which he became a corresponding member.[5]

By 1903 Idress Head, who ultimately replaced Dalton as librarian and curator for the Missouri Historical Society, emerged as Houck's primary research assistant in the state, biding her time on his payroll between Cape

5. *St. Louis Post-Dispatch,* March 1, 1925; Louis Houck to Clarence Alvord, September 17, 1906, Houck Papers, Box 1544, Correspondence–Outgoing, September 14–29 1906, Folder 3; Mary Louise Dalton to Louis Houck, November 13, 1903, Houck Papers, 1903 Box 1528, Correspondence, November M-Z, Folder 28.

Girardeau, Jefferson City, St. Louis, and Ste. Genevieve. Louis entrusted
Idress with the exasperating, but key, job of exploring the tangled records
of the Spanish Land Grants. More specifically, this meant tracking down
the personal histories of the people who received land grants, the actual
surveys and plats for all settlements situated on the grants, and the
"assembly of the inhabitants" or rather how early forms of territorial gov-
ernance chose leadership and made rules for public improvements such as
building fences and bridges. The young woman, who lived for long periods of time at Elmwood and became close friends with Rebecca Houck,
scoured countless rolled-up maps, dusty illustrations, and thick deposi-
tions archived at the state supreme court and the secretary of state's office.
In researching in the Ste. Genevieve Catholic Church, Idress exhaustively
translated French records from the 1760s to 1806 pertaining to marriages,
deaths, and baptisms for both whites and "savages."

Per Houck's "kind and patient" instructions, she hand-copied these
documents—before Louis finally consented to a typewriter—always careful to retrieve too much information as opposed to too little so that he
could make the final determination as to an item's historical value. Miss
Head certainly had more of the temperament necessary for this type of
work than did her employer, and while she found it "interesting," the
"tedious" chores took her almost four years.[6]

On occasion Louis took his own research trips, which actually seemed
to coincide with vacations. While visiting Rebecca at school in Pennsylvania, Houck often left the women together and ventured alone to Washington, D.C., to pore over Thomas Jefferson's papers and the early
territorial collections at the Library of Congress. Mary accompanied Louis
back to Madison, Wisconsin, for the first time in almost fifty years, and
while she joined in the social circles around the state capital for several
weeks, Louis called on the State Historical Society of Wisconsin in order to
sample their substantial collection of territorial testimonials.

More often than not, in their older age the Houcks sought out warmer
climates to escape winter's chill. From time to time this meant a stay in
New Orleans—the historical center of the Lower Louisiana territory—and
an appointment with William Beers, the noted librarian of Howard Memorial Library. Yet during his work on the histories, the couple routinely
spent a few months each year in the Caribbean. Though admittedly "not
what is called a good sailor," he was still captivated by the sapphire-blue

6. Idress Head to Louis Houck, June 2, 1903, Houck Papers, 1903 Box 1528, Correspondence, June K-S, Folder 16; *Cape Girardeau Democrat*, February 29, 1908; Doherty,
Jr., *Houck, Missouri Historian and Entrepreneur*, 113.

ocean and tropical beaches, especially those in Jamaica. On the north side of the island, Houck enjoyed taking daily "ocean baths" and resting on the veranda of his hotel, from which he could gaze at the tropical vegetation covering the landscape from the sea to the top of a seven-thousand-foot mountain. One local plantation, Parsley Gardens—with some 5,000 cacao trees, 1,000 banana trees, and 500 coconut trees—intrigued him to the point that he offered its owner, a British sea captain, £2,000, or roughly $15,000, to make the charming beachfront property his and Mary's permanent vacation residence. Although, disappointingly, the deal never materialized, Louis never ceased to believe that Jamaica would become a great winter resort for Americans.[7]

Little in the way of substantive research got done in Jamaica, but the Houcks did return to Cuba periodically as well, and in this recently liberated Spanish possession, Louis uncovered the trail of a critical cache of colonial history. In Havana, he learned that immediately after the Spanish-American War in 1898, Spain removed a large collection of its documents on the early administration of Upper Louisiana back to the Archivo General de Indias (General Archives of the Indies) in Seville. These "Papers from Cuba" were actually stored in disorganized piles in the basement of the Archives and as yet no American scholar had been given access to review them. Through his association with Dr. James Alexander Robertson at the State Historical Society of Wisconsin, an expert on the Seville archives and their methodologies, Louis hired a Spanish archivist, Don Jose Gonzalez Verger, to examine the material for him.

The Houck-Robertson-Verger arrangement worked something along the lines of Louis sending written research agendas to Wisconsin, which were then translated into Spanish and forwarded to Seville to be carried out. For $15 a month, plus $1.50 for each record uncovered and 30 cents per every four pages of text duplicated, Verger and a small clerical staff hand-copied all the documents he thought met Houck's criteria and then mailed the packages back across the Atlantic to be translated into English by Robertson and his Romance language colleagues. After the translations were completed in Madison—including the calculations for all tables— they were typewritten, proofread, and sent to Cape Girardeau.

The time-consuming process exhausted the better part of two years, especially given that Verger had to follow up related leads in the Spanish

7. Louis Houck to Edward Hidden, February 24, 1903, Houck Papers, Box 1541, Correspondence–Outgoing, February 23–28 1903, Folder 17; Louis Houck to N. R. Snyder, April 6, 1903, Houck Papers, Box 1541, Correspondence, April 1903, Folder 21.

Archives (Archivo General de Espana) in Simancas and on one occasion back to the Cuban Archives. Additionally, the Seville documents themselves were classified only in the academic sense in that they were tied up in paper bundles and loosely divided into first "Audiencias" (supreme court districts) such as Audiencia of Santo Domingo, Floridas, and Luisiana and then often further divided by Ecclesiastical or Secular branches. Others were sorted into special subjects delineated by date ranges. Related to this, delays often also arose when intentions were lost in translation, as sometimes happened regarding more geographically specific research inquiries because, as Robertson confidentially explained to Louis, "the trouble with Spaniards is that not many of them understand the different divisions of our country . . ."[8]

Nevertheless, from this triangular scholarship, Houck uncovered an extraordinary chronicle of the nearly forty years of Spanish colonial control west of the Mississippi in the late eighteenth century: official correspondence among French and Spanish nobility, military reports, journals from expeditions into the continent, detailed geographic descriptions, governmental projections on social and economic growth, position papers encouraging settlements along the Mississippi followed by suggestions for dealing with land-hungry Americans, and eyewitness observations of indigenous tribes.[9]

Study and contemplation agreed with Louis, and many noted that he looked ten years younger when working on the histories. Ironically, they thought that "stern old Houck" found such joy and relaxation in what most considered a truly boring and cumbersome enterprise. Those who encountered him on the Elmwood grounds, at the new Fredrick Street depot, or the work site around Academic Hall could readily attest to his sheer delight in regaling everyone with a full and complete accounting of each new tidbit of historical fact he was uncovering. "The longer I work," Houck would say with the peculiar zeal of the scholar, "the more I find out."[10]

---

8. J. A. Robertson to Louis Houck, December 27, 1905, Houck Papers, 1905 Box 1531, Correspondence, December K-Z, Folder 33; J. A. Robertson to Louis Houck, March 15, 1906, Houck Papers, 1906 Box 1532, Correspondence, March J-R, Folder 9. A graduate of Western Reserve University, J. A. Robertson was a Romance language specialist who worked for another territorial historian, Reuben Gold Thwaites, on his multivolume *The Jesuit Relations*. Doherty, Jr., *Houck, Missouri Historian and Entrepreneur*, 107.

9. J. A. Robertson to Louis Houck, August 13, 1906, Houck Papers, 1906 Box 1532, Correspondence, August P-Z, Folder 25.

10. Louis Houck to M. R. Smith, January 16, 1906, Houck Papers, Box 1543, Correspondence–Outgoing, January 2–29 1906, Folder 20.

As Academic Hall drew closer to completion the following year, Louis maintained a stricter writing regimen and with characteristic intensity began organizing the presumably countless pages of notes and documents while synthesizing them into a coherent manuscript. "The whole thing is what you might call a mosaic," he explained of his methodology, "a thousand and one isolated facts scattered through all kinds of books . . . old newspapers, letters, travels, etc . . . being gathered together and worked into . . . a harmonious whole."[11] New material continued to come in unabated, and the prospect of not exhausting every last Spanish resource made him shudder. "When a fellow gets up a history and information is available and he does not use it," his adage went, "he is guilty of a crime mala per se."[12] Even so, for the next three years Louis's principal focus was on writing some twelve hundred pages of original text.

Houck's preferred routine for writing usually involved breakfast with Mary before sequestering himself in the study just off the library that he referred to as "the history room."[13] Here he labored uninterrupted until lunch. Idress Head remembered that when Houck concentrated, he was not to be disturbed and servants were told not to clean the history room. Because Louis understood that people found it nearly impossible to "decipher my peculiar chirography," he painstakingly wrote out his manuscript in longhand first and then dictated to a live-in stenographer—first Idress Head and sometime later Christine Wheeler—to be typed. He studied these transcriptions over and over and would edit his work according to the same pattern. In this way, Louis said that he "talked" history.[14] Owing to his abiding fear of fire—drawn from memories of the untimely demise of his *Missouri Reports* notes back in 1870 and the more immediate tragedy of Academic Hall—three copies were always typed; one remained in the history room, one in his Cape Girardeau depot, and the other in the Sturdivant Bank vault.

Besides being Louis's mealtime companion, Mary's chief role appears to have been as muse for his historical pursuits. Although a perpetual struggle

11. Louis Houck to L. H. Davis, April 10, 1905, Houck Papers, Box 1543, Correspondence–Outgoing, April 1–17 1905, Folder 7.

12. Louis Houck to J. A. Robertson, February 16, 1906, Houck Papers, Box 1543, Correspondence–Outgoing, February 12–28 1906, Folder 22.

13. Idress Head to Louis Houck, December 19, 1906, Houck Papers, 1906 Box 1533, Correspondence, December C–L, Folder 1.

14. Doherty, Jr., *Houck, Missouri Historian and Entrepreneur*, 110–14; Maynard C. Willis, "Red Letter Books Relating to Missouri," *Missouri Historical Review* (1940): 84; Louis Houck to Robert Sturdivant, October 27, 1904, Houck Papers, Box 1542, Correspondence, October, 1904, Folder 29.

apparently existed between husband and wife over lighting—Mary preferred it dark in Elmwood and kept the draperies closed, while Louis demanded they be open and the house bright—she fulfilled very practical duties as well. Vigilantly she kept her eye out for any material that might be salient to Missouri history in her wide readings and then maintained a scrapbook of these potential contributions, which she organized by subject.

So too did it fall on her to ward off wayward staff and rambunctious toddlers from the history room since, conceivably, the prohibition on disturbance would have applied equally to the two newest members of the Houck clan, little Andy and Alex Juden. Just as Irma seems to have provided the sparkle in the family as a child, her young sons, born in 1901 and 1903 respectively, brought "comfort, entertainment and satisfaction" to their "Grand Pap." Irma and her husband, Charles Juden, of whom the Houcks thought a great deal, divided their time after 1907 between a home near the depot in Cape and the beautiful Briarwood estate on old Giboney land. But the boys spent plenty of their youth around Elmwood, and while other members of the family and the African American and Irish help conducted themselves largely with respectful silence and obedience toward the master and mistress of the manor, Louis conceded that his grandchildren often had the run of the place "as large as life."[15]

Usually after a light meal around noon, Houck would take off his gold-framed glasses, which he kept attached around his neck with a string, and lie down for a brief nap. Business matters sometimes intruded into his afternoons, but on most days Louis donned a hat and cape, and with the aid of his walking stick headed out for a constitutional through the primeval beauty of "El Bosque de los Olmos." The walks served as both rejuvenation and inspiration for chronicling Missouri's bygone heritage, and upon his return to the library, Louis took up the pen until well into the night.

In regard to writing—as opposed to railroading, some might say—Houck could be considered a perfectionist, worrying incessantly that incorrect factual details and small mistakes would go undetected in the manuscript and, once published, would undermine its impact. He demanded his Chicago publishers R. R. Donnelley and Sons return his drafts of each new chapter immediately with critical notes in the margins and corrections in the text. Houck received these editorial criticisms regarding the style of composition, organization, and grammar fairly well

15. Louis Houck to Robert Sturdivant, August 17, 1903, Houck Papers, Box 1542, Correspondence, August 15–29 1903, Folder 4; *St. Louis Republic*, May 10, 1908.

and per their specifications reorganized some longer chapters by breaking them apart at logical breaks, rebuilt the chapter on France ceding Louisiana to Spain, ceased his repetitive use of so many land-grant petitions, and greatly condensed the chapter on missionaries. The accompanying reconfiguration of notes and citations, and of indexing, was a whole other dreadful ordeal in and of itself.

Just as a trained historian would, Louis also routinely solicited the opinions of experts in the field, making use of their critical eyes in matters of both form and content. Portions of the manuscripts were sent out to scholars such as Edward Shepard at Drury College in Springfield and Clarence Alvord at the University of Illinois, who later married Idress Head. "I have rewritten and rewritten the chapter so often that I am quite sure I am incapable to perceive all the finer defects," he despaired to Walter B. Douglass, the former president of the Missouri Historical Society, in seeking his critique of the particularly troublesome first chapter, the "Probable Origin of the Name of the State."[16]

In much the same way, Houck shored up persistent holes in his research, in particular regarding Native Americans, by consulting directly with Thomas Beckwith, an amateur archeologist whose impressive collection of pottery, effigies, and stone tools from the Paleo-Indian to late Mississippian periods positioned him as the dean of southeast Missouri scholars when it came to the Mound Builders. Early on Louis fretted over his own limited understanding and general lack of information concerning prehistoric tribes like the Hopewell and Mississippians who left their earthworks and mounds along the state's rivers in the centuries before European contact. In fact, Houck had so little material that at first he contemplated not even covering the topic of these Native Americans. He said that if he wrote too much about their cultures, "I might get into deep water" and expose his ignorance. "I don't propose to say anything about them," he initially confessed to Beers, "because I don't know anything about them."[17]

The collaboration with Beckwith largely solved this dilemma, as the Charleston, Missouri, man eagerly extended his vast knowledge of the earliest civilizations in the region along with photographs and diagrams of some twenty-eight thousand documented mounds. Beckwith also made

16. Louis Houck to Walter B. Douglass, May 10, 1906, Houck Papers, Box 1543, Correspondence–Outgoing, May 3–10 1906, Folder 27.

17. Louis Houck to William Beer, February 2, 1906, Houck Papers, Box 1543, Correspondence–Outgoing, February 2–12 1906, Folder 21.

Houck a standing offer to loan ancient ceramic vessels and other pottery pieces he had excavated on his own land in Mississippi County. In frequent recommendations for chapter 2 covering the mound builders, Thomas Beckwith strongly suggested that in order to make the histories a truly comprehensive and complete account, Louis should tell Missouri's early story from a more geological perspective, including prehistory with a lot of maps to chronicle the arrival of man.[18]

Armed with Beckwith's contributions, including frequent proofreading of various drafts, Louis gained confidence in presenting material on Native Americans, even speculating that "this chapter may give me the reputation of being somewhat of an archaeologist, although undeserved. I don't know anything more about mounds than about Sanskrit. But I am studying up the subject and the longer I study the more I find out."[19]

In due course, Louis assembled so much material that his original vision of a readable one-volume text inevitably gave way to a multivolume work. As the three volumes that would make up *A History of Missouri* and the two volumes of accompanying documents called *The Spanish Regime in Missouri* arduously came together, their author wrestled frequently with conflicting waves of self-doubt and his own mortality. On one hand, he vacillated, as authors do, over the quality of his art. "Sometimes," he confessed, "I think that what I have is not worth anything and at other times I will say frankly that I am pleased with it."[20]

During one blue period in late 1906, when Mary, Giboney, and Rebecca vacationed in the Mediterranean and Egypt, Louis instead stayed in the history room to work through the endless revisions, explaining to Mary Louise Dalton, "I have a good many doubts about it and with some hesitation ordered the printers to start work. It seems to me there is so much that might be improved. I am not half as sanguine about the work as I used to be. Wish really I could give all of my time to it for another year but that is out of the question. No telling how long a fellow lives anyway."[21]

This second impulse reflected the ominous, but very real, prospect that the histories might well outdistance him, just as he had worried that he

18. Thomas Beckwith to Louis Houck, March 13, 1904, Houck Papers, 1903 Box 1528, Correspondence, March A–E, Folder 6.

19. Louis Houck to Father Thomas A. Shaw, February 28, 1906, Houck Papers, Box 1543, Correspondence–Outgoing, February 12–28 1906, Folder 22.

20. Louis Houck to L. H. Davis, April 10, 1905, Houck Papers, Box 1543, Correspondence–Outgoing, April 1–17 1905, Folder 7.

21. Louis Houck to Mary Louise Dalton, December 27, 1906, Houck Papers, Box 1544, Correspondence–Outgoing, December 15–29 1906, Folder 8.

might orphan Academic Hall. His beloved brother George—always devoted to Louis and his dreams—passed away in 1907, leaving Houck "much bereaved." Now with his seventieth birthday on the horizon while he faced nagging respiratory problems, he felt a familiar urgency.[22] "There is no telling when a fellow is going to die . . . ," Louis reiterated to Robert Sturdivant. "You remember when I went into the railroad business a long time ago I asked you to go in with me and you then said that you felt as if you were too old to go into such enterprises and you were then just about as old as I am now . . ."

Accordingly, in April 1908 he mailed the full manuscript to Chicago, resigned that "one cannot be always polishing a jewel; it must sometime be put in its setting and given to the world."[23]

Within the pages of A History of Missouri, published in 1908, and The Spanish Regime in Missouri the next year, Houck proved that for all his shortcomings as a historian, he was a good, and sincere, storyteller. He faithfully, if sometimes incorrectly, chronicled the prehistoric mound builders and the intrepid De Soto, Coronado, Penalosa, Radisson, and Grossellier, complete with maps to outline the European exploration as well as the trails and pathways of the natives. Commemorating the life of early French settlers, Houck traced the nearly one hundred years their crown ruled the territory Robert de La Salle named Louisiana in honor of King Louis XIV, following especially the hardships and labors of early Catholic missionaries. Equally he outlined the Spanish organization of the five districts of Ste. Genevieve, St. Louis, St. Charles, Cape Girardeau, and New Madrid after the Treaty of Fontainbleau brought this region of Upper Louisiana under Spanish control in 1762, laying out the twisted lineage of the land grants and how they were later adjudicated by the Americans.

As was customary for recreational historians of his day, Houck identified most of the American immigrants and where they settled under Spanish control—especially in southeast Missouri—providing celebratory biographical sketches of these early pioneers, the development of their social life, and their Protestant churches. To supplement accounts of how counties were organized and the story behind the founding of many towns and cities, he also noted all leading territorial lawyers, doctors, banks and

22. M. R. Smith to Louis Houck, September 17, 1907, Houck Papers, 1907 Box 1533, Correspondence, September L-Z, Folder 28.

23. Louis Houck to Robert Sturdivant, July 5, 1905, Houck Papers, Box 1543, Correspondence–Outgoing, July 3–31 1905, Folder 13; Mary Louise Dalton to Louis Houck, December 31, 1906, Houck Papers, Box 1558, 1903–1906, Loose Files, Folder 22.

bankers, manufacturers, newspapers and editors, mail routes and postal workers, hotels and inn keepers. In the same way he detailed duels in Upper Louisiana and provided the only history of military operations in Missouri during the War of 1812 and the Indian wars, accompanied by the names of officers and various regiments in the territory.

The Spanish Regime contained Robertson's translations of the original documents relating to Upper Louisiana with such notable papers as a list of loyal eighteenth-century vassals who contributed support to Carlos III's military conquests and the muster rolls of some of his majesty's militia companies in 1780. Thanks to Idress Head, the volumes also contained the census of the colonial districts complete with the names and businesses of all inhabitants at the time of the Louisiana Purchase.

Fred and George Naeter, who with Houck's considerable moral, professional, and monetary support had since 1904 been publishing the *Cape Girardeau Southeast Missourian*, acted as agents and handled all sales for the volumes. Per Houck's instructions, sales were conducted by subscription only and not in retail bookstores. Nevertheless, the publication of "Houck's Histories," as they became known, immediately resounded with contemporary scholars, students, and readers, elevating Louis to the lofty stature of Missouri's "Foremost Historian" in the public imagination.[24] Academics such as Clarence Alvord judged it "certainly one of the soundest and most carefully written state histories in existence."[25] Jonas Viles, the chair of the University of Missouri History Department, praised this first published comprehensive treatment of the period for its readability and the author's authentic fondness for the material. "Unless one is familiar with the unorganized condition of the materials and the lack of preliminary studies, he cannot appreciate the difficulties of the subject, nor how successfully, on the whole, Mr. Houck has surmounted them."[26]

Floyd C. Shoemaker, later the secretary of the State Historical Society of Missouri, echoed the veneration. "It is undoubtedly the greatest compilation of facts relating to the early history of this State that exists today and is a veritable encyclopedia in that line . . . No student of history, and especially of Missouri history, can be too complimentary in his expression of

24. *St. Louis Post-Dispatch,* March 1, 1925; Doherty, Jr., *Houck, Missouri Historian and Entrepreneur,* 95–101.

25. Clarence Alvord to Louis Houck, September 28, 1908, Houck Papers, 1908 Box 1534, Correspondence, September A-C, Folder 27.

26. Jonas Viles, review of Louis Houck, *The History of Missouri,* in *American Historical Review* 14 (1909): 834–35.

appreciation of Mr. Houck's *History of Missouri* and there is no praise that would be too generous to bestow on the author."[27]

The only real weakness contemporaries found in Houck's broad treatment lay in the inescapable fact that, after all, English was his second language. "The literary style is that of one to whom the English language comes after the idiom of another tongue has become familiar," a reviewer pointed out. "Yet, despite this somewhat irksome manner, the work speedily becomes absorbing."[28]

If Louis did not consider the histories within the context of his patronage of the arts, the public certainly understood them as such. Just as the *St. Louis Republic* headlines proclaimed "Wealthy Missourian Spends Fortune in Compiling Authentic History of State," it was generally believed, erroneously, that Louis spent nearly $100,000 of his own money writing and publishing the books—a figure Houck disclaimed in its degree but not in its kind. As he made it clear, though, it was never his intention to make this a commercial venture, and indeed during Missouri's centennial in 1921, he gave free copies to almost 260 high schools.[29]

Louis also thoroughly enjoyed giving signed copies of the histories as gifts to scores of friends, associates, scholars, and politicians, and many readers who knew Louis only for his other ventures expressed their amazement at his versatility. "I must assure you that I was very agreeably surprised to find that you were such a thorough historian," one business associate congratulated. "I have known of you as a prominent railroad builder and fighter for many years, but never dreamed that you were all that time gathering most interesting data for a real live history of Missouri."[30]

In Cape Girardeau the histories, and their particular emphasis on southeast Missouri, encouraged many civic-minded townspeople to believe that the region's image might finally be redeemed in the public eye statewide. Concomitantly, the books stimulated a rekindling of sorts regarding the town's Spanish colonial heritage. This renewed interest manifested itself perhaps most obviously in the Spanish Colonial Revival–style architectural influences on several of the prominent commercial structures built in

27. *St. Louis Republic*, July 29, 1913, quoted in Doherty, Jr., *Houck, Missouri Historian and Entrepreneur*, 97.

28. *Saturday Evening Post* (Burlington, Iowa), August 1, 1908, Houck Papers, Box 1558, 1908, Loose Files, Folder 24.

29. *St. Louis Republic*, May 10, 1908; *Cape Girardeau Democrat*, May 23, 1908; *Cape Girardeau Southeast Missourian*, January 24, 1919.

30. A. M. Wolleson to Louis Houck, September 25, 1908, Houck Papers, 1908 Box 1534, Correspondence, September L–Z, Folder 29.

the early twentieth century, including the Marquette Hotel, the Southeast Missourian building, and even the B'nai Israel Synagogue.[31] It also raised the profile of Elmwood, as it was the only estate in Upper Louisiana still in possession of the original land grantee, a phenomenon Mary found uncomfortable.

Inasmuch as the publication of the histories cemented Louis as the state's leading authority on the territorial period, the demand for speaking engagements at colleges and both of the state's historical societies also increased, as did frequent requests that he continue his writings. Besides the Missouri Historical Society's plea that he undertake a new project covering the years since statehood, a mutual friend of Houck and David Rowland Francis also encouraged Louis to write the long-overdue history of the American corporation, thinking him uniquely qualified to do so as a lawyer, capitalist, and historian. All these requests went for naught.

While calling for the corporate history, E. S. Hoch offered a unique glimpse into Louis's character when comparing Houck and David Francis, the onetime "Boy Mayor" of St. Louis, governor, organizer of the St. Louis World's Fair, and soon-to-be U.S. ambassador to revolutionary Russia. Hoch wanted the two Democratic associates to become better acquainted and wrote to Louis that Francis was "a really big man . . . being of extraordinary physical capacity as well as of superior mind and culture and great nervous force. I am sure that if you knew him well and he also knew you, you would become fast friends, and that the friendship would yield mutual compensation to both of your lives. Francis is really worth while; not as an ordinary success but as a concrete and brilliant example, like yourself, of the 'survival of the fittest.'"[32]

In due course, Houck's histories slipped in esteem and relevance, primarily because of changes in the historical profession. As another biographer, William Doherty, pointed out in tracing the historiography of Missouri, Louis benefited initially from writing during a period when expectations for history books were simply much lower. Most readers really only sought a celebratory historical encyclopedia of facts with complimentary and commemorative biographical sketches of early settlers. Louis considered his histories to be of a different class from these so-called popular county or regional histories, such as *Goodspeed's History of South-*

31. Melinda Winchester, National Register of Historic Places nomination of B'nai Israel Synagogue, Cape Girardeau, Mo., 2003, section 8, page 4.

32. E. S. Hoch to Louis Houck, n.d., Houck Papers, Box 1534, Correspondence, Folder 5.

east Missouri, and in part that is why he did not want them commonly ped-
dled around in retail outlets. But in fact they had much in common, and as
later generations of state historians began deemphasizing this commemorative approach in favor of more objective interpretation, they became
far more critical of Houck.

In truth, for Houck's generation, historians still embraced an inclusive
array of practitioners, similar to people "reading" the law or midwives
delivering babies. But within just a few years of *A History of Missouri,* as the
larger trend of professionalism took hold in this and other American voca-
tions—that is, as formal training, the application of standardized sets of
objective knowledge and skills, and the institution of rigorous professional
standards to regulate the practice became requirements—academics
squeezed out the amateurs and redefined what it meant to be a historian.
By the end of his life, the term "historian" effectively meant only those
with a doctoral degree from a research institution and an academic
appointment on a campus somewhere. Accordingly, most of the later cen-
sure centered around Houck's lack of graduate training, and therefore,
somewhat ironically, his lack of attention to detail, hurried writing style,
lack of reference sections, and the problematic nature of publishing translations without originals.

These later reevaluations, of course, should in no way lessen the accomplishment or the contemporary impact of the histories. Whatever the real
significance of his books, Louis can be taken at his word in his sincere conclusion that they would stand the test of time as the definitive work on the
subject. "Many men desire nothing better for a monument to their memory than an ornate headstone at the head of their last resting place. I
believe this early history of Missouri, where I and my family have resided
so long, will live longer in the minds of the living than any gravestone that
I might provide for in my last will or which may be erected to my memory
by my family."[33]

A noble, albeit ambitious, epitaph to be sure, yet it was another impressed
reader, W. C. Russell, whose amendment to Houck's requiem perhaps
struck a more poetically formidable chord. "I sincerely hope that after you
have passed into the great beyond, there will be some person possessing the
ability to write a similar history of your life . . ."[34]

33. *St. Louis Republic,* May 10, 1908.
34. W. C. Russell to Louis Houck, August 31, 1915, Houck Papers, Box 1559, Folder
10.

CHAPTER 11

Cape Girardeau Northern

Know how it is when a man gets away from the business in which he has been engaged in all his life. Somehow or other he wants to get back in that business. I was raised in the printing office and it took me a long time to get "weaned."[1]

Later in life when he rewarded himself with one of those guarded moments to daydream, Louis Houck often filled his mind with thoughts of voyages across the glorious "Spanish Main" and wading along the beaches of Port Antonio, Jamaica. These flights of fancy were especially keen since after the sale of the St. Louis and Gulf in 1902 he felt liberated, released from the "state of slavery" he knew as railroading. His son Giboney reminded him more often that he was increasingly "feeling the effects of 'the strenuous life,'" and could not realistically expect to "go under a full head of steam *all* of the time." Of his railroads, only the little Chester, Perryville, Ste. Genevieve and Farmington remained, and perhaps it was time to liquidate that as well. Indeed, even Louis admitted that "while I don't feel old and am as ready to take up schemes as ever my good sense admonishes me as a matter of fact I am getting along in years and ought not involve myself in great and new enterprises."[2]

1. Louis Houck to Casper Edwards, September 4, 1903, Houck Papers, Box 1542, Correspondence–Outgoing, September 4–8 1903, Folder 5.
2. Louis Houck to M. R. Snyder, February 16, 1910, Houck Papers, Box 1545, Correspondence–Outgoing, January–February 1910, Folder 14; Gerard Fowke to Louis Houck, April 1, 1910, Houck Papers, 1910 Box 1536, Correspondence, April A–L, Folder 9; Louis Houck to Casper Edwards, May 22, 1905, Houck Papers, Box 1543, Correspondence–Outgoing, May 18–31 1905, Folder 10.

Be that as it may, just as Madison Smith once observed, Louis had iron in his blood, and instead of winding down construction, as most small railroaders were doing in these twilight years of midwestern railroad promotion, Houck rededicated himself to the expansion of the northern route he had begun in 1895. To the reorganized Chester, Perryville and Ste. Genevieve, Louis soon added the Cape Girardeau and Thebes Bridge Terminal Railroad, the Cape Girardeau and Chester Railroad, and the Saline Valley Railroad. By 1913, when these lines were consolidated into the Cape Girardeau Northern, he operated a system of track covering slightly more than one hundred miles, from the Thebes Bridge just a few miles south of Cape Girardeau to Perry County and headed toward the Mississippi River and St. Louis.

Like all of his ventures, Houck's third railway was never really a fully comprehensive system as such. Instead, it came together piecemeal, with each of the four components constructed more or less with their own distinctive reasons for being rather than as objectives within a coherent, premeditated strategy. The only common denominator—aside from aiming at St. Louis—seems to have been Louis's overriding desire to avoid the mistakes of the past by owning the roads outright, that is, to operate them debt-free, relatively unbeholden to banks and subscribers, and whenever possible to have new construction pay for old construction.[3] Such was certainly the case with the initial Chester, Perryville, Ste. Genevieve and Farmington, which after a hopeful opening in 1895 had lurched along, its abysmal earnings and bonded indebtedness conspiring to keep the line perpetually operating near the red. By 1898, Houck had come to the realization that under its present configuration, the road simply would never make enough money to pay interest on the $300,000 of bonds it owed, and thus to adjust the indebtedness to the actual earning capacity of the road it would have to be reorganized under a receivership. So for the third time in five years, a judge, in this case James D. Fox of the Perry County Circuit Court, appointed a receiver for a Houck road. Not coincidentally, Fox named E. F. Blomeyer, a friendly bondholder, as the temporary custodian to oversee the railway until it could be sold at auction in the fall.[4]

3. M. R. Smith to Louis Houck, October 20, 1899, Houck Papers, 1899 Box 1522, Correspondence, October P-S, Folder 26; Doherty, Jr., "Missouri Interests of Louis Houck," 185, 241.

4. Poor's Manual of Railroads 1900 (New York: H. V. and H. W. Poor, 1900), 534, John W. Barriger III National Railroad Library; Houck, "Story of the Railroad Work, Volume II," 114–15.

As its largest bondholder, Louis never intended to let go of the Chester, Perryville, Ste. Genevieve and Farmington, and instead he purchased his own railroad on the courthouse steps to personally administer its restructuring. A competitor's opening bid of $100,000 forced Houck to spend a little more than he originally hoped—$105,000—but once the line was back in his control, Louis conveyed all its property to a brand-new company: the Chester, Perryville and Ste. Genevieve Railroad. Via this comparatively litigation-free reorganization, two things changed besides the name. The bonded indebtedness decreased as the old bonds were cancelled and replaced with a new issue for a more manageable $140,000. Correspondingly, with the revenue generated from a portion of these new bonds, a planned extension could now finally be built from St. Mary's along the Mississippi north to Ste. Genevieve.[5]

Since Ste. Genevieve had no railway at the time, the determination to invest in additional construction may well have made sense, especially considering that the ultimate destination nominally remained St. Louis. But given the northern system's disappointing bottom line up to this point, the little outlet to Ste. Genevieve was not without its share of risk, at least in the short term. Both the Saline and Aux Vases rivers had to be crossed, and despite initial promises of modest cash subscriptions and free rights-of-way from locals, Louis soon found neither forthcoming. As crews built the road from start to finish in the fall of 1898, financial backers became timid and Houck ended up spending several thousand dollars in unforeseen legal expenses, having some of the properties along the right-of-way condemned while paying out cash settlements for the other lands. Some of this resistance Houck chalked up to shortsighted land owners, while others were obviously motivated by a combination of greed and the common perception that he was in cahoots with the deep-pocketed Frisco. When writing out bank drafts for the contested rights-of-way at prices he judged hopelessly out of proportion to the value of the land, Louis grumbled, "Pecan trees, according to these people, and they swore it, were worth a hundred dollars a tree."[6]

Likewise, once open, this line did not prove profitable either, primarily because most commerce from the area still headed north to St. Louis on packet boats instead of the Chester, Perryville, and Ste. Genevieve's rail

5. *Cape Girardeau Democrat,* January 14, 1899.

6. Houck, "Story of the Railroad Work, Volume II," 118–20; *Twenty-Fifth Annual Report of the Railroad and Warehouse Commissioners of the State of Missouri, Year Ending June 30, 1900.*

transfer. For the next four years, with Houck's attention focused primarily on fashioning the St. Louis, Kennett and Southern and Allied Lines in the Bootheel, the railway once again barely managed to stay in the black. Yet this time, as Louis increasingly came to understand it, survival depended not on another reorganization, but rather on securing additional capital for an extension up the Saline River valley to a connection with the St. Louis, Iron Mountain and Southern and its uninterrupted rail access to Missouri's first city.

In 1902, as part of that much larger consolidation of regional lines by the Frisco—including his own St. Louis and Gulf—Houck indeed seized upon an unexpected offer to sell the Ste. Genevieve branch for $140,000 in St. Louis and San Francisco bonds, or just enough to retire his bonded debt. Due to the substandard conditions of the rails, the deal allowed Louis to keep them as well.[7] It was actually Newman Erb's new St. Louis, Memphis, and Southeastern—in reality the first Houck road—that bought the roughly eleven-mile section from St. Marys to Ste. Genevieve. However, since Erb's railroad was effectively controlled by the Frisco, the acquisition of this little riverfront line from Houck represented just one more facet of the Frisco's overall scheme of fashioning a route from St. Louis to Memphis along the western bank of the Mississippi out of existing railroads.[8]

While the northern system diminished physically with the subtraction of the Ste. Genevieve branch in 1902—temporarily reducing Houck's once sizable network to a two-decade low of only twenty miles—three new ventures once again extended the railway. The first of these, the spanning of the Mississippi River with a rail bridge, would eventually emerge as the north-south axis from which Houck's third system emanated. As it turned out, though, the Cape Girardeau and Thebes Bridge Terminal Railroad was hardly a fresh idea as its origins could be traced either directly or indirectly to Houck's ill-fated relationship with the Grand Tower and Cape Girardeau transfer business in 1890 and his antagonism with the Cotton Belt and Missouri Pacific following the receivership quarrels.

It seems that although the old Grand Tower and Cape Girardeau Railroad never became a money-making proposition for Houck, its operation did attract the attention of the Cotton Belt and Missouri Pacific railroads,

7. Unidentified and undated newspaper, Houck Papers, 1898 Box 1521, Correspondence, Misc A-G, Folder 22.

8. Houck, "Story of the Railroad Work, Volume II," 123–25; Newman Erb to Louis Houck, January 22, 1902, Houck Papers, 1902 Box 1526, Correspondence, January P-Z, Folder 11; *Cape Girardeau Democrat*, January 18, 1902.

both of which recognized the economic potential that large coal shipments from Illinois could generate if the inherent problems of the transfer boats could be solved by replacing them with a permanent rail bridge. Taken at face value, the erection of such a bridge at Cape Girardeau should have pleased Louis, because one of his primary motivations all along had been to develop the town into southeast Missouri's undisputed railroad terminus on the Mississippi.

The timing was not fortuitous, however.

Up until the Cotton Belt's president, Samuel W. Fordyce, was named as receiver of the St. Louis, Kennett and Southern in 1896, Houck and Fordyce had amicably negotiated trackage and terminal lease agreements that would have allowed Cotton Belt trains to enter Cape Girardeau via the Houck roads from a junction where the two railways connected in Delta. Fordyce's dialogue with Houck reflected his railroad's desire for a shorter and more lucrative outlet over the Mississippi to Chicago than their current transfer business between Bird's Point, Missouri, and Cairo, Illinois, allowed. But the receivership had abruptly, and understandably, squelched this proposed trackage arrangement and poisoned the well in regard to any future cooperation. So too did the subsequent flirtation carried on by some prominent Cape Girardeau businessmen and the Cotton Belt as the local suitors sought to woo the bigger railroad into building a line, independent of Houck, into the town with the offering of a $25,000 incentive bonus. Both incidents offended Louis's rigid sensibilities when it came to loyalty and fair play, and he retaliated by obstinately refusing to permit any rail access into the Cape or to grant the Cotton Belt a right-of-way of their own through Mary's vast landholdings that guarded virtually the entire southern approach to the town. As a result of his recalcitrance, instead of fixing Cape Girardeau as the consensus choice for a rail bridge over the Mississippi, the Cotton Belt simply circumvented it by building a fifteen-mile extension from Delta to Gray's Point further below. Within a couple of years Fordyce was successfully operating his own competing transfer business between Gray's Point and Thebes, Illinois, in preparation for spanning the river there.

Matters became even more contentious in 1900 when a consortium of officers from the Cotton Belt, Missouri Pacific, Iron Mountain, Chicago and Eastern Illinois, and Illinois Central railroads incorporated the Southern Illinois and Missouri Bridge Company to finally construct the railroad bridge at Gray's Point, or what is today Illmo, Missouri. Since such a venture required congressional authorization, the moment Louis caught wind of the new Illinois corporation he swiftly moved to regain the initiative by working with Willard Vandiver on a resolution designating Cape Girardeau, not Gray's Point, as the logical location of any proposed Mississippi bridge. Indeed in April, U.S. Congressman Vandiver introduced the enabling bill into the House of Representatives just slightly ahead of rival bills being offered in the House and Senate calling for the bridge to be situated at Gray's Point and Thebes.

Ultimately the Cotton Belt and Missouri Pacific's politicians—Representative George W. Smith of Murphysboro, Illinois, and Senator William E. Mason of Chicago—were just better situated than Houck's. Vandiver's bridge bill passed the House but died on the vine in the Senate. The Thebes legislation made its way through both houses and was signed into law by President William McKinley in January 1901. By all appearances, the Cotton Belt, Missouri Pacific, and Illinois Central had gotten the best of Louis, and just to keep from being left out entirely he formed the Cape Girardeau and Thebes Bridge Terminal Railroad in 1902 to run an extension from a junction on his St. Louis and Gulf road to Gray's Point. Still, once this railway reached the bridge, he would in essence be arriving with his hat in hand, completely beholden to the Southern Illinois and Missouri Bridge Company for access and almost sure to be greeted with some type of retribution. Still, Houck had one more trick up his sleeve. On April 24, 1902, the same day articles of incorporation were filed for the Cape Girardeau and Thebes Bridge Terminal Railroad, L. B. Houck, Giboney Houck, and John H. Crowder purchased the large Stone family farm in Scott County, a sizable piece of riverfront real estate that just so happened to encompass all the land to the north, west, and south of the bridge's Missouri approach. This sale of course came just hours before the Southern Illinois and Missouri Bridge Company sought to have the courts condemn the same Stone Farm lands through eminent domain for the bridge's use. Although he had not been able to dictate the de jure placement of the bridge, Louis now quietly controlled de facto access to it. With this powerful fulcrum, Houck could effectively force the bridge's relocation back to Cape Girardeau if he chose to deny all rights-of-way to Gray's Point over his land. Then again, if he wanted the bridge to remain in Gray's Point, he alone could build the approaches and operate them at his discretion.[9]

With neither side willing to blink, the inevitable legal showdown over the Stone lands commenced between the Cape Girardeau and Thebes Bridge

9. Doherty, Jr., *Houck, Missouri Historian and Entrepreneur*, 48–51; Houck, "Some Reminiscences," 59–60; *Cape Girardeau Democrat*, May 24, 1902.

Terminal Railroad and the Southern Illinois and Missouri Bridge Company. For southeast Missourians, it was as if the crusade against the Goulds had been rejoined. Although a good six years removed from the receivership fight, given that the House of Gould still effectively controlled the Missouri Pacific and the Cotton Belt, the *Cape Girardeau Democrat* naturally recycled much of the same symbolism when interpreting the Thebes Bridge skirmish. "The Bridge Company people went after this little railroad company laughing," the editor concluded with a flourish, but those "smiles changed to frowns . . . when the attorneys for the bridge spied Louis Houck sitting on the hill top near the west end of the proposed bridge, gazing down toward the river with the monarch of all he surveyed look upon his face . . ."[10]

After trading injunctions, writs of prohibition, affidavits of prejudice, and accompanying changes of venue, in May 1902, Louis offered what he considered a suitable compromise: in exchange for the Missouri land he would receive a one-sixth proprietary interest in the Thebes Bridge. He was flatly rebuffed, and in fact, despite the colorful hyperbole and boosterism from the hometown paper, there would be no last-minute legal heroics this time by Houck's attorneys M. R. Smith and his son, Giboney, against the big Wall Street lawyers. The Supreme Court of Missouri eventually upheld the bridge company's right of eminent domain through the Stone farm, and after an exponentially complicated series of appeals all the way to the U.S. Supreme Court proved equally futile, Houck finally turned over the rights-of-way to Gray's Point for a modest court-determined cash settlement.[11]

In 1905 the Thebes Bridge, a twenty-eight-hundred-foot structure with five alternating cantilever and anchor spans designed by the noted Polish-American bridge builder Ralph Modjeski, was opened to passenger and freight train traffic. Instead of being in on the ground floor of the new enterprise, much to his chagrin, Houck's Cape Girardeau and Thebes Bridge Terminal Railroad lined up as just another one of its paying cus-

10. *Cape Girardeau Democrat,* May 31, 1902.
11. The major legal question underpinning the protracted court battles heard variously by the Missouri Supreme Court and U.S. Supreme Court between 1903 and 1907 involved the right of an Illinois company, the Southern Illinois and Missouri Bridge Company, to exercise the right of eminent domain to condemn lands in the state of Missouri. For a full treatment of the legal history of the Thebes Bridge, see Doherty, Jr., "Missouri Interests of Louis Houck," 202–8; *Southern Illinois and Missouri Bridge Company, Appellant, vs. Stone, et al.,* Missouri Reports (174): 1–53; *Southern Illinois and Missouri Bridge Company vs. Stone, et al., Appellants,* Missouri Reports (194): 175; *Stone vs. Southern Illinois and Missouri Bridge Company,* United States Reports (206): 267; *Cape Girardeau and Thebes Bridge Terminal Railroad vs. Southern Illinois and Missouri Bridge Company,* Missouri Reports (215): 286.

tomers. This matter remained a sore one, and only rarely did Louis ever broach the bitter subject of the Thebes Bridge. When he did, his only explanation for the defeat lay in what he considered the treacherous and corrupting influence of the monied interests over an underhanded judiciary in Jefferson City and Washington, D.C., that resulted in the courts making bad law. Those "sycophants of the corporate power" now residing in America's courtrooms, he remarked to attorney friends, made "the Czar of all the Russias" look like "a democratic hobo" by comparison.[12]

That being said, the Thebes Bridge gave Houck his first and only unferried rail access over the Mississippi River, and to a degree his Cape Girardeau and Thebes Bridge Terminal Railroad influenced the timing and direction of the next railway. In 1902 Louis organized the Cape Girardeau and Chester Railroad to connect the Chester, Perryville and Ste. Genevieve to the Thebes Bridge by building a forty-mile line from Cape Girardeau to Perryville.[13] For the next four years, he uncharacteristically moved "slowly and economically" on the line, because as he explained it to the Chester, Perryville and Ste. Genevieve's president John Tlapek, at this point in his career he was "not over-anxious any way about putting in a lot of money into railroads and do not care about asking anybody else to put in money."[14] Indeed, the sale of the Ste. Genevieve branch had afforded the opportunity to launch the Cape Girardeau and Chester with relatively balanced books, and by reinvesting funds from the sale of his St. Louis and Gulf to the Frisco along with any modest earnings the northern system might take in, Louis thought he had enough money to build the entire line without going into debt. To buttress this belief, however, he capitalized the new railway for $500,000 and took out a mortgage of another $500,000 for good measure.[15]

Though slow, the physical construction of the Cape Girardeau and Chester advanced without much incident. All along the survey line, staked

12. Louis Houck to M. R. Smith, April 6, 1903, Houck Papers, Box 1541, Correspondence–Outgoing, April 1–13 1903, Folder 21; Houck, "Some Reminiscences," 58.

13. Houck had actually incorporated a St. Louis, Cape Girardeau and Southern Railroad in November 1900 to in effect fulfill the same function of the Cape Girardeau and Chester Railroad, but the company remained a paper railway only and construction never took place. *Cape Girardeau Democrat*, December 1, 1900.

14. Louis Houck to R. L. Alexander, May 18, 1903, Houck Papers, Box 1541, Correspondence–Outgoing, May 12–19 1903, Folder 25; Louis Houck to John Tlapek, November 21, 1903, Houck Papers, Box 1542, Correspondence–Outgoing, November 18–30 1903, Folder 10.

15. *Cape Girardeau Democrat*, March 8, 1902; Houck, "Story of the Railroad Work, Volume II," 126–28; Louis Houck to G. H. Walker and Company, November 13, 1906, Houck Papers, Box 1544, Correspondence–Outgoing, November 1–14 1906, Folder 5.

out by his new chief engineer, Dennis M. Scivally, crews spread out simultaneously north of Cape La Croix Creek, connecting first with the Iron Mountain in Jackson before moving on to Fruitland. From there the road wound its way to within a mile or so of Pocahontas, Oak Ridge, Daisy, Friedheim, Hilderbrand, Biehle, and Schumer Springs on to Perryville. In some places high trestles were built over the ravines in the hilly country through northern Cape Girardeau and Perry counties, but aside from the many creeks and sinkholes, the alignment was generally good and none of the work excessively heavy.[16]

In the summer of 1904, while still optimistic that the remaining roads would be profitable, Houck revisited a shelved scheme to build a line from a junction on the Chester, Perryville and Ste. Genevieve west along the Saline River valley to connect with the St. Louis, Iron Mountain and Southern. His Saline Valley Railroad, the last of the four railroads that constituted the northern system, joined the Perryville road about four miles north of that place at the Saline Junction, near what is today Lithium. From this point Louis constructed up the Saline valley, taking advantage of an existing old grade, toward the little town of Minnith. The exact terminus was not fixed initially, as engineers weighed the options of linking with the Iron Mountain at either Farmington or Fredericktown, both roughly forty miles away.[17]

In Cape Girardeau, Houck opened his railroad's new headquarters in 1905 near the intersection of Independence and Middle streets in that area known as Happy Hollow, approximately where the Federal Court Building stands today. The three-story J. B. Legg–designed limestone depot housed waiting rooms and a ticket office on the first floor and the general railroad offices of the Houck roads on the second and third floors. Like every depot along his lines, gambling, whiskey and beer drinking were strictly prohibited. In truth, because Louis suspected many of his employees to be known frequenters of Cape Girardeau and Perryville taverns, notices were posted on all Houck railroad properties warning that "any man in the train service, whether on or off duty, who is seen in a saloon, or either, loafing, or drinking therein, will be discharged."[18]

---

16. N. C. Frissell to Louis Houck, January 15, 1901, Houck Papers, 1901 Box 1525, Correspondence, January F-K, Folder 3.

17. Houck, "Story of the Railroad Work, Volume II," 129–31; Doherty, Jr., "Missouri Interests of Louis Houck," 228.

18. Notice to Employees of the Chester, Perryville and Ste. Genevieve and the Cape Girardeau and Chester, June 13, 1907, Houck Papers, Box 1544, Correspondence–Outgoing, June 1–15 1907, Folder 15.

To the south toward William Street, the railroad's terminal yard of tracks, switches, concrete engine houses, maintenance shops, and water tanks stretched for another two and a half blocks. Two seventy-foot concrete viaducts underneath Morgan Oak and Good Hope streets and a concrete wall between the two blocks protected the yard's main southern approach. Around this complex, Houck also constructed modest housing and hotels on Mary's land throughout the adjoining neighborhoods of Cape's working-class Haarig district. In offering affordable housing "for laborers who are gentlemen and not toughs" in the neighborhoods from Fredrick to Spanish streets, Louis hoped to sustain Cape Girardeau's population boom by creating an attractive environment for the right sort of working-class employees, white and black. With a modest five-dollar-a-year lease for ninety-nine years—1906 to 2005—Houck announced that laboring people could now buy their own property in Cape Girardeau cheaper than running off to Oklahoma to get what Indian lands were still left from the latest land rush. There were only two chief provisions: "no saloon or disreputable house shall be established on the lots," and only married men or widows with families could apply. Violations resulted in immediate termination.[19]

Inasmuch as the construction of these final Houck roads generated enthusiasm and optimism for all those with a vested interest, the fact remained that Louis was never able to offset the tremendous disadvantages of building north of Cape Girardeau in the early twentieth century. Consequently, by the time the Thebes Bridge and Independence Street depot opened in 1905, the lines had already reached something of a turning point, as thereafter the development of this last railroad became progressively more problematic. Whether or not age played a substantive role is unclear. But with each passing year the same mindfulness of his own mortality that explicitly drove his pursuit of Academic Hall and the histories naturally seeped into railroading. Perhaps this explains his conscious decision to begin phasing himself out of the business while crafting a clearly defined line of succession to a younger generation. Just a few years prior, L. B. might well have assumed command, but this logical choice was precluded by the nephew's pursuit of a number of entrepreneurial endeavors in his own right, journeys which led him away from southeast Missouri toward Memphis and later California. Hence, twenty-seven-year-old Giboney emerged

19. J. Maul to Louis Houck, November 29, 1904, Houck Papers, 1904 Box 1530, Correspondence, November A-H, Folder 30; Undated Handbills, Houck Papers, 1906 Box 1533, Correspondence, Misc. A-H, Folder 3.

as the rightful heir to his father's operations, and by 1905 Louis was already leaning heavily on his son to attend to much of the railroad's dealings. In expressing to Robert Sturdivant his determination to pass on this legacy to Giboney, Louis revealed a genuine pride in seeing his only son following in his footsteps but also a father's accompanying anxiety over the young man's readiness to enter such a treacherous arena. "Giboney is, however, taking a very great interest in business affairs and I think will develop into a first class business man," Louis wrote to Sturdivant. "In fact I think he is a young man of fine business capacity and instinct now. The only objection that I can possibly find is that he is perhaps too arbitrary and uncompromising. But you know in business matters it won't do to be either arbitrary or uncompromising. You have got to let things go the best way you can, try to steer them right. You rarely succeed if you try to force things to go your own way."[20]

Giboney too had his own learning curve when it came to matters of railroading; in this regard at least, like father, like son.

Another salient factor in the troubles rested on the hard truth that the road never came anywhere close to approaching those earlier rose-colored fiscal projections. Quite frankly, be that as it may Louis was a much better judge of timber's potential for profit than he was at gauging the earning power of hauling produce out of this predominantly agricultural economy.[21] Houck was certainly unaccustomed to the added costs of putting up the legally required fencing and cattle guards along the rights-of-way that were not really necessary in the less farming-oriented swamps. Numerous court-awarded damages to local farmers and ranchers whose crops were eaten or livestock killed because of his tardiness in providing such safeguards compounded the lack of revenue. Adding insult to injury, even after he readjusted earnings strategies by shifting the railway's emphasis to passenger traffic—with substantial stone depots along the route and expensive new coaches—the rapid ascendancy of the automobile outflanked him. By 1915 there were some 76,000 cars in the state of Missouri and 297,000 by 1920 as travelers increasingly embraced this more independent form of transportation.[22]

---

20. Louis Houck to Robert Sturdivant, July 5, 1905, Houck Papers, Box 1543, Correspondence–Outgoing, July 3–31 1905, Folder 13; Louis Houck to Julius Houck, February 3, 1906, Houck Papers, Box 1543, Correspondence–Outgoing, Folder 21.

21. Financial Statements, Chester, Perryville and Ste. Genevieve and Cape Girardeau and Chester, 1910, 1911, Houck Papers, 1911 Box 1537, Correspondence, Folder 32.

22. Richard S. Kirkendall, *A History of Missouri, Volume V 1919–1953*, 36.

On top of the actual operating and building costs, which were not inconsequential, Louis also felt blindsided by the exorbitant amounts locals continually demanded for rights-of-way. What had started in Ste. Genevieve was especially true around Perryville, where the demand for money obliged Houck to again try and have some lands approaching town condemned through eminent domain. Failing this, Louis ended up paying damages and court costs of up to tens of thousands of dollars for some parcels of land, at times over $1,000 an acre. Eventually, when the Cape Girardeau and Chester joined rails with the Chester, Perryville and Ste. Genevieve road in 1905—marked by nineteen-year-old Rebecca driving the last spike—it was not within the city limits of Perryville at all because for financial reasons Houck bypassed the town by almost a mile.

Out west, around what became the community of Coffman on the Saline Valley road, rights-of-way prices drove construction cost to nearly $4,000 per mile for the land alone by 1909, which began to break the back of the operation. In his typical caustic manner, Louis decried one particular instance of being "held up by an old villain named Bede Pratte" about two miles north of Minnith who gouged him for $2,000, while "another worthy citizen named E.E. Swink of Farmington" wanted $5,000 for his place which was out in the woods fifteen miles from anywhere. "I was held up by almost every land owner from Coffman to Farmington," Louis boiled, believing that the sworn testimony land owners gave the courts as to the value of their land "no doubt astonished Belzebub [sic] in the infernal regions."[23]

To tighten their belts, Louis cracked the whip on his nephew Julius, the superintendent of the Chester, Perryville, and Ste. Genevieve, alternatively chastising him for his myopic, "slip shod" management style and preaching the necessity of fiscal constraint. In business, Louis had always preferred to surround himself with a relatively small circle of family and friends, on whom he relied heavily and to whom he remained fiercely loyal. But once a member of this cadre's actions led them outside of his circle of trust for whatever reason, they incurred the old German's wrath. At one point proclaiming himself "perfectly astonished to find how you are neglecting my business," Louis scolded Julius over the paradox of mounting bills amidst a general lack of maintenance on the line. Now more than ever "economy" was the watchword on the Houck roads, and with Louis

---

23. Houck, "Story of the Railroad Work, Volume II," 130–31; Louis Houck to Thomas West, June 3, 1905, Houck Papers, Box 1543, Correspondence–Outgoing, June 2–13 1905, Folder 11; Louis Houck to G. H. Walker and Company, November 13, 1906, Houck Papers, Box 1544, Correspondence–Outgoing, November 1–14 1906, Folder 5.

putting every dollar of earnings back into them, it fell to Julius to assure that the underachieving Chester, Perryville, and Ste. Genevieve operated with the utmost efficiency. Explicitly this meant conserving coal, issuing fewer passes, improving customer satisfaction, and overseeing stricter ticket taking. All freight trains were to be completely loaded to capacity before sending them out, and turnaround times would have to be slashed. Moreover, spending was to be drastically curbed, with all purchases being cleared with Giboney in the Cape Girardeau office by telephone and all salaries cut from the superintendent on down.[24]

In further squeezing every available drop of revenue from the line, around 1908 Houck also initiated regular passenger service between Cape Girardeau, Jackson, and Claryville using a gasoline-powered Stover Motor Car. Locals called the contraption the "Old Gray Goose," and it ran along the same track as his locomotives, but did so far more cheaply than the old coal-burning "tea kettles." For a time, he entertained the idea of having the Westinghouse Corporation convert the Cape and Jackson route into an electric trolley, but balked at the alteration costs.

These initiatives notwithstanding, before long Louis found himself compelled to drum up other people's money to finance the railway—precisely the outcome he had hoped to avoid and at quite an inopportune time. "I am blowing my money into my railroad so fast it makes my head swim," he pessimistically wrote to sympathetic associates of the unanticipated expenses. "I am just now in a tight row of stumps for money . . . am up against it hard and strong. Need money the worst in the world."[25] Unfortunately, the Panic of 1907, an economic downturn many Americans attributed to President Teddy Roosevelt's Progressive antitrust stance, meant that the region itself was suffering through financial hard times, and the resultant scarcity of money only aggravated his predicament as banks had little cash on hand to lend.

In the darkest moments, that old ambivalence, or "zwei meinungen," overtook him once more. "Frankly, nobody but fools now build railroads," he reckoned when second-guessing his lamentable decision to pursue the northern route when most of the region's railroad map had long since

24. Louis Houck to Julius Houck, January 2, 1904, Houck Papers, Box 1542, Correspondence–Outgoing, January 2–29 1904, Folder 13; Louis Houck to Julius Houck, n.d., Houck Papers, Box 1541, Correspondence–Outgoing, November 15–29 1902, Folder 12.

25. Louis Houck to N. A. McMillan, May 31, 1905, Houck Papers, Box 1543, Correspondence–Outgoing, May 18–31 1905, Folder 10; Louis Houck to George Houck, March 10, 1906, Houck Papers, Box 1543, Correspondence–Outgoing, Folder 23.

jelled. "If a man's foresight were as good as his hindsight, no mistakes would be made."[26] Regret and sanguinity tugged at him from both directions, leaving Louis to mull over a unique paradox of railroading as he understood it. "It is easy to put money in," he revealed to his late brother George's son, George, Jr., "it is hard to get it out. In fact, you have to wait until the storm is over until you can sell at an advantage, and when the storm is over, and everything looks serene and the sea smooth, you don't feel as if you want to quit then, and that is the trouble."[27]

Owing to the railroad's financial purgatory, or, to use one of Louis's favorite phrases, its unfortunate tendency to "hang fire," he suspended construction for almost two years between 1909 and 1911 merely to keep the line a going concern. When work resumed in 1911, primarily it seems because Swink sold his Coffman farm to a party Louis considered more reasonable, it took another year before the line linked up with the Iron Mountain in Farmington.

On a positive note, Louis had laid the final rails of his career on September 10, 1912, and as he recalled, "I now had a railroad one hundred and six miles long." Conversely, he conceded that it "cost me over $2,000,000, and which did not at first even make operating expenses."[28]

Over the previous several years, his desire to see the northern lines constructed debt-free and unencumbered by partnerships had indeed vanished amid bleeding expenditures.[29] By 1913 nearly $1 million of the cash and stocks from the sale of his railroads south of Cape Girardeau were invested in this new road, along with another $130,000 the family received from the Little River Drainage District. Per his uncle's request, George, Jr. had also sold many thousands of dollars worth of Louis's real estate in the Bootheel and a number of Mary's lots in Cape to generate extra capital. Moreover, Louis took out additional loans from the St. Louis Union Trust, putting up the Cape Girardeau and Chester's first mortgage bonds as collateral along with several thousand dollars in Japanese government bonds he and Mary had purchased earlier. To compensate for the currency famine in southeast Missouri, Houck also spread out his credit applications, giving

26. Louis Houck to Julius Houck, November 18, 1907, Houck Papers, Box 1544, Correspondence–Outgoing, November 12–30 1907, Folder 24.

27. Louis Houck to George Houck, Jr., January 18, 1908, Houck Papers, Box 1544, Correspondence–Outgoing, January 14–31 1908, Folder 27.

28. Houck, "Story of the Railroad Work, Volume II," 132; *Cape Girardeau Southeast Missourian,* October 3, 1929.

29. Louis Houck to George Houck, March 10, 1906, Houck Papers, Box 1543, Correspondence–Outgoing, March 1–10 1906, Folder 23.

his personal notes for small sums here and there at various rural banks from Cape Girardeau to Farmington, Gordonville, Perryville, and Pocahontas. Together, he managed to leverage himself under a total debt of nearly $500,000 in principal with interest payments on top of that.

In his heart—which was almost surely broken by his beloved daughter Irma's tragic death from an apparent miscarriage in August 1911—Louis still believed that regardless of the line being a failure financially at present, it might ultimately prove to be the most valuable line of railroad he ever built if only given enough time. However, the seventy-three-year-old Houck just did not have enough time any more to be "playing" what he considered "a losing game." "I know," he had written earlier, "that if my property was in the hands of someone else that was young and had more financial backing it might be made a factor of very great importance."[30] Giboney surely qualified for the first but did not possess the latter. And so Louis approached both the Iron Mountain and Cotton Belt, which he thought might be receptive to the possibility of buying him out.

For whatever reasons, the rivals played their cards close to the vest, and if they had any real interest in unburdening Houck, they never let on. Each railroad nibbled, but no bona fide deal materialized until J. Hunter Byrd, the son of lumberman A. R. Byrd, stepped forward to help facilitate the sale. The junior Byrd, a St. Louis investment banker, also had his own substantial interests in the mills at Jackson, which gave him more than a passing fancy in regional railroad speculation. He was in fact a young man with financial backing. When he could not interest the Missouri Pacific's New York financiers, Byrd contacted the Frisco, a move that brought Houck back together with Yoakum and B. L. Winchell of the St. Louis and San Francisco, and Thomas West from the St. Louis Trust Company.[31] By deftly maneuvering himself into the Frisco camp, the young entrepreneur ultimately acted as the big railroad's proxy in the execution of a familiar contract with Louis in February 1913. Immediately after consolidating the Cape Girardeau and Thebes Bridge Terminal Railroad, the Chester, Perryville and Ste. Genevieve, the Cape Girardeau and Chester, and the Saline Valley railroads into one Cape Girardeau Northern, Houck sold this entire new corporation and all his interest in it to a syndicate headed by J. H.

30. Louis Houck to J. C. Crawford, February 9, 1907, Houck Papers, Box 1544, Correspondence–Outgoing, February 2–28 1907, Folder 10.

31. J. H. Byrd to Louis Houck, May 15, 1912, Houck Papers, 1912 Box 1538, Correspondence, May A-J, Folder 7; J. H. Byrd to Louis Houck, December 24, 1912, Houck Papers, 1912 Box 1538, Correspondence, Folder 27.

Byrd for $1,025,000 in Cape Girardeau Northern bonds that were guaranteed by the St. Louis and San Francisco.

This milestone, or at the very least partial victory, should have been celebrated if for no other reason than that at long last Louis Houck had—almost in spite of himself—turned the wolf loose. In marking the occasion privately, he spoke to the rather dubious nature of his retirement, revealing to James Brooks that the railway had "been a hot potato on my hands for the last four or five years, and I was finally compelled to let it drop. I should have let it drop years ago. But you know we are all subject to delusions, and I am not exempt."[32]

Yet, these sentiments turned out to be painfully premature, leaving Louis to reassess that "I thought I was out of this railroad business for good, with a big loss, but a loss that I could stand. Far from it."[33] As fate would have it, in May the Frisco's nearly fifteen-year-long policy of reckless expansionism finally drove the railroad into bankruptcy and receivership, an outcome arguably hastened by its acquisition of the Houck roads. The first receivers were friendly—Yoakum, Winchell, and West—but subsequent appointees were less so, and the new management repudiated the purchase arrangement. These developments returned the insolvent Cape Girardeau Northern to Houck's possession by the year's end, effectively guaranteeing that Louis would never really let go of this critter, even if it was now more albatross than wolf.

32. Louis Houck to James Brooks, December 18, 1912, Houck Papers, Box 1546, Correspondence–Outgoing, December 12–31 1912, Folder 20.
33. Houck, "Story of the Railroad Work, Volume II," 137–39.

CHAPTER 12

The Big Ditch

I suppose I will have to have lawsuits as long as I live.
There is no dodging that.

—Louis Houck

In what passed for retirement, Houck's life flowed with a certain seasonal rhythm of the gentleman farmer. As he waited to finally get his
money out of the Cape Girardeau Northern, Louis was "compelled," in his
words, "to wait and saw wood."[1] For most of the 1910s what he really
meant was springtime in the seat of a new gas-powered tractor, summers
vacationing in cooler climates and feasting on his beloved tomatoes, hog
killing and harvesting in the fall, sending out turkeys to friends for
Thanksgiving, and wintering in Texas before planting again the next year.
In looking at this stage of life "philosophically," Houck confided to Madison Smith that "so far as material things are concerned I have lost a world
of money in the last ten years, but that don't bother me. I think 'I am a
cheerful loser' . . . I expect now to devote myself to the improvement of
farms that I have long neglected, and do the best I can in that direction. Perhaps I will be harassed more with the farms than I ever was worried with
the Railroads."[2]

The Houcks were truly some of the wealthiest planters in southeast Missouri, and thus deeply implicated—for better or worse—in the region's

1. Louis Houck to A. J. Crum, November 7, 1916, Houck Papers, Box 1547,
Correspondence–Outgoing, November–December 1916, Folder 14.
2. Louis Houck to M. R. Smith, January 3, 1912, Houck Papers, Box 1546,
Correspondence–Outgoing, January 1–31 1912, Folder 7.

plantation economy that developed in the early twentieth century.[3] At any one time no fewer than sixty-four tenant farmers worked on the Elmwood estate itself, not counting the family's other substantial properties in this section of the state. Yet Louis never considered himself a disengaged absentee landowner like the kind that came to dominate agriculture in southeast Missouri. The genuine satisfaction he took from trying his hand tilling the soil and his natural curiosity for horticulture consumed many days with another enjoyable diversion. Often in consultation with state and federal departments of agriculture, Houck intently investigated new varieties of crops and experimented with adapting them to the peculiar southeast Missouri climate for the highest yields. When he convinced himself that regional farmers should abandon wheat altogether—believing it a "lazy man's crop" with those growing it getting "lazier and lazier all the time"—he recruited Kentucky families to come raise tobacco on his farms. Southeast Missouri was ideal tobacco country, Louis bragged, and the crop would simultaneously make tenant farmers more industrious and prosperous.[4]

Regardless of the season, one constant thread still wove its way through the tapestry of Houck's remaining years, and although it twisted into many forms and assumed varied hues, it was always present: litigation. "I suppose I will have to have lawsuits as long as I live," he had earlier prophesied with bemusement. "There is no dodging that."[5] Indeed, the Frisco receivership and subsequent uncertainty surrounding the ownership of the Cape Girardeau Northern necessitated it. Technically speaking, the bargain between Louis and J. H. Byrd stipulated that after the Cape Girardeau Northern's consolidation the Frisco would assume control of the railroad in exchange for $1.5 million in Cape Girardeau Northern bonds: $1.025 million for Houck and $475,000 for the Byrds. It also fixed the bonded indebtedness of the new corporation at $2.5 million, of which half a million was earmarked for improvements, including forty thousand new ties and the purchase of five locomotives. What sealed the deal for Houck was the Frisco's promise to guarantee the value of these bonds with their own money.[6]

The rub turned out to be Byrd's role in the arrangement, or rather the fact that he was not a duly elected officer of the St. Louis and San Francisco.

3. Stepenoff, "'The Last Tree Cut Down,'" 72–73.

4. Louis Houck to John Tlapek, July 22, 1912, Houck Papers, Box 1546, Correspondence–Outgoing, July 1–31 1912, Folder 13.

5. Louis Houck to Eleneious Smith, August 8, 1904, Houck Papers, Box 1542, Correspondence–Outgoing, August 2–13 1904, Folder 25.

6. *St. Louis Post Dispatch,* January 11, 1914; *St. Louis Globe Democrat,* January 16, 1913.

And it was largely on this pretense that the receivers sought to renege on the deal. Their lawyers claimed that despite B. F. Winchell's signature on a contract guaranteeing the bonds, no existing company records officially designated J. H. Byrd to act as an agent on behalf of the Frisco, nor were there any board minutes confirming that a purchase of the Cape Girardeau Northern had ever been made. According to the Frisco's legal department, the railroad never even physically accepted Houck's properties. In other words, the receivers effectively refused paternity of this bastard railroad, which meant that by not living up to their financial obligations, the bonds of the insolvent Cape Girardeau Northern were not worth much at face value and had practically no hope of bearing interest.

These revelations naturally left Houck over a sizable barrel because by early 1914 the Cape Girardeau Northern had already spent nearly $200,000 upgrading the lines based on the contract and, probably more importantly, the interest on the $1.5 million worth of bonds was coming due. As one might expect, Louis commenced a series of intervening lawsuits in the federal court over the next several years designed to force the receivers into finally taking over the operation of the Cape Girardeau Northern as a mandatory part of the Frisco's larger reorganization. Finally, in 1916, a U.S. district court ruled that the reorganized St. Louis and San Francisco was in fact liable under the original contract and awarded Houck a settlement of $212,000 in cash, $250,000 in Frisco first preferred stock, and $750,000 in common stock—in total worth half a million dollars in cash.

After Louis paid off $110,000 in old loans to the Mississippi Valley Trust Company and the Perryville Bank, "the balance, about 30 cents on the dollar, was paid on the bonds outstanding, about $1,100,000 and,"—and this was the real kicker—"the road was given back to the bondholders" by the Frisco.[7]

As the largest bondholder, Houck essentially found himself right back where he started, in control of an unprofitable road that still owed around $400,000 to the St. Louis Union Trust Company and every month got further and further behind. What had seemed like a salvation in 1913—a bargain that Louis and Mary felt would "free us from further trouble"—now placed them in an even more "precarious position" as "the whole burden of the road rested on" the two. Both husband's and wife's names were on the paper that endorsed the heavy debt, and what is more, the Houcks had

7. Houck, "Story of the Railroad Work, Volume II," 141–43; *Poor's Manual of Railroads 1921* (New York: H. V. and H. W. Poor, 1921), 224, John W. Barriger III National Railroad Library. Louis actually held $879,000 of the Cape Girardeau Northern bonds.

to start paying interest on the bonds out of their own pockets. Every thirty, sixty, and ninety days these payments came due, and soon Louis cashed out the preferred Frisco stock and sold off some more Scott County land to meet their liabilities. J. H. Byrd had been invaluable in helping keep the property together through patience, money, and credit, but there were finite limits to what even he could do. "I felt," Louis noted, "that my railroad situation was more involved than it ever had been. . . . The question then was what to do."[8]

Receivership offered the only practical solution, and toward that end in 1918 Giboney instituted a suit in the Cape Girardeau Court of Common Pleas whereby John Wallace Fristoe, who still led the T. J. Moss Tie Company, was appointed for that purpose. The next year a new receiver, George W. Cross, prudently cut operating expenses by suspending traffic between Jackson and Perryville and from Saline Junction to Farmington. Gradually, more and more of the Cape Girardeau Northern's mileage was taken out of service, the track dismantled, and the rights-of-way abandoned until only fifty-eight miles remained in 1927, twenty by 1928, and only twelve in 1930. Sometime in the midst of the Great Depression, after the last section between Perryville and the Mississippi River closed, the Missouri hinterland simply reclaimed the last Houck road.[9]

"The longer the road was operated the less business. It is the only road I ever built that instead of going up has gone down," Houck acquiesced. "No fool like an old fool and that man that goes into business after he is 65 ought to be killed with a club."[10]

Louis did not live to see his railroad vanish from benign neglect, but he nevertheless sensed that with its passing, an era was coming to an end. "I am convinced," he observed just a few years before, "that the day for small railroads in this country is over."[11] To his way of thinking, the tendency toward centralization in railroading, that is, a few larger concerns squeezing out the various smaller ones—a process Houck had undoubtedly both anticipated and facilitated—weighed most heavily on rural communities

8. Houck, "Story of the Railroad Work, Volume II," 144–45.

9. *Poor's Manual of Railroads 1930* (New York: H. V. and H. W. Poor, 1930), 1703, John W. Barriger III National Railroad Library. The Missouri Pacific actually bought a portion of the railroad in 1934 while building a new line into Cape Girardeau.

10. Louis Houck to "My Dear Joe," July 19, 1917, Houck Papers, Box 1547, Correspondence–Outgoing, July–August 1917, Folder 18; Louis Houck to J. W. Fristoe, May 7, 1919, Houck Papers, Box 1547, Correspondence–Outgoing, 1919, Folder 25.

11. Louis Houck to John P. Denny, December 17, 1912, Houck Papers, Box 1546, Correspondence–Outgoing, December 12–31 1912, Folder 20.

like those in southeast Missouri. Railways operated by national interests, he believed, were generally strangers to the local populations, customs, and geography, and their disregard for personalized customer service was regrettable. When setting their schedules and timetables, "all towns look alike to them"—sometimes just an insignificant blur in the middle of the night—and they rarely bothered to know, for instance, which communities were even the county seats, the traditional hotbeds of county life.[12] Of all his railroading experiences, one of the lessons he kept coming back to in retirement was how difficult it had been to convince the people of a small town that little roads like his, operated in their local interests, were worth more than a thousand-mile-long railroad operated in the interest of a big city. It seemed that across the region, invariably small towns "either laid out and built up by me and again towns into which I had built the first railroad and breathed the breath of life into" immediately coveted a big railroad to come through their community, only to lament it afterwards.[13]

He certainly detected as much in Cape Girardeau, where the city initially prospered from being a hub on the Frisco's main line, but suffered a major blow when the railroad began moving its division facilities, offices, and shops to Chaffee in 1906. Thereafter, the tumultuous relationship between the Frisco and the town proved stormy as the relocation engendered hard feelings and lawsuits.

Similarly, the specter of centralization in government troubled Houck as well as he considered the Progressive political culture of the first decades of the twentieth century inhospitable—perhaps even hostile—to the same economic individualism that had driven little railroading concerns a generation or so before. The sundry reform impulses known as Progressivism generally sought to ameliorate the social, economic, and political ills of industrialization and Gilded Age corruption, to in other words create social progress in America on par with the nation's dramatic commercial and technological progress. For Progressives, this translated into a general abandonment of traditional conceptions of laissez-faire political philosophy in favor of an unprecedented application of governmental power to create a modern regulatory state. And as the size and scope of government expanded at the local, state, and federal levels, lawmakers claimed new responsibility for policing corporate behavior, consumer safety, health, the environment, transportation, education, morality, and the assurance of democratic procedures.

12. Louis Houck to Thomas West, October 21, 1904, Houck Papers, Box 1542, Correspondence–Outgoing, October 1–31 1904, Folder 29.
13. "Louis Houck Memoirs," 141–42.

Just as he had earlier cherry-picked those planks in the Populist platform he found economically expedient, like "free silver," Louis did not dismiss Progressivism—Populism's ideological progeny—out of hand. He vigorously supported Missouri's leading Progressives, governors such as Joseph W. Folk and the Republican Herbert Spencer Hadley, along with the ubiquitous "Missouri Idea" that politicians have a civic obligation to uphold the public trust by using the law to aggressively eradicate the corruptive influence of special privilege. He embraced Holy Joe Folk's call for "principles above men, morals above money" and sincerely hoped that the crusade of this "champion of civil reform" would smite all of those having the "deplorable" "brand of bribery and boodle stamped on their forehead."[14] Like many former "silver Democrats," Louis too worried about the government's need for effective antitrust legislation against huge national corporations operating in the state, like Standard Oil of New Jersey. Needless to say, he found no philosophical quarrel with the Missouri Progressive's focus on strict enforcement of the state's existing liquor laws.

Where he drew the line, however, was not only the dangerous principle of centralizing governmental power, but moreover, in his opinion, the resulting potential for an overly intrusive government to abuse that power. Here again, his aggregate life experience—as a large landowner, entrepreneur, and railroader—only buttressed an enduring conservative, state's rights orientation. For instance, he held particularly serious reservations about the Progressive reliance on constitutional amendments to make sweeping national changes. Although a "dry," Louis opposed the "cranky" Eighteenth Amendment, which prohibited the manufacture and sale of alcohol nationwide. Likewise, despite an honest belief that "in these days women claim the same rights as men," he could not support the Nineteenth Amendment, which gave Mary the right to vote, because in his opinion, "the Constitution of the United States does not have anything to do with it."[15]

Certainly, this was also the case with corporate regulation, in particular the dozens of laws Missouri Progressives passed to variously supervise and tax railroads.[16] Houck chafed under mandatory safety regulations

14. Louis Houck to the "Editor Cash Book," n.d., Houck Papers, Box 1542, Correspondence–Outgoing, January 2–29 1904, Folder 13; Louis Houck to T. R. R. Ely, March 9, 1904, Houck Papers, Box 1542, Correspondence–Outgoing, March 3–16 1904, Folder 15.

15. Louis Houck to George Houck, Jr., January 18, 1908, Houck Papers, Box 1544, Correspondence–Outgoing, January 14–31 1908, Folder 27; Louis Houck to B. S. Curd, February 24, 1923, Houck Papers, Box 1547, Correspondence–Outgoing, Folder 31.

16. *Weekly Republican*, October 23, 1914.

because in his opinion they were patently unnecessary, since short and impoverished railways like his by their very nature ran much slower—and therefore more safely—than big roads. Moreover, besides requiring these costly precautions, the state further cut into his oftentimes nonexistent profit margin by reducing maximum freight-hauling rates by an average of 25 percent and lowering passenger rates by another 30.[17]

When it came to the thorny issue of taxation, Louis wailed each time Progressives ratcheted rates up, steadfast in his belief that the taxes on railroads were "already so enormous that they can hardly exist." "It seems to be the practice of the Legislature," he critically observed, "to cut the earnings down as much as possible and on the other hand to raise the taxes as high as possible." Progressive Missourians, he thought, labored under the delusion that all railroad owners were millionaires, living in lavish luxury and riding around in fancy private cars. In southeast Missouri, this was not the case and, if anything, locally owned railroads desperately needed the types of state assistance then being directed toward highways and drainage, not more regulations and taxes. If the same cumbersome Progressive laws had been on the books when he started, Louis at one point regretted, "nobody but an idiot would have undertaken to build" the Houck roads.[18]

Louis's resistance to much of Progressivism led historians to the conclusion that he was "out of historical step" with changing conceptions of public policy in the reform era of the late nineteenth and early twentieth centuries.[19] Without question, contemporary critics in the Bootheel, particularly the significant socialist movement that fermented out of the region's extensive land clearance, rapid population increases, and high rates of farm tenancy, thought so. Regarding his apparent hypocrisy when it came to issues of private interest versus public good, detractors took his railroads to task for being the most "abominable rapacious monopoly in this State" and cynically labeled him an exact reverse barometer for the general welfare of the people. "Anything that endangers Louis Houck's railroad and landlord graft sufficiently to excite his protest must be a thing that will be for the benefit of the people of the whole region upon whom

---

17. Christensen and Kremer, *A History of Missouri, Volume IV,* 179, 182–84.

18. Doherty, Jr., "Missouri Interests of Louis Houck," 243–44, 277; Louis Houck to Thomas F. Lane, February 22, 1909, Houck Papers, Box 1545, Correspondence–Outgoing, January–February 1909, Folder 5; Houck, "Story of the Railroad Work, Volume II," 117.

19. Doherty, Jr., *Houck, Missouri Historian and Entrepreneur,* 56.

he has fattened for more than a generation."[20] One man's David was another man's Goliath.

In truth, there was no real dissonance in Houck's political footwork. Although he might rationalize or justify his views with sincere objections to an affirmative government using its police powers irresponsibly or overstepping its bounds in regard to restricting personal freedom and using private property, Louis simply remained faithful to the course he charted long ago—support of the public good extended out only to the boundaries of his own self-interest and no further. His obstinate preference for privately owned toll roads instead of publicly operated "good roads" and outright defiance of the Little River Drainage District's encroachment on his property rights present two instances that illustrate this business creed clearly.

Since 1872 Houck had been in control of the Cape Girardeau and Scott County Macadamized Road—or Rock Levee Road—extending south from Cape Girardeau to Scott County. By virtue of a 1901 Missouri law, possession and operation of all private gravel and macadamized roads in the state were to be turned over to the respective county courts when their original charter life expired, which in the case of Houck's particular toll road meant in 1903. Within days of this mandated transfer, however, Louis conveyed all of the Cape Girardeau and Scott County Macadamized Road's real estate, right-of-way, franchises, and toll booths not to the Scott County Court, but to the newly incorporated Scott County Macadamized Road Company under the direction of Giboney. The county's attorneys immediately prosecuted Houck's blatant evasion of the law, and consequent litigation revolved around Louis's interpretation of private interest versus public good and his Fourteenth Amendment rights.[21]

As the case made its way to the Missouri Supreme Court, Houck's attorney Madison Smith maintained that the road's 1853 charter superseded the new Progressive legislation by granting "perpetual succession" of the company at the pleasure of its directors, meaning that after owning it for fifty years, Louis could sell it to whomever he wished. Failing that strategy, Smith reinforced his flank with the contention that if the county took

20. Stepenoff, "'The Last Tree Cut Down,'" 72; *Mirror* (St. Louis), September 12, 1912, quoted in Stepenoff, 73; Leon Parker Ogilvie, "Populism and Socialism in the Southeast Missouri Lowlands."

21. Doherty, Jr., *Houck, Missouri Historian and Entrepreneur,* 58–60; Houck, "Some Reminiscences," 68–70; Louis Houck to William Penny, July 15, 1903, Houck Papers, Box 1542, Correspondence–Outgoing, July 1–16 1903, Folder 1.

the toll road from Houck, due process of law required that he be compensated. Ultimately, neither argument convinced the state's highest court, which ruled in 1907 that "perpetual: did not mean eternal" and that by virtue of collecting tolls for thirty years, Louis had been more than compensated already.[22]

The passing of the Rock Levee Road from private to public hands served as a prologue of sorts to the progressive "Good Roads Movement" of the 1920s that further centralized governmental authority over a statewide highway system of improved hard surface roads in Missouri. By 1919, Cape Girardeau County had passed its own million-dollar bond to do its part in lifting Missouri "out of the mud." Yet as local good roads clubs convinced Missourians that even county control of the state's antiquated "patchwork quilt" of dirt and gravel roads must give way to a centralized highway authority, Houck's predilection for privately owned transportation and decentralized road administration cast him as an even more embattled dissenter of this imminent element of modernization.[23]

While not a Progressive initiative per se—although its development did involve the reformers' application of modern scientific thinking to conquer an age-old problem—the Little River Drainage District unquestionably represents the clearest example of Louis's steadfast defense of private interest, even at the expense of potentially spectacular progress. The mammoth engineering project revolutionized southeast Missouri by successfully draining the region's wetlands, and, contrary to Houck's denigration, it did in fact turn the Bootheel into one of the most productive agricultural regions of the state, if not the nation, within a generation. Of course, there had been talk of draining the vast swamps in this geographic catch basin since the late nineteenth century—Houck's railroads dabbled in some of these individual reclamation efforts—but comparatively little had been accomplished until the Little River Drainage District incorporated in 1907. Actual construction did not begin until seven years later, with some of the brightest engineering minds in the country overseeing the work, including Otto Kochtitsky, the district's first chief engineer, and others who had

22. Doherty, Jr., "Missouri Interests of Louis Houck," 245–54.

23. *Cape Girardeau Southeast Missourian*, December 12, 1919. See Richard C. Traylor, "Pulling Missouri Out of the Mud: Highway Politics, the Centennial Road Law, and the Problems of Progressive Identity," 47–68. In 1907, the same year the state supreme court ruled against Houck, the General Assembly passed a law preparing for the eventual statewide consolidation of road improvements by providing for a highway engineer to be appointed in each county, creating a "general state road fund," and designating a state highway engineer to serve in an advisory role.

worked on the recently completed Panama Canal. Between 1914 and 1928, when initial construction concluded, these men took advantage of the region's natural boundaries to drain the Bootheel with an elaborate network of ditches, canals, and levees. The basis is a forty-five-mile headwater diversion channel extending across Bollinger County east to the Mississippi River. As the name implies, this channel protects southeast Missouri from water running off the Ozark foothills by diverting it into the river below Cape Girardeau. An accompanying levee and three holding basins north of the diversion channel make sure that no water enters the region from the north. Below the diversion channel, the lower district then drains the Bootheel through a series of five parallel floodway ditches extending north and south.

The statistics were, and are, impressive. At an original construction cost of $11.1 million, the drainage system—said to be the largest such project in the world—runs some one hundred miles long, from Cape Girardeau to the Arkansas line, and is ten to twenty miles wide. Within its borders there are 957 miles of ditches and 304 miles of levees, most of which were originally carved out by electric and steam draglines, floating dredge boats, and backbreaking labor that moved more than a million cubic yards of earth—more than the Panama Canal. Today the district encompasses around 540,000 acres over seven counties, but drains 1.2 million acres, some as far north as Fredericktown. This means that while less than 10 percent of the region's land was cleared of swamps before 1907, afterwards nearly 96 percent has remained relatively free of water.[24]

In fairness, this magnificent triumph of the Little River Drainage District was anything but a foregone conclusion during its infancy, and there were in fact many southeast Missouri landowners who adamantly opposed the project. Some criticized its unrealistic scope, while others feared that the district's uncertain benefits might never balance the cost in terms of the enormous expenditures in money and manpower. Louis certainly shared some of these initial reservations from an engineering standpoint, mainly that the diversion channel would simply create a new swamp to its north in order to drain the old one to the south and the possibility that once the swamps were drained the Mississippi might just alter its course to the west and once again fill in the lowlands.[25]

24. *The Little River Drainage District of Southeast Missouri, 1907-Present* (Cape Girardeau, Mo., 1989).

25. Louis Houck to Charles Miller, March 28, 1910, Houck Papers, Box 1545, Correspondence–Outgoing, March 2–30 1910, Folder 15.

But Houck nevertheless advocated drainage in principle and begrudgingly acknowledged Kochtitsky's overall "visionary idea."[26] It seems he also bought thousands of dollars worth of Little River Drainage District bonds around 1905 through George, in a special deal his brother worked out with Kochtitsky whereby the district promised Louis some reciprocal relief on his yearly drainage taxes as a bonus. Even as late as 1900 he assisted Kochtitsky in presenting the merits of the drainage project to hesitant associates such as R. B. Oliver and the "indifferent" A. R. Byrd. In truth, he later admitted that the construction alone would boom Cape Girardeau and the region for years by pouring millions of dollars into the local economy and attracting laborers from all over the nation to take part in the dig.[27]

It might appear, then, that the reasons Louis came to passionately oppose "the Big Ditch," as most called it, did honestly have something to do with practical concerns of feasibility, cost, and risk, but may well have chiefly stemmed from how he came to understand the ways in which the district might adversely affect the Houck family.

First, the Little River Drainage District—a public agency—wielded quasi-governmental powers that allowed it to levy taxes, determine benefits, and exercise eminent domain.[28] Here Louis blamed the Missouri General Assembly for being intoxicated with this latest "drainage craze": in its haste to empty southeast Missouri, he charged, the state legislators had quickly passed ill-considered and complicated drainage laws that unconstitutionally empowered the Little River Drainage District to trample individual land owners' property rights without due process of law. For example, not only did Missouri law allow for those who held the majority of acreage—lumbermen—to effectively dictate to the relatively smaller landowners—like Houck—in matters of policy, but once landowners signed the articles of association to be included in the district they could not bring suit to have themselves dismissed. What is more, after an issuance of bonds funded the initial construction, maintenance of the system would be paid for through annual drainage taxes assessed on property owners within the district based on the benefits each would receive from drainage.

If Houck did not particularly fancy the notion of engineered drainage at taxpayer expense in the first place, he really disliked it when, before the

26. T. B. Whitten to Louis Houck, January 31, 1911, Houck Papers, 1911 Box 1537, Correspondence, January M-Z, Folder 3.

27. Otto Kochtitzky to Louis Houck, January 27, 1900, Houck Papers, 1900 Box 1523, Correspondence, January D-K, Folder 9; Louis Houck to E. F. Blomeyer, September 3, 1912, Houck Papers, Box 1546, Correspondence, September 2–13 1912, Folder 16.

28. Ronald S. Reed, Jr., to Joel P. Rhodes, July 26, 2006, in possession of author.

first shovel full of dirt could even be moved, the Little River Drainage District levied a preliminary tax for organization and to "project" what each landowner's benefits might be. Legally speaking, Louis found this taxation power "clearly unconstitutional" and the "thoroughly impractical" system highly questionable. What would happen if, after each landowner had been assessed for benefits and that money collected—generally $4 to $40 an acre—the actual construction of the drainage district revealed in a decade or so that the projections were wrong and they did not benefit at all? Suppose that in reality, some lands were harmed instead? Then, of course, what about the collateral damages to existing roads and railways? Who would bear the hidden costs of bridging the ditches: the individual landowners, county taxpayers, or the railroads?[29]

Most of Houck's well-researched and reasoned arguments may have been framed hypothetically for the press, but without question he and Mary's lands were foremost on his mind. Thousands of acres of Houck land were already improved and yearly producing handsome crops. What future benefits could the family realistically expect in his lifetime, or, put another way, why should they pay for something in the future that they already had? If anything, the wide diversion channel cut directly across their lands south of the Cape from Dutchtown to the Mississippi, disfiguring the fields and taking valuable acreage out of cultivation. Perhaps most significantly, because Missouri law did not require judicial findings of benefits to form the basis for levying the assessments, Houck wondered what legal safeguards or recourse existed to keep the Drainage District from saying that their farmland would be benefited as much by the drainage work as would stagnant swamps. In his mind, there were no safeguards, because the drainage district, not the landowners, had the right to decide who would benefit and who would not.

At this juncture, Louis thought he smelled an unholy conspiracy of avarice between the Little River Drainage District, big lumber firms such as Himmelberger-Harrison and International Harvester, real estate speculators, outside investors, and their allies in county and state government. The ringleaders of this "wild cat scheme" were the lumber companies, his old customers whom he had gotten sideways with during the last days of the St. Louis, Kennett and Southern. These timber tycoons—"a gang of the

29. Louis Houck to George Murray, December 5, 1910, Houck Papers, Box 1545, Correspondence–Outgoing, December 1–17 1910, Folder 26; Louis Houck to A. Graham, October 21, 1911, Houck Papers, Box 1546, Correspondence–Outgoing, October–November 1911, Folder 5; *Daily Republican*, December 9, 1909.

biggest rascals I think that ever struck Southeast Missouri"—were playing, Houck believed, "jokes" on the region's unsuspecting landowners.[30]
Why else had International Harvester and Himmelberger-Harrison initially gerrymandered district boundaries to exclude their most valuable
acreage in Pemiscot, Dunklin, Stoddard, and New Madrid counties?
Could it be that these "jokers" wanted only the best farmlands in Cape
Girardeau and Bollinger counties to be included at first so as to make Little River Drainage bonds more attractive to investors on the open market?
Conceivably, the lumbermen were farsighted enough to recognize that
after all the timber had been exhausted by the late 1920s, their vast holdings—by then stripped of their only commodity—would be worth relatively little, unless the district could appreciate regional land values
overall in the meantime.[31]

Therein lay the punch line of the joke: the thirty-some-mile-wide upper
portion of the district north of the diversion channel would be exploited
and maybe even sacrificed in order to increase the price of the hundred-
mile-long bottomlands in the lower end of the district to the south. In
Houck's mind, even the "dullest" southeast Missourian should see that
the "specious" Drainage District was promoted principally to drain the
swamps of lumber companies so that after their timber was gone the firms
could unload their land in the overflow of the Little River on an unsuspecting public.[32]

While not opposed to drainage, Louis reiterated constantly that "all is not
gold that glitters" and "we are opposed to exploiting our Country up here
for the benefit of Himmelberger and the International Harvester Company."[33] That being said, "I am satisfied," he wrote to Cape Girardeau's *Daily
Republican*, "that the ditch industry and bond industry is busily engaged to
fasten a rope around the necks of the land owners of Southeast Missouri.
Endless litigation will be the only alternative."[34] Indeed, after first publicly

30. *Daily Republican*, March 3, 1911; Louis Houck to George Houck, Jr., September 18, 1903, Houck Papers, Box 1542, Correspondence–Outgoing, September 8–30 1903, Folder 6.

31. Louis Houck to Editor, *Republican*, January 9, 1911, Houck Papers, Box 1545, Correspondence–Outgoing, January 3–30 1911, Folder 28.

32. Louis Houck to Fristoe, December 9, 1910, Houck Papers, Box 1545, Correspondence–Outgoing, December 1–17 1910, Folder 26; Louis Houck to E. F. Blomeyer, February 8, 1911, Houck Papers, Box 1545, Correspondence–Outgoing, February 1911, Folder 29.

33. Louis Houck to Edward Deal, January 20, 1911, Houck Papers, Box 1545, Correspondence–Outgoing, January 3–30 1911, Folder 28.

34. *Daily Republican*, March 3, 1911, Houck Papers Accretion, Box 1913, Folder 4.

coming out against the Little River Drainage District in 1909, Louis waged this bitter crusade for the rest of his life. In contesting every inch of ground, at times he called a truce long enough to enlist the help of the Cotton Belt and Missouri Pacific, along with other landowners, to take the battle into the region's halls of justice and courts of public opinion. After his death, Mary and Giboney doggedly carried on the fight.

Since most of Houck's fundamental objections regarding the constitutionality of state drainage laws that provided for tax collection were settled early on in favor of the Drainage District by the Missouri and U.S. Supreme Courts, the family spent years devising new and ingenious strategies to frustrate the Little River people.[35] Sometimes this subterfuge took the form of neglecting to pay annual drainage taxes. Other times the tactics were more overt, as in the case of Giboney's 1918 election to the Missouri House of Representatives on the singular platform of amending state drainage laws so that Cape Girardeau County taxpayers would not have to pay for bridges across the diversion channel.[36] Still, although the Houcks never beat back this tide of progress either, their fierce defense of family lands was not always entirely in vain. In what might be considered a consolation or concession to soften his personal attacks on the project, by 1919 the Little River Drainage District had paid out $130,000 to Louis for what they maintained were "alleged damages" done to some of the Houcks' Cape County lands. Maybe more satisfyingly, instead of condemning the family's property immediately south of Cape Girardeau and vesting itself with free title, the Drainage District ultimately settled for accepting deeds by which Louis retained title and granted the district "flowage rights." Thus the diversion channel of the Little River Drainage District is still owned entirely by the Little River except where it flows though former Houck lands.[37]

35. Ronald S. Reed, Jr., to Joel P. Rhodes, July 26, 2006, in possession of author; *Weekly Republican*, October 29, 1915. See *Louis Houck, et al., Appellants vs. Little River Drainage District et al.*, Missouri Reports 248: 373–94, and *Houck vs. Little River Drainage District*, United States Reports 239: 254–67.

36. *Cape Girardeau Southeast Missourian*, November 1, 1918, February 14, April 25, 1919. Even with Louis's substantial backing, the Drainage District prevailed in this round as well as on the "Houck-Speer" bill to protect Cape Girardeau County taxpayers from paying for bridges across the diversion channel, which failed to pass in the Missouri legislature.

37. *Bulletin of the Little River Drainage District* 18 (February 1919), Little River Drainage District Papers—Bulletins 1914–1949, Box 1951, Special Collections and Archives, Southeast Missouri State University, Cape Girardeau, Mo.; Ronald S. Reed, Jr., to Joel P. Rhodes, July 26, 2006, in possession of author.

Besides opening Louis up to public denunciations of "old fogy" and "moss back," in a more meaningful way the drainage fight destroyed his friendship with R. B. Oliver—whose family law firm enthusiastically served the Little River Drainage District as its chief legal counsel. In turn, this uncomfortable animosity between the two proud lawyers almost certainly contributed at least indirectly to the controversial dismissal of Dr. Washington S. Dearmont as president of Southeast Missouri State Teachers College in 1921.

While not intimates, Houck's and Dearmont's collaboration had formed an integral part of arguably the most prolific administration in school history. Their working relationship certainly continued to pay tremendous dividends for Southeast throughout the 1910s, as the men labored unselfishly to expand the curriculum, establish a college farm, strengthen cultural offerings, and assiduously milk appropriations from the state whenever possible. On a more personal level, although unbeknownst to Houck, it had been Dearmont's private appeal to Elliott Major that probably saved Louis's seat on the board of regents in 1913 when the incoming Missouri governor was not inclined to reappoint him.[38] Similarly, Dearmont also faithfully stayed by Houck's side at St. Francis Hospital after a serious buggy accident in the summer of 1915 permanently blinded the seventy-five-year-old regent in one eye. The mishap occurred near the Juden home, Briarwood, during one of Louis's morning rides into the Cape when the horse came out of its shaft and turned the buggy over, throwing him face down into the gravel of the Bloomfield Road. As he lay convalescing for almost five weeks from the near fatal wreck, with both of his blue eyes bandaged, he could not distinguish day from night. In his "nervous" and "restless" state Louis frequently insisted on Dearmont reading the college library's copies of the *Edinburgh Review* or *London Times* or entertaining him with updates concerning school goings-on. Often these impromptu meetings required Giboney to transport both Dearmont and the college's secretary, Christine Wheeler, to Louis's room at odd hours, but as Wheeler later recalled, "of course we never refused to go, even if between midnight and dawn."[39]

World War I began to strain the relationship between the president and head regent, however. As Democrats, both supported America's entrance

38. Mattingly, *Normal to University*, 110; John Atkinson to Louis Houck, May 11, 1921, Houck Papers, 1921 Box 1540, Correspondence, May–June A-Z, Folder 18; Ivan Lee Holt to Louis Houck, June 3, 1921, Houck Papers, 1921 Box 1540, Correspondence, May–June A-Z, Folder 18.
39. Heil, "Recollections."

into the Great War in 1917, although Louis remained less than enthusiastic for a conflict with European roots that was being fought on European battlefields and would surely have only European consequences. Yet despite his skepticism of the jingoistic fervor the war elicited, he and Dearmont set about mobilizing the campus: patriotic demonstrations were orchestrated, young men voluntarily trained for military service, war bonds sold, and, with Louis's blessing, the teaching of German suspended.[40] What set them at odds was not the justness of America's crusade to make the world safe for democracy, but rather President Woodrow Wilson's postwar vision of a new world order. Sometime around 1917 Louis had become intimate friends with Missouri Senator James A. Reed, an isolationist firebrand and vitriolic opponent of American membership in Wilson's League of Nations. Both Houck and Reed detested Wilson's messianic drive to export American Progressivism, and during Reed's frequent visits to Elmwood they railed against the League of Nations—a proposed global forum whereby civilized nations could solve geopolitical crises through international cooperation—as a dangerous adventure to create a worldwide regulatory state devised by that "damned school teacher we have as President."[41]

Conversely, Dearmont and many other Democratic faculty, like most out-state Missourians, and in fact most Americans, vigorously supported Wilson—the former political science professor—along with his League of Nations. This rift over the League, exacerbated by resentment over Reed's perceived disloyalty to Wilson, positioned Dearmont and Houck firmly within the larger internal schism inside the ranks of Missouri Democrats that by the election of 1920 threatened to dramatically weaken the party's hold on state power. As tempers heated up that fall, local opponents of the League had begun grumbling in Cape Girardeau that Dearmont and other faculty were using weekly chapel periods at the college to imbue students with pro-Wilson views. Even more controversially, Katherine Martin, the outspoken suffragette and wife of Professor W. W. Martin, a dean at Southeast, delivered a bitter polemic against Reed and his animosity toward Wilson at the San Francisco Democratic National Convention. Missouri Democrats had already demonstrated their ire toward the renegade Reed

40. Board of Regents Minutes, vol. 1, 1873–1925, 320; Louis Houck to Senator W. J. Stone, July 30, 1917, Houck Papers, Box 1547, Correspondence–Outgoing, Folder 18.
41. Louis Houck to "My dear Senator," July 16, 1916, Houck Papers, Box 1547, Correspondence–Outgoing, June–August 1916, Folder 12; Louis Houck to A. R. Ponder, January 4, 1921, Houck Papers, Box 1547, Correspondence–Outgoing, January–March 1921, Folder 27; Cape Girardeau Southeast Missourian, April 22, 1925.

by refusing to select him as a delegate to the convention, and many anti-Reed conventioneers credited Martin's highly publicized speech with convincing the national committee to reject the senator's demand that he be seated anyway.[42]

Indeed, these divisions among Missouri's Democrats permitted substantial inroads for Republicans in 1920. As part of the greater national Republican victory, which put Warren G. Harding in the White House, the GOP carried 85 of Missouri's 114 counties and voters elected Arthur Hyde governor. For the first time since the Civil War, the GOP also claimed ownership of both houses of the state legislature.[43] While significant in and of itself, the Republican sweep boded particularly ill for Dearmont on several fronts. First, Governor Hyde's subsequent Progressive agenda to further consolidate many state governmental functions included a controversial plan to eliminate the board of regents for each of the state's five teachers' colleges in favor of a single state board. This initiative put Dearmont in direct opposition to the new governor because as a small college president he felt duty bound to challenge any measure that could severely compromise the autonomy of each institution. Then too there was Hyde's concomitant general purging of political opponents at all levels.

By aggressively opposing Hyde's ultimately ill-fated education reorganization plan, Dearmont was left particularly vulnerable to the new governor's retribution, especially after the chief executive's appointment of two new Republican members to Southeast Missouri State's board of regents gave that body a distinct GOP majority and decidedly anti-Dearmont flavor.[44] In previous years, the powerful Houck—long considered to be the straw that stirred Democratic politics in Cape County—might have been counted on as an ally. But the League ordeal had isolated Dearmont from the head regent's support or protection. And here is where the Houck and Oliver and Drainage District feud enters into the equation. Russell L. Dearmont, Washington Dearmont's son, had married Marie Marguerite Oliver, the only daughter of R. B. and Marie Oliver, thus joining the families into what Houck viewed as the same pro-drainage, anti-Reed crowd.

All things considered—and there are several schools of thought regarding the exact reasons behind Dearmont's sacking—it appears highly likely

---

42. *Cape Girardeau Southeast Missourian*, June 30, 1920, June 6, 1921.
43. Kirkendall, *A History of Missouri, Volume*, 28–30.
44. Simmons, "Dearmont and His Impact," 82–84; Mattingly, *Normal to University*, 111–16. The two new members of the regents appointed by Governor Hyde in 1921 were James A. Finch of New Madrid and H. J. Talbot of St. Louis.

that when the president's contract expired at the end of the spring term in 1921, partisan politics, personalities, and his professional estrangement from Houck cost Dearmont his job.

Amid speculation and rumors surrounding Dearmont's inevitable firing, the regents' postponement, without explanation, of their routine "election"—or hiring—of faculty touched off a groundswell of public support for the popular president in the late spring—so much so that when the regents finally convened in June, a delegation of concerned townspeople and students filled the corridors of Academic Hall to appeal to the board for a hearing regarding Dearmont's future. Houck begrudgingly allowed this unorthodox intrusion by reconvening the entire assembly in the spacious Academic Hall auditorium. But the strict parliamentarian pointedly warned Dearmont's supporters that they had only two hours to say their piece, and while the board was willing to listen in regard to hiring faculty, they would not "abdicate their power to act in these matters."[45]

Eloquent speeches on Dearmont's behalf resounded through the packed house, with several students speaking out vigorously and Professor Martin even offering his own resignation if it would help Dearmont's cause. To place an exclamation point firmly behind their sentiments, those in attendance concluded by calling for a "rising vote" of confidence. Everyone in the noisy auditorium stood up, except the regents. Instead, Louis briskly led the board back across the hall to their formal regent's room and called to order a private executive session.

Out of curiosity and loyalty to Dearmont, Christine Wheeler worked out an elaborate secret code with Russell Dearmont whereby she could communicate the board's decision ahead of time to President Dearmont before the regents adjourned. With Dearmont's son standing outside the boardroom door, which had a glass panel covered by a net curtain so that he could see in without the regents noticing, Christine stayed inside the room and at the moment of the vote walked to the closet by the window, pretending to get a shorthand tablet, but instead picking up the college's blue catalog. If Dr. Dearmont was reelected she would put the catalog into the closet, signifying "he was in." If the board determined to not reelect him, the secretary would lay the catalog flat on the windowsill—"he was out." Either way, Russell could then go to his father's private office and inform him of the outcome.[46]

45. Board of Regents Minutes, vol. 1, 1873–1925, 348, Special Collections and Archives, Southeast Missouri State University.
46. Heil, "Recollections."

Though the official tally is unknown, accounts indicate that the vote was probably unanimous. Christine Wheeler laid the catalogue down on the ledge.

Houck's vague public explanations for not reelecting Dearmont, and for the subsequent hiring of Joseph Serena, a Republican, as the college's eighth president, avoided all mention of politics or Dearmont's qualifications. Nevertheless, in response, popular sentiment immediately recast Dearmont's removal squarely back into the arena of partisanship. "The official head has been severed at the neck," a *St. Louis Post-Dispatch* editor observed, "and the League of Nations apostasy has been extracted, root and branch, from the Cape Girardeau institution."[47] Others wove politics and personalities together with at least a healthy allusion to the Houck and Oliver rivalry. "The League of Nations may boast another martyr and the victors of last November's election a fresh killing," a southeast Missouri newspaper declared. Even though "there seems to be many angles to his personal opposition," the editor continued, "it all has its seat in the local and complex quarrels of the citizens of Cape Girardeau." Ultimately, in placing principles over "the expediency of maintaining peace and concord with all political elements upon whom he might become dependent for his job," Dearmont had virtually assured his ouster.[48]

Aside from the generic official statement concerning the board's decision, Louis did not retort in the media, and in actuality, does not seem to have ever tipped his hand regarding what really went on in the board's executive session. Still, his handling of the subsequent dissent on campus is quite telling.

On the morning after the firing, Southeast Missouri State students expressed their displeasure by holding "Dearmont Day," a nearly spontaneous protest to boycott classes and essentially shut down the normal operations of the school. In preparation for the scheduled resumption of the regents' annual meeting, a group of students arrived on campus before daybreak and "forced" the head janitor Charles Fricke to lock Academic Hall. With the keys safely in Fricke's pocket, they tied "his arms to his body and laid him under a tree on the front campus." Meanwhile, before any of the faculty, librarians, or staff arrived for work, male students from Albert Hall hung effigies bearing the name of each regent between the stone pillars at the main entrance to the campus.[49] By this time a crowd of

47. Reprinted in *Cape Girardeau Morning Sun*, June 11, 1921, quoted in Doherty, Jr., *Houck, Missouri Historian and Entrepreneur*, 86.
48. *Sikeston Standard*, June 14, 1921, quoted in Mattingly, *Normal to University*, 115.
49. Heil, "Recollections."

almost seven hundred students had gathered on the stone steps leading up to Academic from the sidewalk on Normal Avenue to take part in the spectacle. Under a large banner that read "Dearmont Day: in honor of our martyred president," they were eventually joined by college employees who found their offices locked.

When the regents began stepping out of their cars on Normal Avenue, the effigies were set on fire. In their outrage, most of the men refused to walk under the burning effigies, and a standoff soon developed as the regents remained on the plaza and the milling crowd moved to block the sidewalk. But the appearance of Louis Houck apparently broke the brief impasse and summarily put matters of Dearmont Day to rest.

When Louis arrived with Giboney, he barked orders to the staff that the ropes around Fricke be cut and Academic Hall immediately opened. From there he quickly led his colleagues through what he undoubtedly considered a churlish mob, up the grand steps of Academic, and toward the board room. Once inside, however, the crush of students following them compelled Louis to direct the members to the nearby Faculty Room. Because this meeting was to dispense with the customary business of electing teachers, one by one all members of the faculty and staff were summoned before the board and queried as to whether they desired to retain their positions. As the chair, the cranky Houck cautioned each that no faculty would be kept on if they did not cooperate with President Serena and the board of regents. Before exiting he required their promise of continued good and loyal service. All pledged, but some later resigned. Following the employees, the suspected student organizers of the protest along with the matron of Albert Hall were called on the carpet before Houck. None would confess to any role in the demonstration and were dismissed with a strongly worded reprimand.[50]

When his fellow regents finally broached the subject of what to do about the effigies, Louis is said to have yelled back, "Oh, who cares about that nonsense. Let 'em burn. I just hope the owners of those pants will need them."[51]

50. Farmer, "Southeast Missouri State Normal," 237.
51. Heil, "Recollections." Like other colorful folktales surrounding Houck, this too may be apocryphal as an examination of photographs taken during Dearmont Day appears to show that the effigies were not actually dressed, but instead were simply stuffed burlap bags with each regent's name attached.

CHAPTER 13

A Quiet Religious Mood

I am satisfied that . . . you will be much happier and more likely to remain in a quiet religious mood than if you should again undertake to run the Cape Girardeau road.

—Eleneious Smith

"I would not object to old age if I could preserve my activity and interest in human affairs," Louis once told Robert Sturdivant, "but I want to be able to move around and keep moving."[1] With each rapidly passing season, however, the octogenarian found that sentiment more difficult to satisfy, and during the last three or four years of his life, the once well-traveled Houck rarely left the farm. Aside from intermittent board of regents meetings, he largely left it to his son, Giboney—a lifelong bachelor—to manage his business affairs, and with power of attorney, his son also now shouldered the heavy burdens of railroading, debt, and real estate. Louis had always enjoyed deer-hunting excursions and trout fishing at his Greer Springs property in Oregon County—although admittedly he was a poor fisherman—but trouble breathing increasingly precluded even these activities as well. And while he missed the theater and fine hotels of St. Louis a good deal, what he really longed to see again was the Caribbean. "I would rather go to Guatemala any time than to Europe," he had told the anthropologist D. I. Bushnell when apologetically begging out of an invitation to tour that country. "All the states of Central America have an interest and fascination for me."[2]

1. Louis Houck to Robert Sturdivant, September 7, 1903, Houck Papers, Box 1542, Correspondence–Outgoing, September 4–8 1903, Folder 5.
2. Louis Houck to D. I. Bushnell, November 28, 1910, Houck Papers, Box 1545, Correspondence–Outgoing, November 19–30 1910, Folder 25.

An occasional good cigar remained a welcome friend, and likewise Louis acquired a taste for lithium water, which he had delivered regularly from the natural spring along the northern railway. The mood-enhancing lithium carbonate eased his mind while worsening his scholarly absentmindedness. Conversely, he seems to have been a little grumpy when it did come in on time. For a while he thought a great business could be made selling jugs of the water in Cape, perhaps right off the depot platform.[3]

Sunshine and warm weather still lured him outdoors, and together with Mary, Louis busied himself as best he could in the garden tending to the various potatoes, peas, beans, radishes, lettuce, and cabbage she raised. Sometimes while "Mama" looked after her beautiful violets, jonquils, and hyacinths, "Papa" strolled through the large orchard, stopping to exactingly trim a raspberry bush, grapevine, or one of the many apple and peach trees. Often, while leaning on his trusty walking stick, the lord of the manor gazed lovingly across the pastoral fields surrounding Elmwood at the farmers in the field, or the hired hands whitewashing fences, repairing outbuildings, and tending to stock. The dogs who lived on the estate usually tagged along, chasing pigs, turkeys, and, to Houck's sly delight, generally trying to dispose of the large number of cats residing there as well.[4]

Grandchildren similarly roamed free, as the family affectionately knew Elmwood as "grandmother's hotel."[5] By this time the oldest grandchildren—Andy, Alex, and Sally Juden—were young adults and off at school. But even after their mother Irma's untimely death, the Judens remained very close to their grandparents, as did their widower father, Charles. While Alex went to medical school to become a doctor, Louis envisioned a career in railroading for Andy instead. Actually, Houck intended Andy to study law, seeing in his devoted grandson "the making of a fine lawyer" with "sufficient aggressive ability."[6] But an eye ailment that left Andy temporarily blind as a child prohibited the boy from reading or studying for long periods of time, and so the elderly patriarch decided Andy should follow the other family vocation. Accordingly, Houck tried to arrange a sort of apprenticeship for Andy with A. R. Ponder, who by now operated the San Antonio, Uvalde and Gulf railway in Texas. Someday, Andy would

3. Louis Houck to R. J. Hiatt, July 25, 1912, Houck Papers, Box 1546, Correspondence–Outgoing, July 1–31 1912, Folder 13.

4. Giboney Houck to Mary Hunter Giboney Houck, March 21, 1920, Houck Papers, 1920 Box 1540, Correspondence, March A-Z, Folder 9; Rebecca Frissell to Louis Houck, March 29, 1920, Houck Papers, 1920 Box 1540, Correspondence, March A-Z, Folder 9.

5. Mary Hunter Giboney Houck to Louis Houck, March 28, 1920, Houck Papers, 1920 Box 1540, Correspondence, March A-Z, Folder 9.

6. Louis Houck to A. R. Ponder, May 31, 1922, Houck Papers, Box 1547, Correspondence–Outgoing, January–December 1922, Folder 30.

make a great foreman, superintendent, or manager, his grandfather believed, but before then he would have to learn the ropes from the ground up with jobs that would teach him all aspects of railroading, and at a modest salary that would simply keep him out of the poorhouse.[7] Although the apprenticeship never materialized, after briefly attending Southeast Missouri State Teachers College, Andy joined his uncle Giboney in the Independence Street depot to run the various Houck and Juden enterprises.

The baby of the clan was little Mary Giboney Frissell, the only child of Rebecca and her husband, Pat Frissell. Born in 1916, "Little Curly Head," as Louis and Mary knew her, grew up at Elmwood after Pat, an army pilot, died in a crash near Port Jervis, New Jersey, during preparations for a transcontinental air race when she was three years old. Louis had often warned his son-in-law about the dangers of leaving the ground, yet like most pilots, Major Frissell—a career military man and onetime aide in the American embassy in China—felt perfectly at home in the air, even wowing crowds with daring aerial demonstrations in Cape Girardeau just prior to the fatal crash. For her part, Rebecca, who had always been a fragile soul and frequently under a doctor's care, never truly recovered emotionally from the tragedy, and after taking up permanent residence in Elmwood with her daughter became more insecure, irascible, and dependent on her parents. Little Mary, on the other hand, returned to Elmwood the joys of a small child, whether hunting "rabbit eggs" on Easter with Giboney—likewise an enduring occupant of the estate—or mimicking her grandfather's increasingly awkward walk.[8]

When colder temperatures drove Louis indoors—even if Mary habitually kept Elmwood cooler than it was outside by resisting the use of the furnace and drawing all the shades—he usually returned to his labor of love: history. During his last fifteen years or so, Louis occupied himself as health would allow with various smaller scholarly projects and tried to stay engaged in the historical community.[9] He was widely regarded as the most knowledgeable man around when it came to all things concerning southeast Missouri, and many historians—and botanists—made the pilgrimage to Elmwood seeking his guidance. Similarly, he served in a more official advisory capacity as trustee and second vice-president of the State

7. Louis Houck to A. R. Ponder, May 31, 1922, Houck Papers, Box 1547, Correspondence–Outgoing, January–December 1922, Folder 30.
8. Mary Hunter Giboney Houck to Louis Houck, April 4, 1920, Houck Papers, 1920 Box 1540, Correspondence, April A-Z, Folder 11; Ronald S. Reed, Jr. to Joel P. Rhodes, September 22, 2006, in possession of author.
9. Doherty, Jr., "Missouri Interests of Louis Houck," 371.

Historical Society of Missouri until 1923, when he respectfully declined reelection to both positions because of his age. And in another emblematic, albeit earlier, initiative on behalf of the college, Houck used his friendship with Thomas Beckwith to secure the Beckwith Collection, a compilation of several thousand artifacts of the "Mound Builders," including items used by these Native American people for domestic purposes, warfare, agriculture, ceremonial, and personal adornment. This priceless collection, which made up the archeologist's life's work, had been rumored to be on its way to the Smithsonian, but as Louis had proclaimed at the 1914 grand opening of the newly established Beckwith Archeological Museum on campus, its permanent place at Southeast Missouri State assured that "at all hours . . . students" could "enter, study and acquaint themselves with the invaluable treasure of our school."[10]

Houck never summoned the considerable energy and focus necessary to fulfill the Missouri Historical Society's standing request that he continue *A History of Missouri* beyond statehood, primarily due to advancing age and disappointment over poor sales that in his mind relegated the histories to quiet oblivion. Quite frankly, neither did Louis fancy the inevitable criticism he thought sure to follow when scholars discovered that he was not a great admirer of Senator Thomas Hart Benton, a towering figure during the formative years of Missouri politics. "For a Missourian not to admire Benton," he knew, "is something like petit treason."[11]

Nevertheless, the passion for writing by no means waned. In 1915 the Naeter brothers published his parochial *Memorial Sketches of Pioneers and Early Residents of Southeast Missouri,* another collection of commemorative biographical entries. Within its pages, mostly cobbled together from speeches and newspaper obituaries he had penned over the years, Louis affectionately celebrated the region's founding fathers and mothers, most of whom he had personally known. In the spirit of *Memorial Sketches,* Louis also finally turned his historical talents inward with a memoir of his life. "The Story of the Railroad Work of Louis Houck in Southeast Missouri

10. Mattingly, *Normal to University,* 83, 84; *Weekly Republican,* October 16, 23, 1914; Farmer, "Southeast Missouri State Normal," 189. As part of the agreement for the college acquiring the collection, Houck delivered the institution's first annual address on archeology. He also agreed to edit Beckwith's unpublished manuscript, "The Story of the Settlement and Settlers of Mississippi County, Missouri." In a similar undertaking, Louis facilitated the Academic Hall exhibition of the Chatham Firearms Collection, a vast array of weaponry from around the world collected by Dr. A. T. Chatham of Kennett.

11. Louis Houck to C. H. McClure, December 17, 1916, Houck Papers, Box 1547, Correspondence–Outgoing, November–December 1916, Folder 14.

From 1880 to 1920," a two-volume set, and "Some Reminiscences of Louis Houck" probably began at the insistence of Mary, who strenuously desired a comparable memorial of their own history. She did not, however, want it published, but rather coaxed her husband into undertaking his last three books solely to privately preserve the Houck legacy for future generations of the family.

In preparing the manuscripts, Louis returned to the familiar routine that had seen him through the writing of the histories two decades before.[12] Usually working on Sundays, Christine Wheeler again took dictation as Louis paced the history room, summoning to mind the colorful chronology of an extraordinary life. From breakfast till lunch the stories unfolded as he talked history: the Cossacks, the *Volksblatt*, Robert Sturdivant, T. J. Moss, Jay Gould, Newman Erb, and thirty-some years of sewing a ribbon of steel through Swampeast Missouri. After lunch, a short nap, and a stroll around the grounds, the two reconvened for the rest of the afternoon. At times the old lion kept his composure, but when the recollection of certain dealings and personalities agitated him, his gait quickened and torrents of obscenities flew. This would have undoubtedly brought a stern rebuke from Mary had she not been quite hard of hearing by now.

Giboney thought that, maybe unconsciously, these were his father's best works. If so, perhaps Giboney detected that the palpable sense of nostalgia which underlies so much of the reminiscences and *Memorial Sketches* originated quite genuinely from an aging nineteenth-century man's uncertainty at the dissonance between the bygone southeast Missouri portrayed so fondly in his writings and its modern corruptible appearance. The economic maturation of southeast Missouri—from forces Louis unquestionably helped set in motion—accompanied a cultural and social coming of age as well during the 1920s. In particular, just a few miles down the Bloomfield Road in Cape Girardeau, much of the town's modern appearance and identity was being forged. But there was a great deal of tension in this transformation, and like the nation as a whole, Houck's Cape Girardeau found itself torn between two centuries. On one hand, the twentieth century and the powerful forces of modernization were quickly propelling Cape Girardeau into becoming the region's cultural and entertainment center on top of being its commercial and transportation core. On the other hand, the nineteenth century and the powerful forces of tradition kept Cape a rural, isolated, southern rivertown at heart. Drawn to the responsibility of being

12. Doherty, Jr., "Missouri Interests of Louis Houck," 3; *Cape Girardeau Southeast Missourian*, February 18, 1925.

a modern regional hub, but insecure in that role, the town struggled to reconcile its identity crisis in Houck's last years; a process that in large measure continues into the twenty-first century.[13]

Louis finished the Reminiscences near the beginning of 1925 and soon thereafter accompanied Christine Wheeler to the regular midwinter board of regents meeting in early February. He had missed several of the previous gatherings, and attendees noted that not only had his absences robbed the proceedings of "pep," but with his chair vacant it took them three times as long to dispose of the business. On this day, most regents failed to notice how sickly he appeared. And for a final time they followed his lead in deciding to purchase the Matteson estate south of campus for $11,000 because the old rock quarry there would make an excellent athletic field or natural amphitheater. Ironically, this last impression of their determined president strongly advocating the physical expansion of the college compelled the regents to name the fieldhouse and stadium eventually built on the property after Louis Houck, a man who admittedly "knew little and cared less about athletics."[14]

Louis was already suffering from a minor cold for most of that disagreeable and gloomy February 1925, and within a few days of the regents' meeting, bronchial pneumonia set in. Yet despite being tormented almost every night with a fever and persistent cough, Louis managed to get out of bed each day at the usual 7 a.m. and make it around the house. On the morning of the eighteenth, a Tuesday, he arose from a particularly bad night to have breakfast with the family. Giboney was preparing to go to Perryville for the day on business, and Louis quizzed his son about the trip. As the two conversed, Giboney thought his father ate his egg and toast and drank a little glass of milk "with relish," but suspected that he must be feeling greatly depressed because Louis mounted no objection when informed that unless his cough improved that day, they would summon a nurse.[15] As he left his parents at the table, Giboney later regretted having told them "good-bye only in the most casual way, never dreaming that this would be the last time that I should see him alive and conscious."

---

13. Neumeyer, Nickell, and Rhodes, *Historic Cape Girardeau*, 49–51.

14. Christine Wheeler to Louis Houck, February 23, 1920, Houck Papers, 1920 Box 1540, Correspondence, February A–Z, Folder 9; Heil, "Recollections."

15. Giboney Houck to David Landsen, February 26, 1925, Houck Papers, Box 1589, Giboney Houck, Outgoing Correspondence, Folder 6; Giboney Houck to Louis Moeder, March 4, 1925, Houck Papers, Box 1589, Giboney Houck, Outgoing Correspondence, Folder 7.

Just the day before, Louis had felt well enough to stand in his study window and direct the servants planting new trees around Elmwood. However, on the eighteenth he was "harassed incessantly" with coughing, and after joining Mary in the dining room for dinner sometime in the middle of the day he finally consented to having a doctor brought to the estate. In preparation for his arrival, Houck weakly ascended the magnificent stairway, past the huge oil paintings of Irma and Giboney as children, to his bedroom, where he removed his coat and slippers to lie down. Sometime near 3 p.m. servants escorted the doctor to Louis's bedside. With Mary anxiously looking on, the physician prescribed an opiate—probably morphine—to provide some restful relief from the cough. After being injected, Louis lay peacefully for a time. Finally, he turned his drowsy eyes to Mary and as he had done countless times before called her attention to the partially drawn curtains. "Put up those curtains," Louis murmured before losing consciousness. "I have got to have light."[16]

He never awoke from the influence of the narcotic, and by the time Giboney returned to his side that evening, his pulse began to fail rapidly. About nine o'clock the end came. Louis at last reached that long-anticipated "jumping off place."[17]

At Louis's request, Father M. J. LeSage, a Catholic priest from St. Vincent's church, presided over a modest service for the immediate family at Elmwood the following Saturday. In a plain wooden casket trimmed in black, his body lay in state during the week in the library, surrounded by his books. After the service, local farmers living around the estate served as pall bearers, conducting him to the Giboney and Houck family burial plot in Cape Girardeau's historic Old Lorimier Cemetery overlooking the Mississippi River.[18]

Almost immediately, though, Southeast Missouri State Teachers College President Joseph Serena and the regents approached Mary regarding a more substantial, public memorial service in Academic Hall to allow citizens to pay him their respects. Initially Mrs. Houck balked, explaining to Serena that "Mr. Houck was a very modest man in regard to any personal publicity and I am sure such a meeting would not meet with his approval, if held at this time, if he could pass it on now. I remember a conversation of Mr.

16. Giboney Houck to James M. Seifert, February 25, 1925; Giboney Houck to J. W. Fristoe, February 25, 1925, Houck Papers, Box 1589, Giboney Houck, Outgoing Correspondence, Folder 6.
17. Louis Houck to A. T. Chatham, June 30, 1922, Houck Papers, 1922 Box 1540, Correspondence, June–December A-Z, Folder 23.
18. Cape Girardeau Southeast Missourian, February 19, 1925.

Houck and a former President of the College on this subject of honoring the dead: Mr. Houck said wait two years and then you will find how soon a man is forgotten." But she soon relented given the spontaneous outpouring of sympathy by so many of Louis's "friends, and some of his enemies," who came to Elmwood from near and far with generous "expressions of the influence of his character and activities."[19] A memorial service was planned for April in Academic Auditorium.

In the meantime, Giboney commenced the laborious challenge of executing Louis's estate. The Houcks had always been uneasy about mixing their financial affairs too closely, and all of their personal property and real estate holdings—virtually all of their financial dealings, really—were kept in separate books. Most of the value of their respective estates was tied up in a fortune of real estate. Mary had virtually no personal property to speak of but owned sizable land holdings worth hundreds of thousands of dollars, while Louis had more personal property but most of it was in bonds, mortgages, stocks, and notes. Therein lay the real difficulty for Giboney, since most of these paper assets were not liquid and remained disputed within a tangle of debt and liens. Louis passed away with a little more than $200 in cash and bequeathed his extremely valuable real estate holdings fairly evenly among Charles Juden, Giboney, Rebecca, and his grandchildren. The only personal property mentioned specifically in the will was his gold watch, which went to Andy Juden. But as executor and heir to the remaining railroad holdings, Giboney inherited all the liabilities that went with the estate and spent a great deal of his life selling off property and liquidating assets in order to pay off various creditors. Years later, when the family considered the question of whether Giboney felt overwhelmed by his father's many accomplishments, they concluded that perhaps in truth he had been more "overwhelmed by Mr. Houck's debts."[20]

The memorial service hosted by the board of regents on Sunday afternoon, April 26—almost a month to the day after Newman Erb died in New York—brought together a capacity crowd of some fifteen hundred, including an impressive gathering of prominent Missourians. Mary arrived on Giboney's arm shortly before the service opened, accompanied by Charles, Andy, and Sally Juden, and little Mary Frissell. Ushers escorted

19. Mary H. G. Houck to Joseph Serena, March 22, 1925, Houck Papers, Box 1582, Giboney Houck, Incoming Correspondence, Folder 7.
20. Louis Houck, folder CP-1453, Mary H. G. Houck, Box 214, Bundle 3901, Probate Records, Cape Girardeau County Archives, Jackson, Missouri; Ronald S. Reed, Jr., to Joel P. Rhodes, September 22, 2006, in possession of author.

them to the front row of the packed auditorium. Dignitaries and the board of regents sat on the stage, which was decorated with spring flowers. After those in attendance sang "Nearer, My God, to Thee," Father LeSage gave the invocation and turned the rostrum over to Fred Naeter, the publisher of the *Cape Girardeau Southeast Missourian*. Following the newspaperman's address—"Mr. Houck, the Neighbor"—Dr. R. S. Douglass, a dean at Southeast, articulated the theme of "Mr. Houck, the Historian." Governor Sam A. Baker, a former Southeast Missouri State student, addressed "Mr. Houck, the Educator," and finally, U.S. Senator James A. Reed delivered his eulogy of "Mr. Houck, the Citizen."[21]

All paid sincere tributes to the many facets of the renaissance man soon to be called "The Father of Southeast Missouri," but perhaps the board of regents' sentiments offered eloquently "In Memoriam of Louis Houck" would have pleased Houck above all.

A few years earlier, Louis had articulated the abiding theme of his life. "You know we are sometimes better than our reputation," he admitted. "We are all selfish, more or less, but no man can help himself and not help others—help his fellow citizens. The hundreds of miles of railroad I have built in this section of Missouri I can truly say have helped others more than myself. So also my work in this Normal School—which it may also be said proceeds from my selfish motives . . ."[22] In venerating his commitment to the college, the regents acknowledged Houck's line of reasoning and in doing so seem to have brought it to a proper conclusion.

The interests of higher education found in him a devoted friend and a staunch advocate. He was an empire builder who brought to the cause of education the same indomitable spirit with which he built the highways of progress through the swamps of the section of Missouri . . . In the years of richest life experiences he more and more turned aside from a development of the natural resources of Southeast Missouri to pioneer in developing the intellectual and spiritual power of the youth of this new empire. It is not an exaggeration to say that in his last years this college became the ruling passion of his life, and that in the years to come the Southeast Missouri State Teachers College, for which he wrought so well, and did so much, will be his proudest monument.[23]

21. *Cape Girardeau Southeast Missourian*, April 27, 1925; Board of Regents Minutes, vol. 1, 1873–1925, 405.
22. Louis Houck to F. C. Brown, June 6, 1910, Houck Papers, Box 1545, Correspondence–Outgoing, June 3–27 1910, Folder 18.
23. Board of Regents Minutes, vol. 1, 1873–1925, 402–3.

Mary Hunter Giboney Houck lived in Elmwood almost twenty more years with her son and daughter before her death in November 1944 at the age of ninety-six. In true Houck fashion, she resisted a sedentary life, riding sidesaddle around the estate until blindness and a broken hip compelled her to finally stop in her nineties. Likewise, she remained active in the Daughters of the Confederacy and Daughters of the American Revolution. Elmwood's fertile gardens were immaculately tended until the end, and she was said to have never missed a Cape Girardeau District Fair, including the one just weeks before her death. After her sight failed, the diminutive lady allowed Giboney and Rebecca to read to her for hours on end in order to slake her incessant desire to keep up with town, county, and national affairs.[24]

When she passed, the Reverend C. A. Higgins of Christ Episcopal Church conducted the funeral inside her lifelong home, and six African American servants—some descendants of Andrew Giboney's slaves—bore her casket to the hearse. At Old Lorimier Cemetery the men laid her to rest with her parents, brothers, and sisters, and with Irma and Louis.

There, with his wife and the other dignitaries of Cape Girardeau history, Louis Napoleon Houck rests, fittingly, with the Giboney family behind him, just as their resources had been behind him in life.

24. *Cape Girardeau Southeast Missourian*, December 21, 1944.

Bibliography

Primary Sources

Board of Regents Minutes. Volume I, 1873–1925. Special Collections and Archives, Southeast Missouri State University, Cape Girardeau, Mo.
Christina Wheeler Heil Papers. Special Collections and Archives, Southeast Missouri State University, Cape Girardeau, Mo.
Houck, Louis. "Some Reminiscences of Louis Houck." Unpublished manuscript in possession of C. A. Juden and Jeanette Juden, Cape Girardeau, Mo.
———. "The Story of the Railroad Work of Louis Houck in Southeast Missouri From 1880 to 1920, Volume I." Unpublished manuscript in possession of C. A. Juden and Jeanette Juden, Cape Girardeau, Mo.
———. "The Story of the Railroad Work of Louis Houck in Southeast Missouri from 1880 to 1920, Volume II." Unpublished manuscript in possession of C. A. Juden and Jeanette Juden, Cape Girardeau, Mo.
———. "Louis Houck Memoirs." Unpublished manuscript in possession of C. A. Juden and Jeanette Juden, Cape Girardeau, Mo. "Louis Houck Memoirs" is an edited version of "Story of the Railroad Work," which in some passages is slightly different in regard to text and has different page numbering.
Unpublished letters in possession of Patrick and Cheryl Evans, Cape Girardeau, Mo.
Louis Houck Papers Accretion, 1843–1950. Special Collections and Archives, Southeast Missouri State University, Cape Girardeau, Mo.
Louis Houck Collection. Special Collections and Archives, Southeast Missouri State University, Cape Girardeau, Mo.

Poor's Manual of Railroads. John W. Barriger III National Railroad Library, St. Louis Mercantile Library at the University of Missouri–St. Louis.

Report of Committee on Charges Preferred against Honorable John Walker, State Auditor, Together with the Testimony of Witnesses, 34th General Assembly of the State of Missouri. Jefferson City, Mo.: Tribune Printing Company, State Printers and Binders, 1887. Missouri State Archives.

Seventh Annual Report of the Railroad Commissioners for the State of Missouri Being for the Year Ending December 31st 1881. Jefferson City, Mo.: Burch and Ferguson, State Printers, 1882. Missouri State Archives.

Eighth Annual Report of the Railroad Commissioners for the State of Missouri Being for the Year Ending December 31st 1882. Jefferson City, Mo.: State Journal Company, State Printers, 1883. Missouri State Archives.

Ninth Annual Report of the Railroad Commissioners for the State of Missouri Being for the Year Ending December 31st 1883. Jefferson City, Mo.: State Journal Company, State Printers, 1884. Missouri State Archives.

Tenth Annual Report of the Railroad Commissioners for the State of Missouri Being for the Year Ending December 31st 1884. Jefferson City, Mo.: Tribune Printing Company, State Printers and Binders, 1885. Missouri State Archives.

Twelfth Annual Report of the Railroad Commissioners for the State of Missouri Being for the Year Ending December 31st 1886. Jefferson City, Mo.: Tribune Printing Company, State Printers and Binders, 1887. Missouri State Archives.

Fourteenth Annual Report of the Railroad Commissioners of the State of Missouri for the Year Ending December 31st 1888. Jefferson City, Mo.: Tribune Printing Company, State Printers and Binders, 1890. Missouri State Archives.

Fifteenth Annual Report of the Railroad Commissioners of the State of Missouri for the Year Ending December 31st 1889. Jefferson City, Mo.: Tribune Printing Company, State Printers and Binders, 1890). Missouri State Archives.

Twenty-First Annual Report of the Railroad and Warehouse Commissioners of the State of Missouri, Year Ending June 30, 1896. Jefferson City, Mo.: Tribune Printing Company, State Printers and Binders, 1897. Missouri State Archives.

Twenty-Second Annual Report of the Railroad and Warehouse Commissioners of the State of Missouri, Year Ending June 30, 1897. Jefferson City, Mo.:

Tribune Printing Company, State Printers and Binders, 1898. Missouri State Archives.

Twenty-Fifth Annual Report of the Railroad and Warehouse Commissioners of the State of Missouri, Year Ending June 30, 1900. Jefferson City, Mo.: Tribune Printing Company, State Printers and Binders, 1901. Missouri State Archives.

Newspapers

Capaha Arrow (Cape Girardeau, Mo.). October 19, 1949.
Cape Girardeau Democrat. 1891–1909.
Cape Girardeau Morning Sun. 1921.
Cape Girardeau Republican Special Anniversary Edition. October 1, 1909.
Enterprise Courier (Charleston, Mo.). February 26, 1925.
Missouri Republican (St. Louis). 1868–1888.
The Daily Republican (Cape Girardeau, Mo.). October 3, 1904–February 28, 1918.
Cape Girardeau Southeast Missourian. August 8, 1902–February 18, 1925.
St. Louis Globe-Democrat. 1890–1925.
St. Louis Post-Dispatch. 1885–1925.
St. Louis Republic. 1888–1919.
Wall Street Journal. January 5, 1894.
Weekly Republican (Cape Girardeau, Mo.). 1908–1918.

Secondary Sources

Barnes, Harper. *Standing on a Volcano: The Life and Times of David Rowland Francis.* St. Louis: Missouri Historical Society Press, 2001.

Bogart, Ernest Ludlow, and Charles Manfred Thompson. *The Centennial History of Illinois, Volume IV: The Industrial State, 1870–1893.* Springfield, Ill.: Illinois Centennial Commission, 1920.

Calhoun, Charles W., ed. *The Gilded Age: Essays on the Origins of Modern America.* New York: Scholarly Resources, 1997.

Christensen, Lawrence O., and Gary R. Kremer. *A History of Missouri, Volume IV 1875–1919.* Columbia: University of Missouri Press, 1997.

Clarke, Thomas Curtis, et al. *The American Railway: Its Construction, Development, Management, and Appliances.* New York: Bramhall House, 1889.

Cole, Arthur Charles. *The Centennial History of Illinois, Volume III: The Era of the Civil War, 1848–1870.* Springfield, Ill.: Illinois Centennial Commission, 1919.

Degler, Carl. *The Age of Economic Revolution: 1876–1900.* New York: Scott, Foresman, 1977.

Doherty, William T., Jr. *Louis Houck, Missouri Historian and Entrepreneur.* Columbia: University of Missouri Press, 1960.

Evans, Cheryl. "El Bosque de los Olmos." In *Biography of Historic Cape Girardeau County.* 1975. Special Collections and Archives, Southeast Missouri State University.

Fietsam, Robert C., Jr., Judy Belleville, and Jack Le Chien. *Belleville: 1814–1914.* Charleston, S.C.: Arcadia Publishing, 2004.

Grodinsky, Julius. *Jay Gould: His Business Career, 1867–1892.* Philadelphia: University of Pennsylvania Press, 1957.

Gutman, Herbert G. *Work, Culture and Society in Industrializing America.* New York: Vintage, 1977.

History of Southeast Missouri. Chicago: Goodspeed Publishing Company, 1888.

History of St. Clair County, Illinois, 1881. St. Clair County Historical Society, Belleville, Ill.

Houck, Louis. *A History of Missouri from the Earliest Explorations and Settlements until the Admission of the State into the Union.* Chicago: R. R. Donnelley and Sons, 1908.

———. *Memorial Sketches of Pioneers and Early Residents of Southeast Missouri.* Cape Girardeau, Mo.: Naeter Brothers, 1915.

———. *The Spanish Regime in Missouri: A Collection of Papers and Documents Relating to Upper Louisiana Principally within the Present Limits of Missouri during the Dominion of Spain, from the Archives of the Indies at Seville, Etc., Translated from the Original Spanish into English, and Including also Some Papers Concerning the Supposed Grant to Col. George Morgan at the Mouth of the Ohio, Found in the Congressional Library.* Chicago: R. R. Donnelley and Sons, 1909.

Kirkendall, Richard S. *A History of Missouri, Volume V 1919–1953.* Columbia: University of Missouri Press, 1986.

Klein, Maury. *The Life and Legend of Jay Gould.* Baltimore: Johns Hopkins University Press, 1986.

Lears, T. J. Jackson. *No Place of Grace: Antimodernism and the Transformation of American Culture.* Chicago: University of Chicago Press, 1981.

McCandless, Perry. *A History of Missouri, Volume II 1820–1860.* Columbia: University of Missouri Press, 2000.

Local Road Administration in Missouri: An Interpretation in Terms of Its Historical Development. Jefferson City, Mo., July 1936.

Lopata, Edwin L. *Local Aid to Railroads in Missouri.* New York: Arno Press, 1981.

Mattingly, Arthur H. *Normal to University: A Century of Service.* Cape Girardeau, Mo.: Southeast Missouri State University, 1979.

Million, John W. *State Aid to Railways in Missouri.* Chicago: University of Chicago Press, 1896.

Missouri State Planning Board. *Local Road Administration in Missouri, and Interpretation in Terms of Its Historical Development.* Jefferson City, Mo., July 1936.

Neumeyer, Tom, Frank Nickell, and Joel P. Rhodes. *Historic Cape Girardeau: An Illustrated History.* San Antonio, Tex.: Historical Publishing Network, 2004.

Parrish, William E. *A History of Missouri, Volume III 1860–1875.* Columbia: University of Missouri Press, 2001.

———. *Missouri under Radical Rule, 1865–1870.* Columbia: University of Missouri Press, 1965.

Pease, Theodore Calvin. *The Story of Illinois.* Chicago: University of Chicago Press, 1949.

Piott, Steven L. *The Anti-Monopoly Persuasion: Popular Resistance to the Rise of Big Business in the Midwest.* Westport, Conn: Praeger, 1985.

Ripley, William Z. *Railroads: Finance and Organization.* New York: Longmans, Green and Company, 1923.

Scott, Franklin D. *The Political Career of William R. Morrison.* Reprinted from the Transactions of the Illinois State Historical Society. Danville, Ill.: Illinois Printing Company, 1926.

Shrader, Dorothy H. *The City of Hermann, Missouri Presents Hermann: 1836 A Dream in Philadelphia, 1986 A Town in Missouri.* Hermann, Mo.: Sesquicentennial Committee, 1986.

Shortridge, James R. *The Middle West: Its Meaning in American Culture.* Lawrence: University Press of Kansas, 1989.

Snider, Felix Eugene, and Earl Augustus Collins. *Cape Girardeau: Biography of a City.* Cape Girardeau, Mo.: Ramfre Press, 1956.

Taylor, George R., and Irene D. Neu. *The American Railway Network, 1861–1890.* Cambridge, Mass.: Harvard University Press, 1956.

Thelen, David. *Paths of Resistance: Tradition and Dignity in Industrializing Missouri.* New York: Oxford University Press, 1986.

Trachtenberg, Alan. *The Incorporation of America: Culture and Society in the Gilded Age.* New York: Hill and Wang, 1982.

Journals

Dalton, John Hall, Jr. "Dunklin County, Charles P. Chouteau, and the Courtship of the Iron Horse." *Missouri Historical Review* 82 (October 1987): 71–96.

Doherty, William T., Jr. "Louis Houck: Opponent and Imitator of Jay Gould." *Business History Review* 30 (March 1956): 46–56.

Dunn, Joe P. "A 'Damn Yankee' in Rebel Territory: James Hutchison Kerr's Reflections on his Southeast Missouri Years." *Missouri Historical Review* 101 (October 2006): 1–16.

Grace, Karen. "For a Man's House Is His Castle." *Preservation Issues* 5, no. 6 (November/December 1995): 1, 12.

Grant, H. Roger. "Courting the Great Western Railway: An Episode of Town Rivalry." *Missouri Historical Review* 76 (July 1982): 405–20.

Hansen, Bradley. "The People's Welfare and the Origins of Corporate Reorganization: The Wabash Receivership Reconsidered." *Business History Review* 74 (Autumn 2000): 374–405.

"Louis Houck." *Bulletin of the Missouri Historical Society* 7, no. 3 (June 1950).

Miner, H. Craig. "The Colonization of the St. Louis and San Francisco Railway Company, 1880–1882: A Study in Corporate Diplomacy." *Missouri Historical Review* 63 (April 1969): 345–63.

Ogilvie, Leon Parker. "Populism and Socialism in the Southeast Missouri Lowlands." *Missouri Historical Review* 65 (January 1971).

Piott, Steven L. "Missouri and Monopoly: The 1890s as an Experiment in Law Enforcement." *Missouri Historical Review* 73 (October 1979): 21–49.

Reigel, Robert. "The Missouri Pacific, 1879–1900." *Missouri Historical Review* 27 (1924): 173–96.

Rhodes, Joel P. "The Father of Southeast Missouri: Louis Houck and the Coming of the Railroad." *Missouri Historical Review* (January 2006): 72–86.

Stepenoff, Bonnie. "'The Last Tree Cut Down': The End of the Bootheel Frontier." *Missouri Historical Review* (October 1995): 61–78.

Traylor, Richard C. "Pulling Missouri Out of the Mud: Highway Politics, the Centennial Road Law, and the Problems of Progressive Identity." *Missouri Historical Review* (October 2003): 47–68.

Violette, E. M. "The Missouri and Mississippi Railroad Debt." *Missouri Historical Review* 15 (April 1921): 487–518, (July 1921): 617–47.

Wollman, Henry. "The Strange Story of the Cape Girardeau Railroad." *Commercial Law Review* (June 1933): 1–16.

Dissertations and Theses

Doherty, William T., Jr. "The Missouri Interests of Louis Houck." Ph.D. diss., University of Missouri, 1951.

Farmer, Ernest Kent. "Southeast Missouri State Normal, 1873–1921." Ph.D. diss., Southern Illinois University, 1987.

Fitzsimmons, Margaret Louis. "Railroad Development in Missouri, 1860 to 1870." Master's thesis, Washington University, 1931.

Harris, C. Donald. "Louis Houck and His Role in the Economic Development of Southeast Missouri in the Late Nineteenth Century." Master's thesis, Southeast Missouri State University, 1994.

Konold, Donald. "Silver Issue in Missouri Politics." Master's thesis, University of Missouri, 1950.

Muraskin, Jack David. "Missouri Politics during the Progressive Era, 1896–1916." Ph.D. diss., University of California–Berkeley, 1969.

Murphy, James Lee. "A History of the Southeastern Ozark Region of Missouri." Ph.D. diss., Saint Louis University, 1982.

Ogilvie, Leon Parker. "The Development of the Southeast Missouri Lowlands." Ph.D. diss., University of Missouri, 1967.

Simmons, Benjamin W. "Washington S. Dearmont and His Impact upon Southeast Missouri State University." Master's thesis, Southeast Missouri State University, 2008.

Willis, Maynard Cameron. "The Construction of Railroads in Southeast Missouri." Master's thesis, University of Missouri, 1933.

Young, Leilyn M. "The Southeast Missourian and the Naeter Brothers, A Study of Community Service in Cape Girardeau, Missouri, by a Newspaper and Its Publishers." Master's thesis, University of Missouri, 1949.

Unpublished Manuscripts

Albert, Lee L. "Memories of Cape Girardeau and Old Man River."

Jensen, Peggy Ashcraft. "Life on the Edge of the Great Dark Cypress Swamp: The Brownwood, Missouri Community History." Unpublished manuscript in Center for Regional History, Southeast Missouri State University, Cape Girardeau, Mo.

"Riding the Rails Through Time." HP 200, Southeast Missouri State University, Spring 2002.

Index

Able, Barton, 38, 39, 41
Adams, Elmer B., 175, 176
Advance, Mo., 81, 82
Albert, Harry L., 201
Albert, Leon J., 83, 212, 218, 219
Allen, Russell, 70
Allenville, Mo., 58, 60, 70, 71
Alton, Ill., 13
Anderson, William P., 194
Anzieger des Westens (Western Gazette), 3
Arbyrd, Mo., 190

Baker, Sam A., 282
Bard, Albert S., 188
Barnum, William, 25, 26, 28, 29, 31, 32, 34, 53, 66
Beckwith, Thomas, 231, 232, 277
Bedford, Henry H., 45, 46, 49, 50, 58
Belleville, Ill., 5–7, 15–17, 19, 22, 24, 26, 27, 32, 34, 111
Belleville Beobachter (Belleville Observer), 5
Belleville Volksblatt (Belleville People's Sheet), 15–17, 21–26, 29, 30, 31, 32
Belleviller Zeitung (Belleville Newspaper), 1, 5, 10, 11, 12, 13
Berry, Richard, 75
Bird's Point, Mo., 242, 243
Bissell, William H., 13
Block, Zalma, 93
Blomeyer, Edward F., 145, 183, 189, 239
Bloomfield, Mo., 45, 49, 158
"Bloomfield Crowd," 49
Bollinger County, Mo., 45, 105
Boone, Banton G., 94
Boundaries of the Louisiana Purchase: A Historical Study, The, 199, 225. *See also* Houck, Louis; as historian

Boynton, C. A., 67, 171, 190, 221
Brazeau, Julia, 28, 29
Brooks, James Francis, 81, 82, 106, 108, 144, 145, 146, 149, 170, 172, 181, 216
Brown, Daniel S., 107, 110, 131
Brown, William, 67, 81, 82, 85, 87, 92, 93, 103, 105, 107
Brownwood, Mo., 82
Brownwood City and Northwestern Railway. *See* St. Louis, Cape Girardeau and Fort Smith Railroad; Zalma division
Bruihl, C. F., 88
Burrough, Jacob, 62
Butler County, Mo., 45, 50
Byrd, Abe R., 190, 252, 264
Byrd, J. Hunter, 252, 253, 255, 256, 257

Cairo and Fulton Railroad, 50, 57, 59. *See also* St. Louis, Iron Mountain and Southern Railway
Cairo, Ill., 33, 35–38
Caligoa, Mo., 190, 191
Campbell, Mo., 151, 193, 194
Cape Girardeau, Mo., 9, 79, 104, 144, 145, 174, 180, 181, 195, 198, 204, 206, 209, 235, 242, 246, 247, 258; in Civil War era, 35, 36; post–Civil War era, 42, 43, 46, 47, 58, 60, 62; effects of Panic of 1873, 61; and Cape Girardeau Railway Company, 70
Common Pleas Court, 159, 160, 201; early twentieth-century development of, 220, 221, 222, 264, 278, 279
Cape Girardeau and Bloomfield Gravel Road Company, 80
Cape Girardeau and Chester Railroad. *See* Cape Girardeau Northern

293